THE LOEB CLASSICAL LIBRARY
FOUNDED BY JAMES LOEB 1911

EDITED BY
JEFFREY HENDERSON

[QUINTILIAN]

The Lesser Declamations

II

LCL 501

[QUINTILIAN]

THE LESSER DECLAMATIONS

VOLUME II

EDITED AND TRANSLATED BY

D. R. SHACKLETON BAILEY

HARVARD UNIVERSITY PRESS
CAMBRIDGE, MASSACHUSETTS
LONDON, ENGLAND
2006

Copyright © 2006 by the President and Fellows
of Harvard College
All rights reserved

LOEB CLASSICAL LIBRARY® is a registered trademark
of the President and Fellows of Harvard College

Library of Congress Catalog Card Number 2005046792
CIP data available from the Library of Congress

ISBN 0-674-99619-4

Composed in ZephGreek and ZephText by
Technologies 'N Typography, Merrimac, Massachusetts.
Printed and bound by Edwards Brothers, Ann Arbor, Michigan.

CONTENTS

CONTENTS

CONTENTS

CONTENTS

DECLAMATIONES MINORES

Heredes de deposito

Quidam a commilitone eiusdem ordinis depositum petebat. Negavit ille se accepisse. Cum res sine teste esset, ⟨iudicio victus petitor⟩[1] occidit eum a quo petebat et se. Petitoris heres petit ab herede alterius commilitonis.

1   DECLAMATIO

Si pecunia tantum in causa litis esset, parem videremur litigandi habere rationem; nunc[2] illud quidem nobis extra ordinem accidit, quod litigandum est etiam propter hoc ipsum, ne ⟨ille⟩[3] sine causa perierit.

Plurimum autem fallitur si quis eandem condicionem putat huius iudicii ac prioris. Desiit lis esse sine teste. Ergo ⟨quod⟩[4] illi in[5] priori non erat satis pro se dicere, mihi non mediocre argumentum est. Si quis enim testis idoneus fuisset, videretur huius fiducia calumniatus. Quid in causa est praeter veritatem ut aliquis id petat quod probari non possit? Et infitiandi quidem depositam pecuniam manifesta ratio est, cupiditas[6] lucri; petendi etiam non depositam,

---

[1] Ro.   [2] Aer.: ne Aβ   [3] SB[1]   [4] Sch.
[5] i. in Ro.: iam Aβ   [6] Sch.: -tatis A (ex cupiditis), β

---

[1] Equal to the previous claimant's, from whom the speaker inherited.

[2] The original claimant was not believed because he had no proof in the shape of a credible witness. The present claimant has a witness (the original claimant) and that witness is credible be-

Heirs concerning a deposit

A person was claiming a deposit from a fellow soldier of the same rank. The latter denied receiving it. Since there were no witnesses to the matter, ⟨the claimant lost the case and⟩ killed the man from whom he claimed and himself. The claimant's heir claims from the heir of the other fellow soldier.

DECLAMATION

If money was the only cause of the dispute, we might seem to have an equal[1] cause to go to law. As it is, something outside the ordinary has happened to us: we must go to law just so that ⟨he⟩ has not died for no reason.

But if anyone thinks that this trial and the other are on a par, he is very much mistaken. The case is no longer without a witness. So ⟨the fact that⟩ in the former it was not enough for him to speak for himself is an important argument for me. For if there had been a good witness, he would be thought to have brought a false charge in reliance upon him.[2] Why should anyone claim what could not be proved except because it is the truth? There is a clear reason for denying money deposited, greed of gain; the same motive would exist for claiming money not deposited, if

---

cause he would not have brought an unprovable claim if it had not been true. But the argument that lack of proof is evidence of *bona fides* does not become more credible by being offered at second hand.

si quae probationis spes, eadem causa sit. Cum quidem aliquis dicit 'deposui apud te, scis ipse', quid aliud quam videtur advocare[7] deos testes? Dicite igitur causam quare petierit si non deposuerat.

Habere pecuniam potuit, manifestum est: et ipse reliquit heredes et is qui eiusdem ordinis fuit. Multas deponendae pecuniae intervenire rationes inter milites manifestum est: longum iter incidit, periculosa expeditio. Si deponenda sit, ubi credibilius est deponi quam apud hominem eiusdem ordinis? Nam, praeter id quod facilior speratur fides ex pari, est quaedam eiusdem ordinis coniunctio: ⟨nec apud superiorem⟩[8] nec apud inferiorem deponi solet ⟦cum ideo deponatur ut recipiatur⟧.[9] Credibile
6 est ergo apud hominem eiusdem ordinis deposuisse. 'At sine teste.' De omnibus depositis loquar. Misera hercule condicio mortalitatis, quando omnibus iam quae agimus videtur opus esse teste. Ita parum facit veritas, ita nullum numen[10] est Fidei? Non satis videri potest probatum quod duo sciunt?

7   Veniamus tamen, ut dixi, ad probationem. Occidit eum a quo pecunia negabatur. Iterum quaero: qua ratione, qua causa? 'Odium fuit.' Unde? Ego quare occidere debuerit dico: infitiabatur. Tu, ut hanc causam occidendi excludas, substituas aliam necesse est. Satis argumenti erat si occidisset clam, si ex insidiis, si tamquam negaturus. Quae causa hominem in scelus egit? Quid fuit quod tantam rabiem
8 concitaret nisi illud, quod sciebat se dedisse? Cum dicenti

[7] q. v. a. *SB*[2]: v. a. q. Aβ   [8] *Ro., Ri.*
[9] *ita secl. SB*[4]
[10] *SB*[2]: nomen Aβ

---

[3] Fides was a deity in Rome from time immemorial.

4

there is a hope of proving it. But when someone says "I deposited it with you, you know it yourself," what does he appear to be doing except calling on the gods as witnesses? So give us a reason why he claimed if he had not made the deposit.

He could have had the money, that's clear. He left heirs himself and so did the other of the same rank. It is clear that many reasons may arise among soldiers for depositing money: a long journey came up, a dangerous mission. If money were to be deposited, where is it more likely to be deposited than with a man of the same rank? For beside that good faith is more easily expected from an equal, there is a kind of bond between the same rank. It is not usual for a deposit to be made ⟨with a superior⟩ or with an inferior ⟦since the deposit is made so that it may be returned⟧. It is credible therefore that he deposited with a man of his own rank. "But without a witness." I shall speak of all deposits. Sad, upon my word, is the condition of mortality when a witness seems to be needed nowadays in everything we do. Is truth not enough? Is there no divinity in Faith?[3] Can't what two people know be regarded as sufficiently proved?

However, let us come, as I said, to the proof. He killed the man who was denying the money. Again I ask, for what reason, what motive? "It was hate." Why? I give a reason why he should have killed: the denial. For you to exclude this motive for the killing, you must substitute another. It would have been proof enough if he had killed in secret, from ambush, as though he were going to deny it.[4] What motive drove the man into crime? What was it that aroused such fury—except that he knew he had given the money?

[4] Even so, there would be no other plausible motive.

'apud te pecuniam deposui' respondebatur 'quis testis est, quae probatio est?', quanti animi aestus agebantur! Non vobis videtur, cum feriret, illa dixisse: 'ita non deposui?'? Optime mehercule mihi videtur[11] in[12] militari[13] facinore illa exclamasse: 'i nunc et nega, i nunc et alienam pecuniam

9 converte in tuas cupiditates: non uteris tamen.' Erat argumentum ergo tantum quod occidit. Quam ultra desideratis probationem? Occidit statim moriturus. Frequenter iudicia huiusmodi ‹ita›[14] exercentur, ut, si res in notitia dicitur esse servulorum, torqueri mancipia videamus. Si mos civitatis et condicio militiae pateretur, se in tormenta obtulisset, illum poposcisset. Non tibi videtur praebuisse de animo suo[15] quaestionem?

313

Falso caedis damnatus

Qui caedis reum accusaverit neque damnaverit, ipse puniatur. Damnatorum supplicia in diem tricesimum differantur. Accusavit quidam et damnavit. In diem tricesimum dilata †damnatio†[1] est. Intervenit is qui occisus dicebatur. Petit reus poenam accusatoris.

1 SERMO

Non erit alienum advocatum dare huic accusatori: fecit rem, ut parcissime dicam, paenitentia dignam. Et fortius

---

[11] *Fr.*: -ebatur Aβ [12] *SB1*: ac Aβ [13] *anne* tali ?
[14] *SB4* [15] *Aer.*: tuo Aβ
[1] β: domin- A: poena damnato *Hå.2*: poena *coni. Wi.*

---

[5] Cf. 313.15 *ita non erubescis?*
[6] I translate *in tali*.

When he said "I deposited the money with you" and got the answer "Who's your witness, what proof is there?" what tempests surged in his mind! When he struck, don't you think he said: "Really? Didn't I deposit?"[5] Upon my word, I think in such a crime[6] he might very appropriately have exclaimed: "Go on, deny it now, take another man's money for your lusts: but you shan't spend it." So the mere fact of the killing would have been proof. What further proof do you want? He killed when he was going to die straight away. Trials like this are often <so> conducted that if the facts are said to be known to slaves, we see slaves tortured. If the custom of the community and the rules of the service had so allowed, he would have offered himself for torture and demanded the other man. Do you not think he has provided an examination of his conscience under torture?[7]

313

Wrongly convicted of homicide

Let whoso prosecutes another for homicide and does not convict him be punished himself. Let the punishments of persons convicted be delayed thirty days. A man prosecuted and convicted. The punishment[1] is deferred for thirty days. The person who was allegedly killed intervenes. The defendant claims the death of the prosecutor.

DISCUSSION

It will not be out of place to give this prosecutor an advocate. He did something, to say the least, calling for regret.

---

[7] As *quaestionem* implies. The killing spoke for his veracity as powerfully as evidence under torture.

[1] See crit. note.

defendetur ab alio et maiore cum verecundia patronus
confitebitur si quid confitendum est. Et quotiens causa
plus iuris habet quam pudoris, ad eum transferenda est qui
non erubescit.

2   DECLAMATIO

Reum capitis arcessitis in ea civitate in qua hoc grave et
indignum videtur, et reum capitis arcessitis qui ipsi intole-
rabilem hanc crudelitatem vocatis. Conveniebat eos[2] qui
temeritatem accusationis incusant nihil nisi certum ex-
3   ploratumque deferre. Ergo lege occidi vultis hunc statim
qui reum caedis detulerit (hactenus agnosco: detulit enim
quem defendo) neque damnaverit[3]: hoc iam ad nos non
pertinet; hic enim damnatus est. Sequitur ergo ut aliam
legem adferas,[4] aut hanc mutes, aut hoc audeas dicere, ius
aliquod tibi esse constitutum.

4   Ad interpretationem nos vocas et ex hac lege qua litigas
aliam constituere conaris. Non est ista res iudicum, non
horum qui ad certa iura, et quidem iurati, consederunt.
Deflecti iura ne pro defensione quidem aequum est; legem vero mutare ut occidas, et crudeliter interpretari ius
5   quod a maioribus[5] scriptum est, cuius animi est? Ego legem habeo adversus eum demum scriptam qui detulerit

  [2] *Aer.*: -batis A[1]β: -bat is A[2]
  [3] n. d. *Ri.*: dam(p)navit qu(a)e A (*ex* –tquem), C: -tque BD
  [4] *Gron.*: -amus Aβ
  [5] *SB*[3]: magistratibus Aβ

---

[2] Not to malice, as Wi. assumes, but to haste or carelessness.
Even so, such an admission would throw away the defense that the
charge was justified by the facts as then known.

He will be more vigorously defended by someone else, and if a confession[2] is to be made, it will come with better grace from his attorney. Whenever a plea has more to do with law than with decency, it should be transferred to someone who doesn't blush.

You people summon a defendant on a capital charge in a community in which this is deemed grave and shocking and you summon a defendant on a capital charge when you yourselves call this an intolerable cruelty.[3] It would have been fitting that those who accuse the rashness of a prosecutor should make no charge that is not certain and verified. So you want this man killed at once under the law who charged a man with homicide (so far I agree, for my client did bring the charge)—and did not convict him.[4] This is no longer our concern, for he *was* found guilty. It follows then that you must bring us another law or change this one or else dare to say that some legal right has been constituted just for you.

You summon us to interpretation and try to lay down another law out of this one under which you bring your case. That is not a matter for the jury, not for these gentlemen who have sat down according to fixed laws and under oath. It is not fair that laws should be bent even for the defense; but to change a law in order to kill, and to interpret in cruelty a law that has been written by our ancestors, what sort of mentality is that? I have a law written only against a person who has laid a charge and failed to

---

[3] Assuming the defendant to be innocent.
[4] The words of the law.

neque damnaverit. Non scrutor quid voluerit legum lator; neque enim possum: sera[6] inquisitio in praeterita est. Id sive voluit esse quod scripsit sive aliud aliquid cogitavit,

6 hoc scripsit, hoc iure viximus, hoc spectamus.[7] Nihil minus ferri oportet in civitate quam ut lex decipiat. Innocentem accusavi; satis est quod damnavi. Neque enim lex ita scripta est ut qui innocentem accusaverit capite puniatur, sed ut puniatur qui accusaverit nec damnaverit. Quomodo ergo nihil prodesset accusatori si non damnasset, postea nocentem esse compertum eum quem accusavit, ita ei qui fortunam secundam iudicii tulit non debet nocere quod postea

7 accidit. Lex talem condicionem iudicii facit in quo caedis accusatur reus ut utique adversus alterum[8] pronuntietur: aut reum damnari oportet aut accusatorem. Tu quid vis? Ut uterque damnatus sit [an ut istud verum sit, ut damnatus sit reus et accusator][9]? 'Illud tamen lex voluit.' Transeo quod perniciosum sit interpretari legem et ad ingenia utriusque converti, id quod scriptum est ne dubitaretur dubium fieri postquam scriptum est.

8 Descendo ad hanc quoque contentionem[10] (non quia necesse est, nec quia ad vestram religionem pertinet, nec quia solvit ista res ius iurandum, sed quia victori optinentique causam facile est et libet disputare[11]): recte fecit

---

[6] *Gron.*: s(a)eva Aβ   [7] hoc (*anne* huc ?) s. *SB*[3]: hoc –avit Aβ   [8] *Gron.*: alium Aβ   [9] *SB*[1]
[10] *Gron.*: inten- Aβ   [11] l. d. *Ro.*: debet –ari Aβ

---

[5] The advocate identifies with his client.

[6] A reiteration. Wi. may have been right to double-bracket the rest of the section.   [7] *Hanc* looks forward. The declaimer has argued that the law must be followed as it stands, not inter-

convict. I don't scrutinize what the lawgiver intended, for I can't; inquisition into bygones comes too late. Whether he meant what he wrote or whether he had something else in mind, this *is* what he wrote, this is the law we have lived with, this is what we look to. Nothing should be more intolerable in a community than for a law to deceive. I[5] prosecuted an innocent man: it's enough that I convicted him. For the text of the law does not say that he who has prosecuted an innocent man shall be capitally punished, but that he shall be punished who has prosecuted and not convicted. So just as a prosecutor who had failed to convict would gain nothing if it was later discovered that the man he accused was guilty, so something that happened later ought not to damage a prosecutor who had good fortune in the trial. This is the scenario set by the law for a trial in which a defendant is prosecuted for homicide: verdict has to be given against one side or the other; either the defendant is to be convicted or the prosecutor. What do you want? That both be convicted [or that this be fair (?), that the defendant and the accuser be convicted]?[6] "But that is what the law intended." I pass over that it is pernicious to interpret a law and twist it to suit the ingenuities of both parties and that what is written to preclude doubt should become doubtful after it has been written.

I come down to this other contention[7] (not because it is necessary or because it is relevant to your religious duty nor because this factor[8] releases you from your oath, but because as winner, successful in my case, it is easy and agreeable to make the argument): the lawgiver did right

preted. He now argues that it is equitable as it stands, and so intended (s.13).   [8] Of equity.

legum lator, qui ita scripsit legem ut non puniretur si con-
demnasset. Quare? Noluit accusatorem esse calumnia-
9 torem, noluit accusatorem dare aliquid odio. Alioqui scimus multa vera quidem non esse, credibilia tamen esse.
Accusator quid debet nisi[12] ut eum deferat adversus quem
argumenta habeat, adversus quem testes habeat: alioqui
nocentem[13] an innocentem qui scit? Ipsi iudices hoc non
pronuntiant, sed se ex animi sui[14] sententia facere pro-
fitentur. Quis autem miratur si ea res accusatorem decepit
quae decipere iudices potuit? Accusator, cum id effecit ut
reus damnandus videretur, reddidit rationem accusationis.
10 Nullus autem tam inicus[15] legis lator fuit ut errorem accusatoris punire vellet.

Oportet esse in civitate et accusatores: alioqui omnia
mittuntur ad manus, omnia mittuntur ad ferrum. Per se
difficilem rationem vindictae et ultionis ‹difficiliorem›[16]
facimus, paene licentiam grassatoribus et latronibus da-
mus, quod nemo accusare sine periculo capitis sui potest.
11 Sed tamen adversus haec illud remedium est, quod accusator cogitat quid obiecturus sit. Si ne hoc quidem prodest,
vidisse aliquid in accusatione, motum esse probabilibus ar-
12 gumentis, in totum iudicia ista tollemus. Hunc autem habuisse quare accusaret credite iudicibus qui damnaverunt.
‘Hic inimicus.’ Quid illi qui cognoverunt? Quo vultis motos
esse iudices ut damnarent? Non enim moti sunt auctoritate ipsius accusatoris: argumentis moti sunt, illis, credimus, testibus moti sunt quos[17] habebamus. Et mihi videtur
ideo constituta esse lex quae damnatum post tricesimum

[12] Sch.: tibi Aβ   [13] nocentem] sc. deferat
[14] a. s. Aer.: -mis ut Aβ   [15] Gron.: inimicus Aβ
[16] Aer. (om. et ult.)   [17] Aer.: hos Aβ

when he wrote the law in the form that a person should not
be punished if he had won a conviction. Why? He did not
want a prosecutor to be a calumniator, he did not want a
prosecutor to give any latitude to hate. We know in general that many things are untrue but nevertheless credible. What is the prosecutor's obligation except to accuse
one against whom he has proofs, against whom he has
witnesses? Apart from that, whether guilty or innocent,
how does he know? The jury themselves do not so pronounce but declare that they are acting in their sincere
judgment. Who is surprised that the prosecutor was deceived by something that could deceive the jury? When
the prosecutor made the defendant appear to deserve conviction, he justified the prosecution. And no lawgiver was
ever so unfair as to wish to punish a prosecutor's mistake.

Prosecutors too are needed in a community. Otherwise
everything comes to violence, everything comes to the
sword. The business of punishment and vengeance is difficult in itself; we make it <more difficult>; we almost give
license to footpads and brigands because nobody can prosecute without risking his life. But there is a remedy for this:
the prosecutor thinks about what he is going to charge. If
even this does not help, the fact that he has had something
to go on in his prosecution, was influenced by probable evidence, we shall do away with these trials altogether. That
he had reasons to prosecute, believe the jury that convicted. "He was an enemy." What about those who tried
the case? What do you want us to think influenced the jury
to convict? They were not influenced by the prosecutor's
own personal authority: they were influenced, we believe,
by evidence, by those witnesses we had. And it seems to
me that the law which required the person convicted to be

diem puniri voluit, quoniam videbat legum lator posse fieri
ut deciperetur accusator. Itaque eius qui non damnasset
13 praesentem poenam esse voluerunt: nulla dilatio est. Quid
te movit? Quid attulisti ad iudicem? Hoc enim vult lex,
prius causam[18] approbari ipsi accusatori. Ergo etiam voluntas legis pro nobis est, et non tantum scriptum, quod satis erat nisi ita recedamus ab eo quod proprie[19] nostrum est
ut concessisse videamur. Sed ut †transissetis†[20] rursus id
quod dicebam: cum suspectus esset reus, boni erat civis
accusare; neque aliter stare leges possunt, neque aliter
civitas. Accusavit quoniam homo occisus videbatur.
14 Quid postea?[21] 'Hic tamen perire potuit [et occidi po-
tuit][22] et hoc indignum est.' Primum omnium durum est
unam indici utrique fortunam et occidi hominem quia aliquis occidi potuerit. '<At>[23] huius culpa.' Ita magna poena
15 est causam bene dicentis[24]? Deinde hoc non tantum accusatoris culpa factum est. Fortasse ita vixeras: multa petu-
lanter, multa temere, multa cruente commiseras. Turpissi-
mi hominis argumentum est innocentem posse damnari.
Non enim dicis[25] corruptum esse iudicium, non versatam
pecuniam. Ita non erubescis? Homicida visus es. Tu porro
tantum accusatori irasceris? Non idem de te iudices sense-

18 *SB*[1]: etiam Aβ: rem *Gron.*
19 *Sch.*, *Gron.*: propter te Aβ   20 recenseatis *SB*[1]
21 q. p. *huc transp. Watt*[1]: *ante* quoniam (*supra*) Aβ
22 *SB*[3], *auct. Watt*[1]   23 *SB*[2]
24 c. b. d. *SB*[2] (c. d. *Ro.*, *auct. Obr.*): c. edicitis A(β)
25 *Gron.*: dicit Aβ

9 The argument is elliptical. The prosecutor who loses his case
gets no stay of execution because, even if later evidence were to

punished after thirty days was so constituted because the lawgiver perceived the possibility that a prosecutor might be deceived. So they wanted[9] the punishment of a prosecutor who had failed to convict to be immediate; there's no delay. What influenced you? What did you bring to the jury? The law wants the case first approved by the prosecutor himself. So even the intention of the law is on our side, and not only the text, which would have been sufficient if we were not to draw back from what is properly ours so as to seem to have conceded. But to let you review again[10] what I was saying: since the defendant was under suspicion, it was a good citizen's part to prosecute; laws cannot stand otherwise, neither can the community. He prosecuted because it seemed that a man had been killed.

What follows? "All the same, he could have died and this is shocking." To begin with, it is hard that two be given one fate and a man be put to death because somebody might have been put to death. "<But> it was his fault." So heavy a punishment for pleading a case well? Next, the prosecutor was not alone to blame for what was done. Perhaps it was the way you had lived: you had done many aggressive things, many rash things, many bloody things. For it to be possible for an innocent man to be found guilty argues a very ugly reputation. For you don't say that the trial was corrupt, that money was involved. Are you really so brazen? You were thought to be a murderer. And are you angry only with your prosecutor? Did not the jury have the

prove the accused's guilt, he would still have been culpable for bringing a charge which he could not prove. The plural *voluerunt* where the singular would be proper seems to be due to *legum*.

[10] See crit. note.

runt, non omnium sententiae?

314

Ego te, pater, occidi

‹Magistratus de confesso sumat supplicium.›[1] Parricidii reus paribus sententiis absolutus furere coepit et dicere per furorem frequenter: 'ego te, pater, occidi.' Magistratus tamquam de confesso supplicium sumpsit. Reus est caedis.

1   SERMO

Si qua erunt quae a me in divisionibus controversiarum dicantur eadem frequentius, intellegite fieri primum propter interventum novorum, deinde propter condicionem divisionum; nam hi qui antea non audierunt pertinentia ad plures controversias debent cognoscere, et ad praesentis materiae controversias nonnihil[2] interest quomodo ego diviserim.

2   Est autem commune cum[3] aliis controversiis huius materiae illud, quod reus magistratus, de cuius personae dignitate haec ipsa res satis pronuntiat. Videtur etiam de ante acta vita probari eo modo[4] quod creatus est. Secundum illud aeque commune, quod nullas simultates executus est, nullam spem ex caede eius quem occisum accusator queritur concipere potuit, et officio impulsus, etiamsi lapsus est,

3 tamen veluti legis consilio deceptus est. Ut haec commu-

---

[1] *SB*[2]
[2] *Ro.*: nihil Aβ
[3] *Ranc.*: -nis cura Aβ
[4] modo (= tantum *ut vid.*)] *del. SB*[1]

same opinion about you, was not the vote unanimous?

314

I killed you, father

‹Let the magistrate punish a confessed offender.› The defendant in a parricide case, acquitted on an equal vote, started to go mad and often in his madness say "I killed you, father." The magistrate punished him as a confessed offender. He is accused of homicide.

DISCUSSION

If in what I say about the division of controversies I often repeat myself, understand that this is firstly because new auditors come in and secondly because of the nature of divisions. For those who have not previously heard matter pertaining to more than one controversy need to learn of it and with regard to controversies based on a current theme it is of some consequence how I divide.[1]

It is common to other controversies so based that the defendant is a magistrate, a fact which in itself declares his personal high standing. Also the mere fact that he was elected seems to show that his past life is approved. Second is another point equally in common, that he has not pursued any feuds, had nothing to hope for from the killing of the man of whose execution the prosecutor complains. Motivated by his duty, even if he made a slip, he was deceived as it were by the advice of the law. As these are

---

[1] Obscure, if not lacunose. He goes on to list two points common to this type of controversy and one special to this particular one.

nia, ita illud iam proprium: etiam[5] si ullum adversum hunc adulescentem habuisset odium magistratus, magis insania eius vindicabatur. Sic,[6] cum ita praeparaverit causam, incipit de iure suo loqui.

4   DECLAMATIO

'Magistratus de confesso sumat supplicium.' Durum ministerium et iniucunda honoris huius necessitas. Sed quis potius leges exequetur et hominum commissa nisi qui rem publicam administrat[7]? Nemo istud faceret libenter, ‹nemo›[8] nisi necessitate. Ergo non solum licuit mihi occidere confessum, sed etiam, si nollem, necesse fuit.

5   Videamus an ille confessus sit. Testes praebeam vobis? Tota civitate audita vox est. Ne ipsos quidem accusatores negaturos esse confido ipsius voce, ipsius lingua esse dictum: 'ego te, pater, occidi': et non semel dictum, ne casus 6 videretur. 'At enim confessio habenda non est nisi quae a sano proficiscitur.' Non video cur ad hanc interpretationem deducatur vis istius verbi, quod lege comprehensum est. Ego enim confessionem existimo qualemcumque contra se pronuntiationem; nec me scrutari lex iubet qua quis 7 causa confessus sit. Immo ea natura est omnis confessionis ut possit videri demens qui de se confitetur. Furore[9] impulsus est: alius ebrietate, alius errore, alius dolore, quidam quaestione. Nemo contra se dicit nisi aliquo cogente. Quod enim genus confessionis exigitis? Ut aliquis securus, quieta mente, nullo adigente, dicat 'ego patrem occidi'?

---

5 *Wi.*: ut Aβ   6 *Obr.*: si Aβ   7 *Ro.*: -rarit A (*ex* -raret), B   8 *SB*[1]   9 *anne* ‹alius› f.?

---

2 "Confess." *Fateor* implies reluctance.

common, so this is particular: even if the magistrate had borne a grudge against this young man, he was better avenged by his insanity. So having thus prepared his case, he starts talking about the law in his favor.

DECLAMATION

"Let a magistrate punish a confessed offender." A hard function and a disagreeable necessity of this office. But who will enforce the laws and punish men's offenses rather than the man who manages the business of the commonwealth? No one would do it willingly, ⟨no one⟩ except of necessity. Therefore not only was I entitled to execute a confessed offender but, even if I did not wish to, I had to.

Let us see whether he confessed. Should I give you witnesses? His voice was heard all over the community. I am confident that even the prosecution will not deny that with his own voice, his own tongue, came the words "I killed you, father;" and not said once, as might seem chance. "But it must not be considered a confession unless it comes from a sane man." I do not see why the sense of that word, included in the law as it is, should be drawn to that interpretation. I judge a confession to be a declaration, no matter of what nature, against oneself; and the law does not tell me to scrutinize the reason why a man confesses. Or rather, it is in the nature of every confession that a man who confesses about himself can seem to be out of his mind. He was impelled by madness; another by drunkenness, another by pain, somebody by torture. Nobody speaks against himself unless somebody forces him. For what sort of confession are you demanding? That anyone in security, his mind composed, nobody driving him, should say "I killed my father"? And yet the very word[2]

Atqui ipsum verbum videtur habere vim coactae veritatis. Quid ergo aliud intueri debeo[10] quam vocem? Si semel hoc audissem, lex tamen me iam appellaret: saepius dixit, in eadem voce perseveravit. Viderimus an in aliis partibus de-

9 mens fuerit: hic tamquam sanus perseveravit. De confesso ergo sumpsi supplicium, atque ad me non pertinet an is qui confessus est nocens fuerit. Fingite enim esse aliquem qui aliquo modo confessus sit, hunc a magistratu occisum, postea apparuisse aliquo casu falsum fuisse quod dixisset: num agi cum magistratu potest? Lex quae confessum puniri iubet sententiam ipsi relinquit.

10 Descendamus tamen eo, quoniam confessus[11] est, ut quaeramus an ille etiam parricida fuerit. Nec mihi necesse est dicere illa quae ab accusatore dicta sunt. Habuerit ille causas propter quas deferret, habuerit testes suos, habue- rit argumenta (et profecto creditis non sine magna fiducia delatum esse tanti criminis reum); mihi in argumentum sufficit genus absolutionis: paribus sententiis absolutus

11 est. Hoc in alio genere causae dubium est, in parricidio vero, quod probari nemo voluit, quod falsum esse ad vota pertinebat, diversam habuit pronuntiationem. Obiectum est alicui mortalium quod patrem occidisset, quod eum cui lucem, cui haec beneficia rerum naturae debebat, sua ma-

12 nu trucidasset—et hoc pars iudicum credidit? Ego vero illos et probo nec[12] miror qui absolverunt: pars tamen iu- dicum pronuntiavit factum esse parricidium, pars incre- dibile esse.[13] Hos movit quod probari poterat, illos quod

---

[10] *Sch.*: debes Aβ   [11] *SB*[3]: filius Aβ   [12] *SB*[1]: et Aβ
[13] parricidium . . . esse *om.* A[1], pars . . . esse *del. Ri.*, *SB*[3]

---

[3] He pronounces his own guilt.

seems to have the force of truth compelled. So what do I have to look at but his utterance? If I had heard it only once, still the law would thereupon call on me. He said it often, kept on repeating the same words. We shall see later whether he was mad in other contexts: here he kept on track, like a sane man. Therefore I punished the confessed offender, and I am not concerned as to whether the person confessing was guilty. For imagine that somebody somehow made a confession and was executed by the magistrate, and that it later appeared through some accident that what he had said was untrue: can the magistrate be prosecuted? The law which requires that a confessed offender be punished leaves the verdict to the person himself.[3]

However, let us come down to the question: since he has confessed, was he also a parricide? And I do not have to say what has been said by the prosecutor: grant that he had his reasons for bringing the charge, that he had his witnesses, that he had evidence (and I am sure you believe that a man would not have been charged with so terrible a crime if the prosecutor had not been very confident): for me the nature of the acquittal is proof enough. He was acquitted by equal votes. In another kind of case this leaves doubt, but in a parricide, which no one wanted proved, where it was a thing to pray for that the charge be false, it declared something different. A human being is charged with murdering his father, of slaughtering with his own hand the one to whom he owed the light of day, these benefits of nature—and half the jury believed it. For my part I applaud them, but I am not surprised at those who acquitted. However, half the jury declared that parricide was committed, half that it was unbelievable. One half was swayed by the fact that it could be proved, the other by the

negari. Reus ergo suspectus, et in eam partem potius accipiendus, ut fecerit.

13   Quid superest? 'Per dementiam confessus est.' At mihi pro causa mea summum videtur argumentum ipsa dementia, etiam si confessus non esset. Non sine causa videlicet vetus illa et antiqua aetas tradidit eos qui aliquod commiserunt scelus Furiis agitari et per totum orbem agi. Ut nomina mentita sint, ut aliquid fabulae fingant, ab aliquo tamen

14   men exemplo ista ‹et› experimento[14] venerunt. Factum esse aliquid necesse est ut hoc credibile videretur, sive istud di immortales, qui non iudiciis falli, non gratia circumveniri, non ignorantia decipi possunt, constituerunt. Ego vero gratulor mortalitati. Colite, homines, innocentiam et nullam spem impunitatis ex secreto scelerum conceperitis.

15   ceperitis. Licet nulli hominum prospexerint oculi, licet nulla cuiusquam mortalium conscientia intervenerit, sub caelo tamen fecistis, et ille fusus per omnes rerum naturae partis spiritus adfuit. Erat, erat illic potentior testis: non quidem apud iudicem dicet nec oratorum interrogabitur

16   artibus, sed loquetur ore vestro. Tu forsitan, cum miserum patrem trucidares, tollentem ad sidera manus risisti; inane hoc supra nos vacuumque cura caelestium putabas. Sunt illa vera quae extremo miseri spiritu dicebantur: 'dabis mihi, scelerate, poenas: persequar, quandoque et occurram.' Et quod ad me quidem pertinet, iudices, non aliam huius dementiae putem fuisse rationem, quae coepit post

17   absolutionem. Nec tamen illa mihi vana quorundam vide-

---

[14] *Sch.*: -nta Aβ

---

4 And denial could seem easier to believe than that such a crime had been committed.   5 "A stoic touch" (Wi.).

fact that it could be denied.[4] So the defendant is under suspicion and rather to be regarded as having done it.

What remains? "He confessed when he was out of his mind." But I regard this very dementia, even if he had not confessed, as a capital argument for my case. With good reason, it seems, did the old, antique time hand it down that those who have committed a crime are harassed by the Furies and pursued through all the world. Names may have been falsified, legends may be part invention, but these stories come from some example <and> experience. Something must have happened to make this seem credible; or was it that the immortal gods, who cannot be deceived by trials or hoodwinked by influence or misled by ignorance, so ordained? For my part I congratulate the human race. Men, cultivate innocence and set no hope of impunity on the secrecy of your crimes. Though no human eyes may have seen you, no mortal's knowledge entered in, yet you did it under the sky and the breath that is spread through all parts of nature[5] was there. Yes indeed, a more potent witness was on the scene; one that will not talk in front of a judge or be questioned by the skills of pleaders, but will speak through your own mouths.[6] You perhaps, when you were slaughtering your poor father as he raised his hands to the stars, laughed; you thought this above us was a void, empty of sky-dwellers' care. But what the poor man said with his last breath is true: "You criminal, you will pay me a penalty; I shall pursue you one day and meet you." And so far as I am concerned, gentlemen, I think there was no other reason for this dementia, which began after his acquittal. And yet the persuasion of some folk

---

[6] "The mouths of the guilty" (Wi.).

tur esse persuasio, qui credunt non extrinsecus has Furias
venire nec ullius deorum impulsu hanc mortalibus incidisse dementiam, sed nasci intus: conscientiam esse quae
torqueat, animum esse qui urat. Iterum gratulor: bene
hercule factum est quod, etiam si omnes fefellerimus, ef-
18 fugere non possumus nos. Ite nunc et dicite: 'demens erat
cum confessus est.' At mihi videtur demens fuisse cum
occidit. Ergo quodcumque illud furoris genus aut poena
a diis immortalibus constituta aut confessio quaedam no-
19 centis animi videretur. Videamus tamen quomodo insanie-
rit. Si per praecipitia ferretur, dicerem: agit aliquis deorum; si in obvios occurreret, dicerem: ultionis quaeritur
materia. Nunc vox una, vox eadem ad iudices et per totam
civitatem: 'ego te, pater, occidi.' Indicare[15] liceat quid factum sit. Non est dementia. 'Ego te, pater, occidi.' Hoc si
vos furorem vocatis, idem pars dixit iudicum. Nihil varia-
tum, nihil ex more aliorum insanientium mutatum est.
'Ego te, pater, occidi.' †Longa confessio est repetita totiens
confessio est.†[16]

20   Ecquid concipitis animis imaginem illam quae hoc
coegit? Stabat profecto ante oculos laceratus et adhuc cru-
entus pater, ostendebat effusa vitalia; totus ille ante oculos
locus, totum scelus mente et cogitatione †perflexum†.[17]
⟦Non potest fieri ut per dementiam videatur totiens con-

15 *SB*[1]: invenire A[2]CD (inv- . . . occidi *om.* A[1]B)

16 ⟨plura ne requiratis.⟩ longa . . . repetita totiens [confessio
est] ⟨*del. Ro.*⟩ *tempt. SB*[2]: ⟨non⟩ longa confessio est: rep. tot. longa
est *Watt*[2]

17 perspectum *Sch., alii alia*

seems to me not without foundation: they believe that
these Furies do not come from outside and that this dementia has not befallen mortals by any impulse of the gods
but is born within; it is conscience that torments, the mind
that burns. Again I congratulate: well it is that, even if we
elude everyone else, we cannot escape ourselves. I challenge you people, say it: "He was out of his mind when he
confessed." But *I* think he was out of his mind when he
killed. So whatever sort of madness that was, it would seem
to have been either a punishment ordained by the immortal gods or the confession of a guilty spirit. But let us look at
the manner of his madness. If he had jumped over a preci-
pice, I should say: "Some god drives him." If he attacked
people who came in his way, I should say: "Matter for retribution is sought." [7] As it is, there is one and the same utterance addressed to the jury and throughout the community:
"I killed you, father." Let a man be free to give information
about something done. It is not dementia. "I killed you, father." If you call this madness, half the jury said the same.[8]
Nothing varied, nothing changed after the fashion of other
lunatics. "I killed you, father." <Don't ask for more.> A
confession so often repeated is lengthy.

Can you imagine the picture that made him do this? His
father no doubt was standing before his eyes, torn and still
bleeding, he was showing his vitals poured out. That whole
place was before his eyes, the whole crime scanned in
mind and thought. [[It cannot be that he be thought out of

[7] The gods are making him commit acts for which he will be
punished.

[8] That he killed his father.

fessus qui numquam negavit.]] Ite nunc et paribus absol-
vite.

315

Fortis pater desertoris

Vir fortis desertorem sua manu occidat. Eodem proelio
quo pater fortiter fecit eiusdem filius deseruit. Petit praemii nomine ut eum non ipse occidat.

1   DECLAMATIO

Fortis praemium peto.

2   SERMO

Illa communia nostis.

3   DECLAMATIO

Scriptum est.

4   SERMO

Et[1] illud commune.

5   DECLAMATIO

Merito scriptum est: magno labore, multis periculis consecutus sum.

6   SERMO

Est aliquid proprium controversiae huic.

[1] *Ro., Ri.*: est Aβ

---

[9] Irrelevant to context but well enough *per se*. A real madman
would have confessed one day and denied the next. No reference
to the trial for parricide (see SB[2]).

his mind when he confessed so often with never a denial.[9]]
Acquit now—on an equal vote![10]

315

The hero father of a deserter

Let a hero kill a deserter with his own hand. In the same
battle at which a father became a hero his son deserted. He
asks as a reward that he not kill him himself.

DECLAMATION[1]

As a hero I claim my reward.

DISCUSSION

You know the commonplaces.

DECLAMATION

It is written.

DISCUSSION

This too is commonplace.

DECLAMATION

Rightly it is written. I won it by long effort, by many
dangers.

DISCUSSION

There is something particular to this controversy.

---

[10] Addressed in scorn (*ite nunc*) to the acquitting jurors in the
parricide trial, not the present jury (unbelievably disrespectful).

[1] Here and in the following items we have only the opening
words.

7

DECLAMATIO

Peto praemium fortis qui senex fortiter feci, qui iam pater fortiter feci, qui in ea acie fortiter feci in qua et filius meus fugit. 'Sed contra legem petis.'

8

SERMO

Iterum illa communia: omne privilegium contra reliqua iura esse; viris fortibus non posse praemia persolvi nisi cum aliqua inclinatione legis alicuius. Haec iam prompta ut comparemus: etiamsi contra legem optamus, utram tamen magis servari legem placet: utrum eam quae honorem dat bene meritis an eam quae constituit poenam peccantibus? Deinde specialiter: utrum eam quae honorem viro

9 forti dat an eam quae poenam desertori constituit? In utraque re speciosus et apertus tractatus est; nam describere possumus quanta cum difficultate fortiter pugnetur et quanto cum periculo, et excusare et dare veniam aliquam †ut natura dignum sit et difficile fortiter pugnare†: quid[2] mirum esse aliquem qui <sibi> parcat[3]? Hic clamor ille utriusque exercitus, tela illa in os et in oculos venientia et cadens secundum latus commilito, tum gemitus vulneratorum et fragor ille armorum et nitor ferri. Deinde, cum comparaverimus leges, nihilominus et molliamus quaes-

10 tionem. Non utique perit lex. Quare? Quoniam plurima accidere possunt ut desertorem non vir fortis occidat.[4]

[2] *Ro.*: quam Aβ
[3] *Ri.*: pereat Aβ
[4] non utique . . . occidat *in serm. transp. coni. Ri.*: *declam. tribuunt* Aβ

I claim a hero's reward: I became a hero as an old man, I became a hero when I was already a father, I became a hero in the battle in which my son fled. "But your claim is against the law."

DISCUSSION

Again those commonplaces: that every law *ad hominem* is against other laws, that rewards cannot be paid to heroes without bending some law or other. These are now ready to our hand for comparison: even though an option is against a law, which law do we more want to observe, that which gives honor to the well-deserving or that which lays down a punishment for wrongdoers? Then in particular: that which gives honor to a hero or that which lays down a penalty for a deserter? On either subject the treatment is attractive and open; for we can describe how difficult it is to fight bravely and how fraught with danger, and excuse and in some sort forgive.[2] What wonder that there is someone who spares ⟨himself⟩? Here we have the shouting of both armies, the missiles coming at mouth and eyes, the comrade falling at our side, then the groans of the wounded and the clash of arms and the gleam of steel. Then, when we have compared the laws, let us nevertheless soften the question. The law does not necessarily perish.[3] Why? Because many things can happen to prevent the hero killing the deserter.

[2] Obelized words not translated.

[3] Which law is more important? The question loses its edge if the opposing law is not necessarily violated.

DECLAMATIO

Haec autem[5] sic dixi tamquam impunitatem desertoris peterem; nunc de poena nihil detraho desertoris, de ministro
11 tantum, de manu tantum quaeritur. Frequenter autem
necesse est accidat ut desertorem non vir fortis occidat.
Finge deseruisse aliquem et neminem fortiter fecisse: incolumis erit desertor? Finge fortiter pugnasse aliquem,
sed in ipsa pugna debilitatum, ita ut manum amitteret:
numquid non necesse est subire aliquem hoc ministeri-
12 um? Hoc de alienis. Praeterea lex quae desertorem a viro
forti occidi iussit nihil cogitavit de hac necessitate. Quaedam, etiamsi nulla significatione legis comprehensa sint,
natura tamen excipiuntur. An hoc cogitatum esset, ut pater
filium occideret? Ut frater fratrem occideret? Nam id quidem profecto vix natura ipsa videbatur admittere, ut in ea-
13 dem acie pater fortiter faceret, filius desereret. Itaque si
illud non praemii nomine peterem, si aliter gratiam mihi
rettulissetis, recusarem; dicerem: 'non utique occidere debeo.' Plus est quod opto. Lex desertorem et virum fortem
nominavit. Mutata sunt omnia: filius deseruit.

14   Ergo haec dixi adhuc: debetur[6] mihi quodcumque
praemium, debetur vel contra legem; mea lex utilior est rei
publicae; non utique contra legem peto, quoniam multa
accidere possunt ut non vir fortis occidat; non contra legem peto, quoniam fieri non potest ut lex hoc voluerit, ut a
patre filius occidatur.

15   ⟦Renuntio, res publica,[7] non utor honore constituto.
Nemo queratur de iniquitate praemii mei, nemo me im-
potenter uti fructu virtutum existimet. Non feci fortiter.

---

[5] *coni. Ri.*: enim Aβ   [6] *Ro.*: dice- Aβ
[7] *Ro.*: rei p(ublicae) Aβ

I have said all this as though I was asking for immunity for the deserter. In fact I abate nothing of the deserter's punishment, the question is only as to the executant, the hand. It often necessarily happens that a hero does not kill the deserter. Suppose somebody has deserted and nobody has become a hero: will the deserter go free? Suppose somebody has fought bravely, but has been crippled in the fight itself, so as to lose his hand: isn't it necessary for someone else to take on this function? So much as to strangers. Furthermore, the law which required a deserter to be killed by a hero never thought of this compulsion. Some exceptions are made by nature, even though they are not covered by any intimation in the law. Would it have been considered that a father kill his son? Or a brother kill his brother? Surely nature herself hardly seemed to admit that in the same battle a father should become a hero and his son desert. So if I were not asking for this as reward, if you had repaid me in some other way, I should refuse; I should say: "I am not necessarily obliged to kill." My option is additional. The law has spoken of a deserter and a hero. Everything has changed: my son deserted.

So this is what I have said so far: any reward is due to me, even against the law; my law is more useful to the commonwealth; I do not necessarily claim against the law, since many things can happen to prevent a hero killing; I do not claim against the law, since it is impossible that the law intended a son to be killed by his father.

⟦Commonwealth, I renounce. I am not using the established honor. Let no man complain of the disproportion of my reward, no man judge that I am making excessive use of the fruit of valor. I did not become a hero. You are in error,

Erratis, commilitones: blanditus est mihi imperator; decepit te fama, civitas. Ego fortiter, homo senex? Ego fortiter,
16 desertoris pater?⟧ At putate me hoc optinere non posse:
non utor honore virtutis, non subeo onera viri fortis. Nolite
mihi dare praemia: non occido desertorem tamquam vir
17 fortis. Dimittite me a merito meo, liberate me nomine. ⟦Et
sane quam habetis aliam vindictam.⟧ Lex occidi a viro forti
desertorem voluit tamquam inutilissimum, tamquam in-
imicissimum. Neque enim poenam hanc viro forti constituit, neque imposuit recusanti, neque ullam necessitatem
nolenti. Quid enim facietis si non occidero? Quis est huius
18 constitutionis exitus? Legem nullam habetis. Sed vindicare vos vultis: adhibete carnificem, occidite utrumque.
Bene hercule exhortamini: est quare arma senex resumam.
'Fortiter fecisti, plurimum rei publicae tuae praestitisti,
velis nolis.' Quid igitur haec ad parricidium? 'Et filium oc-
cide, et parum sit tibi perdere.' Vehemens erat si dicerem:
'nolo occidere'; ignoscetis mihi dicenti: 'non possum; manus illa, quae fortis dicebatur, defecit.'

19   Scio nunc me, iudices, reprehendi a bonis patribus
tamquam praemium optare nesciam. Melior enim et in-
dulgentior pater hoc diceret: 'Donate meritis meis filium.
Ita ego quod fortiter feci, quod tantum hostilis sanguinis
fudi, quod inter momenta victoriae fui, non est pro opera
20 duorum?' Ego, si melior essem pater, illud quoque simpliciter confiterer, deseruisse filium mea culpa. Quid enim
necesse fuit educere in aciem adulescentulum? Quid necesse fuit rudes annos cum gravissimo hoste acerbissimo
proelio componere? Aut certe si tantus gloriae amor, si

---

4 Double-bracketed by Wi. as an alternative to s.16.
5 But why by a "hero"?   6 Or "brave"? He was *vir fortis*.

comrades; the general flattered me. Community, rumor
has deceived you. I a hero, an old man? I a hero, the father
of a deserter?]][4] But suppose I cannot have this: then I
don't use the honor of valor, I don't take on the burdens of a
hero. Don't give me rewards. I am not killing the deserter
as a hero. Discharge me from my merit, free me from the
name. [[And you certainly have another punishment.]] The
law wished the deserter to be killed by a hero, as a thoroughly useless, thoroughly hateful being.[5] It did not lay
this down as a penalty for the hero, nor impose it on him if
he refused, nor any other compulsion against his will. For
what will you do if I don't kill him? Where does this ordi-
nance take us? You have no law. But you want to avenge
yourselves: get an executioner, kill both of us. Upon my
word, I like your urging: there's a reason for me to take up
arms again in my old age. "You became a hero, you did
great service to your commonwealth, like it or not." What
then does this have to do with parricide? "Kill your son too,
don't think it enough just to lose him." It would be too
strong to say: "I don't want to kill him." You will forgive me
if I say: "I can't; my hand, which used to be called strong,[6]
has failed."

I know, gentlemen, that good fathers now blame me, as
not knowing how to opt for reward. A better, more loving
father would say: "Give me my son for my services. I became a hero, shed so much enemy blood, was one of the
factors in victory: won't that do for the work of two?" If I
was a better father, I should frankly admit that it was my
fault my son deserted. What need was there to lead a strip-
ling into battle? What need was there to pit tender years
against a very formidable enemy in a very bitter fight? Or
at least, if love of glory, desire for praise was so great, I

tanta cupido laudum, recedere a filio meo non debueram.
21 Et feci, iudices, primum, et, tamquam instituerem filium
rudem militiae, non procul a latere reliqui. Decepit me ardor ille belli; ut primum signa canere coeperunt, ut primum *,[8] totum animum percussit patria, *[9] sola virtus.
Adulescentulus interim rudis in illa nube pulveris, in illa
confusione permixtarum utrimque legionum virum fortem sequi non potuit. At ego infelix etiam invidiam filio
feci, et spolia rettuli quo minus illi ignosceretur.

22 Quo me ducis, anime? Quo me trahis, adfectus? Pla-
cent ista[10]; sed aliud optavi. Nihil est quod ex meo favore
speres, iuvenis infelicissime; nullam fiduciam ex hac quan-
tulacumque operae meae gratia capias. Moriendum est.
Debetur hoc sane disciplinae militari, debetur castrorum
23 severitati. Infelix exeuntium omen miseraeque primitiae!
Si alterum utique ex domo nostra ⟨Fata⟩[11] destinabatis,
cur non senem potius traxistis? Quid nunc tibi proderit,
miserrime adulescens, quod modestus in pace, quod pius,
et, si contigisset civitati[12] felicior quies, optimus filius eras?
24 Moriendum est. Quid tibi praestare infelix pater possum?
Cum duceris, flebo, plangam. Hos quos sumpseram modo
ex victoria publica laetos habitus abducite. Metui[13] ambitiosus pater scilicet ne quid de militari severitate detrahe-

---

[8] *lac. ind. Ri.*
[9] *lac. ind. SB[3] (remansit in pectore add. SB[1])*
[10] *SB[1]*: placet causa Aβ   [11] *SB[3]*
[12] *Ranc.*: felicitati A(β)   [13] *Sch.*: merui Aβ

---

[7] See crit. note.

[8] As Wi. says, the Manlius Torquatus who executed his son for
a breach of military discipline is in mind; cf. 349.8. This father "no

ought not to have gone away from my son. And at first, gentlemen, I didn't; as though I was initiating my son, ignorant as he was of soldiering, I did not leave him far from my side. The ardor of war led me astray, when first the trumpets began to sound, when first *, my country struck my whole mind, <in my whole heart remained>[7] only valor. Meanwhile, in that cloud of dust, in that confusion of legions mingled on both sides, the untried youth could not follow the hero. But I, alas, made my son look bad and brought back trophies to make it harder for him to be forgiven.

My soul, where are you leading me? Emotion, where are you taking me? All this is very well, but I opted for something else. Hapless young man, you have nothing to hope for from my popularity; don't put any faith in this favor, whatever little it amounts to, accruing from my service. You must die. Military discipline demands it to be sure, army rigor demands it. Unhappy omen as we went forth, miserable firstfruits! If you <Fates> were settling on one of us and it had to be from my house, why did you not rather drag off the old man? What good will it do you now, most unfortunate young fellow, that you were well-behaved in peacetime, dutiful, and if the community had enjoyed a happier repose, an excellent son? You must die. What can I do for you, your hapless father? When you are led to execution, I shall weep, I shall beat my breast. Take away that garb of joy that I had just put on after the public victory. No doubt as a father eager to shine[8] I was afraid of

doubt" wanted similar kudos, but his real motive was fear of criticism. *Ambitiosus* (pace Wi.) has nothing to do with his high hopes for his son.

rem, ne viderer vir fortis desertori ignoscere. Contentus
fui post tot merita, favente tota civitate, ut tantum inno-
25 cens essem. Et ecce iam miserantes video iudicum vultus;
quorundam deprehenduntur lacrimae. Potui plus optare,
potui. Sic quoque ego te, fili, occidi. At tu, quisquis es in
quem transferetur hoc infelix ministerium, supremas audi
patris miserrimi voces. Hoc saltem fortunae meae praesta:
semel ferias.

316

Flens luxuriosi pater

Flens pater per publicum filium luxuriosum sequebatur.
Dementiae reus est.

1   SERMO

Hoc genus controversiarum paene divisionem non exigit.
Illa communis fere omnibus ex lege dementiae pendenti-
bus controversiis quaestio est, quid dementia sit; et an
haec dementia sit. In eo quo quaerimus quid sit dementia,
et finitionibus utrimque positis et omni tractatu, hanc controversiam dividemus ut quaeratur utrum dementia ea demum accipi debeat quae habeat aequalem mentis errorem
2 an etiam ex singulis vel paucis intellegi possit. Haec saepe
tractata sunt: ad crimen ipsum veniamus. Intellego et indi-
gnari posse hunc patrem quod reus dementiae a luxurioso
fiat et eum multa graviter et aspere dicere contra filium
posse: recipit adversarii persona; sed videamus an recipiat
nostra. Nam sicut paulo ante praecipiebam vobis ut perso-

detracting from military rigor, of seeming (a hero) to pardon a deserter. After so many services, the darling of the whole community, I was content just to be innocent. And look, I now see pity in the faces of the jury; some are caught weeping. I could have opted for more, I could. This way too, son, I killed you. But you, whoever you are, on whom this sinister function shall devolve, hear the last words of a most wretched father; do this much for my fortune: strike once!

316

The father of a loose-liver weeping

A father used to follow his loose-living son in public weeping. He is accused of dementia.

DISCUSSION

This type of controversy has almost no need of division. The question common to almost all controversies depending on the law of dementia is: "what is dementia?" and "is this dementia?" When we ask what dementia is, in definitions laid down on both sides and in general treatment, we shall so divide this controversy that it be asked whether dementia is to be recognized only when there is consistent mental wandering or can also be diagnosed from individual items or a few. All this has often been handled; let us come to the charge itself. I realize that this father can be outraged at being charged with dementia by his loose-living son and that he can say many severe and bitter things against his son. The adversary's persona is open to that, but let us see whether ours is. For just as I told you a little while

nam intueremini eius apud quem dicenda esset causa,[1] sic
nunc quoque admoneam necesse est ut intueamur perso-
3 nam quam nobis induimus. Pater hic qualis est? Non acer:
luxuriosum non abdicavit, non conviciatus est; etiam cum
aliquid admonendi gratia faceret, tacuit tamen. Non durus: flevit enim. Quidquid contra colorem talis animi dixe-
rimus, quodam modo contra thema dicemus. Consilium
itaque totius actionis ex iis capere debemus quae praeces-
4 serunt. Quid aliud praecessit ⟨quam⟩[2] mollis invidia? Ergo cum approbaverimus non uno facto dementiam esse
convincendam, veniemus ad ordinem defensionis. Ante
actae vitae ratio constet. Hoc non propterea tantum dicendum est quod sic defendi reus potest, sed etiam quod invidia redit ad accusatorem: omnia enim quae pro se dixerit
in filium dicet.

5   DECLAMATIO

Quid feci dementer? Iuvenis frugaliter vixi, patrimonium
auxi, uxorem duxi, filium sustuli, hunc amo. 'Flens' inquit
'me per publicum sequeris.' Poterant ista et separata defendi; nam neque admirationi profecto cuiquam mortalium esset quod pater filium sequerer et separatae ab hoc
6 lacrimae poterant videri non ad te pertinere. Sed ne ulla
arte suffugere crimen accusatoris mei videar, totum hoc

---

¹ *SB²*: sententia A*β*   ² *Aer.*

---

¹ Not in our collection.   ² The judge or jury. *Sententia*,
"verdict," seems to have replaced *causa* (*cā*).

³ A mild rebuke and sign of a soft heart.

⁴ Before the charge of *dementia* was brought.

⁵ *Invidia* towards the son caused by his father's behavior.

ago[1] to look at the persona of him before whom the case is to be pleaded,[2] so too I must now also warn you to look at the persona which we are assuming. What is this father like? Not harsh: he did not disown the loose-liver or scold him; even when doing something by way of admonishing him he said nothing. He is not hard: for he wept.[3] Whatever we say against the "color" of such a disposition will be in some sort said contrary to the theme. So we ought to take the plan of our whole plea from what came before.[4] What did come before other ⟨than⟩ a certain mild embarrassment?[5] So when we shall have made our point that a conviction of dementia must not be reached from one action, we shall come to the process of our defense. Let us be clear about the earlier life; not only because the defendant can thus be defended but because the embarrassment recoils upon the prosecutor.[6] For everything he says on his own behalf he will say against the son.

DECLAMATION

What did I do dementedly? As a young man I lived frugally, I increased my patrimony, I married a wife, I acknowledged a son, I love him. "You follow me in public," he says, "weeping." These items could be defended separately; for nobody in the world could be surprised because as a father I followed my son and, separated from this, the tears might seem to have nothing to do with you. But lest I be thought to be sliding out of my prosecutor's charge by any device, I will join what is brought against me in its en-

[6] This son who says that he is embarrassed by his father's weeping will indeed be embarrassed by the recital of his father's irreproachable past as contrasted with his own.

quod obicitur iungam. Lacrimae sunt in culpa. Fleo fortasse supervacuo[3]: sic me consolaris, sic lacrimas patris tui siccas? Flendum mihi hodie foret, etiam si hoc antea non fecissem.

7   SERMO

Nolo quisquam me reprehendat tamquam vobis locos non dem. Si ampliare declamationem voletis et ingenium exercere, dicetis quod ad causam huius nullo modo, ad delectationem aurium fortasse pertineat.

8   DECLAMATIO

Nondum privatas ac peculiares lacrimarum reddo causas; interim, quis miratur flere hominem? Hinc infantia incipit, in hanc necessitatem plerumque Fortuna deducit. Quis enim est dies qui non triste aliquid et flebile nobis mine-

9   tur? Si nullam aliam rationem lacrimarum haberemus, conspectus tamen hominum et ratio mortalitatis poterat elicere fletus. Hae amicitiae, hae propinquitates, hi congressus, haec studia laudesque intra breve temporis momentum occident atque labentur. Quotus quisque transit dies quo non funus aspiciamus[4]?

10   'Flens me sequeris, et per publicum sequeris.' Non totum crimen obicis: diu hoc antea domi feci. Quantulum temporis spatium est quod[5] talem me vides! Fleo[6] secreto,

11   ubi cubiculum et nox et animus sibi relictus est. 'Flens me sequeris.' Quid[7] possum? Miror equidem illos fortissimos patres qui hunc animi dolorem semel recidunt et in universum flere definito aliquo temporis spatio semel

3 *Dingel*: -ua Aβ
4 *Hå*.²: accipi- Aβ   5 quo *Aer.*
6 *Wi.*: flere Aβ   7 *Sch.*: quod Aβ

tirety. The tears are blamed. Perhaps I weep superfluously: is this how you comfort me, this how you dry your father's tears? I would have good cause to weep today, even if I had not done so before.

DISCUSSION

I don't want anyone to criticize me for not giving you topics.[7] If you want to expand the declamation and exercise your ingenuity, you will say what has nothing to do with this man's case, but may perhaps have something to do with pleasuring the ear.

DECLAMATION

I don't yet give private and particular reasons for the tears; meanwhile, who wonders that a human being weeps? Infancy starts from that, Fortune mostly leads into this compulsion. For what day but threatens us with something sad and lamentable? If we had no other reason for tears, the survey of mankind and the consideration of mortality could elicit weeping. These friendships, these family bonds, these gatherings, these studies and achievements will die and slip away in a brief moment of time. How few days pass in which we do not see a funeral?

"You follow me weeping and you follow me in public." You don't bring the charge in full: I did this before at home for a long time. How brief a space of time it is in which you see me thus! I weep in secret where bedchamber and night and spirit is left to itself. "You follow me weeping." What can I do? For my part I admire those stalwart fathers who cut back this mental anguish once for all and can weep

---

[7] *Loci communes*, general themes for rhetorical embroidery.

queunt.[8] Flens te per publicum sequor. Quid ergo? Non misereris? Gratulor crimini meo si movi. Si haec tibi gravis videtur invidia, quid opus erat accusatione, quid iudicibus, quid hac probatione dementiae? Sanare poteras.

12   Exigis tamen causas lacrimarum mearum. Non me pecunia movet (divites aliquando fuimus), non illos late quondam patentes agros desidero, non faenus nec ingens pondus argenti. Nuper sine modo[9] desideravi vernulam meum.

317

Imperator provocatus a filio

Qui provocatus ab hoste non pugnaverit, capite puniatur. Filius imperatoris ad hostes transfugit. Provocavit patrem. Ille non descendit in certamen solus, sed acie commissa vicit hostes: in quo proelio et filius eius cecidit. Accusatur quod provocatus ab hoste non pugnaverit.

1   SERMO

An quisquis ab hoste provocatus non pugnaverit puniri debeat; an haec lex ad imperatorem pertineat; an hic ab hoste provocatus sit; an pugnaverit.

2   DECLAMATIO

'Qui ab hoste provocatus non pugnaverit, capite puniatur.' In omnibus quidem legibus solam spectari oportet scri-

---

[8] *SB*[2]: queant Aβ   [9] s. m. *Fr., Obr.*: in domo Aβ

---

[8] *Sine modo*: probably not, as I formerly suggested, imperative and adverb ("with your kind permission"); Wi. cites Apul. *Met.* 4.7. It is implied that the tears need not have been on account of

once for all in a definite space of time. I follow in public weeping. What then? Are you not sorry for me? I am thankful to my charge if I have moved you. If this embarrassment seems severe to you, what was the need for a prosecution, a jury, this proving of dementia? You could have cured me.

But you demand reasons for my tears. Money does not move me (we were rich at one time), I don't miss those widespread lands or the income or the massive weight of silver. Lately I missed extravagantly[8] a little slave of mine.

317

A general challenged by his son

Whoso being challenged by the enemy does not fight, let him be capitally punished. A commander's son deserted to the enemy. He challenged his father. The latter did not come down to fight alone but joined battle and defeated the enemy; in which battle his son too was killed. He is prosecuted because being challenged by the enemy he did not fight.

DISCUSSION

Ought whoever being challenged by the enemy does not fight to be punished? Does this law apply to a commander? Was he challenged by the enemy? Did he fight?

DECLAMATION

"Whoso being challenged by the enemy does not fight, let him be capitally punished." In all laws only the intention of

the son's misbehavior. The slave may have died or been sold under financial pressure.

bentis voluntatem. Verba enim ambigua et in plures intel-
lectus ducta sunt, scribendarum legum causa voluntas fuit.
Ergo id unum spectari convenit propter quod scriptae
3 sunt. Huius autem legis manifestum est hanc voluntatem
esse, uti puniatur quotiens commissum est propter quod
constituta poena est: supervacuum supplementum est. Ut
contra verba interpretatio sequatur aliquid, frequenter accidere potest, cum in aliis legibus tum in hac praecipue.
4 Fingamus enim ab hoste provocatum aliquem aegrum,
fingamus provocatum eum qui proximo proelio debilitatus
sit, fingamus esse provocatum quem imperator in aliam
partem expeditionis[1] ire iusserit; profecto adversus neminem horum actio ex hac lege dabitur.
5   Atqui mihi satis est efficere ut alicui non pugnare liceat.
Nam si ulli potest dari haec venia, non dubitabitur quin
patri detur. Sed antequam naturam defendo, imperatoris
6 volo defendere dignitatem. Contendo hanc legem ad milites pertinere: primum quod inter hos fere provocatio fit,[2]
deinde quoniam legum lator numquam profecto tam
iniquus[3] fuit ut periclitari ex eventu pugnae unius civitatem summamque[4] rei publicae[5] vellet. Fingamus enim
ab aliquo ultimo militum provocari ducem: idem discri-
7 men, idem periculum, impar[6] eventus est. Adice quod
inter praecipuas virtutes est imperatoris[7] non pugnare

[1] *del coni. SB*[3]: *anne* nomine *vel* ducem (*Watt*[2]) *addendum?*
[2] *Hå.*[2]: sit Aβ
[3] *Gron.*: inimicus Aβ
[4] *Aer.*: summa Aβ
[5] rem –am *Gron.*
[6] *Hå.*[2]: par Aβ
[7] *Gron.*: -torem Aβ

the writer is to be looked at. For words are ambiguous and drawn into various interpretations, the reason for writing laws was the intention. So the one thing to be looked at is the reason why they were written. The meaning of this law is clear: that there be punishment whenever the act for which punishment is laid down is committed. No supplement is needed. It can frequently happen both in other laws and especially in this one that interpretation contrary to the words makes sense.[1] For let us imagine that some sick person was challenged by the enemy, let us imagine that someone disabled in a recent battle was challenged, let us imagine that someone was challenged whom the commander had ordered to go to another part of the operation: surely no action under this law will be given against any of these.

And yet all I need do is to show that someone is free not to fight. For if this permission can be given to anybody, there will be no doubt about giving it to a father.[2] But before I defend nature, I want to defend the dignity of a commander. I contend that this law applies to soldiers: first, because challenging is usually between them; second, because the lawgiver was surely never so unfair as to want the community, the commonwealth itself, to be staked on the issue of a single combat. For let us imagine that the commander is challenged by some soldier of the lowest rank: the critical situation, the danger, is the same, but the issue is unequal. Add that it is among the chief virtues of a commander *not* to fight sometimes. Thus the enemy is kept in

[1] Lit. "follows something." Not "makes headway."
[2] Of the challenger.

aliquando. Sic extrahitur hostis, sic impetus subitos partis adversae frangit mora, sic interclusos commeatibus in deditionem venire fame cogimus. Itaque hercule rnilitem legimus robustum, legimus iuvenem: imperatorem facimus senem. In illis enim vis corporum et manus sola spectatur, in his consilium et ratio, quae bona procedentis

8 aetatis in locum virium subeunt. Ipsum praeterea nomen imperatoris satis significat non exigi[8] manum ipsius: imperare enim debet et praecipere. In summam, ab eo qui provocatus ab hoste non pugnaverit supplicium optime exigit imperator. Ergo si hoc solum apud vos dicerem: 'non pugnavit dux, non pugnavit senex, non fecit summae rei discrimen', satis tamen iusta defensio videretur.

9 Adhuc tamen propius accedere ad interpretationem legis volo et, quatenus pars diversa scripto innititur, etiam ipsa verba scrutari. Quid tandem dicit lex? 'Qui ab hoste provocatus non pugnaverit.' Ab hoste igitur, non a transfuga: nec umquam habuerim hunc ego perditissimo parricidae honorem, ut illum in numero ponam eorum homi-

10 num qui pro re publica sua, qui pro patria pugnabant. Et si verba ipsa intuemur, hoc satis est; si vero introspicere voluntatem voluerimus, ecquid manifestum est non hoc sensisse legum latorem, ut ulla necessitate posset cogi pater cum filio dimicare? An vero is qui scripsit hostem non videtur scripsisse[9] alienum? Summa hac nominis utique

8 *Gron.*: -gere Aβ
9 voluisse *Watt*[2]

---

3 Who is kept in suspense and so inhibited from any initiative.

suspense, thus delay frustrates sudden pushes on the part of the adversary,[3] thus we force the besieged, cut off from supplies, to surrender from hunger. And therefore, upon my word, we choose a strong young soldier but appoint an old man commander. In the one only force of body and hand is regarded, in the other judgment and reason, the gifts of advancing years which take the place of physical strength. Moreover, the very name "commander"[4] sufficiently indicates that his own hand is not required: his job is to command and enjoin. To conclude, the punishment of one who does not fight when challenged by the enemy is best enforced by the commander. So if I were saying to you only this: "the commander did not fight, the old man did not fight, he did not risk our all," my defense would seem sufficiently valid.

But in addition I want to come closer to the interpretation of the law, and since the opposing party relies on the text, to scrutinize the actual words. What does the law say? "Whoso being challenged by the enemy does not fight." By the enemy, therefore, not by a deserter and I shall never do honor to an abandoned parricide by putting him into the number of those who were fighting for their commonwealth and country. If we look at the actual words, that is enough; but if we want to delve into intention, is it not clear that the lawgiver did not mean that a father should be forced by any compulsion to fight with his son? Or when he wrote "enemy," does he not seem to have written "stranger"? In this ultimacy of the noun he necessarily in-

[4] *Imperator.*

minora complexus est. Non ergo cogi potest quisquam lege ut cum filio suo pugnet.

11   Hic tamen non defenditur adfectus et pietatis simulatione. 'Ego vero' inquit 'pugnavi, sed quo modo pugnare oportebat vestrum imperatorem. Unius sanguinem exigitis: exercitum cecidi. Par gladiatorum simile postulatis: totius civitatis victoriam rettuli. Numerate captivos, numerate spolia, et aestimate an damnari debuerim quia plus

12 praestiti. Quae sunt enim quae lex postulet? Illa quidem pugnam tantummodo meam. Verumtamen videtur tacitum hoc scribentis fuisse votum, ut et hostis occideretur. Utrumque praestiti: et ego pugnavi et ille occisus est.

13   'Sed non continget ea perditissimo iuveni quam quaerebat invidia, ut videretur scelere occisus, ut nobilem facinori suo exitum daret: iaceat in turba. Vos oro qui illud pugnae genus exigebatis, utrum tandem eventum concepistis animo? Vicisset iuvenis senem, vicisset sceleratus pium? Quantum res publica detrimenti, quantum lacrimarum, quantum luctus amisso duce haberet et fractis

14 militum animis et inclinata in posterum spe! An vero imperator vester[10] occidisset illum temerarium iuvenem et sceleratum? Eratne tanti ut publice commissum parricidium videretur? Non iram numinum, non sterilitatem morbosque et alia quibus magna scelera expiari solent timeremus? Ab hoc omine commisissem[11] aciem?'

[10] *Ro.*: nos- A*β*
[11] *Fr.*: -et *fere* A*β*

---

5 An exercise in false logic? *Hostis* includes *alieni* (i.e. in this context nonrelatives); therefore by implication it excludes relatives? So Wi. The conclusion is nonsequential and the concept of

cluded lesser items.[5] So nobody can be forced by any law to fight with his son.

However, he is not defended by any pretence of affection and family feeling. "Yes," he says, "I fought, but as your commander ought to fight. You require one man's blood: I slew an army. You demand a matching pair of gladiators: I brought back the victory of the whole community. Count the prisoners, count the booty, and judge whether I should be found guilty because I provided more. For what items are demanded by the law? Only my personal fight. All the same, the writer's silent prayer seems to have been that the enemy be killed too. I provided both: I fought and he was killed.

"But the abandoned young man shall not get the scandal he aimed for: that it seems as though his killing was a crime, that he gave a spectacular outcome to his wickedness. Let him lie in the multitude. I ask you folk who were pressing for that sort of combat, which outcome did you conceive of? Would the young man have beaten the old, would the criminal have beaten the decent fellow? What damage would the commonwealth have suffered, what tears, what mourning, with her general lost, her soldiers' spirit broken, hope for the future downgraded? Or would your commander have killed that rash and criminal young man? Was it worth it, that the spectacle of parricide should be seen? Should we not have been afraid of the anger of the gods, of a crop failure and epidemics and the rest of it—the usual expiations of heinous crimes? Was this the omen with which I would have joined battle?"

alieni as a smaller group within *hostis* bizarre. What would be the other *minora*?

318

Legatum inter libertos

Testamento quidam instituit heredem amicum et petît ab eo ut ex duobus libertis quos relinquebat utri vellet decem milia daret. Unus ex libertis petît; iudicio contendit. Victus est. Petit alter.

1 DECLAMATIO

Quae mihi iura, quam vetera cum patrono eorum fuerint, non est dicendum: heres sum. Quantopere hi post libertatem satisfecerint, videlicet hac contumelia qua mecum consistunt aeque manifestum. Neuter apud illum meruit ut decem milia acciperet. Quare ergo hoc testamento cavit ut darem hanc summam utri vellem? Non poterat aliter 2 efficere ut mihi isti obsequerentur. Excogitavit ergo optimus omnium amicorum quomodo isti tamquam patrono mihi obsequerentur, cum alioqui praedivinaret hoc quod accidit, nullam apud istos fore amicitiae suae,[1] nullam nostrae coniunctionis reverentiam.

3 Ratio ergo testamenti talis est; ne ius quidem dubium erat, etiam antequam veniret in iudicium.[2] Petis a me decem milia ex testamento patroni tui. Interrogo an dari iusserit tibi. Quantaelibet sis impudentiae, non mentieris. 4 Quare ne illa quidem tibi actio quae invidiam facere solet legatum non solventibus relicta est, ut dicas: 'quod ego merui, quod ego iure peto.' Repetis quod tibi non est relic-

1 *Obr.*: summae Aβ
2 *Sch.*: dubium Aβ

318

Legacy between freedmen

A man made his friend his heir and requested him to give ten thousand to whichever he wished of two freedmen whom he was leaving. One of the freedmen claimed; he went to trial and lost. The other claims.

DECLAMATION

I do not have to speak of what bonds I had with their patron and how long-standing. I am his heir. How appreciative these men showed themselves after their freedom is equally clear, I presume, from this insult, their going to court with me. Neither deserved in his view to get ten thousand. Why then did he provide in this will that I give this sum to whichever of the two I wanted? In no other way could he make sure that they would defer to me. So my best of all friends thought of a way to make them defer to me[1] as a patron, since otherwise he prognosticated what happened, that these two would pay no respect to his friendship or to our connection.

So the rationale of the will is as I have said; nor was the law in doubt, even before the case came to trial. You claim ten thousand from me under the will of your patron. I ask whether he ordered that it be given to you. However impudent you may be, you will not lie. So even that plea which usually creates odium for those who do not pay legacies is not open to you—you can't say "what I earned, what I lawfully claim." You reclaim what was not left to you. That this

---

[1] The freedmen had no legal obligation to their former master's heir. *Obsequi* is used both of slaves vis-à-vis masters and freedmen vis-à-vis former masters (*patroni*).

tum. Verum hoc esse manifestum est: petît alter prior, qui
sibi magis dignus videbatur; quo petente tacuisti; non
tamen optinuit id quod nullo iure poterat optinere, ut acci-
5 peret legatum incertum. 'Sed hoc ipso apparet' inquit 'deberi mihi, quod ille cum iudicio contendisset victus est.'
Nondum diligenter verba testamenti legis. Non enim hoc
scriptum est tantum, ut alteri ex libertis darem, sed illud,
quo mihi et plena et (quo magis doleas) perpetua libertas
6 relicta est: darem utri vellem. Ergo si hoc non cadit in rerum naturam, ut ego illi malim dare qui mecum contendit,
sperares; aut, si hoc probare potes, me tibi malle, forsitan
iudicio quoque non inique contendes. Si quidem neutrum
horum tale est ut contra me sit, satis sit utrique vestrum se-
7 paratim dicere: tibi nolo. 'Sic ergo hoc respondebis semper?' Puta me dicere: 'Querere de te atque officiis tuis, qui
non aliter meruisti.' Fortasse vexare vos voluit et legatum
sperare semper et alternis desperare. Sic tueri me volo ut
dicam 'semper': ante omnia enim testamento tempus non
est cautum quo solvam. Ac ne caveri quidem oportuit[3];
nam qui dicit 'utri malueris' et tempus non adicit, manifesto illud quoque significat, cum volueris utri volueris solves.
8 Adhuc ergo ambo improbi estis, ambo calumniatores.
Quam sapienter tacueras! Si in hoc perseverasses, videreris mihi verecundior, sperarem futurum ut diligentius
servares pecuniam quam non cupide acceperas; nunc incipit mihi videri minus ille peccasse. Litigavit ante experimentum, litigavit ante sententiam; tu non credis iudicibus.
9 'Neuter ergo accipiet? Cum voluerit patronus alteri dari,

---

[3] *Watt*[2]: potuit Aβ

---

[2] As he is doing.   [3] The present claimant.

is true is evident: the other claimed before you, thinking himself the more deserving. When he claimed, you said nothing. But he did not succeed in what he could not succeed in under any law, in getting an uncertain legacy. "But this very fact," says he, "that when he claimed he lost, shows that it's due to me." You are still not reading the words of the will carefully. It was not written just that I give to one of the freedmen but that I give to which of them I wish, thereby leaving me freedom both complete and (what irks you more) perpetual. So if it is not in the Nature of Things that I should prefer to give to the one who fought me in court, you might hope; or if you can show that I prefer to give to you, perhaps you will fight me not unfairly in court even.[2] But if neither of these is such as to work against me, let it suffice for me to say to each of you separately: "I don't want to give it to you." "So will you always make this answer?" Suppose I say: "Blame yourself and your services. You deserved nothing else." Perhaps he wanted to tease you, wanted you to hope for the legacy always and despair by turns. I say "always" wishing to protect myself; for, first of all, the will lays down no time for me to pay. Nor should it; for he that says "to whichever you prefer" and adds no time clearly also intimates "You will pay when you wish to which of the two you wish." So far then you are both rascals, both false claimants. How wise you[3] had been to say nothing! Had you so persevered, I should have thought you were the more modest, hoped that you would take better care of the money that you had received without grasping. As it is, I begin to think that the other one was less to blame. He went to law before the test, before the verdict: you don't believe the jury. "So will neither get it? Since the patron wanted it given to one of the two,

non potest ab altero hoc legatum peti ex voluntate defuncti?' Neuter vestrum dicere potest: 'hoc patronus dari mihi voluit.' Habuit hunc honorem mihi, ut istud esset beneficium meum. Me ergo emereri debet nec[4] a me istud petere quod a patrono non petisset.

10   Detegam vobis propositum amici mei: meliori dari voluit. Hoc sciri ex praeterita vita vestra non potest: alioqui ipse scisset et, si ulla inter vos fuisset differentia, nominatim reliquisset. Hoc legato patroni vestri necesse est utrique vestrum diligentius vivere. Utri dabo? Uter vestrum patronum magis desideraverit, uter vestrum frugalius vixerit, uter vestrum modestior fuerit: quid vos diutius traham?—utri voluero. Interim similes estis, eandem causam habetis. Non magis ego de vobis iudicare possum quam patronus vester.

11

319

Adultera venefica

Qui uxorem adulterii ream detulerat dixit communem filium testem fore. Inter moras iudicii adulescens ambiguis signis cruditatis et veneni decessit. Vult maritus agere cum uxore veneficii. Illa postulat ut praeferatur iudicium adulterii.

[4] *SB*[3]: et Aβ

cannot this legacy be claimed by one of the two, as intended by the deceased?" Neither of you can say: "The patron wanted this given to me." He did me the compliment of making it my favor. So he should deserve well of *me* and not claim from me what he would not have claimed from his patron.[4]

I shall unveil what my friend had in mind. He wanted it given to the better man. This cannot be known from your past lives; otherwise he himself would have known, and if there had been any difference between you, he would have named the legatee. With this legacy of your patron's you both have to live more carefully. To which shall I give it? Which of you will have missed your patron more, which of you will have lived more frugally, which of you will have been the more respectful? Why should I keep you waiting any longer? To which of you shall I wish? Meanwhile, you are alike, you have the same case. I can no more judge between you than could your patron.

319

The adulteress poisoner

A man who had charged his wife with adultery said the son they had in common would stand witness. During the delays of the trial the young man died with ambiguous signs of indigestion and poison. The husband wants to take his wife to court for poisoning. She asks for the trial for adultery to be taken first.

[4] Had he been alive—nobody can claim under a will during the testator's lifetime. *Petere* refers to legal action as does *peti* above (also in the theme and ss.3, 4), requiring *nec* for *et*.

1

DECLAMATIO

Antequam criminum facimus comparationem, sic agere possum: veneficii accuso, responde[1]; occisum a te filium dico, defende.[1] Sint paria quae obicio, non possunt uno iudicio cognosci; aequum est ream respondere ad id quod obicitur.

2 ⟦Puta omittere me quod antea obiecerim, non perseverare in eo propter quod detuli.⟧[2] De vita cogitari aequum est, de maiore ⟨re⟩[3] quaeri prius. Postea dicam ex qua diffidentia praeferri iudicium adulterii velit; interim duo crimina apud vos proponuntur, adulterium et parricidium:

3 de utro prius cognosci oportet? Hocine aequum est, sceleris gravissimi, sceleris atrocissimi dilationem impetrari quia et adultera est? Si nihil illi ante obiecissem, continuo rationem redderet; quoniam ad parricidium prioris crimi-

4 nis diffidentia venit, huc trahit[4] propter quod occidit. Filium ab hac occisum esse dico: quamdiu, iudices, sinetis hoc esse dubium? Vivit interim in civitate, inter nos est femina inter prodigia numeranda, implet numerum civitatis: et vivet dum bis rea sit, praesertim in hac civitate in qua

5 iudicia diu differuntur. De me utique mirari non potestis si omnes moras odi, omnes dilationes: liceat vindicare filium dum vivo, antequam ad accusatorem transeatur a teste. An hoc aequum, hoc cuiquam vestrum iustum videri potest,

[1] *Aer.*: -des Aβ
[2] *ita secl. SB*[3]
[3] *Gron.*
[4] *Sch.*: -tur Aβ

[1] The capital charge—poisoning.

Before we compare the two charges, I can plead thus: I accuse you of poisoning, answer; I say you killed my son, defend yourself. Suppose my charges are equal, they can't be taken in one trial. It is fair that the accused reply to what is charged.

⟦Suppose I drop my earlier accusation, don't persevere with it because of what I have charged.⟧ It's fair that life be considered, that the greater ⟨matter⟩[1] be taken first. I shall tell you later on what misgiving makes her want the adultery trial taken first; meanwhile, you have two charges before you, adultery and parricide: which of the two ought to be tried first? Is it fair that she should be granted delay of a most grave, most atrocious charge because she is also an adulteress? If I had brought nothing against her previously, she would answer to it immediately; since she came to parricide because of her misgiving about the former charge,[2] she pulls that way, that being the reason for her murder. I say that this woman killed my son: how long, gentlemen of the jury, will you leave this in doubt? Meanwhile she lives in the community, a woman who should be categorized as a monster is among us, makes up the number of the community, and she will live until she stands trial twice, in this community too in which trials are long put off. As for me, you certainly cannot be surprised if I hate all delays, all deferments. Let me be permitted to avenge my son while I am alive, before she moves from witness to prosecutor.[3] Can it seem fair or just to any of you to decide

---

[2] Of adultery. She had made away with the witness, who was her son.   [3] Himself. Having murdered the witness, her son, she will murder the prosecutor next.

ut censeatis adulterium esse inter crimina, parricidium inter maledicta?

6   'Causam dicere adulterii volo.' Hoc est, perît ille testis. Mihi autem vacat hoc tempore curam agere lectuli mei? Flens et orbus querar quod uxor mea alium amaverit, alium mihi praetulerit? Ego ne priore quidem tempore istud crimen ad iudicem perduxissem nisi quod sciebat filius

7 meus. Si amisissem tantum optimum iuvenem, excusate tamen omnibus aliis causis renuntiarem; verum confitendum est: ego occidi, ego, qui palam nominavi, qui omnem iudicii prioris fiduciam in hoc esse confessus sum. Tua porro quid interest? Utere hoc argumento, quod tibi obicere adulterium nolui, pone hoc inter praeiudicia accusationis, dum ego ago meo iudicio. Dic legem qua vindicari potest utrumque.

8   Nempe hoc inter alia dictura es[5]: 'Quam causam dandi veneni filio meo habui? Adultera non eram.' Illic videbimus, illic reddemus rationem. Nec te hoc fefellit. Sed naturalis improbis hominibus dilationis est cupiditas. Hic infamiae vides poenam. Quid autem fama ad te aut opinio?

9 Sed occurrunt illae cogitationes: 'Quaeretur de adulterio et quaeretur diu, et extrahetur[6] iudicium, sicut adhuc extrahitur,[7] ut sequatur adulterii poenam alia subscriptio, alii iudices et alia sortitionis fortuna. Interim ut nihil artes valeant, multum Fata possunt: multum citra scelus quoque

---

[5] *SB*[3]: dictum est Aβ   [6] *Ri.*: -et Aβ
[7] *Sch.*: -it Aβ: *del. coni. SB*[2]

---

[4] Until she is tried for murder, the charge will only be talk.

[5] Addressing the wife.   [6] At the poison trial, where adultery would be proved despite the loss of the witness. The wife

that adultery counts as a charge, parricide as defamation?[4]

"I want to plead on adultery." Which is to say, that witness is dead. And am I at this time at leisure to worry about my bed? Weeping and bereaved, shall I complain because my wife has loved another, preferred another to me? Even earlier on I should never have brought that charge into court except that my son knew. If I had merely lost that fine young man, still I should be excused if I called off all other cases. I must confess the truth: I killed him, yes, I, when I named him openly, when I confessed that my confidence about the earlier trial lay entirely in him. Further, what does it matter to you?[5] Use the argument that I did not want to tax you with adultery, make it one of the points prejudicial to the prosecution—so long as I get *my* trial. Tell me of a law under which both offenses can be punished.

I expect you will say among other things: "What reason did I have to poison my son? I was not an adulteress " We'll see *there*;[6] we'll put our case *there*. And you were well aware of it. But desire for delay is natural to wicked people. Here[7] you see infamy as the punishment. But what is reputation or public opinion to you? But certain thoughts occur: "There will be argument on the adultery and it will take a long time and the trial will be dragged on, as it is so far. The penalty for adultery will be followed by another indictment, another jury, and another drawing of lots.[8] Meanwhile, if tricks don't work, the Fates can do much.

knew it, but hoped that an adultery trial could be dragged out and ultimate punishment postponed.

[7] At an adultery trial.

[8] In jury selection? See Mommsen, *Römische Strafrecht*, 214f.

impedimenti per se ipsa mortalitas adfert. Ut nihil prosit,
vixero tamen, et, quod mihi vita ipsa iucundius est, tamdiu
superstes testi vixero.'

320

Multati socius

Sociorum communia sint damna et lucra. Ex duobus sociis
alter in civitate erat, alter peregre. Cum bello laboraret
civitas, decrevit ut intra certum diem reverterentur qui
abessent, qui non venisset multaretur publicatione bonorum. Exacta est pars a praesente negotiatore absentis ‹loco›.[1] Reversus ille partem petit reliquorum bonorum.

1

SERMO

Saepe vobis dixi quomodo ad inveniendum statum facil-
lime perveniretis. Qui sint omnes novistis. Primum singulos repetite; sublatis iis quos certum erit non esse, inter
residuos quaeremus. Quaerendi autem via haec erit. Videamus quid proponat petitor, quid respondeat possessor vel
reus: ex eo quaestio nascitur; ea nobis ‹statum›[2] demons-
2 trabit. Neque hoc dico, quid primum dicat petitor, quid
ille respondeat. Non enim ex prima quaestione ducendus

[1] a. ‹loco› *Hå.*: ‹nomine› a. *Watt*[1]: *del. coni. Wi.*
[2] *Aer.*

---

[1] Of the joint property.
[2] See crit. note.
[3] *Status*, a technical term of rhetoric; cf. Quint. 3.6.
[4] The one we are looking for.

Mortality itself brings a lot of impediment short of crime. If nothing works, I shall at least have lived that long surviving the witness, and that is sweeter to me than life."

320

A fined man's partner

Let losses and gains of partners be in common. Of two partners one was in the community, the other abroad. When the community was in trouble in war, it decreed that absentees return before a certain date and that anyone who had not come back be mulcted by confiscation of his property. Half[1] is exacted from the business man on the spot <in the name of>[2] the absentee. When he gets back, he claims half the remaining assets.

DISCUSSION

I have often told you how you may most easily find out the basis.[3] You all know what they are. First go back to them one by one. After removing those that are certainly not it,[4] we shall look among the remainder. The method of looking will be as follows: let us see what the plaintiff puts forward, what answers the man in possession (or the defendant) makes; from that arises the question,[5] and that will show us the <basis>. I do not mean, what does the claimant say first, what does the other answer? For the basis is not to be deduced from the first question, but from the most impor-

---

[5] "The *quaestio* is mysterious; it is not dealt with in the declamation" (Wi.).

est status, sed ex potentissima. Videndum erit an post divisionem socii sint.

3   DECLAMATIO

'Sociorum damna et lucra communia sint.' Fortasse videri potest supervacuum laudare legem. Nam et apparet prudentissimos maiores et constitutores huius civitatis sapienter rogasse et, cum hoc iure civitas tamdiu usa sit, iam approbatum est. Veruntamen causa exigit ut aequitatem quoque legis intueamur, non ut vos religiosius iudicetis,

4 sed ut appareat quam improbe socius meus faciat. 'Sociorum communia damna et lucra sint.' Sacra res est et quaedam fraternitas compositorum[3] animorum. Consortes enim potest facere casus; ceterum quidem cum duo homines omnes fortunas suas contulerunt, omnes casus miscuerunt, unum quoddam factum est. Quid est iustius quam compositum patrimonium habere condicionem[4]

5 unius? †societatis hoc enim est unitas† Vides ergo et damna et lucra communia esse debere; et nihil non aequum est quod utrique parti scriptum est.

6   Eventus nos diduxit; sed de sociis loquitur ‹lex, non de sociis›[5] ibidem[6] agentibus. Illud suo loco imputabo, quod hic domi semper et custos tantum pecuniae fuit, ego sum ille qui longas terras et ignotas regiones peragravi, ego ille qui tam longe abieram ut in patriam redire non possem. Ex hac igitur lege postulo ut communia sint quae in bonis[7] sunt aut[8] dividantur.

    3 *SB*[1]: propos- Aβ   4 *Gron.*: -e Aβ
    5 *SB*[1] (lex *ante* loquitur *Aer.*)
    6 *Sch.*: idem Aβ   7 *Aer.*: vobis Aβ
    8 *SB*[1]: ut Aβ

tant. We shall have to see whether they are partners after the division.[6]

"Let the losses and gains of partners be in common." Perhaps it may seem superfluous to praise the law. For it is evident that our very prudent ancestors and founders of this community legislated wisely, and since the community has used this law so long, it has already been approved. However, the case demands that we look also at the equity of the law, not so that you may give your verdict in better conscience but to make it evident how unconscionably my partner is behaving. "Let the losses and gains of partners be in common." It is a sacred thing, a sort of brotherhood of amalgamated minds. For chance may make co-heirs, but when two men have combined all their fortunes, mingled all chances, a kind of unity is created. What is more just than that a fortune put together be treated as a unity?[7] You see, therefore, that both losses and gains ought to be in common; and nothing is unfair that applies to both parties.

The event separated us; but ‹the law› speaks of partners, ‹not of partners› operating in the same place. In the proper place I shall take credit for the fact that he was always at home, merely the custodian of the money, whereas I am the one who travelled through distant lands and regions unknown, I the one who had gone so far away that I could not return to our country. So under this law I demand that the assets be either in common or divided.

[6] Of the joint property, assuming the claimant wins. But "what happens after the *divisio* seems altogether irrelevant" (Wi.).

[7] The obelized words are thought to be a corrupt gloss.

7   Quid ais? Perisse patrimonii partem, et mihi perisse;
adicis mea culpa perisse. Omnia haec interim confiteri
libet: commune tamen damnum est. Negat hoc esse dam-
8   num et poenae nomen imponit. Ego porro damnum existimo esse amissionem eorum quae habueris; neque enim
veniet in dubitationem quin amiserimus aliquid ex iis quae
habebamus. Hic poenam appellat. Possum non negare,
cum et ipsa poena damni genus sit. Nam mihi ex hoc quod
plerisque criminibus pecuniae poena imponebatur appel-
9   lata[9] etiam ipsa damnatio videtur. ⟦Ablatum est aliquid
mihi; sane etiam confitear (quid interest quomodo ablatum sit?), ego perdidi. Nam et si latro abstulisset, mihi
abstulerat, et si in piratas ego incidissem mercator, ego
10 amiseram; peribat hoc utrique nostrum.⟧ Quid si etiam
poenae id genus est quod casus attulit? Sane enim feramus
hanc tuam finitionem, ut damnum credamus esse fortui-
tam rerum amissionem: quid tam fortuitum potest esse
quam quod accidit? Non enim ⟨factum est⟩[10] lege vetere
et ante profectionem meam scripta et quam ego nosse pos-
11 sem et in quam mea culpa inciderem.[11] Quid fortuito accidit? Bellum. Quid fortuito accidit? Ignorantia mea. Non
est tale quale si in furto deprehensus quadruplo damnatus
essem. Tum[12] enim diceres: 'noveras damnum, noveras
12 legem, vitio tuo incidisti in hanc.' Haec non eo pertinent
⟨ut intersit⟩[13] quo genere damni adflictus sim. Nam si nau-
fragium fecissem, diceres: 'vitio tuo; navigabas enim,' et si

9 *Aer.*: -atio Aβ   10 *Ro.*   11 *Aer.*: acc- Aβ
12 *Obr.*: tu Aβ   13 *SB*[3]

8 "Conviction," as connected with *damnum* ("loss," especially
pecuniary).

What are you saying? That half of the property was lost and lost to me; you add, lost by my fault. For the time being I choose to admit all this: still, the loss is in common. He denies that it is a loss and applies the name of penalty. I on the other hand consider a loss to be the losing of things you had; for there can be no doubt that we lost part of what we used to have. He calls it a penalty. I need not deny that, since a penalty is itself a species of loss. For I think the term *damnatio*[8] itself derived from the fact that a pecuniary penalty was imposed for many offenses. ⟦Something was taken from me; yes, I will even confess (for what matter how it was taken?), I lost it. For if a robber had taken it, he would have taken it from me, and if as a trader I had fallen in with pirates, it would have been I that had lost it; but the loss was to both of us.⟧ What if even the penalty is of such a kind that chance brought it?[9] For let us put up with this definition of yours and believe that a loss is a fortuitous losing of things: what can be so fortuitous as what occurred? It ⟨was⟩ not ⟨done⟩ under an old law, one written before my departure, one which I could have known and fell into by my own fault. What happened fortuitously? The war. What happened fortuitously? My ignorance. It is not as if I had been caught in a theft and sentenced to pay fourfold. Then you would have said: "You knew the penalty,[10] you knew the law, you fell into it by your own misdoing." I do not mean that ⟨it matters⟩ what kind of loss struck me. For if I had been shipwrecked, you would have said: "By your misdoing; you were at sea." And if I had

---

[9] *Abstulit* (Gronovius) was a false improvement.
[10] See *OLD damnum* 4.

spoliatus essem a latronibus, diceres: 'vitio tuo; parum dili-
13 genter custodiebas.' Quotumquodque damni genus est cui
non applicari reprehensio possit? Si mancipiorum mortes
sunt, 'parum curasti, medicinam non adhibuisti.' Hoc habent gravissimum damna, quod vix ulla sine paenitentia
sunt. Ergo tunc quoque si vitio meo factum esset, si lege
vetere, damna tamen communia erant.

321

Invicem veneficii ⟨rei⟩[1] frater et medicus

Fratres consortes inimici esse coeperunt. Diviserunt. Alter ex his medicum instituit heredem. Postea redierunt in
gratiam. Is qui medicum amicum habebat, cum cenasset
apud fratrem et domum redisset, dixit suspicari se venenum sibi datum. Respondit medicus potionem se daturum
remedii, et dedit; qua epota ille decessit. Invicem se reos
deferunt veneficii frater et medicus.

1   DECLAMATIO
Etiamsi causa unius hodie agnoscitur, tamen, cum eum
de cuius morte agitur constet veneno perisse, idque inter
duos litigantes conveniat, alterutrius[2] eum veneno perisse,
ita committenda utrimque causa est ut non minor nobis
2 defensionis quam accusationis habenda sit ratio. Itaque,
etiamsi dolor fratris amissi et condicio iudicii quo accuso

1 *coni. Ri.*
2 *Sch.*: -iusque Aβ

---

1 See *OLD potio* 3b and s.28 *potionem dedisti aut remedii aut*
veneni.

been robbed by brigands, you would have said: "By your misdoing; you didn't guard carefully enough." How few kinds of loss are there for which no blame could be attached! If there are deaths of slaves: "You didn't look after them enough, didn't give them treatment." The worst thing about losses is that hardly any are without remorse. Therefore then too, if it had been the result of my misdoing, with an old law, still the losses were in common.

321

Brother and doctor <accuse> one another of poisoning

Brothers sharing an inheritance became enemies. They divided. One of them made a doctor his heir. Later they were reconciled. The one who had the doctor as his friend, after dining with his brother and returning home, said he suspected he had been given poison. The doctor replied that he would give him a potion as an antidote[1] and did so. Having drunk it the man died. The brother and the doctor accuse each other of poisoning.

DECLAMATION

Even though one man is on trial today, yet, since it is agreed that the person whose death is at issue died of poison and both litigants say the same, that he died of poisoning by one or the other, the case is so to be joined[2] on both sides that we have to take account of our defense no less than of our accusation. Therefore, even though my grief for my lost brother and the set-up of the trial in which I am

[2] Wi. takes *committenda* as "quasi-military," as in *committere pugnam*.

hoc videtur exigere primum ac paene solum, ut ea quae obieci probem, ignoscetis tamen mihi si primum defensionis meae putavero habendam esse rationem, neque hoc eo tantum, quod pertinet ad pudorem hodie[3] meum, sed eo etiam, quod plus auctoritatis habiturum me in accusatione scio si ad illam innocens venero.

3 Quaeritur ergo, iudices, venenum ego fratri dederim an iste alieno. Non me fugit nomen quo utitur [amicus][4]; et rogo sciatis, iudices, de hoc ipso quaeri hodie, an amicus fuerit. Sine dubio, etiamsi certa utriusque nominis fides esset, neminem vestrum praeteriret quantum praeferri 4 fratrem amico oporteret. Nam quae potest amicitia esse tam felix quae imitetur fraternitatem? Certe quotiens blandiri volumus iis qui esse amici videntur, nulla adulatio procedere ultra hoc nomen potest, quam ut fratres vocemus: adeo inane etiam nomen et umbra quaedam naturae ⟨valere⟩[5] videtur †simile amicitiae[6] nomen imponere†. 5 Cum vero me fratrem constet esse, ⟨iste⟩,[7] si venenum (ut probabo) dedit, amicus utique non fuerit, quae comparatio esse personarum potest? Ac si tantum de amore quaereretur, iudices, multum natura vinceret; nunc plus est aliquanto de quo apud vos agitur: quaeritur enim an ego fratrem potuerim occidere. Ergo inter homicidium et 6 parricidium cognoscitis. Nondum de persona loquor utriusque, non de causa; interim quaero, iudices, utri parti

---

3 hodie *del. Ro.*   4 *SB*[1], *Wi.*   5 *SB*[1] (valet *ante* et *Ro.*)   6 s. ⟨erat quaestui⟩ a. *SB*[1]   7 *Ri.*

---

3 "Friend."

4 See crit. note. Calling a friend "brother" is like calling a professional adviser "friend"—a hit at the doctor.

prosecutor appear to require first and almost solely that I prove my charges, you will nonetheless forgive me for thinking that I must first take account of my own defense; not only because it concerns my honor but because I know I shall carry more weight in my prosecution if I come to it as an innocent man.

So the question is, gentlemen of the jury, whether I gave poison to my brother or that man to a non-relative. I am well aware of the name[3] he uses, and I ask you to know, gentlemen, that the question today is just this, whether he *was* a friend. Without doubt none of you would overlook how much preference should be given to brother over friend, even if the good faith of both names were assured. For what friendship can be so happy as to imitate fraternity? Sure it is that when we wish to make up to those who appear to be our friends, no flattery can go beyond this name—we call them brothers. So ⟨powerful⟩ appears to be even the name and a sort of shadow of nature; it would be like putting the name of friendship on making a living (?).[4] But since it is agreed that I am his brother whereas ⟨that man⟩, if he gave the poison (as I shall prove), was certainly not his friend, what comparison can there be between the two personae? If the question were only about affection, gentlemen, nature would come far ahead; but as it is, something considerably more is before you. For the question is whether I could have killed[5] my brother. So your enquiry is between homicide and parricide. I am not yet speaking of our respective personae, nor of the case; I ask meanwhile, gentlemen, which side you favor, on which

[5] Was not such an unnatural crime incredible?

faveatis, utrum verum esse pro civitate, pro temporibus velitis. Equidem, iudices, admirari me confiteor aut constitutas esse de tantis sceleribus leges aut ullos inveniri po-

7 tuisse mortalium in quos caderet ista suspicio. Fratrem suum potuit aliquis occidere? Non obstitit tacita natura, non sanguinis vis? Non sceleribus manus suas obiecit quaecumque est illa, quae certe creditur esse, Pietas? Fratrem occisuro non succurrit communis uterus, non eadem causa vitae, non una primordia, non illa [consuetudo][8] quae alienos etiam ac nulla necessitudine inter se coniunctos componere et adstringere adfectibus possunt,[9] consuetudo actae pariter infantiae, pueritiae studia lusus,[10] tris-

8 tia[11] ioci? Membra hercule inter se citius pugnaverint et si qua in nobis natura geminavit diversos ceperint adfectus. Nam quid est aliud fraternitas quam divisus spiritus et quae ad tuendos nos natura concessa sunt multiplicata?— eo quidem felicius quod diversis etiam ac distantibus[12]

9 locis esse ibidem[13] ac plura simul obire possumus. Huic necessitudini qui dare venenum potest non oculos effodiet suos, non manus in viscera sua armabit? Habet ergo hoc primum (ut parcissime dixerim) admirationem. Neque ego ignoro, iudices, quanto me onere premam: ipse confiteor nullis suppliciis, nullis poenis, nulla me omnium hominum ira posse pensare, si feci.

10 Vult detrahere fraternitati auctoritatem: 'discordes' inquit 'fuistis.' Nondum rationem huius criminis reddo; illud interim testor, hunc bonum amicum utrique maledicere.

---

[8] *Gron.*   [9] *SB*[1]: potest Aβ
[10] B[1]: ludus Aβ   [11] *Ro.*: tristitia Aβ
[12] ac d. *Bu., auct, Gron.*: assista- A: assistentibus β
[13] *Aer.*: idem Aβ

you want truth to lie for the sake of the community and the times. For my part, gentlemen, I confess I am surprised that any laws were made about such heinous crimes or that any mortals could have been found to whom such a suspicion could attach. Could anyone kill his brother? Did not silent nature, the force of blood, stand in the way? Did not Piety, whoever she is, who is certainly believed to exist, put out her hands to block the crimes? A man is about to kill his brother—will not the womb they had in common come to his mind, the same life-origin, the beginnings in one, those things that can combine and link in affection even persons unrelated, joined by no family connection—the intercourse of an infancy lived together, the studies and play of boyhood, the serious things, the jests? Upon my word, our limbs would sooner fight one another, all that nature has duplicated in us would sooner develop opposite feelings. For what is fraternity but a spirit divided and a multiplication of those items which nature has allowed us for our protection?—all the more happily because even in diverse and distant places we can be in the same one and perform many actions together.[6] Will not one who can give poison to such a relationship gouge out his own eyes and arm his hands against his own vitals? So this first (to say the least) is something to be wondered at. And I am not unaware, gentlemen, of how great a load I place upon my own shoulders: I myself confess that no tortures, no punishments, no anger of all men against me can compensate—if I did it.

He tries to strip brotherhood of its authority: "You were at loggerheads," he says. I am not dealing with this charge yet. Meanwhile, I call to witness that this good friend is

[6] How this comes about is not clear to me.

Nunc mihi, frater, in quacumque parte naturae es, agenda
11 causa et tua est. Aliquid ex summa fraternitatis gratia de-
fuisse visum est aliquando, dum forsitan uterque alterius
animum magis exigit fiducia sui. Bene hercule Fortuna
quod uterque tunc incolumis, quod penates sine lacrimis
fuerunt, nulla parricidii suspicio tempore illo quo minus
12 amabamus. Non tamen ista nostri animi culpa fuit, nisi
quia vitium est humanae mentis nimia ‹amicorum›[14] cupiditas. Hi sunt qui coniunctos separant animos, qui summae
concordiae virus suum interponunt, qui hereditates captant, qui se testamentis parant, qui ita demum spem aliquam in posterum vitae habent si eos quos amicos appella-
13 verunt carissimis pignoribus abduxerint. Quis fecerit illud
inter nos sic quaerite: nullam iste spem hereditatis habuisset si numquam dissedissemus. Hoc igitur primum veluti
mentium animique temptati veneno sumus. Sed dii melius: neque longum istud fuit neque quicquam ex eo secu-
tum est quod emendari non posset[15]: divisio sola, ut sciat
is[16] cui heres sit, sed postea (quod satis est) gratia et rursus
solida fraternitas, immo hercule maior artiorque coniunc-
14 tio post paenitentiam. Nesciunt homines quantum boni
fraternitas habeat qui numquam dissederunt. Ut dulcius
serenum post tempestatem est, ita nostris animis laceratis
et diu[17] castigatis velut portus ille fraternitatis occurrit.
Amabamus etiam in praeteritum, nec caritas fuit illa sed

[14] *SB*[1]   [15] *SB*[1]: -sit Aβ
[16] *SB*[3]: sciatis Aβ   [17] *SB*[1]: domi Aβ

---

[7] More than he gave or more than the other was prepared to
give?

[8] False friends.

libeling both of us. Now, brother, whatever part of nature
you are in, I must plead your case too. Some degree of
brotherly good will at its utmost seemed at one time to
have been lacking, perhaps because each of us, confident
in his own feelings, demanded more of the other's.[7] Fortune was kind in that each of us was in good case at that
time, our homes without tears, no suspicion of parricide at
that period when we were less fond of one another. But
it was not the fault of our own hearts, except that over-
eagerness for ⟨friends⟩ is a vice of the human heart.
These[8] are the folk who separate minds conjoined, insert
their virus into the height of harmony, hunt inheritances,
get into position for wills, have some hope for the rest of
their lives only if they lead away those they call friends
from their dearest relations. Who did that between us, enquire thus: he would have had no hope of the inheritance if
we had never disagreed. So this was the poison, as it were,
of minds and feeling with which we were first attacked. But
the gods willed better: it did not last long and nothing followed from it that could not be put right; only the division,
to let him know whose heir he is.[9] But afterwards (and
that's enough) good will and once more solid brotherhood;
or rather, upon my word, greater and closer association
after repentance. Men who have never disagreed do not
know the blessing of brotherhood. Just as fair weather is
the sweeter after a storm, so to our hearts, torn and long
chastened, comes the haven as it were of brotherhood. We
were loving even in retrospect; it was not affection,[10] but

[9] Ironical, almost facetious. The doctor, who had engineered
the split, would now have everything cut and dried.

[10] Not *just* affection.

invicem satisfactio. Utinamque hoc non palam, non manifeste fecissemus, ut videretur frater meus nullo modo mu-
taturus testamentum.

15   Personae igitur nullo modo comparantur, alienus et frater. Supervacua mentio discordiae, cum et illo tempore
constiterit innocentia et id tempus quod in culpam deducitur non solum sine discordia fuerit, verum etiam maior
atque artior caritas post illam de qua locutus sum paenitentiam increverit.

16   Proximum est, ut opinor, excutere causas. Et quod ad
me quidem pertinet, videor de his satis locutus. Nam si inimicitiae eo tempore non fuerunt quo frater meus accepit
venenum, mihi certe hoc faciendi ratio non fuit: qui, si essem malus frater, uti tamen bonitatis simulatione debebam
usque ad mutationem testamenti: nam quid obstabat quo
minus non ultionem tantum sed etiam lucrum consceque-
17 rer? Si ego non habui rationem dandi veneni fratri, videbo
an hic habuerit. Heres est: hoc per se potens est. Omnia
quaecumque toto orbe terrarum committuntur scelera
circumspicite, iudices: pleraque ex cupiditate nascuntur.
18 Haec latrones facit, haec piratas, haec intra muros etiam
atque intra domos nostras et templa sicas percussorum
acuit, inde nata sunt venena; ut mihi videatur rerum natura omnibus in hominem collatis bonis unum malum[18]
opposuisse. Tolle pecuniam: bella sustuleris, sustuleris se-
19 ditiones. Hanc ergo causam habuisti. ⟦Et aliud est aliis

---

[18] *Ro.*: metum Aβ

---

[11] The period after the reconciliation, ending in the alleged
murder.

mutual apology. And I only wish we had not done this openly and manifestly so that there might not have seemed any chance of my brother altering his will.

So the personae are in no way comparable, an outsider and a brother. Mention of the disagreement is superfluous since innocence at that time is unquestioned and not only was the time that is faulted[11] clear of discord but affection had grown up even greater and closer after the repentance of which I have spoken.

The next thing, I suppose, is to examine motives. So far as concerns myself, I think I have said enough about them. If there was no enmity at the time when my brother took the poison, I certainly had no reason to do it. If I was a bad brother, I ought still to have made pretence of being a good one until the will was changed. For what was to stop me from achieving[12] not only retaliation but profit as well? If I had no reason to give my brother poison, I'll see whether *he* has. He is the heir: that's a powerful motive in itself. Look around all the crimes that are committed the world over, gentlemen: most of them have their root in greed. Greed makes robbers, greed makes pirates, even inside the walls and inside our homes and temples greed sharpens assassins' daggers, thence poisons come into being; so that the Nature of Things seems to me to have set this one evil against all the good she has conferred upon mankind. Abolish money, and you will have abolished wars and civil strife. This then was your motive. [And money means dif-

---

[12] By reinstatement in his brother's will to the exclusion of the doctor. "Retaliation" assumes that as a "bad" brother he had a score to settle.

pecunia. Si de cupiditate sola loquendum mihi foret, dicerem: 'hereditatem concupisti, homo locuples.' Nunc hereditatem concupisti id solum habiturus quod scelere acquisisses. Quid enim? iam te metiri incipis et longam domus nostrae patientiam calcas? Ecquid scis quid paulo ante fueris? Nunc te circumfluens pecunia, nunc ista mancipia et quidquid quaesisti scelere ditabunt?⟧[19]

20   Venenum dicor dedisse in cena mea. O di immortales! Erat quidem honestius illa defensione patrocinari causae meae. Venenum aliquis inter lares suos, inter sacra mensae, coronatis pariter quos colebamus dis immortalibus, venenum aliquis hilaris hilari dedit? Non hoc ipsum obsti-

21   tit conatibus meis, quod non credebatur? Venenum aliquis circumstante familia, praesentibus ministeriis daret, foedaturus continuo cadavere illud convivium suum? Ut severa nobis antiquitas tradidit, infestos animos placavere mensae, et homines qui inter se armis atque exercitibus

22   conflixerant tuti tamen iacuere media cenae fide. Sic defendi decebat innocentiam. Sed quatenus tamquam maligni loquimur, quatenus tamquam suspecti, in praesentia seponite mentem meam, seponite fraternitatem, seponite ante actam vitam. Tamquam de venefico[20] loquor. Quo minus loco, quo minus tempore dare fratri meo debuerim

---

[19] *ita secl. SB*[4] (*cf. SB*[3])   ·   [20] *Ro.*: -cio Aβ

---

[13] An apparently unwarranted assumption. Nothing indicates that the doctor was rich, quite the contrary (cf. s.30, *subito locuples*), and one is tempted to add a negative, *homo ⟨non⟩ locuples*. But this was not a case of simple greed but of greed that could only be served by a crime, and *locuples* makes a point, though at variance with the scenario. Hence double brackets.

ferent things to different people. If I had to speak only of greed, I should say: "You set your mind on a will, a rich man."[13] As it is, you set your mind on a will, with nothing to expect except what you acquired by crime. Come! Are you starting to take your measure[14] and trample on the lengthy patience of our family? Don't you know what you were a little time ago? Moncy flowing around you, those slaves and everything you got by crime, shall it now enrich you?]

I am said to have given the poison at my dinner. Immortal gods! It would have looked better to plead that[15] for the defense. Did somebody give poison at his hearth, amid the sacred rites of the table, with the immortal gods[16] whom we both[17] worshipped in their garlands, cheerful giver to cheerful taker? Did not the very fact that it was not credited block my attempts?[18] Would someone have given poison with the household standing around, servants present, to befoul that dinner party of his right away with a dead body? As austere antiquity had handed down to us, tables placated hostile feelings and men who had clashed with arms and armies yet reclined in security; the faith of the banquet was their intermediary. So it would have been seemly for innocence to be defended. But since I am speaking as an evil man, a suspect, put aside for the present my feelings, my brotherhood, my past life. I speak as of a poisoner. What place, what time would have been less suit-

[14] Apparently = "to realize your new affluence." But the whole of s.19 looks like a maladroit elaboration.

[15] The setting of the alleged crime.   [16] Their images.

[17] *Pariter*: not "as well as the guests" (Wi.).

[18] A clumsy way of saying that what made such an attempt incredible would also block its inception.

23   venenum? Neque enim quisquam dubitat, iudices, quin
faciendi sceleris consilium non unam viam intueatur, ut ad
summam cogitati inchoatique perveniat, sed illam alteram
vel magis necessariam et quae penitus in cogitationibus se-
deat, ut scelus quod commisit neget. Venenum do: et unde
scio an exhausta potione statim concidat? Venit ad mensam
meam, inter convivas meos expirat frater meus: in quem
scelus translaturi,[21] quem deorum hominumque invocatu-
24   ri[21]? Non fuit ergo locus idoneus, non fuit tempus. Adice
quod ego daturus venenum potui timere ne deprehende-
rer, ne praesentiret, ne intellegeret, ne colore venenum
25   deprehenderet, ne qua vis odoris [se][22] ostenderet. Ergo
nullum consilium sceleris mei est; at tui quanta occasio!
Nulli venenum facilius dari potest quam qui accipit utique
tamquam medicamentum.[23] Quamquam de hac postea loquar; paulum enim me interpellat ordo, ut illud defenden-
26   dum existimem, quod fratrem meum ait suspicatum. Ante
omnia, iudices, quod sit illud suspicionis genus non intellego. Postquam biberat, fingamus cibos redundasse, fingamus aliquem sensum interiorum[24] fuisse: haec tamen
omnia accidere etiam ex innocenti convivio possunt. Unde
ergo suspicio est? Unde illae simultates, unde illa discor-
27   dia. Simul et illud vos, iudices, intueri oportet, epota huius
potione fratrem meum continuo perisse: non potest videri

21 *SB*[2]: -rus Aβ   22 *SB*[3]

23 nulli . . . m. *huc transp.* *SB*[1]: *post* ostenderet *habent* Aβ

24 interiorem *coni.* *SB*[3]

19 The plot (above) becomes the plotter.

20 The genitives go with *mei* (pronoun) understood with the
preceding possessive adjectives.

able for me to poison my brother? For nobody doubts, gentlemen, that a plot to commit a crime does not simply look at the means to accomplish what is planned and begun, but also at that other means, even more necessary, deeply embedded in the planning, how to deny what he[19] has done. I give poison: and how do I know whether he will collapse at once after draining the potion? My brother comes to my table, expires among my guests. On whom am I going to shift[20] the crime, whom of gods and men am I going to invoke? So the place was wrong and the time. Add that on the point of giving the poison I could fear that I might be caught, that he might have a presentiment, might realize, might detect the poison by its color, that some odor might make it apparent. So my crime has no plan. But yours—what an opportunity! Poison can be given to no one more easily than to someone who takes it without suspicion. However, I shall speak of this opportunity later on; for the order interrupts me[21] a little—I think I must deal with his allegation that my brother had a suspicion.[22] To begin with, gentlemen, I don't understand what sort of suspicion that would be. After he had drunk, let us suppose that food came back into his mouth, that he felt something inside him; but all such things can happen from an innocent dinner too. So whence came the suspicion? Whence came that enmity, that quarrel?[23] You should also look at something else, gentlemen: when he had drained this man's potion my brother died right away. He cannot be

[21] He has got ahead of the order of events and must go back a little.

[22] According to the theme, he did suspect.

[23] The former falling-out. Answer: from the doctor.

eo veneno perisse in quo ante momentum mortis suspicio fuit. Verum haec ex huiusmodi causis orta suspicio plenissimam deferendi veneni occasionem dedit. Prima illa, quod habebas cui obiceres, altera illa, quod qualemcumque potionem accepturus erat frater: etsi illam tristem visu, etsi[25] illam gustu asperam, bibendum est tamen cum dicas remedium.

28   Sed quid ego diutius? Si venenum a me accepisset, tu sanasses: nam et pollicitus es ⟨et⟩[26] habebas medicamentum et tale medicamentum dicebas quo propere reduceres[27] spiritum, quo vita reponi posset, quo venena fugarentur, quo transmitterentur. Potionem dedisti aut remedii aut veneni. Si remedii dedisses, viveret. Non id apparet. Ergo venenum dedisti.

29   Multa sunt, iudices, quae minus clare verbis atque actione exprimi possunt. Utinam quidem Fortuna praestitisset ut frater meus viveret: ostendissem vobis medicum; hoc enim ante omnia dico, iudices: medicum. Ostendissem potionem hanc non cotidianam et qua omnes utimur,

30   sed medicamentis permixtam et oneratam. Dat medicus medicamentum. Qui acceptam bibit potionem, statim expirat. Quid tandem hic argumentandum erat, quid tandem hic probandum? Non oculis iudicassetis, non continuo

---

25 etsi . . . etsi *Gron.*: si et . . . si ad A: si ad (si et D) . . . si et β
26 *SB*³   27 D²: ducere(s) Aβ

---

24 There was no good reason to suspect that the deceased had been poisoned by his brother, but the suspicion was started by the doctor as suggested in s.26 fin. and gave the doctor his opportunity. But this flouts the theme.

25 Watt's *ostendisset* (twice) is no help. Neither the speaker

thought to have died of a poison which gave rise to suspicion prior to the moment of death. But this suspicion, arising from causes of this nature,[24] gave an ideal opportunity for presenting the poison: first, because you had somebody you could charge, and second, because my brother would take any potion whatsoever. It might be unpleasant to look at and bitter to taste, but when you say it's medicine there's no choice but to drink.

But why do I go on? If he had taken the poison from me, you would have cured him. You promised ⟨and⟩ you had a medicine and you said it was a medicine by which you swiftly brought back breath, by which life could be restored, by which poisons were put to flight or passed through. You gave him a potion either remedial or poisonous. If remedial, he would be alive. That does not appear. So you gave him poison.

There are many things, gentlemen, which are less clearly expressed by words than by action. Would that Fortune had let my brother live! I should have shown[25] you the doctor—I say this first of all, gentlemen: the doctor. I should have shown you this potion, not an ordinary one such as we all use, but one compounded and loaded with medicaments. The doctor gives the medicine: the man who takes the potion and drinks dies immediately. What need was here for argument, what need here for proof? Would you not have judged with your eyes, would you not

nor his brother could have shown the jury these things. Instead of wishing his brother were alive, the speaker should have wished that the jury had been there to see what happened rather than hearing it from himself. They could not even have *heard* all of it from the brother—there would have been no death.

81

strictis faucibus rapiendus ad supplicium veneficus videretur, qui nunc etiam spolia occisi hominis tenet et, subito
locuples, ait se tantundem habere quantum me qui nuper
divisi?

31   Mihi quid relictum est praeter luctus et lacrimas? Ultimum ergo illud nobis, frater miserrime, convivium erat?
Sicine digressi sumus? In has spes discessimus? ⟦Habui
occasionem †merendi diu† insidiatus essem. Potui tibi
venenum dare de quo nihil suspicareris.⟧[28]

322

Abdico te nisi desinis

Stricto gladio et cruento processit adulescens in contionem et dixit occisum a se patrem quod ab eo tyrannis
adfectaretur. Perduxit magistratum in domum, ostendit
apparatum tyrannidis. Cum excuteretur corpus, inventae
sunt tabellae ad filium, in quibus erat hoc: 'abdico te nisi
desinis, et si contradixeris indicabo causas.' Reus est iuvenis adfectatae tyrannidis.

1   DECLAMATIO

Quod circa probationem criminis huiusmodi difficillimum
solet esse, certum est: adfectatam tyrannidem; certum est
adfectatam esse in hac domo; omnisque eo deducitur
quaestio, ut dispiciatis utrum a patre huius an ab hoc sit
adfectata.

2   Nihil de moribus huius adhuc dico: aetates comparate.

---

[28] *ita secl. SB*[3], *auct. Wi.*

---

[1] Used for notes.

have thought that the poisoner should be dragged off to execution with a rope round his neck—he that now holds the spoils of the man he killed and, rich all of a sudden, says that he has just as much as I have, who lately divided?

What is left me except mourning and tears? Was that then our last dinner together, my most unfortunate brother? Did we part thus? Were these the hopes with which we said good-bye? ⟦I had the opportunity to kill you for a long time. I might have plotted against you. I could have given you a poison of which you would have had no suspicion.⟧

322

I disown you if you don't stop

A young man came into a public meeting with a sword drawn and bloodstained and said that he had killed his father because he was planning a tyranny. He led a magistrate into the house and showed the preparations for tyranny. When the body was searched, tablets[1] were found addressed to the son, with the words: "I disown you if you don't stop, and if you oppose, I shall reveal my reasons." The young man is accused of plotting a tyranny.

DECLAMATION

What is usually the most difficult thing to prove in a charge of this kind is certainly that tyranny was plotted. It is certain that it was plotted in this house. The whole question comes to this: that you enquire whether this man's father plotted it or he.

I say nothing as yet about this man's character. Com-

Senex ille et aetatis exactae quam rationem adfectandae tyrannidis habuit?—nisi forte propter filium hoc[1] fecit. Hic adulescens est: omnes cupiditates, omnes impetus in hac aetate facilius convalescunt. Est quaedam praeterea ratio sceleris (si hoc tamen nomen ullum accipit scelus): id 3 temptavit quo frui diu posset. Haec aetatum comparatio, illa morum[2]: pater modestus est: etiam si quid facere severius voluit, minatus est. Hic contra qualis adulescens? Ut nihil aliud obiciam quam quod ipse confessus est, quam quod gloriae loco pro contione dixit, patrem suum occidere potuit. Non quaero an innocentem—erit huius rei procedente oratione nobis locus; interim, occidere patrem 4 potuit. Quid non cadat in hunc animum, quid non recipiat haec temeritas? Minus est quod negat. Si componendus nobis esset aliquis qui opprimere rem publicam, qui libertatem patriae auferre posset, quam tandem mentem aliam existimaremus? Fingamus hominem cruentum, hominem crudelem, hominem apud quem nihil valeant[3] iura naturae. Est quaedam scelerum ipsorum societas, adeo ut vel uno appellari nomine potuerit utrumque parricidium.[4] 5 Ergo et ex aetatibus et ex moribus credibilius est adfectatam ab adulescente quam a sene tyrannidem. Cetera qualia sunt? Ac primum te interrogo, si adfectari tyrannidem a patre tuo existimabas, cur occideris antequam criminareris. Neque enim difficilis damnatio, nec longa iudicii mora sequebatur: apparatus tyrannidis erat in domo.

---

[1] *Aer.*: hoc (hunc D) filium Aβ
[2] *SB*[4] (*cf.* 2 *init.*): animorum Aβ
[3] *Aer.*: habe- Aβ [4] *anne* potuerint: u. p.?

---

[2] Or rather "was."

pare the ages. What reason had that old man, at the end of his life, for plotting a tyranny?—unless perhaps he did it on his son's account. *He* is a young man. All appetites, all urges more easily grow powerful at his age. There is a further sense to the crime—if any crime admits this word: he tried for something he could enjoy for a long time. So much for comparison of ages, now of character. The father is[2] a man of moderation. Even if he wanted to take a stern line, he only threatened. This young man on the other hand, what is *he* like? Suppose I tax him with nothing but what he has confessed himself, what he stated before a meeting as a boast: he could kill his father—whether innocent I don't ask, there will be a place for that later in my discourse. Meanwhile, he could kill his father. What would not fit such a mind, what would such recklessness not be capable of? The thing he denies[3] is less heinous. If we had to put together a being who could crush the commonwealth and deprive our country of freedom, what other mentality could we give him? Let us imagine a bloody man, a cruel man, a man with whom the laws of nature count for nothing. There is an association between the crimes themselves, so much so that both could be called by one name: parricide.

So both their ages and their characters make it more credible that tyranny was plotted by the young man than by the old. What about other points? First, I ask you, if you thought your father was plotting a tyranny, why did you kill him before you accused him? Convicting him would not have been difficult, no long delay of trial was to follow: the preparation for tyranny was in the house. "But he would

[3] Plotting tyranny.

'Deducendus tamen ad magistratus.' Et hoc certe non difficile fuit adversus senem ei qui occidit eum quem cri-

6 minaturus erat ut ⟨non⟩[5] responderet sibi. Non potest ergo videri rei publicae gratia fecisse cui plus aliter praestitisset. Nunc excutiamus qua causa feceris. Ante omnia gratias magistratibus ago quod, non deprehendisse contenti ea quae ostendebantur, aliquid et ipsi viderunt. Gratias ago etiam providentiae deorum immortalium, qui numquam ita opprimi veritatem voluerunt ut non magnis suis

7 vestigiis emineret. Recitentur hae tabulae: 'abdicabo te.' Non lego sequentia. Nego hanc esse fiduciam eius qui de adfectanda tyrannide cogitavit. An ille in iudicium vocare ausus fuisset et ignominia adficere adulescentem omnia scientem? Non enim tyrannis convincenda vestigiis erat neque argumentis eruenda: domi arma, domi apparatus.

8 Et si hanc causam abdicandi te non habuit, dicas oportet quam aliam habuerit. Non consentiebas consiliis eius? Hoc minus te debebat offendere: ille, si te tamquam indicem timuisset, potuit occidere. Satis ergo plenum vel hoc

9 erat argumentum innocentiae, severitas et vindicta. Quid tamen adiectum est? 'Si responderis, causas indicabo.' Quaerite nunc uter malae sit conscientiae. Ille minatur. Cur taceri voluit? Quoniam pater erat, quoniam numquam hi adfectus in tantum vincuntur odio ut non ad naturam suam tamen revertantur. Causas, quas ille se dicturum

[5] ut ⟨non⟩ *SB*[1]: ut A*β*: ne *Gron.*

---

[4] I.e. "never mind what follows," the threat being incredible if the father was plotting. But how *did* the young man explain the note?

have had to be taken before the magistrates." Assuredly that would not have been difficult against an old man for someone who killed the person he was about to accuse so that he should <not> answer him. So he cannot be thought to have done it for the sake of the commonwealth, which he could better have served by another procedure. Now let us shake out why you did it. First of all, I thank the magistrates in that they were not content with discovering what was shown there, they saw something for themselves. Also I thank the providence of the immortal gods who have never wished truth to be so buried but that large traces of it stand out. Let the tablets be read out: "I shall disown you." I don't read what follows.[4] I deny that anyone who thought of plotting a tyranny would be so confident. Would he have dared to take a young man who knew everything to court[5] and put him under stigma? For the tyranny did not have to be proved by traces and dug out by evidence: weapons and preparations were in the house. And if he did not have this motive for disowning you, you should tell us what other motive he did have. You were not an accomplice in his plans? The less reason for offending you. If he had feared you as an informer, he could have killed you. So even the severity and the punishment would have been sufficient evidence of innocence. But what was added? "If you oppose it, I shall reveal my reasons." Ask yourselves now which of the two has a bad conscience. He threatens. Why did he want nothing said? Because he was a father, because these affections are never so overcome by hate but that they return nevertheless to their nature. The reasons

---

[5] Inaccurate. In the situation as envisaged the disowned son would take the father into court to contest the disownment.

minatus est, tu ostendisti. Haec arma detecturus erat si respondisses, hos apparatus protracturus in medium.

10   Satis apparere omnibus arbitror adfectatam ab hoc esse tyrannidem. Ne quem autem vestrum securum faciat hoc, quod oppressa, quod deprehensa est tyrannis; apparatus enim iste testatur adulescentis mentem. Num latro innocentiam accipit si quis illi gladium extorqueat? Minatur aliquis moenibus flammas: num igitur facere securitatem civitati potest si quis faces eius extinxerit? Non habet nunc arma, non habet apparatum: sed habet animum.

11   Nec mihi hoc satis est approbare, iudices, tyrannum futurum, nisi illud quoque ante oculos vestros posuero, qualis sit futurus tyrannus. Ullius hic parcet corpori qui patrem trucidavit? Ullius hic criminis aget verecundiam qui parricidium professus est in contione, qui gladium illum cruentum stillantemque sanguine ostendere populo non recusavit? Quid ille manibus imperabit alienis, tantum suis ausus?

323

Alexander templum dedicans

Qui hosti opem tulerit, capite puniatur. Alexander bello Athenas cum premeret templum extra muros positum incendit. Pestilentia laborare coepit. Responsum est non posse finiri nisi templum restituisset. *[1] Restituto templo

---

[1] *lac. ind. Wi.*

---

[6] I.e., don't acquit him in the belief that he is no longer dangerous.

[1] There was no such war in history.

which he threatened to tell, you displayed. These weapons he was going to expose if you had replied, these preparations he was going to bring out to view.

I think it sufficiently apparent to everyone that this man plotted tyranny. And do not let the fact that the tyranny was crushed and caught make any of you feel secure:[6] that preparation bears witness to the young man's state of mind. Does a robber get innocence if somebody wrenches his sword away from him? A man threatens arson against our buildings: if somebody douses his torches, can he make the community secure? He doesn't have the weapons now, doesn't have the preparations: but he has the mentality.

Nor is it enough, gentlemen, for me to convince you that he will be a tyrant if I don't also put before your eyes what sort of tyrant he will be. Will he spare anybody's person—a man who murdered his father? Will he be shy of any crime?—a man who professed his parricide at a public meeting, who did not refuse to show that sword, bloody, dripping with gore, to the people? What will he command of other men's hands who dared so much with his own?

323

Alexander dedicating a temple

Whoso brings aid to the enemy, let him be capitally punished. When Alexander was pressing Athens hard with war,[1] he burned a temple situated outside the walls. He began to have trouble with a plague. The response[2] was that it could not be brought to an end unless he restored the tem-

---

[2] Of an oracle. Ellipse of *oraculum poposcit* (s.6) is barely credible.

Atheniensis sacerdos, Alexandro pollicente discessurum se ab armis si dedicaret, dedicavit. Discessit ab obsidione Athenarum Alexander. Dicitur sacerdos hosti opem tulisse.

1
SERMO

Quam potest maxima religione iudicum implendus animus est. Nam et sacerdos reus est et datur ei crimini quod dedicaverit templum et [quod][2] utilissimum causae et[3] etiam facile est hoc tempore: nam et praesentia numinis eius de quo agitur approbata est.

2
DECLAMATIO

Deos immortales omnes quidem, praecipue tamen numen et mihi maxime familiare et, sicut proxime experti sumus, praesentissimum, iudices, invoco: ante omnia ut, si respectu sacrorum, si pietate, si religione sola ductus feci quod obicitur mihi, velint impunitum esse sacerdotis officium; tum[4] (quod me aliquando sollicitum habet) ne aspere, ne irate hanc iudicii faciem intueri velint, in qua capitis periculo luitur quod templum dedicatum est. Oro igitur atque obtestor, si fieri potest, ne damnari me velint, si minus, ne vindicari, tueanturque civitatem in hac quam modo habere coepimus pace: immo vero hanc vestris animis voluntatem, hoc propositum mentis inspirent, ne eo tempore

---

[2] SB[1]
[3] c. et. SB[1]: et c. Aβ
[4] Sch., Gron.: nunc Aβ

---

[3] The second part of the response (see note 15) is missing here.   [4] The case. With *praesentia* cf. s.2 *numina . . . praesentissimi*, 20.

ple * .[3] When the temple had been restored, an Athenian priest dedicated it on a promise by Alexander to withdraw from warlike operations if he did so. Alexander withdrew from the siege. The priest is said to have brought aid to the enemy.

DISCUSSION

The jury's mind must be filled with religious feeling to all possible extent. For a priest is accused and the charge against him is that he dedicated a temple and it is highly advantageous to the case and also easy at this time; for it[4] is approved by the activity of the deity concerned.

DECLAMATION

I call upon the immortal gods, gentlemen of the jury, but especially the deity most familiar to me and, as we have lately seen, most present:[5] first of all that, if I was led to do what I am charged with only by respect for sacred things, by piety, and by religion, they may will my priestly duty to go unpunished; next (and this sometimes makes me anxious) that they may be pleased to regard the spectacle of this trial, in which the dedication of a temple is expiated by mortal danger, without bitterness and wrath. Therefore I beg and implore that, if possible, they will that I be not convicted; if not, that I be not avenged, and that they protect the community in this peace we have just begun to have; or rather that they inspire your minds with the will

[5] Apollo (note the oracle and the plague), to whom the former temple will have been dedicated. Evidently the speaker was his priest, probably priest of the temple, though that is not stated explicitly.

deos laedere velitis quo illis iam Alexander satisfecit.

4   Qui, etiamsi bellum contra nos traditum ac relictum a patre usque suscepit, etiamsi non tam propria quam here-ditaria nobiscum constitit contentione, omnia tamen alia impune faciebat: dum res intra caedem hominum stetit, dum intra vastationes agrorum, quamquam totius sancti[5] ac venerabilis soli, secunda res tamen, ac ne illa numina quidem quae semper excubare videntur pro nostra civitate

5 satis ad tuendam urbem profuerunt. Ut vero ignem sacris postibus, ut ferrum vetustissimae religioni admovere au-sus est, intellexit sibi non esse bellum nobiscum. Libenter audio quae ex diversa parte dicuntur: aegrum exercitum, praecipiti morte consumptas copias; quis enim non videt

6 omnia ista facta esse ut rursus templum esset? Ita illius quoque concitati, ut auditis, ac temerarii iuvenis motus est animus. Vidit non aliunde petendum esse quam a dis immortalibus praesidium. Oraculum poposcit. Quae hic culpa nostra est? Accepit. Videlicet dii immortales ut pec-cantibus graves, ita satisfacientibus faciles: si noluissent remedium illi pestilentiae concedere, non indicare potue-

7 runt. Restitui iussere templa. Gratias publice privatimque agamus: dedicare ipsi non permiserunt. Divisum parti-tumque responso est, quid Alexander facere deberet, quid nos. Ille quod debuit fecit: templum speciosius quam fuerat et cultius extruxit animo regis periclitantis; partes

    [5] *Obr.*: soli Aβ

---

    [6] The syntax misleads. There should have been something to the effect that although the war was hereditary, not personal,

and intention not to injure the gods at the same time that Alexander has already made them amends.

Although the war he undertook against us was handed down and left to him from his father, although the conflict in which he stood with us was hereditary rather than personal to himself,[6] all but one thing he did with impunity: as long as the matter stopped at the slaughter of people, the ravaging of fields (though the entire soil is sacred and to be revered), his campaign prospered, and even those deities that always seem to watch over our community were of too little avail to protect the city. But when he dared to set fire to sacred doorposts and bring steel against ancient sanctity, he found that his war was not against us. I am happy to hear what is said on the other side: that his army sickened, his forces were consumed by sudden death. For who does not see that all this was done so that there might be a temple again? So the mind of that young man, excitable and rash as you hear that he is, was moved. He saw that he must seek help from no other source than the immortal gods. He asked for an oracle. How am I to blame here? He got one. It can be seen that the gods are stern to sinners but compliant to them that make amends. If they had not wished to vouchsafe a remedy for that plague, they could have given no indication. They ordered the temple to be restored: let us give thanks publicly and privately. But they did not let him dedicate it himself. The response was divided into two parts: what Alexander should do and what we should do. He did his part: he built the temple grander and more elaborate than it was before, in the spirit of a

Alexander waged it mercilessly; for all that, the gods were with him until he burned the temple.

8 supererant meae. Excuso me vobis, dii immortales, quod
non statim ad condicionem dedicationis accessi: hoc enim
ex responso [et][6] Alexandro satis erat, quod permittebat.[7]
Ego nihilominus magna mercede suscepi hoc officium:
pacem poposci. Impetravi: veluti ore ipsius dei iussus promisit, praestitit. Haec est criminum meorum, iudices,
summa: et templum habemus et pacem.

9   Hosti opem tulisse dicor. Nondum causas facti mei reddo, nondum rationem legis ipsius excutio; interim, quid
vos putatis opem ferre? Neque enim id solum quaeritur
hac lege, an aliquis hosti profuerit. Multa enim quae utilia
sunt hosti et inviti et imprudentes facimus. Ideoque hoc
non complexa lex est, sed adversus eum se destrinxit qui
opem tulisset: illud, ut opinor, tale ‹est›,[8] qui auxilio iuvis-
set, qui armis, qui commeatu. Non sine causa: haec ipsius
verbi proprietas continet. Lex ‹enim›[9] quaeri voluit an
quis[10] opem tulisset; quodammodo[11] manum deprehendit
10 et ferentem coarguit. Causam autem huiusce iuris quis
ignoret? Animus, ut opinor, eius punitur qui hosti prodesse
voluit. Adversus proditorem, adversus hostem rei publicae
conscripta lex est. Quae si talia sunt, quid simile his com-
misi? Templum dedicavi. Viderimus an hoc hosti profuerit; ad causam meam pertinet sciri quid ego fecerim, non
quid ex eo factum sit.

6 *SB*[1]   7 *Gron.*: -ant Aβ   8 D[2]   9 l. e. *Obr.*:
legem Aβ   10 *Sch.*: is Aβ   11 *Aer.*: -dam loco Aβ

---

7 That the new temple be dedicated not by Alexander (i.e. his
priest), but by an Athenian priest—seemingly by the speaker himself (as priest of the old temple?). Cf. n. 15.
    8 Enough to get him off the hook.

king in peril. My role remained. I crave your pardon, immortal gods, that I did not immediately assent to the terms governing the dedication.[7] For it was enough for Alexander according to the response that he was allowing it.[8] Nevertheless I undertook this office for a great price: I asked for peace. I got it: as though commanded by the mouth of the god himself, he promised it and gave it. This is the sum of my offences, gentlemen: we have both temple and peace.

I am said to have brought aid to the enemy. I am not yet giving reasons for my act nor shaking out the purpose of the law itself: meanwhile, what do you understand by bringing aid? For the question under this law is not simply whether a person has been of help to the enemy. For we do many things both unwillingly and inadvertently that are useful to the enemy. For that reason the law did not embrace this, but unsheathed itself against one who had brought aid, meaning I think, one who had helped with reinforcements or weapons or supplies. Not without good reason: this is what the proper use of the word[9] implies. <For> the law wished the question to be whether a person had brought aid; in a manner of speaking it seized his hand and convicted him in the bringing. As for the reason for this law, who would not know it? The intention, I think, of a person who wanted to help the enemy is punished. The law was drafted against a traitor, an enemy of the commonwealth. If these things are as I say, what have I done that resembles them? I dedicated a temple. Never mind now whether this helped the enemy. What matters in my case is that what I did be known, not what came out of it.

[9] *Ops*, "which has a strong concrete connotation" (Wi.).

11 'At enim hoc hosti profuit.' Si ideo feci ut hosti prodessem, sane sim legi isti obligatus. Si cum aliquid facerem pro universa re publica utile etiam hosti fuit, non, ut opinor, damnis contendendum fuit. Videamus ergo an hoc pro re publica fuerit. Nondum dico quae secutura fuerint si non dedicassem; interim cum pietate vestra, Athenienses,

12 loquor. Templum non illud vetus, non illud praesentissimae religionis, non illud [est]¹² a quo totius civitatis nostrae petitur auctoritas, sed novum aliquod et adhuc inexpertum; video in finibus nostris: est dedicandum. Haec enim, priusquam dedicationis accipiant summam religionem, opera sunt tantum: dedicatio est illa quae deum inducit, quae sede destinata locat. Hoc ideo facere non cuicumque permittitur, nisi castae manus, nisi familiaris sacris animus accesserit. Dedicatio solis, ut nunc comperimus, concessa Atheniensibus. ⟦Hinc¹³ ergo fieri reor, iudi-

13 ces, quod, cum ceterarum civitatium templa, in ipsis posita urbibus, frequenter cum totis ruere atque incendi moenibus viderimus, nulla vindicta, nulla religio, nulla eos qui fecerant supplicia consecuta sunt, hic sacrilegium pestilentia vindicatum.⟧ Dedicationem¹⁴ destinabat: neque

14 enim aliter saltem templum esse existimaverat nisi dedicaretur. De quocumque templo loquor: hoc templum non

¹² SB⁴: sit *Ro.*   ¹³ *Aer.*: hoc Aβ
¹⁴ *Aer.*: destina- Aβ

---

¹⁰ Better help ourselves and the enemy than hurt the enemy and ourselves. Not "what they benefited was not comparable to the loss they incurred" (Wi.).

¹¹ From the response.

¹² Transposed from below (see crit. note 15), giving barely

"But this helped the enemy." If I acted in order to help the enemy, then certainly let me be tied to your law. But if, when I did something for the entire commonwealth, it was also of advantage to the enemy, I do not think we should have competed in losses.[10] Let us then consider whether this was in the interest of the commonwealth. I am not saying at this point what would have followed if I had not done the dedication; meanwhile, I speak with your piety, Athenians. I see a temple on our borders, not that ancient one, that temple of the most present sanctity from which our whole community derives authority, but a new one, yet untried. I see it on our borders. It needs to be dedicated. Such structures are mere buildings until they receive their final authority of dedication. It is the dedication that brings in the god, places him on his chosen seat. That is why not just anyone is allowed to perform it; his hands must be clean, his mind conversant with sacred things. The dedication, as we have now learned,[11] was permitted only to the Athenians. ⟦For my part I would believe that a divinity is present in all our religious institutions.[12] Hence I suppose it comes, gentlemen, that we have often seen temples of other communities, located in the cities themselves, collapse and burn along with all their buildings, with no ensuing vengeance, no religious sanction, no punishment of the doers, whereas here the sacrilege was avenged by a plague.⟧ He[13] was purposing dedication; for he had reckoned that otherwise it would not even be a temple unless it was dedicated. I speak of any temple: shall I not dedicate

tolerable continuity. But Wi. perceives signs of double versions in this passage and double-brackets accordingly.

13 Alexander (Rohde added *rex*).

dedicabo? Quam multa adhuc remitto! Taceo quid dii voluerint, taceo quid responsa praeceperint; humanis consiliis locum relinquo: non dedicabo? Procedere ultra volo:
si Alexander ab obsidione tantum Athenarum recessisset,
15 nonne aedificassemus, nonne restituissemus? ⟦Equidem
ego omnibus nostris sacris crediderim inesse numen.⟧[15]
Debetur hoc Atheniensium civitati, debetur vetustissimo
generi, debetur solo de quo contendisse quondam deos
immortales non sine causa creditum est. Cetera tamen
opinioni[16] credimus et coniectura colligimus: in hoc numine sensimus momenta bellorum, hoc pars utraque cognovit, hoc numen scit esse Alexander. Adice quod ⟨dii a
me⟩[17] dedicari voluerunt. Si a quocumque voluissent, oc-
cupandum fuit mihi, cum Atheniensis sim; totum enim ego
16 hunc populum, iudices, puto sacerdotem. 'At enim sic
effectum est ut laborare pestilentia exercitus Alexandri
desineret.' Non dico desiturum alioqui fuisse; periturus
sit Alexander, perituri sint milites omnes: vultis uti hoc
sacrilegii publici beneficio? Si quis nobis[18] hanc poneret
condicionem, Athenienses, ut omnium potiremur gentium

[15] *ante* hinc ergo (13 *init.*) *transp. coni. SB*[4] (*cf. SB*[3])
[16] *Hå.*[2]: -one Aβ   [17] *SB*[4] (dii *Ri.*)
[18] *Sch.*: vobis Aβ

---

[14] Athena (Minerva) and Poseidon (Neptune).

[15] Added *dii* (Ritter) is not enough. Obviously the temple
would have to be dedicated, but the response prescribed who was
to do it. *Si a quocumque voluissent* indicates that a particular person was designated (the priest), not the Athenians generally. So
too ss.7–8 *divisum . . . accessi* implies that the response pointed to
the priest even if it did not actually name him.

this temple? How many things there are that I do not press as yet! I say nothing about the wishes of the gods, the instructions of the response, I leave room for human counsels: shall I not dedicate? Let me go further: if Alexander had merely withdrawn from the siege of Athens, should we not have built, should we not have restored? ⟦For my part I would believe there is deity in all our sacred objects.⟧ This is due to the Athenian community, due to our ancient race, due to the soil for which immortal gods[14] are with good reason believed to have contended. However, in other matters we trust opinion and infer by conjecture; but we have seen that this divinity turns the scale of wars; both sides have found it so, Alexander knows that this is a divine power. Add that ⟨the gods⟩ willed it to be dedicated ⟨by me⟩.[15] If they had willed it done by anybody, I ought to have stepped in first, since I am an Athenian; for I think that this whole people, gentlemen, is a priest.[16] "But the result was that Alexander's army ceased to be troubled by plague." I don't say that it would have ceased anyway; grant that Alexander was going to die, he and all his soldiers: do you wish to take advantage of a public sacrilege? If somebody gave us the option of ruling over all nations, Athe-

---

16 If *cum Atheniensis . . . sacerdotem* was part of the original text it is an aberration. The priest should have claimed the dedication, not because he was an Athenian but because he was an Athenian priest, and the following compliment to the audience is not only irrelevant but stultifying—if all Athenians are priests, why this one in particular? Yet it has the right flavor and I hesitantly leave it with the author, temporarily off balance. But perhaps there is a lacuna after *cum*.

eversis exustisque templis, non profecto acciperemus. Pluris nobis pietas, pluris nobis opinio, pluris disciplina civi-

17 tatis fuisset. Moritur miles Alexandri: sed templum sine numine, sine religione, sed templum adhuc est inter praesidia hostium, sed non adire[19] mihi, non colere, non agnos-

18 cere, non agere gratias licet. Vos porro cur perire exercitum Alexandri, cur perseverare istam pestilentiam vultis? Nempe ne bellum haberetis. Habetis pacem. Beneficium dedistis; ex illo quem gravissimum hostem timebamus ha-

19 bemus potentissimum amicum. Sint sane pertinacia odia, Alexander responso satisfecerat: quod ad ipsum pertinuit, templum restituerat, quod ad secundam quoque partem responsi pertinebat, fecerat potestatem dedicandi. Mercedem quanta maxima dari poterat rei publicae dedit. Tam iniustos vos creditis deos immortales ut non fuerint cogitaturi cuius culpa templum vacaret? Nam, ut dixi, si pestilentiam finiri dii immortales noluissent, aut nullum responsum aut aliud certe dedissent. Demonstrata satisfactio et in hoc valet, ut accipienda sit.

20 Vereor, iudices, ne quid fingere ex necessitate periculi videar, verumtamen me religionis meae dissimulare quae acciderunt non sinit ratio. Alexandrum apud me valuisse solum putatis, aut ullam mercedem? Ego illum recessurum putabam, etiamsi non pacisceretur. Deus, deus ille (testor ipsum et praesentissimi conscientiam numinis), ille adegit, ille iussit, ille in has partes[20] misit: secundum hoc quodammodo fuit responsum.

---

19 *Ro.*: ire Aβ 20 B: preces Aβ

---

17 Peace.
18 Indicated (in the response).

nians, provided that our temples were demolished and burned, surely we should not accept. Piety, public opinion, the discipline of the community would have mattered more to us. Alexander's soldiery is dying: but a temple, without a divinity, without sanctity, but a temple, is still behind enemy lines; I cannot go to it, worship, acknowledge, give thanks. Further, why do you want Alexander's army to perish, why do you want the plague to continue? Surely, in order not to be at war. You are at peace. You have conferred a benefit; the man we feared as a deadly enemy has become a very powerful friend. Grant that hate is pertinacious, Alexander had complied with the response; for what concerned himself, he had rebuilt the temple, for what concerned the second part of the response, he had given us leave to dedicate. He gave the commonwealth the biggest possible price.[17] Do you think the immortal gods are so unjust that they would not have thought about who was to blame for the temple standing empty? For as I have said, if the immortal gods had not wanted the plague to be ended, they would either have given no response, or at any rate a different one. Amends clearly shown[18] carry also the corollary that they be accepted.

I am afraid, gentlemen, that I may be thought to be making up a story under compulsion of danger, but my religious conscience does not permit me to conceal what happened. Do you suppose it was only Alexander who counted with me, or any price? I thought he would withdraw even if he did not bargain. It was the god, yes the god (I call to witness the consciousness of his most present divinity); he made me do it, he commanded it, he sent me to this role. This was, in a manner of speaking, a second response.

101

324

Bona sacrilegi

Qui reum caedis damnaverit, bona eius possideat. Sacrilegi bona templo consecrentur. Damnatus caedis cum torqueretur, dixit et sacrilegium a se commissum. Ambigitur de bonis: sacerdos templo vindicat, accusator sibi.

1   DECLAMATIO

Antequam leges comparamus, intueri personas libet. Nos nullam habemus in litigando propriam cupiditatem: non acquirimus nobis, petimus bona templo, petimus honorem deo. Adversarius sibi vindicat et in praemium operae suae deposcit; ostendit quare accusaverit.

2   Quemadmodum personas comparavimus, ita comparemus et leges. Idem demus utrique tempus,[1] eandem utrique legi causam, ipsae tamen etiam citra defensiones non parem rationem habent: scripta est altera deo, altera homini. Aequum est priorem esse rationem religionis.

3   SERMO

Hic subici poterit et locus in quo laudemus hanc legem.[2]

4   DECLAMATIO

Praeterea et alioqui iustius est sacrilegi bona pertinere ad templum quam damnati ad accusatorem. Quare?[3] Quo-

---

[1] "Time, that is, of passing" (Wi.). The declaimer goes on to argue (s.6) that the circumstances give his law priority, but here he is looking at the laws *per se*.   [2] Presumably that the property of a man found guilty under either law should be suitably disposed of.

[3] Particular arguments supporting one law or the other in a particular case.

324

The property of a temple thief

Whoso convicts a defendant of homicide, let him take possession of his property. Let the property of a temple thief be consecrated to the temple. A man convicted of homicide said under torture that he had also committed a sacrilege. There is a dispute about the property. The priest claims it for the temple, the prosecutor for himself.

DECLAMATION

Before we compare the laws, I should like to look at the personae. We have no personal object in litigating; we are not acquiring anything for ourselves; we claim the property for the temple, honor for the god. The opposing party claims for himself and demands it as a reward for his work; he shows why he prosecuted.

As we have compared the personae, so let us compare the laws. Let us give the same time to each law,[1] the same motive for both,[2] but the laws themselves, even without defenses,[3] are differently based; one is written for god, the other for man. It is fair that the religious basis should have priority.

DISCUSSION

Here can be introduced the commonplace in which we praise this law.

DECLAMATION

Furthermore, it is in general more fair that the property of a temple thief pertain to a temple than that of a convicted man to the prosecutor. Why so? Because in a temple rob-

niam in sacrilegio propria templi iniuria est, in damnatione
rei alienum crimen. Ita illic praemium est, hic solacium;
illic datur ista pecunia, hic quodammodo redditur.

5   Haec comparatio esset si ipsas leges committeremus;
nunc nostra et tempore prior est. Ante enim commisit sacrilegium quam caedem. Accusator hoc nititur, quod ante
damnatus sit caedis quam sacrilegium confessus sit. Non
est autem intuendum quo tempore aperuerit se culpa sed
quo tempore commissa sit, quo tempore hanc poenam de
6   qua quaeritur ille meruerit. Id cum ipsa natura iustum est,
tum etiam legibus apertum. In caede enim spectanda sit
damnatio, in sacrilegio tempus[1] ipsum intuendum. Quare?
Quoniam lex tua ita scripta est ut qui damnaverit bona possideat [possidere non potes],[2] lex mea ita scripta est ut
bona sacrilegi ad deum pertineant. Statim ergo ut fecit
sacrilegium devotus huic poenae est, et ante ista bona ad
7   deum pertinere coeperunt quam lex damnaret. Vide quantum recedas ab intellectu iuris huiusce. Si caedem ante
sacrilegium commisisset, tamen, quoniam postea caedis
damnatus esset, ad deum potius pertinerent. Non enim
prodesset tibi quod prius caedis tempus esset, quoniam lex
tua non ad caedem sed ad damnationem pertinet. Nunc
vero, cum sacrilegium ante commissum sit quam caedes,
non est dubium quin bona ista templi sint.

[1] *anne* crimen *vel* facinus?   [2] *Wi.*

---

[4] The injury to the victim, not the prosecutor.

[5] Of the commission of the theft.   [6] "A pure invention,
beyond the theme" (Wi.). In s.8 the prosecutor states that the
murder was committed in public, which also is not in the theme;
but if that is granted, the sacrilege could hardly have come later.

bery, the injury is special to the temple, whereas in the conviction of a defendant the charge concerns someone else.[4] So in the latter case we have a reward, in the former a consolation; in the one case the property is a gift, in the other it is given back.

This would be a comparison if we were setting the laws themselves in opposition. As it is, our law is prior in time too. For he committed the temple theft before the homicide. The prosecutor relies on the fact that he was convicted of homicide before he confessed to the temple theft. But we must not look at the time when the wrongdoing revealed itself but at the time when it was committed, at which time he earned the punishment in question. That is both just in the very nature and also made plain by the laws. For grant that in the homicide we must look to the conviction, in the temple theft the time[5] itself is to be regarded. Why so? Because your law is so written that he who convicts takes possession of the property, whereas my law is so written that the property of the temple robber pertains to the god. Therefore as soon as he committed the theft, he was devoted to this punishment and that property began to pertain to the god before the law convicted him. See how far you depart from the understanding of this law. If he had committed the homicide before the theft, yet since he had been convicted of the homicide later, the goods would rather pertain to the god. It would not help you that the time of the homicide was prior, since your law does not pertain to the homicide but to the conviction. But as it is, since the theft was committed before the homicide,[6] there's no doubt that the property is the temple's.

8   'At enim praemium mihi debetur. Meo enim beneficio et sacrilegium illud inventum est.' Immo hercule [etiam illa caedes][3] beneficio suo: ex quo semel manus inquinavit, insecutae sunt illae protinus Furiae, ut hunc hominem palam occideret, ut reus deferretur, ut damnaretur, ut tor-

9   queretur, ut confiteretur. An vero tu illum, quod sacrilegium a se commissum esse dixit, praestitisse ignibus quos nos subiecimus aut flagellis putas? Nihil illa tormenta ad confessionem sacrilegii pertinebant, non de hoc torquebatur. Numen erat profecto, numen illud quod subiceret faces, quod acrioribus stimulis agitaret. Vos de caede torquebatis, ille de sacrilegio confitebatur.

325

Hereditas fidei commissa

Pauper et dives vicini erant. Pauperi uxor speciosa. Rumor erat adulterari pauperis uxorem a divite, conscio viro. Delatus lenocinii reus pauper et absolutus est. Dives decessit herede instituto bonorum omnium paupere et elogio tali: 'peto ut hanc hereditatem restituas ei cui rogavi.' Petit a paupere uxor hereditatem tamquam fidei commissam.

1   SERMO

Quid dicimus? Quomodo haec uxor et heres erit et adulte-

---

3 *SB*[3]

---

[7] Cf. s.5 *quo tempore aperuerit se culpa*. The bracketed words will not combine with *suo* and seem best regarded as a reader's comment: the murder too was a consequence of the sacrilege.

"But I am entitled to a reward, for it's owing to me that the theft too was discovered." Rather, upon my word, owing to the theft itself.[7] For from the moment when he fouled his hands, straight away those Furies pursued him, making him kill this man openly, be charged and convicted and tortured and confess. Or do you think that when he said he had committed temple theft he yielded to the fires and lashes which we applied? These torments had nothing to do with the confession of temple theft. He was not being tortured about that. It was surely divine power, that divine power, which applied the brands and stirred him with harsher goads. You were torturing him about the homicide; he was confessing about the sacrilege.[8]

325

An inheritance left in trust

A poor man and a rich man were neighbors. The poor man had a beautiful wife. There was talk that the poor man's wife was in adultery with the rich man, with the husband's connivance. The poor man was charged with procuring and acquitted. The rich man died, making the poor man heir to all his property, with the following rider: "I ask you to restore this inheritance to the person to whom I requested." The wife claims the inheritance from the poor man as having been left in trust.

DISCUSSION

What do we say? How shall this wife both be heir and not

[8] According to the theme, he was tortured after conviction for murder, presumably to make him reveal further details.

ra non erit? Quomodo, si conscius nullius flagitii fuit maritus, illius potissimum fidei haec hereditas mandata est?
Invenienda est enim aliqua causa propter quam heres sit.
Numquid hic dives hanc speciosam adamavit, cum ipsa
loqui nihil ausus est, locutus est cum viro (et inde opinio),
dum captat, fecit testamentum?

2   Quaedam, etiamsi themate non continentur, natura tamen ipsa manifesta sunt: matrimonium ⟨salvum⟩[1] inter
hos non esse qui litigant videtur mihi luce clarius; non
enim ego intellego rem[2] fidei tacite commissam nisi conscio. Hoc eo pertinet, ne quis iudicum manifestas exigat
probationes. Non est causa quae recipiat testem, non est
causa quae recipiat consignationem; scrutamur conscien-
3 tiam eius qui adversarius est. Totum ergo hoc iudicum
opus est, ut inveniant veritatem, quae ita demum poterit
esse manifesta in causis latentibus et natura conditis si nihil existimaverint exiguum quo inveniri veritas possit. Sic
ergo praeparandus est animus iudicum ut etiam levioribus
4 argumentis commoveri possit. Difficile est quidem natura
probare tacitum fidei commissum. Quomodo tamen probamus? Quaedam, etiamsi per se firma non sunt, comparatione vincunt. Hereditas aut ad pauperem pertinet aut ad
uxorem pauperis; si ad pauperem non pertinet, ad uxorem
pertinet. Elogium scriptum est palam. Certe et manifeste
electus hic est ad transitum hereditatis, huius silentium et
fides est utique de restituenda hereditate. Ergo debet re-
5 stituere alicui; si non huic, statim interrogo: cui? Habent

---

[1] *SB*[3]   [2] *Sch*.: litem A*β*

---

[1] The husband.
[2] The rich man.

be an adulteress? How comes it that if the husband did not connive at any outrage this inheritance was consigned to the good faith of him in particular? For some reason must be found for his being heir. Did this rich man love this beautiful woman (and hence the rumor) and as he[1] hunted for a bequest did he[2] make the will?

Certain things, though not mentioned in the theme, are manifest by their very nature. That the marriage between these litigating parties is <in bad shape> seems to me clearer than daylight. For I do not understand how the estate was tacitly left in trust to the husband unless he were conniving. This is to prevent one of the jurors requiring manifest proofs. This is not a case that admits of a witness or an attested document; we examine the conscience of the opposing party. So the whole business of the jury is to find the truth, which can become clear, where motives are hidden and concealed by their nature, only if they think no item petty by which truth can be found. So the mind of the jury must be so prepared that it can be influenced even by trivial pointers. It is by nature difficult to prove a tacit bequest on trust. Nonetheless, how do we prove it? Certain points, even if they are not strong in themselves, prevail by accumulation.[3] The inheritance pertains either to the poor man or to the poor man's wife. If it does not pertain to the poor man, it pertains to the poor man's wife. The rider was written openly. Surely and clearly he was chosen with a view to the passing on of the inheritance; his silence and good faith necessarily relate to restoring the inheritance. So he ought to restore it to somebody; if not to her, I ask

---

[3] *Comparatione* must = *congregatione* (cf. 307.6 fin.). But what follows hardly bears the observation out.

hoc incommodi controversiae scholasticae, quod quibusdam respondere non possunt: sed[3] quaedam incommoda
huius generis etiam in forum aliquando descendunt; et
ideo difficultatibus quoque utendum est.

6   DECLAMATIO

Ergo tibi non debetur. Superest ut alicui debeatur. 'Non'
dicis 'superest ut huic debeatur.' Fidei tuae commissa hereditas est. Quam committendi causam putamus? Necesse
est infirmam esse personam cui restitui oportet. Cum
infirmam dico, non statim infirmiorem dico quam te? Non
aestimabimus[4] per te istam[5] fortunae imbecillitatem? Pau-
7   perem fecit heredem. Ergo oportet inveniri personam
quae possit esse sub tutela tua, cui minus tuto relicturus
fuerit hereditatem quam tibi. Ergo infirmam personam
oportet esse feminae, et, si quid ad hanc infirmitatem adici
8   potest, pauperis feminae. Adsum huic feminae. Duxi ex
tua persona argumentum, ducere ex nostra volo. Dico
hunc animum fuisse divitis, ut hanc faceret heredem.
Cuius fidei committit? Maritum scripsit heredem. Ergo si
neque inveniri persona infirmior potest altera quae tibi
subiciatur quam haec neque familiarior huic quam tua,
credibile est idcirco sic scriptum esse testamentum.

9   ‹SERMO›[6]

Quaedam argumenta etiam ex incommodis petenda sunt.

    [3] *Ri.*: et Aβ
    [4] *Hå.*[2]: est vitavimus A: evit- β
    [5] *SB*[3]: ipsam Aβ
    [6] *Ri., auct. Pith.*

at once: "To whom?" Academic[4] controversies have the disadvantage that they cannot answer certain questions. But some disadvantages of this sort sometimes even come down to the Forum; and so we must make use even of the difficulties.

DECLAMATION

So it's not due to you. Remains that it's due to somebody. "It does not remain," you say, "that it's due to *her*." The inheritance was left to you in trust. What do we think was the reason for so leaving it? The persona to whom it should be restored must be weak. When I say "weak," don't I say in the same breath "weaker than yourself"? Shall we not judge from you of the weakness of the persona's condition? He made a poor man his heir. So a persona has to be found who can be under your tutelage, to whom he would have left the inheritance with less security than to you. So the weak persona should be that of a woman, and if anything can be additional to this weakness, a poor woman. I am here for this woman. I have taken an inference from your persona, I'll take one from ours. I'll say that the rich man's intention was to leave her his heir. To whom does he leave on trust? He made the husband his heir. So if we can find no weaker persona to be substituted for you nor any more familiar to him than yours, it is credible that the will was so written for that reason.

⟨DISCUSSION⟩

Some arguments are to be sought even from disadvantages.

4 I find *habent sqq.* unintelligible.

10   ⟨DECLAMATIO⟩[6]

Fuerit necesse est ratio aliqua et causa propter quam dives non ipsam ad quam pervenire volebat hereditatem scripsit heredem. Obstiterit oportet pudor non ille praetereundi[7] aliquem propinquorum: praeteriit enim; non ille scribendi aliquem extrarium heredem: scripsit enim extrarium; non ille bona sua in aliquem humilem demittendi: demisit

11 enim. Obstiterit oportet familiarior aliqua causa: non poterat salvo pudore hanc scribere heredem. Postea vobis causam verecundiae huius approbabo, postea scribentis animum; interim, fuit aliquid quod obstaret diviti quo minus hanc scriberet heredem.

12   'Quo merito' inquit 'tuo te scripsit heredem?' Vox communis est: isdem verbis interrogare te possum: quid merueras ut te scriberet heredem? Quamdiu enim[8] tertium non exhibes cui debeatur hereditas, inter nos quaestio est. Si nominasses, fortasse et illi dicerem: quo merito? Sed neque nominas ullum extrarium neque vindicare tibi

13 potes hereditatem. 'Proinde nobis responde: quo merito?' ⟨Quid si⟩[9] nullo? Quis ignorat testamentorum fortunam? Et esset fortasse in totum iniquum requiri a nobis mentis alienae rationem. Sunt quidam irrationabiles impetus animorum, quaedam gratuita, ut vulgo vocantur, odia. Quotiens audivimus filium dicentem: 'quo meo merito pater me exheredavit?' Nullam rem frequentior admiratio sequitur.

---

[6] *Ri., auct. Pith.*   [7] *Aer.*: reperiu- Aβ
[8] *Sch.*: etiam Aβ   [9] *SB*[2]

---

[5] That this was the wife is assumed by the "Master" (s.4) and argued by the declaimer (s.6–8).

112

There must be some reason and motive that caused the rich man not to write down as heir the woman to whom he wanted the inheritance to go.[5] Some embarrassment must have stood in the way: not at passing over one of his relations, for he did pass them over; not at naming an outsider, for he did name an outsider; not at passing down his property to one of humble station, for that is what he did. Some more interior reason must have inhibited: he could not name her as his heir without embarrassment. Later I shall approve to you the reason for this coyness and the mind of the writer; meanwhile there was something that inhibited the rich man from writing her down as his heir.

"What had you done," he says, "to deserve that he made you his heir?" That applies to both. I can ask you exactly the same question. How had you deserved that he make you his heir? For so long as you do not show a third party to whom the inheritance might be due, the question is between the two of us. If you had named one, perhaps I should have said to him too: "What had you done to deserve it?" But you neither name any outsider nor can you claim the inheritance for yourself. "So answer us: what have you done to deserve it?" ‹What if› nothing? Doesn't everyone know about the luck of wills? And perhaps it would be in general unfair that we should be asked about what is in someone else's mind. Minds sometimes have irrational impulses, sometimes gratuitous (to use the common word) dislikes. How often we have heard a son saying: "What did I do to deserve to be disowned by my father?" Nothing is more often followed by surprise.[6]

---

[6] Than a will.

14   Sed tolerabile erat si interrogaremur hoc tantum de hereditate: altius convicium quaestio ista habet. Quid si non
communis ista infamia fuisset? Quid ergo? Negem fuisse
rumorem qui aspergeret hanc feminam? Tu scis an vera
sint. Et praesenti fortasse liti vel expediebat confiteri. Nam
si istud quod intellegi vis verum est, utique hereditas nos-
15   tra est. Sed pecunia potius periclitemur: nullum meritum
uxoris tuae adversus divitem fuit. Quasi vero meritis tantum hereditates contingant. Interest an ametur qui amat?
Potuit hanc amasse feminam dives, salva huius conscientia: erat speciosa, erat, potuit in hunc adfectum incidisse.
16   Multi sunt qui testamenta sic scribant tamquam illud ad
vitam eorum pertineat. Sic quidam heredes scribunt eos
quos captant tamquam intellecturos, quamquam[10] secreto
scriptos. Potuit[11] ergo amor in causa esse, potuit ipsa pudicitiae admiratio in causa fuisse. †Sedit†[12] virtutum intellectum rerum natura: nulla tanta vitia sunt quae non
meliora mirentur.
17   Sed quatenus suspicamur, videor perspicere rationem
quare hoc tibi mandaverit. Nondum illa opinio, nondum
accusator; videlicet[13] haec tamquam ab advocatis audies

10 *Aer.:* tamq- A(β)
11 potest *coni. SB*[3]
12 serit *Aer.:* insevit *Watt*[1]: dedit *Ranc.*
13 *SB*[4]: videt Aβ

---

7 The husband would have been even harder on the wife if the
aspersion had not involved himself as well as her.
8 The adultery admitted, there could be no further question
about whom the rich man meant in the rider. What the advocate

But it would be tolerable if we were only asked this about the inheritance. Your question has a deeper slur. What if the aspersion had not applied to both?[7] What then? Should I deny that there was a rumor aspersing this woman? You know whether the talk is true. And perhaps it would have been to the advantage of our present suit to confess it. For if what you want to be thought is true, the inheritance is definitely ours.[8] But let us rather risk the money: your wife deserved nothing from the rich man— as though inheritances only go by deserts! The rich man would have loved this woman without her connivance. Does it make any difference whether a lover is loved? She was beautiful, yes indeed; he could have just fallen into this attachment. There are many that write their wills as though it pertained to their lives. Thus some name as their heirs those whose legacies they are hunting, as though they are going to know, even though named secretly. So love could be the reason, even admiration of her very virtue could have been a reason. The Nature of Things gave (?) us understanding of virtue. No vices are so great that they don't admire better things.

But since we are suspecting, I think I can see why he gave you this commission.[9] That talk came later, the prosecutor came later. You will be hearing clearly as from

does not say is that the jury might still baulk at finding in favor of an acknowledged adulteress.

[9] The advocate tries to get the best of both worlds: his client was loved by the rich man and intended in the rider, but she was innocent of adultery.

⟨quae⟩[14] ego de te suspicarer.[15] Pauper eras, vicinus eras.
18 Huius noti mores, certa sanctitas; argumento probabimus[16]: cum rumor utrumque infamaret, tu reus factus es; a
te lenocinium committi dixit accusator, non ab hac adulterium. Non ergo nova haec erit suspicio mea neque ex me
nata. Id quod accusator tibi obiecit,[17] hodie credo: locutum esse tecum divitem, egisse tecum, promisisse tibi
multa, novissime etiam iactasse testamentum.

326

Legati filius victima pestilentiae

Qui pestilentia laborabant miserunt legatum ad oraculum
petendum. Responsum est ei filium ipsius immolandum
esse. Ille nuntiavit civitati sacra desiderari; filio verum
confessus est. Sacris finitis pestilentia non est finita. Filius
processit in contionem et se ipse interfecit. Finita pestilentia reus est legatus laesae rei publicae.

1   DECLAMATIO

Existimaveram,[1] iudices, consecutum esse me hoc saltem,
ut sanguine meo servata civitas datae salutis grata meminisset, atque eo magis quod filius meus non necessitate im-
2   molatus erat sed voluntate. Verum hoc adeo in contrarium

---

[14] *SB*[4]   [15] *SB*[4] (*cf. K.–S.* II. 186 *sq.*): -cer Aβ
[16] *Ro., Ri.*: -avimus Aβ   [17] *Aer.*: obi(i)cit Aβ
[1] *ed. princ.*: (a)estim- Aβ

---

[10] With some fairly easy textual changes perhaps after all not a
locus desperandus. The advocate puts himself back where he was
before what he suspected had become general talk. Later the hus-

advocates ⟨what⟩ suspicions I had about you.[10] You were a poor man, his neighbor. *Her* character was well-known, her chastity certain. We have an argument to prove it: though the rumor defamed both, *you* were brought to trial; the prosecutor said that *you* committed procurement, not that she committed adultery. So this suspicion of mine will not be new, nor originating from myself. I today believe as the prosecutor charges you; that the rich man talked with you, treated with you, made you many promises, finally even brandished his will.

326

Envoy's son victim of pestilence

A people suffering from pestilence sent an envoy to an oracle. The response was that his own son should be sacrificed. He reported to the community that rites were required, but confessed the truth to his son. The rites were done with, but the pestilence was not done with. The son came into an assembly and killed himself. When the pestilence was done with, the envoy was put on trial for harming the commonwealth.

DECLAMATION

I had thought, gentlemen of the jury, that I had accomplished this much at least, that the commonwealth saved by my son would gratefully remember its deliverance, and the more so because my son was not sacrificed under compulsion but voluntarily. But this has turned out contrari-

band would hear it in court from the prosecutor and now from the declaimer himself.

cessit ut inventi sint in hoc populo qui, rem nescio indigna-
tione[2] magis dolendam an vanitate ridendam, obiciant homini pestilentiam. Et remedium deberi diis immortalibus
putant,[3] si quid vero passi sumus tali remedio dignum,
nostrae infirmitati adsignatur.[4]

3 SERMO

Fere commendatio per haec petenda erit, quae illi difficil-
lima est. Quod ad quaestiones pertinet, primae communes
sunt fere omnibus controversiis quae hac lege continentur.
Quaerendum est enim quid sit laedere rem publicam, et
paulo fortius in hac controversia, in qua tractum esse pestilentiae malum hoc nuntio manifestum est.

4 DECLAMATIO

Postea ergo causam ipsam defendemus, postea factum
commendabimus; interim satis est non esse me hac lege
qua deferor nocentem. Sane credatis imputari mihi posse
civium mortes: sunt iura quae istud defendant. Non esse
explicitam legationis fidem dicitis: habet haec quoque lex
actionem suam. Neque est quaerendum apud vos an alio
iudicii genere damnari possim; interim hoc ius ad me non
5 pertinet. Nam[5] si rei publicae ‹laesae›[6] lex est, haec nihil
ad hominum mortes, nihil ad ea quae privatim quoque vin-

---

2 A*β* (-em ABC): -gnitate *Gron.*   3 *Ro.*: putent A*β*
4 *Ro.*: -abitur *β*: adfirmab- A
5 *Sch.*: aut A*β*   6 *Obr.*

---

1 The son's death, which these people prefer to regard as an act
of weakness rather than a noble expiation.

2 *Per haec* is vague. Has something relative to the son's self-
sacrifice fallen out?

wise, so that in this people are found some who—I don't
know whether one should rather be angry at the outra-
geousness or laugh at the folly of it—tax a human being
with a pestilence. And they think a remedy is due to the immortal gods, but if we have suffered something[1] worthy to
be such a remedy, it is put down to our own infirmity.

DISCUSSION

Commendation more or less will be sought hereby,[2] and
that is very difficult for this speaker.[3] As regards questions,
the first are common to pretty well all controversies coming under this law. For we must ask what it is to harm
the commonwealth, and rather more vigorously in this
controversy, in which it is clear that the evil of pestilence
was prolonged by this report.

DECLAMATION

Therefore we shall defend the case itself later and commend the act later; meanwhile, it is enough that I am not
guilty under this law under which I am prosecuted. Maybe
you believe that I can be blamed for the deaths of our citizens; there are laws to get satisfaction[4] for that. You say
that the obligation of an envoy was not discharged. This
law[5] too has its own legal action. Nor has it to be argued before you whether I can be convicted under another law:
meanwhile, this law does not apply to me. For if there is a
law covering ‹harm to› the commonwealth, it has nothing
to do with people's deaths or with actions that can also

---

[3] His own conduct being so questionable.

[4] See *OLD defendere* 9.

[5] The law *male gestae legationis*; cf. *Decl. Mai.* 12.12.

dicari possunt. Obicias oportet aliquid quo publicum fuerit per me laesum; in hoc nihil obicis mihi praeter mortis
hominum. Quod crimen an verum sit, postea viderimus;
interim, ut dixi, legi et iuri coniunctum non est.

6   Mora tamen mea aliquid detrimenti civitas acceperit.[7]
Si hoc defenderem infirmitate animi mei, satis defensionis
esset non odio me civitatis fecisse. Filium meum immolandum esse dixerat deus. Putate id egisse[8] me, ne immola-
retur: hostias caedi mirabamini? Quid? Vos non maluis-
setis[9]? Exorari[10] posse sollemnibus sacris existimabamus
deos. Quid? Vos haec remedia non temptassetis[11]? Secum
quisque cogitet quantum mihi impositum onus, qualis
7 exacta vox. Sed ne mentitus quidem sum. Sacra exigi a diis
immortalibus dixi: non sacra exigebantur, non sacris placa-
ti sunt? Alioqui nihil me fecisse subripiendae hostiae gratia
cui non manifestum est? Indicavi filio maximi animi. Ergo
ne hac quidem venia dignus est pater, si hoc filio voluit de-
8 beri, quod moriebatur? Quod quidem neque consilii mei
neque voluntatis primum fuit. Credite eum qui legatus
missus sit, credite eum qui responsum acceperit, renuntia-
verit, nihil animo suo, nihil propria mente fecisse: hoc profecto quaerebatur exemplum, ut narraretur iuvenis qui pro
re publica mortem non recusavit, qui in conspectu civium
visceribus suis ferrum immersit. Non potuisse aliter finiri
9 pestilentiam quomodo vultis approbem? Sic finita est. Non
enim profecto dii immortales poenam petebant, nec in

---

[7] *SB*[4]: -pit Aβ
[8] *Aer.*: esse Aβ
[9] *Aer.*: -uistis Aβ
[10] *SB*[3]: -are Aβ
[11] *SB*[3]: -astis Aβ

be punished privately. You must tax me with something through which the commonwealth was harmed through me. Herein you tax me with nothing but people's deaths. Whether that charge is true, we shall see later. Meanwhile, as I have said, it is not connected with the law and statute.

However, ⟨suppose⟩ the community sustained some damage through my delay. If I were to defend this by the infirmity of my spirit, it would be defense enough that I did not act from hatred of the community. The god has said my son must be sacrificed. Suppose I tried to prevent the sacrifice. Were you surprised that animal victims were slaughtered? Well, would you not have preferred it so? We used to think the gods could be appeased by customary rites. Well, would you not have tried those remedies? Let each of you put it to himself what a load was placed upon me, what sort of utterance was required. But I did not even lie. I said that rites were required by the immortal gods: were not rites required, were they not placated by rites? Anyway it is clear to everybody that I did nothing with the object of sneaking away a victim. I told my great-hearted son. So does not a father deserve even this indulgence, if he wanted his son's death to be due to his son? It was not primarily of my doing, of my will. Believe that the man who was sent as envoy, who received and reported the response, did nothing of his own motion, his own mind: this example surely was wanted—that the story be told of a young man who did not refuse to die for the commonwealth, who plunged his sword into his vitals before the eyes of the citizens. How do you want me to show you that the pestilence could not have been ended in any other way? That is how it was ended. For the immortal gods surely were not seeking a penalty, they had not given the

121

supplicium filii hoc responsum dederant civitati. Magna arcessabatur anima; debuit duci honesta via. Quem igitur potius in fine actionis meae invocem quam illum mihi proprium deum?

327

Sterilis trium noverca

Introducta[1] tribus privignis sterilitatis medicamentum bibit. Repudiata iniusti repudii agit.

1 DECLAMATIO

Quod primum pertinet ad pudorem huius feminae, non adulterium obicitur, non aliqua adversus maritum licentia. Necesse est plurimum eius moribus tribuat ex qua liberos 2 quaerit. Omnis repudii causa in crimine uno consistit. Hoc quale sit, postea videbimus; interim, unum est. In quo mortalium tanta felicitas[2]? Nec de femina loquor, cuius infirmior sexus est, sed in ipsis etiam qui prudentia sapien- 3 tiaque gloriari solent habet locum paenitentia. Sed ⟨hoc⟩[3] unum sane sit grave, sit scelestum (et hercule credibile erit in ea quae tres privignos habuit): expecto ex his aliquid novercalibus factis. Venenum paravit, insidiata est liberis tuis, vel, quod levissimum est, expugnare animum tuum voluit? Nihil horum. Novum et inauditum antea crimen:

---

[1] ind- *Ro.*: *anne* superd- (*cf.* 373 *thema*, 381 *thema*)?
[2] *Fr.*: facilitas Aβ   [3] *Aer.*

---

[6] *Duci* has nothing to do with execution here.
[7] His son.
[1] Lit. "was introduced to three sons."

community this response to punish my son. A great soul was summoned: they wished it led[6] by a path of glory. Whom then should I invoke at the end of my pleading but that god[7] peculiar to me?

327

The barren stepmother of three

A woman who married the father of three sons[1] drank a drug causing sterility. Divorced, she brings an action for wrongful divorce.

DECLAMATION

What is first relevant to the honor of this woman, she is not taxed with adultery or any license against her husband. He must needs think highly of the character of a woman from whom he wants children. The whole reason for divorce lies in one charge. What sort of charge, we shall see later; meanwhile, it is the only one. What mortal is so fortunate? And I am not speaking of a woman, whose is the weaker sex, but even in those who are accustomed to boast of their prudence and wisdom repentance has a place. But ⟨this⟩ one charge, let it be grave, let it be criminal (and upon my word that will be believable in a woman who had three stepsons[2]): I expect one of those stepmotherly acts. Did she prepare poison, did she plot against your children, or, what is the least of them, did she try to turn your mind against them?[3] None of these. The charge is novel, never

---

[2] Stepmothers being notoriously prone to murder their stepsons.

[3] Lit. "storm your mind."

noverca nimium dicitur amare privignos.

4 'Sterilitatis medicamentum bibit.' Si tu liberos non haberes, poteram tamen illa dicere: periculum timuit, documentis quarundam infeliciter parientium mota est, fortasse male sensit de temporibus ipsis, vidit eam luxuriam, ea vitia, ut paene educare liberos amentis esset. Tu porro in uxore nihil aliud spectas[4] quam fecunditatem? 'Non

5 parit.' Sed obsequium, sed fidem praestat. Sed iam tempus est propriis eam rationibus defendi. Bibit illud cum tres liberos haberes. Nec statim hoc amore et adfectu defendo; interim tamquam ambitiosam tuebor. Voluit[5] effugere fabulas novercarum, voluit se adversus casus etiam praeparare, voluit nihil in domo habere propter quod privignis

6 invideret. Quid si fecit hoc non modo novercae sed etiam uxoris optimae[6] animo? Plenam invenerat domum, plenum testamentum. 'Quid mihi' inquit 'cum partu erat? Dederat mihi Fortuna iuvenes; neque maritus eius aetatis est ut concupiscere novos liberos possit. Ne fraternitatis quidem eadem iura futura erant [inter tam dissonantes

7 tamque discordes].[7]' At nunc expellitur et, quoniam bona fuit noverca, nec liberos habitura est nec virum.

328

Discordes fratres

Filii familiae duo adulescentes fratres dissidebant. Iuncta

---

4 *Gron.*: exs- Aβ   5 *Gron.*: illam Aβ
6 *Gron.*: -mo Aβ   7 *SB4* (*cf. SB2*)

---

4 I now exclude these words; cf. SB2.
1 Subject to *patria potestas*.

before heard of: a stepmother is said to love her stepsons too much.

"She drank a drug causing sterility." If you didn't have children, I could still say that she feared the danger, was upset by certain examples of women unfortunate in childbirth, perhaps had a bad opinion of the times we live in—she saw such loose living, such vices, that it was well-nigh madness to bring up children. Moreover, do you think of nothing in a wife except fecundity? "She does not produce a child." But she gives obedience, gives loyalty. But now it's time she be defended by arguments special to her case. She drank that drug when you had three children. I am not defending this straight away by love and affection: for the present I shall say on her behalf that she was eager to shine. She wanted to escape the stories about stepmothers, wanted to prepare herself too against ill chances, wanted to have nothing in her home to make her jealous of her stepsons. What if she did it not only in the spirit of an excellent stepmother but of an excellent wife? She had found a full home, a full will. "What had I to do with childbearing?" she says. "Fortune had given me sons; and my husband is not of an age that he can form a desire for new children. Nor would the laws of brotherhood have remained the same [among persons so dissonant, so discordant].[4] But now she is expelled, and because she was a good stepmother, she will have neither children nor husband.

328

Brothers at loggerheads

Two young men, brothers, were at odds, sons of family.[1]

erant eorum cubicula. Quodam tempore audito tumultu in interiore parte domus venit pater in eum locum in quo clamor erat. Invenit alterum ex filiis occisum. Cubicularium eius torsit et occidit in tormentis. Quid compererit incertum est. Interrogavit illum filius quid comperisset. Non indicantem accusavit dementiae. Absolutus est pater. Iuvenis parricidii accusatur; adest illi pater.

1

SERMO

Rei persona ante omnia infirmatur, et necesse est nos ab ea incipere. Prius ergo sumimus id quod prius videtur esse in persona. Occidisse dicitur fratrem: hoc etiamsi non possumus efficere ut in rerum natura non esse videatur, eo tamen perducemus ut non facile credatur.

2

DECLAMATIO

Obicitur reo discordia cum fratre; et hoc, priusquam ad causas pertineat occidendi, ad crimina personae admittimus. [discordia cum patre][1] Ante omnia, commune maledictum est cum eo qui vindicatur; et penes quem culpa fuerit magis potest pater scire quam accusator. Asperiorem esse autem adversus suos interim et fiduciae argumentum est, et hoc adeo non valet ad probationem tanti criminis ut contra sit. Iam enim transimus ad causas.

3

Dicitur occidisse fratrem inimicum. Non dico illa: non protinus, si causae sceleris sint, scelus quoque constat. Utinam enim ita composita esset natura rerum ut omnia facta causas expectarent[2]! Plures erant propter quas non occide-

---

[1] *Ri.*   [2] *SB*[3] (*vel* sp-): superarent Aβ

---

[2] Killing his brother.
[3] That one has done nothing wrong.

Their bedrooms were adjoining. One night the father heard a commotion in the inner part of the house and went to where the noise was. He found one of his sons murdered. He tortured the young man's valet and killed him in the torments. What he found out is uncertain. His son asked him what he had found out. When he did not tell, he accused him of dementia. The father was acquitted. The young man is accused of parricide.[2] His father appears for him.

DISCUSSION

First of all, the persona of the defendant is enfeebled and we must begin from that. So we take first what seems to be first in the persona. He is said to have killed his brother. Although we cannot make this appear to be outside the Nature of Things, we shall bring it to the point of being hard to believe.

DECLAMATION

The defendant is taxed with being at loggerheads with his brother; and we admit this as a charge against the persona before it relates to motives for murder. To begin with, the reproach is shared with him we are avenging; and who was to blame, a father can know better than a prosecutor. To be rather rough towards one's family is sometimes even a sign of confidence,[3] and so far from counting as proof of so great a crime it makes the other way. For now we pass to motives.

He is said to have murdered his enemy brother. I won't say the usual things—if there are motives for a crime, that crime is not automatically proved. Would that the Nature of Things were so constituted that all acts wait for a motive! He had more motives *not* to kill. The fact that he was an

ret. Nam erat occidendi quod inimicus est, non occidendi quod frater est, non occidendi quod periclitaturus, non occidendi quod ipsa per se innocentia satis iustas rationes ha-

4 bet.[3] Ergo non continuo sequitur ut, si quis odio aliquo concitatus est adversus alium, hunc etiam ferro petiturus[4] sit. An vero innocenter inimicitias geri vel inter alienos, vel inter extraneos fas non est? Cotidianis iurgiis forum strepere, adsiduas lites videmus; quis non dies convicia, quis

5 non maledicta adfert? Scelus ex natura mentis oritur. Huic vero etiam ad causas metuendi sceleris accessit, quod iurgium ei cum fratre palam fuerat. Cauta sunt huiusmodi scelera et circumspecta; neque enim est quisquam tam perditus, tam inutilis sibi, ut non ista committat proposito

6 negandi. Et mehercule quam hoc ipsum repugnat, quod ab accusatore pro potentissimo ponitur, quod in cubiculo suo occisus est, quod in lecto suo! Nihil minus commisisset percussurus quam ut hoc ei obiceretur. Latrones longe a receptaculis suis spoliant; ferarum quarundam dicitur haec esse natura, ut procul a cubilibus rapiant. Fratrem discordem in domo, in cubiculo occidit ut qui neget?

7 Sed ne apud ipsum quidem accusatorem hae causae satis valuerunt. *[5] Neque enim servi torquendi ratio erat si fecisse filium existimarem. Desine ergo hoc uti argumento

8 et me testem citare contra eum qui defenditur. Servum torsi: quis nescit hoc accidere nihil indicanti? Servum torsi, cubicularium eius qui occisus est; nihil in servo suspica-

3 *Ro., Ri.*: -eat Aβ
4 D: et it- A¹: et iterus BC: extincturus A²
5 *lac. ind.* SB³

enemy was a motive for killing; for not killing, the fact that he was a brother, that he would be risking his own life, that innocence in itself has sufficiently good reasons.[4] So it does not follow straightway that if one man has been stirred up by some hostility toward another, he will also attack him with steel. Is it not admissible that feuds are carried on innocently even between nonrelatives, even between persons unconnected? We see the Forum loud with daily brawls, we see disputes all the time. What day but brings shouting matches and insults? Crime arises from the nature of a man's mind, but my son had an additional reason for keeping clear of crime—his quarrel with his brother was no secret. Crimes of this sort are cautious and circumspect, for no one is so abandoned, so self-injurious, that he commits them without the intention of denying them. And upon my word, how recalcitrant is that point of which the prosecutor has made so much, that he was killed in his bedroom, in his bed! The last thing an assassin would do is to let that be brought against him. Brigands do their robbing far away from their lairs. It is said to be the nature of some wild beasts to find their prey far from their dens. Does any man kill a brother with whom he is at odds in the house, in the bedroom, expecting to deny it?

But even with the prosecutor himself these motives did not carry much weight. * For I had no reason to torture the slave if I thought my son had done it. So stop using this argument and calling me as a witness against the person being defended. I tortured the slave. Everyone knows this happens to one who tells nothing. I tortured the slave, the victim's valet. I suspected nothing in the case of my other

[4] Better in general be innocent than guilty.

tus sum alterius filii. Nec potest mihi obici neglegentia quaestionis: quaesivi enim ‹nimis›.[6] Nec in hac diligentia suspicio adversus filium alterum[7]: ipse demum qui erat percussus quaesivit.

9 'Quid ergo' inquit '‹in›[8] tormentis confessus est?' Dura est condicio interrogationis huius, cum id quaeritur cui[9] si respondeas non creditur. Vis enim, accusator, voce mea stari? Vis credere iudices quidquid respondero? Das enim[10] mihi fingendi libertatem; propter hoc ipsum perdam necesse est fidem, quod mihi dicere licet quidquid voluero.

10 In alia, inquam, parte filio meo conferam si qua potero advocatus; pro testimonio mihi remittet. 'At ne ipsi quidem[11] filio indicasti.' Quid? hoc colligis noluisse me dicere quod contra ipsum erat? Quae ratio tacendi fuit si filium meum fecisse credebam, quae ratio tacendi apud ipsum? Nam sive irascor, vindicari possum hac voce quam contra illum habeo, sive imputare indulgentiam volo, plus

11 illi praestitero si scierit ‹me scire›[12] se fecisse. Cur ergo non respondi? Iam videor iudicibus reddidisse rationem. Sic enim causam agebam: 'Non respondeo filio nimium curioso. Quid est enim utique cur indicare necesse sit? Non respondeo [nunc][13] quoniam sic instat.' Adiciebam huc[14]: 'Nihil respondeo quoniam nihil certi scio. Non respondeo quoniam non credo aliquid dicenti. Non respondeo quo-

6 *Opitz*: diligenter *Watt*[1]   7 *Opitz*: alia Aβ
8 *ed. Leid.*   9 *SB*[2]: quod Aβ
10 *Ro.*: etiam Aβ   11 ne i. q. *Ro.*: nec siquidem Aβ
12 *Watt*[1]   13 *Obr.*   14 *Ro.*: huic Aβ

5 The slave died.

6 By proxy. The other son was not in his father's mind.

son's slave. I cannot be accused of negligence in the torture. I ⟨overdid⟩ it.[5] And in this zeal no suspicion attaches
to my other son. He himself, the murder victim, only he
applied the torture.[6]

"What then," he says, "did he confess ⟨under⟩ the torture?" Hard indeed are the terms of this interrogation
when the question is such that any answer is disbelieved!
For, Mr prosecutor, do you wish what I say to be accepted?
Do you wish the jury to believe whatever I reply? For you
give me liberty to invent; I must lose credibility from the
very fact that I am free to say whatever I like. "In another
role," I say, "as backer I shall do whatever I can for my son;
as for giving evidence, he will excuse me." "But you did not
even tell your son himself." What? Do you infer that I was
unwilling to say something that was against him? What reason did I have for saying nothing if I thought my son was
the perpetrator, what reason for saying nothing to himself?
If I am angry, I can take my revenge with this utterance[7]
against him that I have; or if I want to take credit with him
for indulgence, I shall have done more for him if he knows
⟨that I know⟩ he did it. So why did I not answer? I think I
have already given the jury the reason. For this is how I
pleaded the case:[8] "I don't answer an over-inquisitive son.
For why should it be absolutely necessary to tell? I don't
answer because he is so pressing." I added: "I make no answer because I know nothing for certain. I don't answer
because I don't believe anything he[9] said. I don't answer

[7] Assuming (capriciously) that the slave did say something
prejudicial to the defendant.

[8] In the first trial.

[9] The slave.

niam adhuc quaero. Non respondeo quoniam hoc inquisitioni meae non expedit. Non respondeo quoniam ⟨non⟩[15]

12 illum ut interrogarem torsi. An vero parum iustas saeviendi causas habebam adversus cubicularium? Dominum suum non defenderat, non servaverat, nesciebat quis dominum suum occidisset.' Sed si argumentum ex his trahimus, non est maius contra filium meum silentium quam pro ipso quod accusavit, quod detulit. Irascor quidem huic eius pertinaciae; sed quandoque vindicabo, quomodo fas est, quomodo oportet. Verumtamen qua fiducia fecit quod

13 me non timuit offendere! 'Iudices' inquit 'cum te absolverunt dementiae, hoc iudicaverunt, a filio fratrem videri occisum.' Nihil minus: nam si filius meus fratrem occidisset, patrem impie accusaret, demens eram, ⟨non tam⟩[16] quod non respondere tam curioso[17] poteram quam si vivere[18] cum eo quem cruentas manus habere sciebam. Erit ergo adeo non damnatio ista filii mei ut possit videri etiam absolutio.

14 Haec ego de causa dico ipsius. Permittetis mihi in summa parte causae uti etiam persona mea. Ego istum si filium meum occidisset defenderem? Qualem me patrem iudicatis? Asperum? Et ego pro filio mentiar? Mitem, indulgen-

15 tem? Et ego non vindicabo illum qui occisus est? Inter liberos haec una differentia est apud animum patris, quod semper maiorem locum habet is cuius miseremur. Neque hic sane meruerat ut a me nisi innocens defenderetur:

---

15 *Wi.*
16 *Ro.*
17 *Obr.*: furiose (for- A) Aβ
18 viverem *Obr., Hå.*[2] (*cf. SB*[2])

because I am still looking. I don't answer because this does not help my investigation. I don't answer because I did <not> torture him in order to interrogate him—did I not have good enough reasons for ferocity against the valet? He had not defended his master, he had not saved him, he didn't know who killed his master." But if we draw an argument from all this,[10] my silence is no more against my son than the fact that he charged me, brought me to trial, is for him. To be sure I am angry at his pertinacity; but I shall punish him one day in the right and proper manner. All the same, what confidence he showed in not being afraid to offend me! "When the jury acquitted you of dementia," says my opponent, "they showed that your son appears to have killed his brother." Not a bit of it: for if my son had killed his brother and impiously prosecuted his father, I *would* have been demented, not <so much> because I could not answer such curiosity as for being able to live with somebody I knew to have blood on his hands. So far therefore from this being a conviction of my son, it can even be seen as an acquittal.

This I say on *his* case. In the final part of the case you will allow me to use my own persona too. Would I be defending him if he had murdered my son? What sort of father do you judge me to be? Harsh? And shall I lie for my son? Gentle, indulgent? And shall I not avenge him that was murdered? In a father's mind there is only one difference between his children: one we pity always has the greater place. Certainly he had not deserved to be defended by me unless he is innocent. He brought me to

[10] From what he did not say at the *dementia* trial and the assortment of possible reasons he gave for his silence.

reum me detulit, sordes mihi induit, ad iudicem vocavit. Sentiet hoc quale sit cum testamentum scribam, sentiet
16 cum frustra[19] indulgentiam meam requiret. Quid est ergo? Mentiri ne iratus quidem possum: est filius contumax, est patris sui accusator, sed fratrem non occidit. Neque ego istum in ulla alia parte absolvendum puto, nec hodie veni in hoc iudicium tamquam advocatus. Nihil rogabo, nihil deprecabor: illud tantum meae pietatis gratia, meae tantum conscientiae causa faciam, ne videar istum silentio pressisse.

17   SERMO

Ne quem vestrum ducat illa species, ut videatur hic esse aliquid momenti habiturus apud iudices si miserabilem se fecerit, si amisso altero filio deprecatus fuerit pro iuvene. Sunt ista in aliis causis potentia; hic pater, nisi propior[20] securo est in hoc iudicio, mentitur pro filio: non tam illi opus est opera advocati quam fide testis.

329

Sepultura tyranni qui se occidit

Qui tyrannum occiderit, in foro sepeliatur. In pestilentia responsum est tyrannum occidendum. Ipse se occidit. Petunt propinqui ut in foro sepeliatur.

---

[19] *Hå.²:* tristitia A: -am β [20] *Ri.:* prior Aβ

---

[11] Again, "judge" and "jury" are used indifferently.

[12] Cf. s.10 init. *si qua potero advocatus.* But in s.14 this seems to be his speech for the defense. The contradiction (as it appears to be) remains in the speaker's lap.

trial, made me put on mourning, summoned me before the judge.[11] He shall feel what sort of behavior that is when I write my will, he shall feel it when he asks in vain for my indulgence. So how do we stand? Angry as I am, I cannot lie: he is a refractory son, prosecutor of his father, but he did not kill his brother. I don't think he deserves acquittal in any other context and I didn't come into this court today as his advocate.[12] I shall ask nothing, beg no mercy. All I shall do, only for the sake of family feeling, only for the sake of my conscience, is not to appear to have crushed him by silence.

DISCUSSION

Let none of you be seduced by a presentation in which the speaker might seem likely to carry some weight with the jury if he makes himself pitiable, if having lost the other son he pleads for the young man. Such tactics work well in other cases: *this* father, unless he is close to confident in this trial, is lying[13] for his son, who does not so much need the services of an advocate as the good faith of a witness.

329

Burial of a tyrant felo de se

Whoso kills a tyrant, let him be buried in the Forum. In a plague it was responded[1] that a tyrant must be killed. He killed himself. His relatives ask that he be buried in the Forum.

---

[13] I.e. "will be thought to be lying."
[1] By an oracle.

1

DECLAMATIO

Ingens calumnia! Pudet mehercule meae actionis. Nunc ego negabo? Quid? Si ostendero eum qui civitati libertatem abstulerit, qui leges sustulerit, qui templa violaverit, qui iniuriis nostris iram deorum immortalium commoverit, tyrannicidam non fuisse, multum alioqui effecisse

2 oratione mea videbor? Interpretanda nobis legis ipsius voluntas est, quid spectaverit ille qui constituebat diligenter, ut res est, et alte exquirendum atque eruendum? Ego mihi arbitror, iudices, pauca pro legum latore esse dicenda, ne

3 tam obscure hoc occulteque scripsisse videatur. An non est hoc omnibus, qui modo ad intellectum sermonis pervenire possunt, lucidum atque manifestum, eum qui legem ita composuerit, ut si qui tyrannum occidisset in foro sepeliretur, locutum de duobus? Non intellegit aliquis alium

4 esse eum qui occidat, alium qui occidatur? Argumentis scilicet agendum est et in exemplum adferendae aliae quoque leges. Dicam nunc ego: 'qui pulsaverit aliquem iniuriarum teneatur, nemo tamen tenebitur qui se ipse pulsaverit'? Nam illud quidem ridiculum, ut opinor, omnibus vobis futurum est, si in exemplum proximam similitudinem adduxero, ac negavero teneri lege ulla eum qui se

5 occiderit. Est porro hoc manifesto reprehendendum, si ad eos existimemus pertinere praemia ad quos poenae ⟨non⟩[1] pertinent.

⟦Bene scilicet de re publica meruit quod aliquando

[1] *Obr.*

[2] That the tyrant was a tyrannicide—a preposterous notion. Cf. SB[2].

A huge quibble! Upon my word, I am ashamed of my plea. Am I now to deny?[2] Come! If I show that the man who robbed the community of freedom, abolished the laws, violated the temples, provoked the anger of the immortal gods by the injuries he did us, was not a tyrannicide, shall I seem to have achieved much by my address anyway? Must we interpret the intention of the law itself? What its author had in view must we, as matters stand, deeply and diligently search out, dig out? I think, gentlemen of the jury, that I must say a few words on behalf of the lawgiver, so that he may not be thought to have written this so obscurely and cryptically: or is it not clear and manifest to all that can attain to understanding of speech that when he so drafted the law that whoso killed a tyrant be buried in the Forum, he spoke of two individuals? Does anyone fail to understand that the killer is one, the killed another? I suppose we must find arguments, bring up other laws too as examples. Shall I say now: "Let whoso beats anyone be liable for injuries, but nobody who beats himself will be liable"? For I think you will all laugh if I bring in the closest parallel for an example and say that a man who kills himself is not liable under any law. Moreover, it is clearly wrong to think that rewards pertain to persons to whom penalties <do not> pertain.

⟦He[3] deserved well of the commonwealth, I suppose,

---

[3] I have kept Wi.'s double brackets for ss.6–9. For all its ironic twists the passage is against the claim, but it goes badly with the straightforward arguments that follow; and the opening suggests a spin-off from s.10 init.

finem imposuit harum calamitatium; illi scripta lex est.
Non ille qui componebat haec iura sic locutus est: 'Non est
satis ei qui servitutem rei publicae detraxerit, qui monstra
haec quibus libertas laborat ⟨sustulerit⟩,[2] qui homines
adversus[3] deorum hominumque iniuriam natos et in exemplum scelerum constitutos quo magis ea odissemus
6 occiderit, dum vivit tantum honorari. Non sufficiunt
magistratus, nec satis sunt tituli: habeatur aliquis etiam
morti honor, et ad exemplum posteritatis ostendatur in
foro sepulcrum, ne quis audeat tyrannus esse, ut omnes
homines monumentis huius sciant quibus praemiis adver-
7 sus tyrannos tyrannicidae armentur'? Ita nunc hic tamquam bonus civis, ita tamquam liberator huius civitatis
honorabitur? Sic est hercule, iudices, sic est: si hunc civitas
non habuisset, serviremus etiam nunc et gravissima illa
8 tempora quae diu passi sumus sustineremus. Expecto mehercule ut cuiuslibet impudentiae adsectatores[4] sic quoque opus eius augere atque exaggerare conentur: 'Occidit
tyrannum non hunc vulgarem et usque ad nomen tantum
9 nocentem: plus aliquid quam ceteris constituamus. Occidit tyrannum crudelissimum, saevissimum, expugnatorem
non pudicitiae modo et patrimoniorum nostrorum et prin-
cipum huius civitatis, sed templorum omnium et caeri-
moniarum, nec hominibus magis quam diis immortalibus
invisum.' Vera sunt quidem ista, iudices; sed si velimus
suum titulum reddere liberatoribus nostrae civitatis, illum
10 dii occiderunt.]] Non enim contenti advocati partis adversae hac legis calumnia, etiam bene meruisse eum de re

2 *Watt*[1]
3 ad *Bu*.
4 *SB*[1]: accusato- Aβ: aucto- *Wi*.: fauto- *Hå*.[2]

because he put an end at last to these calamities; the law was written for him! He that drafted the law, was not this what he said? "It is not enough that a man who relieves the commonwealth of slavery, ‹removes› these monstrosities under which freedom labors, kills those born for the harming of gods and men, formed to be an example of crimes to make us hate them the more—that such a man be honored only in his lifetime. Offices do not suffice, distinctions[4] are not enough: let some honor be paid to his death as well, let a tomb be displayed in the Forum to be an example to posterity, so that no man dare to be a tyrant, that all know by his memorials the rewards that arm tyrannicides against tyrants." Shall *he* now be thus honored as a good citizen, as the liberator of this community? So it is, upon my word, gentlemen, so it is: if the community had not had him, we should still be slaves, enduring those dreadful times which we suffered long. Upon my word I expect that the followers[5] of every impudence will try to maximize and exaggerate his work this wise: "He killed a tyrant, not an ordinary tyrant, guilty of the name only. Let us lay on something special for him. He killed a very cruel and savage tyrant, the ravisher not only of chastity and our private fortunes and of the leaders of this community, but of all temples and ceremonies, not more hateful to men than to the immortal gods." These things are true, gentlemen, but if we wished to give the liberators of our community their true credit, the gods killed him.] For not content with this quibble about the law, the advocates opposing me actually say that he deserved well of the community by killing

---

[4] *Tituli*, such as honorific inscriptions.
[5] Followers rather than instigators (*auctores*: see crit. note).

publica nostra dicunt quod audito responso ipse se percussit. Ego porro etiamsi confiterer plurimum eum rei
publicae morte sua praestitisse, non tamen inter beneficia
ducerem iniuriae finem. Nunc vero quis ignorat quam
multae eum necessitates ad exigendas a se ipso poenas
11 impulerint? Si tantum hoc dicerem: cum salus esset pro-
posita civitati hoc solacio,[5] ut tyrannus occideretur, quis
non nostrum in arcem rueret, quis non subderet faces,
quis non concremare pestem illam rei publicae vellet?
Vidit animos nostros, vidit impetum. Non enim vulgaria
sacramenta ducebant, nec sicut adversus alios tyrannos
[tenebat][6] iniuriae tantum dolore urgebamur. Incredibile
est quid non ausura fuerit libertatis et salutis necessitas.
12 ⟦Quid enim dicam quam invisus ille diis immortalibus fuerit? Nos non ferebant et patientiae nostrae irascebantur.⟧
Igitur si hunc tantum vitasset impetum, nihil tamen ipsi
deberemus. Age, illud, quamquam demens et sceleratus et
furiosus, non vidit, effugere se non posse, quando eum dii
immortales mori vellent? Pestilentia innocentes rapieban-
13 tur. Non mehercule aliam fuisse causam, iudices, existimo
quod huc deducti sumus. Quid ⟨enim⟩[7]? In illa labe totius
civitatis dii immortales non tam tacite intellegi quam pub-
licari[8] poenam tyranni voluerunt. Parum existimaverunt si
illum alius occidisset.
14   Ne quis itaque existimet ultionem nostram tantum[9] ad
animos hominum pertinere. Illam, illam ego, iudices, iam

5 SB[4] (*cf. ad* 252.21): silentio Aβ
6 *Obr.* (*cf. Watt*[1])   7 SB[3]
8 SB[2]: -are Aβ   9 n. t. *Ro.*, *Ri.*: t. n. Aβ

---

6 To common action ("the stampede").

himself after hearing the response. Now even if I confessed that he did the commonwealth a great service by
this death, yet I would not count the end of an injury as a
benefaction. As it is, however, who but knows how many
compulsions drove him to exact punishment from himself?
If I were only to say this: "When deliverance had been offered to the community at this price (?), that the tyrant be
killed, which of us would not have rushed to the castle,
which not have set fire to it, which not have wished to burn
that pest of the commonwealth? He saw our minds, saw
the impetus.[6] No ordinary oaths led us on, we were not
urged only by indignation at our injury as with other tyrants. It is unbelievable what compulsion of freedom and
deliverance would not have dared. [[For why should I say
how hateful he was to the immortal gods? They were losing
patience with us and angry at our long-suffering.]] So if
he had just evaded this impetus, we should still owe nothing to the man himself. Come, demented, criminal, mad
though he was, did he not see that he could not escape,
since even the immortal gods wanted him to die? The innocent were being snatched away by the plague.[7] Upon my
word, I think there was no other reason, gentlemen, why
we were brought to this pass. <For> look you: in that disas-
ter of the whole community the immortal gods wanted the
tyrant's punishment to be not so much tacitly understood
as made public knowledge. They thought it would not be
enough if someone else had killed him.

Let no one therefore suppose that our avenging concerns only human minds. That plague, gentlemen, I see it

[7] The gods did not spare them, much less would they spare the
tyrant himself.

nunc video pestilentiam. Nam si fuit causa morborum quod homo in civitate nostra, sua tamen mente suoque proposito arcem occupasset, quod libertatem abstulisset, quo tandem modo ulciscentur dii immortales id quod nos
15 fecerimus? Corpus illud omnibus sibique ipsi damnatum publicis scilicet exequiis efferemus! Hoc agite: ducatur ingens funeris pompa, eat primus senatus et ordo ille sanctissimus, quamquam recepta modo libertate laetus, vultus tamen habitusque ad maestitiam transferat; tum[10] maxima multitudo equitum,[11] universus denique populus lustret
16 atque ambiat rogum. Adiciamus et lacrimas: 'perdidimus tyrannicidam et vindicem rei publicae et libertatis auctorem!' Tum domum reversi narremus liberis nostris: 'haec virtus habet praemia.' An aliquis etiam rostra conscendet et, qui supremus claris civibus honor habetur, advocata populi contione laudes eius quem in foro sepulturi sumus
17 concinet? Audient haec dii immortales, qui nos pestilentia liberaverunt, qui gravissimos morbos propitii miserunt? Si ulla est dicenti fides, iam nunc in hac cogitatione atque in hac rerum imagine versatur mens mea. Ex illo succenso tyranni rogo surrecturi mihi protinus morbi videntur: et quacumque feralis ille ignis in civitatem diros illos atque execrabiles diffuderit fumos, gravem quandam pestilen-
18 tiae[12] nubem supra domos nostras ac tecta sessuram. Quae tunc responsa petituri sumus, quod auxilium, homines qui hanc quoque diis immortalibus iniuriam facimus, ut videantur salutare illud rei publicae responsum pro tyranno dedisse?

[10] *Gron.*: dum Aβ
[11] *Ro., auct. Gron.*: qu(a)eque dum Aβ
[12] *Bu.*: -lem A¹β: -lemtem A²: ‹ac› -lentem *Sch., Fr.*

at this moment. For if it was the cause of diseases that a man in our community, but by his own will and intention, had seized the castle and robbed us of our freedom,[8] how will the immortal gods punish what we shall have done? So we shall bring out that body, condemned of all and of his own self, in public obsequies! To work! Let a great funeral procession be led, let the senate go first, and let that most venerable order, though happy in the recent recovery of freedom, transfer their countenances and dress to sorrow; then let a great multitude of Knights, finally the entire people, move in a circle round the pyre. Let us add tears also: "We have lost a tyrannicide, avenger of the commonwealth and author of our freedom!" Then let us go back home and tell our children: "These are the rewards of valor." Or shall someone even ascend the rostrum and call an assembly of the people and sing the praises of the man we are about to bury in the Forum—the supreme honor given to illustrious citizens? The immortal gods shall hear it, who freed us from the plague, who sent most grievous distempers—propitious gods! If anyone believes what I say, at this moment my mind is on this thought, this picture: from that tyrant's burning pyre I think diseases will rise straight away, and wherever that ill-omened fire shall disperse its dire and accursed smoke upon the community, I think a pestilential cloud will settle over our houses and roofs. What responses shall we seek then, what aid?—we men who do the immortal gods the crowning injury of making them seem to have given the response that saved the commonwealth for the sake of the tyrant?

[8] The community had not been to blame, but it would be if they buried him in the Forum.

330

Abdicandus qui alit adulteram matrem

Crimine adulterii repudiavit quidam uxorem, ex qua iuvenem habebat filium. Adulescens accessit ad patrem et ait amari a se meretricem. Dedit illi pecuniam pater. Ille matrem egentem alere coepit, patre ignorante. Comperit pater et ob hoc abdicat filium.

1   DECLAMATIO

Non ignoro †expectatione†[1] criminis me onerari ex hoc praecipue, quod abdicat[2] indulgens pater. Itaque ne illa quidem dicere quae initio defensionis sollemnia ceteri habent possum: 'Ecquid peccavi? Numquid luxuriatus sum? Numquid bona paterna consumpsi? Numquid meretricem amavi?' Cum eo mihi patre res est qui remissurus haec 2 fuit. Utinam profutura ista frugalitas esset apud patrem! Nunc omnis iudicii scaena, omne periculum meae dignitatis ex hoc oritur, quod pecuniam non meretrici dedi.

3   In haec[3] enim, ut opinor, omnis criminatio divisa est patris, quod matrem aluerim, quod talem, quod patre ignorante, quod sic. Matrem alui. Blandior mihi adhuc, pater: erat quod in me laudari posset, si ‹aliud›[4] aliquid obiceres. Itaque defensionem huius partis[5] iucundam praeteribo, ne

---

[1] ‹in› purgatione *SB1*: ‹in› explica- *Watt2: fort.* ‹in› excusa-
[2] A2: -ans A1β: -avit *Sch.*
[3] *Wi.*: hac Aβ
[4] *SB2, auct. Aer.*
[5] *Aer.*: patris Aβ

330

Disowned-to-be, the feeder of an adulterous mother

A man divorced his wife, from whom he had a young son, on a charge of adultery. The young man came to his father and said he was in love with a prostitute. The father gave him money. He started feeding his mother, who was in need, without his father's knowledge. The father learns of it and disowns his son for that reason.

DECLAMATION

I am not unaware that in clearing myself (?) of this charge[1] I am chiefly hampered by the fact that I am being disowned by an indulgent father. So I cannot even make the customary points that others have available at the beginning of a defense: "Did I do any wrong? Have I lived loosely? Have I wasted my father's substance? Did I love a prostitute?" I had to deal with a father who would forgive all this. I only wish that my frugality was going to stand me in good stead with my father. As it is, all the scenario of trial, all the threat to my status, comes from the fact that I gave money to a woman who was not a prostitute.

My father's whole accusation, I think, divides as follows: that I fed my mother, that she is what she is, that I did so without my father's knowledge, that I did so in the way I did. I fed my mother. So far I am complimenting myself, father. It was something that might have been praised in me if you were taxing me with ⟨anything⟩ else. So I will pass over this agreeable part of my defense in case I might

[1] See crit. note. As a palaeographical improvement on *purgatione* I would prefer *excusatione* to *explicatione*. Expounding a charge is for the prosecution rather than the defense.

quam quaesisse videar occasionem qua de meis laudibus
4 loquerer. Sed repudiatam tamen crimine adulterii alui. Satis erat mihi respondere, iudices: istud, qualecumque est,
ad filium non pertinet. Mariti mores excutiant, mariti se-
5 veritatem desiderent: liberis satis est quod nati sunt. Et
hercule facilior[6] mihi vindicandi potestas ab isto[7] crimine
est quod non est litigatum, non est quaesitum, non est
pronuntiatum maledictum fuerit an crimen, conscientia[8]
mater discesserit an verecundia, vana[9] te suspicio an certa
aliqua probatio ad hoc duxerit. In utrumque me ratio
ducit. Aliquid audisse te credo: repudiasti. Nihil certum
manifestumque cognovisse te credo: tantum repudiasti.
6 Qualecumque tamen istud est, non mediocrem habet morum suorum defensionem vel ipsam egestatem. Illa prosti-
tuta, quae se omnium amoribus permisit, fame iam perisset nisi filium habuisset. Neque ignoro mea vel tarditate
vel verecundia factum quod mihi causa matris meae hic
agenda est, quod tam sero, quod nunc demum, postquam
7 ipse dum misereor offendi. Utinam dicere[10] apud te voluisset illa quae mihi cotidie [ait][11]: 'ita ego adultera hoc
tempore, in hac potissimum aetate, post filium, et post
filium iuvenem?' Adfirmat ideo se cibos accipere, ideo pro-
trahere vitam, ut tibi de pudicitia sua liqueat. Sunt ista
quae movere te quoque potuerint. Ego tamen in praesentia, omissa omni defensione, illud respondere contentus
8 sum: qualemcumque alui. ⟦Quantulum est enim quod
praestiterim ego illi, etiam invidiosae pietatis filius! Non
plus in matrem contuli quam quod patereris datum esse

6 *Sch.*: -lius Aβ   7 *SB³*: ipso Aβ
8 *Gron.*: constan- Aβ   9 *Bu.*: una Aβ
10 *coni. Wi.*: ad- Aβ   11 *coni. SB³*

seem to have looked for an opportunity to sing my own praises. But I fed her when she had been divorced on a charge of adultery. It would be enough, gentlemen, for me to answer that whatever this may amount to it has nothing to do with her son. Let husbands examine morals, let husbands find a lack of strictness; for children it is enough that they were born. And upon my word it is easier for me to defend myself on this charge because there was no litigation, no one asked or determined whether it was a slander or misconduct, whether my mother left because of a guilty conscience or because she was ashamed, whether idle suspicion or some certain proof made you take this step. Reason takes me both ways. I believe you heard something: you divorced her. I believe you knew nothing clear and certain: you only divorced her. But however this stands, she has no mean defense of her morals: her very poverty. That whore, who gave herself to the passions of all comers, would have starved to death by now if she had not had a son. And I am not unaware that it is through my sluggishness or embarrassment that I have to plead my mother's case here, so late in the day, only now, after I have myself given offense by taking pity on her. I only would that she had wished to say in your presence what she says to me every day: "I an adulteress, at this point of time, at this age in particular, after a son, and after a son who is a young man?" She swears that she only takes the food, prolongs her life, so that you be convinced of her chastity. Such pleas might move even you. But as for me, at present, I leave all defence aside and am content to answer: I fed her whatever she was. [[For how little I gave her, her son, whose affection gets him even into bad odor. I gave no more to my mother than you could have tolerated if it had

147

9   meretrici.]] Sed clam et ignorante te. Unde mihi tantam fe-
licitatem ut hoc crimen sit? Volo itaque interrogare, praesentibus his quos habemus iudices, quid fieri oportuerit.
Rogare te debui? Exoratus igitur fuisses si petissem? Hoc
responde, hoc adnue, et crimen confitebor. Aluisses ergo si
scisses. Credo. Quantulum enim erat cotidianam stipem et
hoc exiguum quo anima in posterum diem prorogaretur

10   praestare filii tui matri! Etsi[12] hoc animo fuisti[13]; tu voluisti, tu dedisti. Nec enim cuiquam credibile videri potest
ignorasse te an ego vere amarem. Me sine dubio et verecundia et metus inhibuit aliquatenus verum statim dicere.
Sed cum[14] pecuniam acciperem, illae me subierunt cogitationes, quam indulgenter, quam prudenter faceres, ut infelicem feminam aleres, nec videreris in gratiam redisse.

11   'Tu tamen' inquit 'mentitus es patri et amorem meretricis
finxisti.' Ita innocentior eram si verum dixissem? Plena est
huiusmodi artibus vita, plena sunt etiam theatra: circum-
scribuntur et servorum artibus patres et mendaciis filio-
rum, et ignoscunt cum meretricibus pecunia datur, cum
aliqua a lenone redimitur ancilla. Dixi amorem esse meretricis, acceptam pecuniam matri dedi. Innocentior ergo
eram si pecuniam matri petitam meretrici dedissem?

12   Possit videri sine dubio durum et asperum me, cum
ipse sim in periculo, etiam ⟨pro⟩[15] alio rogare; quaecum-

---

12 *SB*[3]: et si Aβ   13 *Aer.*: fuit Aβ
14 *Ri.*: ut Aβ   15 *Aer.*

---

2 I.e., that I had a father who would have accepted what I was
doing.   3 A paradox, underscored in s.14. To this father compassion for the mother is cruelty to himself (SB[2]). S.10 is belied in
the fluid fashion of declaimers.

been given to a prostitute.]] But in secret, without your knowledge: I only wish I was so fortunate that this could be held against me.[2] So I want to ask in the presence of this jury of ours, what ought I to have done. Should I have appealed to you? Would you have given way if I had asked? Make this your answer, give your assent, and I will confess your charge. So you would have fed her if you had known. I believe it. What a little thing it was to provide the mother of your son with a daily pittance, the small amount that kept her breathing until the next day! But you *were* of that mind; *you* wished it; *you* gave the money. For nobody can find it credible that you didn't know whether I was really in love. No doubt embarrassment and fear somewhat inhibited me from telling the truth at once. But when I took the money, certain thoughts came to me. How lovingly, how wisely you acted, feeding the unhappy woman while not letting it appear that you were reconciled! "But you," he says, "lied to your father and made up an affair with a prostitute." Would I have been less culpable if I had told the truth? Life is full of such tricks, and so are the theaters. Fathers are cheated by the tricks of slaves and the falsehoods of sons, they forgive when money is given to prostitutes and some slave girl is bought off from a pimp. I said it was love of a prostitute. I gave the money I received to my mother. Then would I have been less to blame if I had asked for money for my mother and given it to a prostitute?

No doubt it may look unfeeling[3] and harsh that when I am myself in danger I should actually be asking ⟨on behalf⟩ of someone else. But whatever the occasion, what-

que tamen occasio, quaecumque tamen necessitas est, si iam ego offendi, si quid quod parum simpliciter rogaverim irasceris, illam commendo miseram: non ut reducas (fuit ista spes aliquando, et forsitan, si felicior essem, maneret [illud]¹⁶ adhuc), ‹sed›,¹⁶ quod egens et abdicatus necesse

13 habeo deprecari, ut alas, etiamsi irasceris. Qualem enim miserae illius existimas vitam, cum cibos cotidianos petit et semper in posterum egens est? Equidem vereor, iudices, ne post hanc meam calamitatem, quam praesertim excepisse me propter misericordiam sui credit, finiat invisam

14 diu vitam et cibos accipere desinat, etiamsi dabis. Nam si perseverabit (rogo ignoscatis, etiamsi hoc forsitan apud animum patris mei asperum videri possit), haerebo miserae comes cotidiano labori.

331

Bis damnatus iniuriarum tertio absolutus

Qui capitis reum non damnaverit, ipse puniatur. Qui ter iniuriarum damnatus fuerit, capite puniatur. Bis damnatus iniuriarum tertio a quodam postulatus absolutus est. Agit cum accusatore tamquam capitis accusatus.

1 SERMO

Bis damnato huic demus oportet patronum; nam etiamsi proxime absolutus est, bis tamen damnatus est.

¹⁶ *Aer.*

---

4 Does he mean "whatever forced you to disown me?"
1 Which does not say much for his forensic skills.

ever the necessity,[4] even if I offended and you are angry
because I did not ask you straightforwardly enough, I commend the poor woman to you—not to take her back (I had
that hope once, and perhaps, if I were more fortunate,
it would still remain), <but> what I have to beg of your
mercy, needy and disowned as I am, that you give her food
even though you are angry. For what sort of life do you
think that poor woman has, asking for food every day and
always with the hunger of tomorrow? For my part, gentlemen, I am afraid that after this calamity of mine, which
moreover the poor woman thinks came upon me because
of my compassion for her, she will end the life she has long
loathed and cease to take food, even if you give it. For if she
perseveres (I ask you gentlemen to forgive me, even if in
my father's mind this would perhaps seem harsh), I shall
keep the poor thing company in her daily toil.

331

Twice convicted of injuries, acquitted the third time

Whoso fails to convict on a capital charge, let him be punished himself. Whoso be convicted of injuries three times,
let him be capitally punished. A man twice convicted of
injuries was prosecuted by someone for a third time and
acquitted. He goes to law with his accuser as though he had
been accused on a capital charge.

DISCUSSION

We ought to give an advocate to this twice convicted person, for although he was recently acquitted, he has twice
been convicted.[1]

2   DECLAMATIO

'Qui capitis accusaverit neque damnaverit, ipse capite puniatur.' Lex haec est qua iudicium continetur, haec est qua ego istum accusem, haec est quae utrumlibet horum occisura sit. Ergo hac lege sola accuso. Nemo dubitaverit hanc legem esse iustissimam; sed quas causas habeat postea dicam.

3   'Non accusavi te' inquit 'capitis sed iniuriarum.' Primum igitur hoc intueri vos oportet: si quid damnatione, si quid ultione dignum non habet ius suum,[1] debet iudex sequi <simile>,[2] debet sequi proximum. Nulla tanta providentia potuit esse eorum qui leges componebant ut spe-

4   cies criminum complecterentur; nam et semper caventes nequitia vicisset et ius ita multiplex atque diffusum esset ut pro incerto haberetur [ignotum].[3] Fecerunt ergo ut rerum genera complecterentur et spectarent ipsam aequitatem. Multa ergo invenientur frequenter quae legum verbis non teneantur, sed ipsa vi et potestate teneantur: quale hoc est.

5   Sane enim concedam in praesentia tibi non fuisse illud iudicium capitis, si tamen eandem vim habuit quam iudicium capitis, eandem poenam habere debet. Fingamus enim plura esse scelera, sicuti sunt, quae morte punienda sint (nam cum lex etiam eum qui falso accusaverit occidi velit, manifestum est occidendum esse eum qui templa incenderit, occidendum esse eum qui patriam prodiderit):

6   quomodo non interest qua lege harum accusaveris (quoniam id demum iure de quo quaeritur comprehensum est, ut qui capitis accusaverit poenam patiatur), ita nihil inter-

---

[1] ius s. *Ri.*: iustum Aβ
[2] *coni. Wi.*
[3] *SB*[3]

"Whoso brings a capital charge and fails to convict, let him be capitally punished himself." This is the law governing the trial, this it is under which I accuse this man. This it is that shall take the life[2] of one or other of these two. So I accuse him under this law alone. No one will doubt that this is a most just law, but I shall speak of its motivation later on.

He says: "I did not accuse you of a capital offense but of injuries." First you must look at this: if an offense deserving of conviction and retribution does not have a law special to itself, the judge should follow what is similar, what comes closest. Those who drafted the laws could not have the foresight to cover the varieties of offenses; for wickedness would always have got the better of their precautions and the law would have been so complex and extensive that it would have been regarded as uncertain. They therefore decided to embrace categories of things and pay attention to actual equity. Many things will therefore often be found that are not covered by the words of laws but are covered by their very meaning and force: as is this. For suppose I concede to you for the present that that trial was not capital, yet if it had the same force as a capital trial, it should carry the same penalty. Let us suppose there are a number of crimes (as there are) that are to be punished by death (for since the law wishes even the author of a false accusation to be killed, it is clear that a temple burner should be killed, that a betrayer of his country should be killed): just as it makes no difference under which law among these you accuse (since what is embraced under the law here in question is that the maker of a capital charge suffer the

---

[2] The subjectives *accusem* and *occisura sit* seem anomalous.

est quod genus iudicii fuerit si eventus eodem rediturus
7 fuerat. Num igitur dubium est quin hic pro quo loquor, si
esset iniuriarum tertio damnatus, periturus fuerit? Extra
quaestionem est. Quid ergo? <Non capitis> accusatum[4]
eum existimari oportet cui damnato capitis poena immi-
net? Non pecunia multabitur, non ignominia, non damno
8 iuris alicuius. Quid ergo futurum erat? Ut occideretur.
Quid interest hoc qua lege, quid interest quo genere iudicii? Fieri non potest ut hic capite periclitatus sit et tu non
capitis accusaveris.
9   Praeterea quam putamus fuisse causam conscribendae
legis huiusce? Hanc enim cum excusserimus, apparebit in
istam quoque partem satis esse cautum. 'Si quis capitis accusaverit et non damnaverit, ipse capite puniatur.' Hoc,
opinor, illi iustissimi legis huiusce latores spectaverunt, ne
quis impune alteri periculum adferret. Homicidii genus
putaverunt petere spiritum hominis quem occidi non
10 oporteret. Tu hoc fecisti: accusasti innocentem; si tibi creditum esset, periturus erat is quem accusasti. Iudices
eodem tempore de te pronuntiaverunt. Non potest omnino ita[5] circumscribi religio et severitas iudicii ut non
poenam det pars utralibet. Hoc absoluto qui periturus fuit,
continuo id quoque consecutum est, ut tibi esset poena
patienda.
11   'At enim [tertio][6] tantum iniuriarum accusavi [et tu bis

[4] n. c. a. *Ri.*: dam(p)natum Aβ
[5] *Aer.*: ista Aβ   [6] *SB²*

---

3 "Under which law" and "the category of the trial" virtually
come to the same thing, the former determining the latter; cf. s.8.

penalty), so the category of the trial[3] makes no difference if the result was going to come to the same thing. Is there any doubt therefore that if my client had been convicted of injuries a third time, he would have lost his life? It is beyond question. What then? Must <not> a man be held to be <capitally> charged if the death penalty hangs over him should he be convicted? He will not suffer a money fine, nor a stigma, nor the loss of some right. What then was going to happen? He was going to be put to death. What difference does it make under what law, in what category of trial? It is impossible that he stood in peril of his life and that you did not make a capital accusation.

Furthermore, what do we think was the motive for drafting this law? When we have shaken that out, it will appear that adequate provision has been made in that direction also.[4] "Whoso brings a capital charge and fails to convict, let him be punished himself." This, I think, was the object of those very just men who proposed this law, that no one should put another in danger with impunity. They considered it a sort of homicide to seek the life of a man who did not deserve to die. This you did. You accused an innocent man. If you had been believed, the man you accused was going to lose his life. The jury gave a verdict on you at the same time. It is quite impossible that the sanctity and strictness of the trial can be so cheated that neither party is punished. When the man who was to have lost his life was acquitted, it followed automatically that you must pay the penalty.

"But I only accused him of injuries." What difference

[4] Meaning apparently that the words of the law, properly understood, duly convey its intention. But the phrasing is nebulous.

iam damnatus eras iniuriarum].⁶ʾ Quid interest quae res
fecerit istud capitis iudicium? Nam et tu crimen gravius
obiecisti quam priores obiecerunt. Vis scire quam hoc verum sit? Semel ‹et iterum›⁷ iniuriarum damnato ignoscitur: illud morte dignum videtur, si is qui bis iam damnatus
est iniuriam fecit. Iam hoc tale videtur quale hominem occidere. Ergo tu id obiecisti quod lex morte dignum putavit,
quod lex capite taxavit; capitis ergo accusasti.

12   Hoc loco iure depulsi ad convicia confugiunt. 'Bis tamen iniuriarum damnatus est.' Poterat mihi satis esse
quod tertio absolutus est. Sed animadvertitis quales inimicitias sortitus sit: scitis illum iam innocentem accusari
solere. Sed facilius fuit ut traheret aliquid gratia, dum id
13   fieri sine periculo videbatur; ideo intentius iudices pronuntiaverunt posteaquam talis pugna commissa est in qua
perire alteri necesse sit. Omnia igitur eius tulit qui reus
capitis accusatur, periculum, sollicitudinem: debet con-
sentire iis etiam ultio.

14   SERMO

Haec ab accusatore existimo satis dicta; contra illa:

15   Pars altera

                          DECLAMATIO

Lex eum qui capitis accusarit neque damnaverit capite puniri iubet. Capitis iudicia certa sunt et vim suam habent.
Semper capitis iudicia sunt iis legibus constituta quibus

6 *SB*²   7 *SB*¹, *auct. Aer.*

---

5 Or rather, given a lesser punishment.
6 The convictions are assumed to have been wrongful.
7 To the *life* of the accused.

does it make what particular factor made that a capital trial? Actually you made a graver charge than your predecessors made. Would you like to know how true this is? Once ‹and twice› the convicted man is pardoned.[5] If a person who has twice been convicted has committed injuries, that appears deserving of death. This seems like actually killing a man. Therefore you charged an offense that deserved death in the eyes of the law, that the law punished capitally. Therefore you made a capital charge.

At this point, dislodged from law, they take refuge in abuse. "But he was twice convicted of injuries." It could be enough for me that he was acquitted the third time. But you gentlemen perceive what kind of enmities have befallen him. You know that he is already used to being accused when innocent.[6] But it was easier for influence to pull something when it seemed as though that could be done without danger.[7] For that reason the jury gave their verdict with more care after a battle was joined in which one or the other had to perish. So he endured all that appertains to a defendant on a capital charge: peril, anxiety. The retribution too should be conformable.

DISCUSSION

This I consider enough said from the prosecutor. Now for the contrary.

Other side

DECLAMATION

The law orders that whoso accuses of a capital offense and fails to convict be capitally punished. Capital trials are definite and have their own system. Capital trials are always constituted under laws by which nobody can be con-

nemo potest damnari plus quam semel. Habent suam
formam, suum iudicum[8] numerum, suum quaesitorem
16 [suum],[9] sua tempora, sua nomina. Responde igitur mihi
tu qui accusatum te capitis esse contendis, qua lege fueris
reus. 'Iniuriarum.' Hic iam ipsos interrogare iudices possum an iniuriarum actio capitalis sit. Sed quid habeo quare
interrogem iudices? Ex te ipso quaero iniuriarum damnatus utrum occidatur. Non ut opinor eius te futurum impudentiae ut hoc contendas. Alioqui dicam: damnatus es
semel, damnatus es iterum; non esse hoc capitis iudicium
vel ex hoc solo apparet, quod vivis.

17 'Sed idem' inquit 'effectura res est quod si capitis damnatus essem, et proximo iure utendum est et similitudine
quadam legis.' Hic iam desinit privata esse lis. Nam si accusatori licet constituere iura et leges ferre, si quod antea
fieri per populum, per senatum licebat, constituitur inter
subsellia pro dolore cuiusque vel pro auctoritate, supervacua erunt suffragia, supervacuus tantus ambitus in con-
18 stituendo iure. Non de eo quaeritur apud hos, an aequum
sit; nos venimus in iudicium quaesituri hoc solum, an ego
ista lege tenear. 'At oportet et iustum est ea quae similia
sunt simili poena contineri.' Adhibe senatum, adhibe populum. Emendandum sit fortasse ius: hoc interim vivimus,
hoc utimur. ⟦Multa autem iura decipiunt, neque ideo conscripta sunt ut ignorantia fallant.⟧[10]

8 *SB4*: -cium Aβ 9 *SB4*   10 *SB3, auct. Wi.*

---

8 *Forma*. "Less mechanical than *formula*" (Wi.).
9 See crit. note. *(Iudicia) habent suum iudicium* has survived
too long.
10 So in s.20, meaning I am not sure what.

victed more than once. They have their own forms,[8] their own number of jurors,[9] their own president, their own times,[10] their own names. So tell me, you that contend you were accused on a capital charge, under what law you were a defendant. "Injuries." Here I can ask the jury themselves whether action for injuries is capital. But why should I ask the jury? I ask you yourself: is a person convicted of injuries put to death? I don't think you will have the effrontery so to contend. Anyway I shall say: you were convicted once, you were convicted twice: that this was not a capital trial is evident from the mere fact that you are alive.

"But the thing will have the same result," he says, "as if I had been convicted of a capital crime, and we must apply whatever formulation comes closest, a sort of similitude of the law." Here this ceases to be a private dispute. For if a prosecutor is allowed to constitute statutes and pass laws, and if what could formerly be done only through the people and the senate is now laid down among the benches[11] according to individual passion and influence, votes will be superfluous, as will all the campaigning that goes on in constituting the law. The question before these gentlemen is not whether it is fair. We have come to court only to examine whether I am liable under this law. "But it is right and just that like offenses be covered by like punishment." Call the senate, call the people. Perhaps the law should be amended. Meanwhile, we live by this law and use it. ⟦Many laws are deceptive, but they were not drafted to mislead through ignorance.[12]⟧

[11] Prosecution and defense.
[12] "Awkwardly tacked on to what precedes" (Wi.).

19

SERMO

Hoc est illud commune, ut dicebam vobis, cum scripto et voluntate.

20

DECLAMATIO

Sed fingamus, ut has demus delicias, ut simili lege, ⟨simili poena⟩[11] utendum sit. Quid hic simile [dixit][12]? Nam[13] illa lege aliud genus actionum, alium quaesitorem, non eadem tempora, ⟨nomina⟩[14] non paria. 'Sed periculum par.' Hoc si fit actione iniuriarum, sane aliquam similitudinem habere videatur. Interrogo enim te, an si ego, qui tecum iniuriarum egi, semel obiecissem tibi hoc idem crimen et tu antea damnatus non esses, num capite fueris periclitaturus. Non, ut opinor. Non[15] ergo ego feci ut tu capite periclitareris, sed illi qui te ante bis damnaverunt. Neque enim

21 senectutem adfert summus dies, sed longus ordo vitae, nec ebrietatem facit illa potio post quam concidendum est, sed tempestivum convivium et aviditas nimia. Non ergo mea actione effectum est ut periclitareris, sed illis actionibus quibus iam damnatus es.

22 'Sed absolutus sum' inquit 'tertio.' Viderimus quantum hoc ad gloriam tuam pertineat; interim, damnatus es saepius. Etenim de petulantia tua hoc illi primi iudices senserunt, hoc secundi senserunt; nunc absolutus es. Nihil de religione eorum qui pronuntiaverunt querar: erant tamen

23 quae te adiuvarent. Non illud dicebatur in iudicio: 'non est

---

11 *SB*³   12 *SB*²   13 *Sch.*: iam A*β*
14 *Ri., auct. Aer.*   15 *Aer.*: num A*β*

---

13 Cf. s.15 fin.
14 Connoting protracted and luxurious, as elsewhere.

DISCUSSION

This is that general topic, as I used to tell you, going with text and intention.

DECLAMATION

But let us suppose (to indulge these fads) that under a like law <a like punishment> is to be applied. What is like here? For in that law we have a different class of actions, a different president, times not the same, <names>[13] not matching. "But the danger matches." If that comes by reason of the action for injuries, I grant that it might seem to have some similarity. For I ask you, if I, who prosecuted you for injuries, had charged you once with this same offense and you had not previously been convicted, whether you would incur a capital risk. I think not. Therefore it was not I that put you in capital danger, but those who convicted you twice previously. For it is not the last day that brings old age but the long course of life, nor that last drink, after which he has to fall down, that makes a man drunk but an early[14] dinner and overmuch greed. So it was not my prosecution that brought you into danger but those prosecutions through which you had already been convicted.

"But I was acquitted," he says, "the third time." We'll see later how much that redounds to your glory; meanwhile, you were more often convicted. This was the verdict of that first jury on your ruffianism and of the second; this time you were acquitted. I shall not complain about the way those who gave that verdict kept their oath. Still,[15] there were some things in your favor. Nobody said at the

---

[15] "I shall not complain" implying "I could complain." All the same there was something to be said for the verdict.

hic talis in quo petulantia credenda sit: modestos mores
habet, nemini umquam fecit iniuriam', sed dicebatur illud:
'Non iam[16] iniuriarum petitur ultio: capite periclitaturus
est. Etiamsi quid commisit, satis tamen poenarum dedit.'
Ipsa hac sollicitudine circumscripsisti misericordiam iudicum, si alterum occisuri erant.

24   ‹SERMO›[17]

In summa parte aestimabitur cui homini et quanta ultio
petatur.

25   ‹DECLAMATIO›[17]

Ultio quae petitur? Quae adversus homicidas scripta est,
quae adversus eos qui ter[18] iniuriarum damnati sunt scripta est. Neque ego ignoro unde isti hic animus. Nova[19] enim
spes fecit hanc litem: homo alioqui petulans quaerit quomodo impune occidat, quomodo manibus suis permittat
omnia. Hoc ergo privilegium habeant qui bis iniuriarum
damnati sunt, ut tertio accusari sine periculo non possint?
26 Hoc aequum mortalium videri cuiquam potest? Vivit ille
qui †semel†[20] iniuriarum damnatus est, qui duabus partibus perît civitati, quem[21] petulantia sua morti iam prope
admovit: hic occiditur qui questus est? Utinam mihi con-
tingeret apud eosdem illos iudices causam dicere qui istum absolverunt, homines mites et misericordes, et qui
turpissimos quoque cives tamen servare maluerint!

---

[16] A[2]: tam A[1](β)
[17] *Pith.*
[18] *Gron.*: bis Aβ
[19] *Ro.*: non Aβ
[20] semel ‹et iterum› *Obr., similia alii*
[21] *Gron.*: qui Aβ

trial: "He is not a person in whose case ruffianly behavior is believable. He's well-conducted, has never done injury to anyone." This is what was said: "Penalty for injuries is not what is asked for here. He will be at risk of his life. Even if he has done wrong, he has been punished enough." With just this worry you tricked the jury's compassion; ⟨they would not have acquitted,⟩ if they were about to kill the other party.

⟨DISCUSSION⟩

In the final part it will be judged from whom retribution is to be claimed and how much.

⟨DECLAMATION⟩

What is the retribution claimed? That written against homicides, against those convicted of injuries three times. Nor am I unaware what lies behind this intention of his. A new hope has made this suit: a ruffian anyway, he is looking for a way to kill[16] with impunity, to put universal license in his hands. So are people convicted of injuries to have the special privilege that they cannot be accused a third time without peril? Can anyone in the world think this equitable? The one that was convicted of injuries once ⟨and again⟩, that perished for the good of the community by two parts out of three, whose ruffianism has already brought him close to death—does he live, whereas the one that brought the complaint is killed? How I wish I had the good fortune to plead my case before the same jury that acquitted him, those mild and compassionate folk who preferred to save even the most infamous of citizens!

[16] "Kill" is illogical. He should have said "commit injury."

332

Divitis et pauperis testamenta

Pauper et dives amici erant. Dives testamento alium amicum omnium bonorum instituit heredem, pauperi iussit dari id quod ille sibi testamento daret. Apertae sunt tabulae pauperis. Omnium bonorum instituerat heredem. Petit totam divitis hereditatem. Ille qui scriptus est heres vult dare tantum quantum in censum habet pauper.

1   DECLAMATIO

Si ad votum meum, iudices, Fata cessissent, optabilius fuerat mihi ut is de cuius bonis contendimus esset heres meus. Ad hanc igitur petitionem invitus et tristis et flens venio.

2   Viderimus enim postea de iudiciis; interim non dubitabitur uter ex nobis illum magis amaverit. Postea iura excutiam, postea scriptum interpretabor; interim, quod ad utriusque nostrum animum pertinet, non esset inter nos quaestio si utrumque eodem titulo reliquisset heredem.

3 Narratio

Habet autem hoc incommodi paupertas, quod quotiens ad amicitiam superioris accessit, adfert aliquid dubitationis fide an utilitatibus amet. Officia adversus se mea noverat dives, adsiduum me haesisse lateri suo sciebat; tenuitas mea adferebat hanc ei dubitationem, ut posset quaerere an 4 istud amicitia fecissem. Itaque cum sciret mortem esse quae de animis diceret verum, testamenta quibus omnem

---

[1] The poor man had proved his affection by his will, not so the rich man's heir.

332

Wills of a rich man and a poor man

A poor man and a rich man were friends. In his will the rich man made another friend heir to all his possessions, but ordered that the poor man be given what *he* gave in his will to himself. The poor man's tablets were opened. He had made the rich man heir to all his possessions. He claims the rich man's whole inheritance. The man who was named heir wishes to give as much as the poor man has in his census.

DECLAMATION

If the Fates had gone according to my prayers, gentlemen, it had rather been my wish that the man whose property we are disputing about had been my heir. So I come to this claim reluctantly, in sadness and in tears.

We shall see later about the dispositions; meanwhile, there will be no doubt about which of us loved him more.[1] Later I shall analyze the law and interpret the text. Meanwhile, what has to do with the sentiments of both of us, there would be no question between us if he had left both of us his heir in the same terms.

Narrative

But poverty has this disadvantage, that whenever it approaches the friendship of a superior it brings a degree of doubt about whether its affection is sincere or self-interested. The rich man knew of my offices towards him, was aware that I constantly stuck to his side; but my humble circumstances made him doubtful—he could ask whether I had done that out of friendship. So, knowing that it is death that tells the truth about men's minds, wills wherein

adfectum fateremur, ita supremas tabulas ordinavit ut adversus ⟨se⟩ me dicere vellet animum meum.[1] Bona interim sua apud istum deposuit, dum sciri posset[2] quid de illo ipse sensissem. Dari mihi iussit id quod ego testamento meo darem. Si cogitationem intra angustias facultatium mearum tenuit, praeter id quod ingratus videri posset[3] amicus, non multum eius interfuit quid ego scripsissem.

5   Lectae sunt tabulae meae: constitit fides amicitiae, omnium bonorum institutus heres erat, hoc planior[4] animus meus quod sine exceptione. Igitur, quod ad me pertinet, aperui pectus et conscientiam protuli et, qua rerum natura patitur, viscera paene mea in conspectu vestro sunt. Iste heres adhuc non ostendit testamentum.

6   Sed scio non esse praesentis temporis disceptationem uter mereatur. Satis enim voluntas defuncti comprehensa tabulis est. Institutus es primo loco heres. Non facio tibi istius honoris controversiam; quaeritur hodie quid debeas mihi. Si iudicia mea adversus amicum intra legatum stetissent, legatum a te repeterem. Heredem omnium bonorum

7   habui: hoc ut sim postulo. Ut scriptum non esset, iudices, iniquum erat offerri mihi quantum habeo, tamquam is qui defunctus est dari mihi iusserit quantum ego illi dare possem. Ingens autem horum differentia est: id mihi dari iussit quod ego illi meo testamento darem. Non habet in

---

[1] ⟨se⟩ me d. v. a. meum *SB*[4]: d. me v. –mo meo Aβ

[2] *Wi., Hå.*[2]: -sit Aβ

[3] *Sch.*: potest Aβ

[4] *coni. Ro.*: plen- Aβ

we confess all our feelings, he drew up his last tablets in such a way that he wanted my own sentiments towards him to speak. Meanwhile, he deposited his property with this man, until it could be known what I myself felt about him. He ordered that I be given what I gave him in my will. If he kept his thoughts within the narrowness of my means, it did not much matter to him what I had written, except that he might be seen as an ungrateful friend.[2] My tablets were read: the sincerity of my friendship was established, he was left heir to all my possessions, and my feelings were all the plainer because I made no reservation. So as far as I am concerned I opened my heart and brought my conscience into view; and so far as the Nature of Things allows, my vitals are almost under your eyes. The heir has not so far shown his will.

But I know that this is not the time to debate which of us is deserving. The intention of the deceased is sufficiently expressed in the tablets. You were made heir in the first instance. I do not dispute that compliment with you. The question today is, what do you owe me? If my dispositions as regards my friend had stopped short at a legacy, I should claim a legacy back from you. I made him heir to all my possessions: I demand that I be that. Even if that had not been written,[3] gentlemen, it would have been unfair that I be offered as much as I possess, as though the deceased had ordered me to be given as much as I could have given him. And there is an enormous difference between these two: he ordered me to be given *what* I gave him in

[2] If "what I gave him in my will" meant what the poor man could leave, the opening of the latter's will (if it proved to be in the rich man's favor) would only put the rich man in a poor light.

[3] As the poor man contends.

hoc interpretationem modus; quantum pensatione constat[5]; numerari[6] potest et recipit comparationem. Quod[7]
8 reliquit, quantum fieri potest, dari voluit. Eadem rei natura est. Itaque si illi pecuniam testamento meo legassem,
pecuniam peterem, nec ferrem te dantem pro pecunia aliquid quod esset tantundem. Si mancipium reliquissem,
mancipium deberes, nec diceres mihi: 'accipe quanto istud
9 est.' Id dari mihi iussit quod ego illi darem. Quid ego autem dabam illi? Hereditatem. Quid peto? Hereditatem.
Quid scripsi? Bona omnia. Quid vindico mihi? Bona omnia. Voluit simile esse iudicium suum meo testamento, et
quodammodo invenit rationem qua posset iudicare post
mortem. Istud vero quale est quod offers? Reliquit mihi
10 dives amicus paupertatem? Non statim de animo loquar;
interim potestis permutata, ut sic dixerim, translataque invicem fortuna aestimare ius. Fingamus enim hoc aliquem
pauperem scripsisse de divite. Quomodo causam explica-
mus? Alium fecit heredem, iussit amico locupleti tantum
11 dari quantum ipse sibi testamento daret. Sit inventum tale
testamentum quale est meum: num ab herede tantam pecuniam peteret quantam ipse possideret? Non, ut opinor;
nam ne posset quidem dari. Sed illud succurreret[8]: 'dari
tibi iussit quod titulo testamenti dabas; dabas autem hereditatem. Nihil ultra hereditatem petere debes.' Atqui ius

5 *Sch.*: -stet Aβ
6 "quantum" p. constat. n. *coni. Wi.*
7 *Aer.*: quid Aβ 8 *Sch.*: -urrit Aβ

---

4 *Quod . . . darem* does not specify a particular item or sum.
5 Neither will so specifies.
6 The rich man's judgment would be expressed after his death

my will. Herein a quantity cannot be interpreted.[4] "How much" is settled by weight; it can be counted and a comparison made. He wanted me to be given what he left, as much as can be made of it. The nature of the thing is the same.[5] So if I had left him money in my will, I should ask for the money and I should not tolerate you giving me something of the same value instead of the money. If I had left him a slave, you would owe me a slave and you would not say to me: "Take as much as that is worth." He ordered that I be given what I gave him. And what was I giving him? An inheritance. What do I claim? An inheritance. What did I write? "All my possessions." What do I claim for myself? All his possessions. He wished his disposition to resemble my will and somehow[6] found a method which allowed him to judge after his death. But what is this you are offering me? Did my rich friend leave me penury? I shall not speak of my intention at this moment; meanwhile, you[7] can exchange, so to speak, and transfer the fortunes and then judge the law. Let us suppose that some poor man wrote this about a rich man. How do we set out the case? He made someone else his heir, but ordered that as much be given to his rich friend as the friend gave himself in his will. Suppose a will was found such as mine: would he[8] ask of the heir as much as he himself possessed? I think not; for it would not even be possible for it to be given. But this would come to mind: "He ordered that you be given what you were giving him in the words of your will; and you were giving him the inheritance. You should not ask anything beyond the inheritance." And yet the law is the same, the

by his will, if the poor man complied with its terms.
[7] The jury.   [8] The rich friend.

idem est, verba eadem sunt; nec cum personis lex mutata est.

12   Nunc ut animum quoque intueamur testantis: hocine illum voluisse existimatis? Ideo inquisivit meam fidem, ideo vitae experimentis credere parum putavit, ideo in ipsum irrupit animum et penitus intuendam omnibus hominibus mentem dedit, ut mihi hoc relinqueret quod habe-

13 bam? 'Est quare aperias testamentum, est quare omnem spem tibi in posterum excidas.' Sciunt propinqui mei nullum alium mihi cariorem fuisse, sciunt si qui alii fuerunt amici totam mentem meam deditam uni fuisse.

    Quid interest animi quantum sit quod totum est? 'Omnium bonorum heres': quidquid habui, quidquid servavi, quidquid longae frugalitati[9] superfuit. Accessissent huic testamento subitae opes, idem erat. Neque ego nunc divitias peto: paupertate consuevi, frugaliter vivere scio, nulla mihi gravis necessitas est. Illum, illum titulum amplector omnium bonorum.

14   Si quid inferi sentiunt, cognosce animum meum, sicut voluisti: tibi vixi, tibi moriturus fui, nulli alii in hoc pectore locus fuit. Hoc[10] te omnium bonorum meorum heredem instituit. Post hoc testamentum dicat aliquis se mereri.

[9] Gron.: -tatis (A)β
[10] hic (sc. animus) coni. SB[3]

words are the same, and the law has not been changed along with the personae.

Now to look at the intention of the testator: do you think this is what he wanted? Did he enquire into my sincerity, did he think it insufficient to believe in the tests of life, did he break into my very heart and give my mind to all men to be inspected down to its depth, just in order to leave me what I had? "You[9] have a reason to open your will, you have a reason to cut off all hope for the future." My relatives know that no other man was dearer to me, they know that if I had other friends my whole heart was devoted to one.

What does it matter to the mind how much if it is the whole? "Heir to all my possessions:" whatever I had, whatever I saved, whatever my long frugality left over. Had some windfall accrued to this will, it would have been the same. And I am not now asking for riches. I am used to poverty, I know how to live frugally, I have no burdensome need. I embrace that wording, yes, that: "all my possessions."

If those below are conscious, then know my mind, as was your wish. For you I lived, for no other was there any place in this heart. This heart made you heir to all my possessions. After this will, let some man say that he deserves!

[9] The poor man, not, as Wi., the first heir. Only the poor man could authorize the opening of his will, which he would do in compliance with the rich man's stipulation. The advocate makes the rich man assume what he did not know, that the poor man's will was in his favor. Opening it would make the poor man wealthy, even though it would cut off any hopes he might have of inheriting from others. Actually, adds the poor man, the relatives already know how matters stand.

333

Pauper impensis divitis disertus

Patronum optare liceat. Ingrati sit actio. Adulescentem dives pauperem impensis suis in Athenas misit. Redît ille disertus. Detulit divitem quidam reum proditionis et optavit patronum pauperem illum qui divitis impensis profecerat. Egit pauper. Non tenuit. Accusatur a divite ingrati.

1   SERMO

Intellegitis huic adulescenti cum summo respectu divitis agendum; ita demum enim videbitur id quod fecit necessitate fecisse [si de illa queretur].[1] Et in totum hoc servare in omnibus controversiis quae ingrati lege continentur debebimus, ut hi qui rei sunt in ipsa actione ingrati non sint.

2   Raro valde intervenient controversiae in quibus hoc quaeratur, an is qui ingrati reus est acceperit beneficium. Pleraeque, sicut haec, devertunt eo ut quaestiones habeant an quisquis acceperit beneficium et non reddiderit ingratus sit; an omnia quaecumque exigebantur praestare debuerit; an potuerit.

3   Gulosos figurarum ducet haec species, ut hic pauper imputet diviti tamquam praevaricatus sit. Id autem si intellexerint iudices, vel propter hoc illum damnabunt, quod praevaricatus sit, vel propter hoc, quod hodie certe, ubi patronus non optatur, accusat illum quem vult videri

1 *SB*3

---

1 "'The Master' is talking about something that one would normally call a color" (Wi.).

333

A poor man eloquent at the expense of a rich man

Let it be permitted to opt for an advocate. Let there be an action for ingratitude. A rich man sent a poor young man to Athens at his own expense. He came back an orator. A certain person charged the rich man with treason and chose as his advocate that poor man who had become proficient at the expense of the rich man. The poor man appeared for him. He was unsuccessful. He is accused by the rich man of ingratitude.

DISCUSSION

You understand that this young man must handle the rich man with the utmost respect; only so will it appear that he did what he did under duress [[if he makes complaint thereof]]. In general we shall be well advised to make it a rule in all controversies that come under the law of ingratitude, that those who are defendants are not ungrateful in the actual pleading. Very rarely controversies will crop up in which the question is whether the party charged with ingratitude received a benefaction. Most of them, like the present one, will come down to these questions: is whoever received a benefaction and did not return it ungrateful? Was he obligated to furnish whatever is demanded? Was it in his power?

Gluttons for figures[1] will be attracted by the angle that this poor man claims that the rich man owes him for having prosecuted collusively. But if the jury so understand, they will convict him: either because he prosecuted collusively or because, today at any rate, when no advocate is opted for, he accuses the man whom he wants to appear as having

173

praevaricatione dimissum. Ergo, quod ad meum consilium pertinet, hic invitus egit: ea quae dicenda accepit pertulit.

4   DECLAMATIO

Est videlicet, iudices, hoc quoque in potestate Fortunae, ut in contrarium bona ipsa convertat. Maximum me a divite accepisse beneficium quod mihi consummare studia contigerat, quis negaverit?—cum interim maximorum mihi malorum causam hoc ipsum attulit, quod videbar disertus: adeo ut si mihi exuere hanc artem[2] persuasionis liceret, amputare vocem et velut omnem usum loquendi perdidisse maluerim quam cum homine de me optime

5 merito iam bis consisterem. Et prioris tamen iudicii manifesta excusatio erat: iussus loquebar. Hodie quem modum teneam actionis, quibus vocibus optime, ut iam saepe dixi, de me merito satisfaciam reperire non possum. Vera sunt enim illa quae dixit.

6 Narratio

Pauper ego natus et contra facultatium rationem mearum infelicis huius eloquentiae studiosus, huius liberalitate, huius opibus peregrina studia, clarissima exempla, otium, quo plurimum studiis confertur, sum consecutus. Utinam non usque ad invidiam! Nam mihi cogitanti cur integerrimum virum, optimum civem calumniator ille proditionis reum fecerit nihil succurrit aliud quod secutus sit

7 quam ut ego agerem. Habebat enim ius optandi patronum,

---

[2] *Watt*[2]: pa- Aβ

---

[2] The allegation of collusion would imply that the rich man had been guilty as charged and that implication would be an act of ingratitude without the excuse of legal compulsion.

174

been discharged through collusion.[2] So, as far as my advice goes, this person took the case against his will. He said what his brief required him to say.

We know, gentlemen of the jury, that this too is in the power of Fortune, to convert even good things into their opposite. That I received a great benefaction from the rich man in that I was able to complete my studies, who shall gainsay? And yet the very fact that I was thought eloquent brought me cause of great calamities, so much so that if it were permitted me to put off this art of persuasion, I would sooner cut out my voice and lose as it were[3] all use of speech than now for the second time appear in court against a man to whom I owe a great deal. In the former trial I had a clear excuse: I spoke under orders. Today I cannot find how to strike a balance, with what words to make amends to one to whom, as I have often said, I owe a great deal. For what he said is true.

Narrative

I was born poor. Contrary to what my means indicated, I devoted myself to the pursuit of this ill-starred eloquence. By his generosity, his wealth, I came by study abroad, the most illustrious models, leisure, the greatest aid to study. I only wish it had not gone so far as to bring me ill will. For as I ask myself why that false accuser charged a most upright gentleman, a fine citizen, with treason, I can think of no other motive except that I should take his case.[4] For he had the right to opt for an advocate, the laws had

---

[3] *Velut* is an encumbrance.

[4] He wanted to bring a professional rival into *invidia*.

[et][3] hanc leges dederant potestatem: et forsitan quaerebat etiam contra absolutionem innocentis rei hunc colorem, ut
8   videretur ideo dimissus quia ego egissem. Hoc ei certe non contigit. Reum offendi, non mehercule supervacua asperitate verborum (ab hac enim me, quatenus fides agendi permiserat, abstinuisse animum confiteor): sed perferenda fuerunt mandata falsa verum criminosa, conficta verum invidiae tamen plena. Quodsi quid esse in ratione dicendi videtur, si quis me infestam attulisse credit orationem, accedit hoc quoque gloriae optimi civis, quod me accusante absolutus est.

9   Ingrati reus sum. De prima parte causae, iudices, non faciam controversiam, neque fas est: accepi beneficium, quantum maximum dare parentes liberis possunt. Non enim si Fortuna infelicissima adhuc officia studiis meis dedit, non tamen ista animo praestantis aestimanda sunt. Accepi pecuniam, otium,[4] spem futurae[5] in posterum vitae: infeliciter, etiamsi mihi hic defendendus fuisset. Accepi beneficium; ne illud quidem infitiabor: non reddidi.

10 Non tamen continuo sequitur ut ingrati lege teneatur qui acceptum beneficium nondum pensaverit. Alioqui nemo est qui non ‹in hoc›[6] calumniae genus possit incidere. Nam ut huiusmodi omittam tempora, statim certe ut ‹aliquis›[7] accepit beneficium accusari potest: nondum enim reddidit.

11 Quod si non continuo ingratus est qui[8] paria non fecit,

---

3 *Ro.*   4 *Watt*[1]: votum Aβ
5 *Gron.*: -am Aβ
6 *Aer.*   7 *SB*[3]
8 *Sch.*: quia Aβ

given him this power; and perhaps he also[5] wanted to suggest with respect to the acquittal of the innocent defendant the angle that he was discharged because I was the prosecutor. In this he certainly failed. I came up against the defendant, not to be sure with unnecessary harshness of language (for I admit that I kept myself from that so far as my prosecutorial duty allowed me), but I had to deliver my brief—false but incriminatory, fabricated but full of prejudice. But if oratory counts for something, if someone thinks that I brought with me an aggressive style of pleading, all the more glory to our excellent citizen that he was acquitted with me as prosecutor.

I am accused of ingratitude. As to the first part of the case, gentlemen, I won't dispute, nor would it be right; I did receive a benefaction, the greatest parents can make to their children. Fortune may so far have given my studies employments very far from happy, but such gifts must nevertheless be valued by the intention of the giver. I received money, leisure, the hope of a future career: unhappily, even if I had had to defend him. I received the benefaction. This too I won't deny: I have not repaid it.

It does not, however, follow automatically that anyone who has not yet balanced a benefaction received is liable under the law of ingratitude. Otherwise there's nobody who could not fall <into this> kind of false charge. For to say nothing of times as long as this, the moment <anybody> has received a benefaction, he can be accused; for he has not yet repaid.

But if one who has not evened the score is not automati-

---

[5] Another reason: if the jury acquitted, they might be thought to have done so because the prosecutor pulled the case.

superest ut illa nobis intuenda sint, an omnia praestari iis qui beneficium dederint oporteat; an id de quo cognoscitis praestari[9] oportuerit; ac postremo, an potuerit.

12   Non omnia esse praestanda etiam parentibus dico. Alioqui nihil est periculosius acceptis beneficiis, si in omnem nos alligant servitutem. Nam etiam scelerum, si ita videatur iis qui nos meritis obligavere, adferunt necessitatem. 13 Quapropter illa in confesso erunt, neque facturum aliquid adversus rem publicam ex voluntate eius a quo beneficium acceperit eum qui acceperit, neque impium erga parentes necessitate tali futurum, neque inhonestum, neque ea quae fieri non poterunt praestaturum.

14   Quod si luce ipsa, iudices, clarius est, iam intueamur an hoc quod me praestare debuisse dicit praestari oportuerit. Fortior sic ageret: advocationem negare contra reum proditionis non debui; oportebat non deesse legibus vocem, oportebat esse aliquem qui in summis rei publicae, ut tum 15 videbatur, periculis excuteret veritatem. Dicebatur proditor aliquis; clamabat delator: 'si mihi vox esset, si quid eloquentiae natura tribuisset, iam vobis ostendissem quae cum hoste commercia, quod discrimen totius rei publicae, quam haec omnia quae in conspectu sunt in ultimo periculo essent.' Hicine eum qui accusare[10] posse videbatur tacere oporteret?

16   Mihi aliter agendum est. Ego utilitatibus publicis con-

---

[9] *Aer.*: praesetari *ut vid*. A[2]: interpraet- A[1]: pr(a)ecari β
[10] *Gron.*: -ari Aβ

cally ungrateful, it remains for us to examine whether all things ought to be furnished to those who have conferred a benefaction, and whether what you are now considering ought to have been furnished, and lastly whether it could have been.

I say that not all things are to be furnished even to parents. Otherwise nothing is more dangerous than benefactions received, if they bind us into all manner of servitude. For they bring compulsion even to commit crimes, if it should seem good to those who have obliged us with services. Therefore it will stand agreed that one who has received an obligation will not do anything to harm the commonwealth because the person from whom he has received it so desires, nor be undutiful to his parents under such compulsion, nor unseemly, nor furnish things impracticable.

If that is clearer than daylight itself, gentlemen, let us now examine whether this thing he says I ought to have furnished should have been furnished. A man bolder than I might put it this way: it would not have been right for me to deny my services against a man accused of treason; the laws ought not to have lacked a voice, there ought to have been someone to shake out the truth in time of utmost peril to the commonwealth, as then appeared. Someone was said to be a traitor. The informer was clamoring: "If I had a voice, if nature had given me a tincture of eloquence, I should already have shown you what contacts he had with the enemy, what a crisis the whole commonwealth was in, how all we see around us was in mortal danger." In such a situation should a man thought capable of prosecuting be silent?

I must take a different tack. I would rather have taken

tra restitissem, ego ruere[11] haec omnia supra me maluissem quam tanta merita asperiore ulla voce violare. Sed necessitati quid faciam? Lex optandi patronum ius dabat: me delator optaverat. Doce quid faciam. Delator ius habet. Contra omnem meam deprecationem publica aucto-

17 ritas nititur. Conscientia mehercule facere hoc viderer ac timuisse ne, si illi causae vox contigisset, in medium scelera prodirent. Ego vero suscepi causam, nec timui ne vincerem.[12] Non igitur obicere debes mihi in quod coactus sum; illa quae fuerunt in mea potestate, si deprehendisti, ostende: si vultus infestus, si vox incitatior, si quid ultra ne-

18 cessitatem. Neque ista ego imputo: non enim poteram, neque erat adversus innocentiam tuam ingenio locus. Itaque discessi a iudicio laetior quam reus ipse et velut editis necessitate operis ad gratulationem cucurri.

Nec me ei in reliquum eximo tempus. Debere confiteor: da quem defendam, da pro quo loquar. Si quid adversus illum nocentissimum delatorem invenire possumus, impera quod vis, in quantumcumque tua ista vox est.

334

Proditoris accusator ex defensore

Cum damnato proditionis patronus exulet. Adfuit reo pro-

[11] *Wi.* (vero ruere *iam Walter*): vere Aβ
[12] *Gron.*: -rer Aβ

---

[1] *Adfuit*: Ritter supplied a subject, *quidam*, perhaps rightly. Wi.'s list of such omissions in *themata* is indiscriminate—e.g. in 309 *deducta* is substantival. Håkanson's edition of 1978 adds *pater* in Calp. 48.

a stand against the interests of the commonwealth, had rather everything here crashed upon my head than violate such obligations by a single harsh word. But what should I do in face of compulsion? The law gave the right to opt for an advocate. The informer had opted for me. Tell me what to do. The informer has the right. Public authority resists all my excuses. Upon my word it might have been thought that I was involved and feared that if that case found a voice the crime would come into the open. Yes, I took the case, and I was not afraid of winning. So you should not tax me for what was forced upon me. As to what was in my power, if you caught me, out with it—a hostile expression, a raised voice, anything over and above what was necessary. Not that I am taking credit for that; it was not in my power and against your innocence there was no place for talent. So I left the court happier than the defendant himself and, having done my necessary job as it were, I ran to offer congratulations.

And I do not exempt myself for time to come where he is concerned. I confess I am in debt. Give me someone to defend, to speak for. If we can find anything against that villain of an informer, order what you will. My voice is yours for however great a service.

334

Defender of a traitor turned prosecutor

Along with one convicted of treason let his advocate be exiled. <A person >[1] appeared for a man accused of treason.

ditionis. Absolutus est ille. Petît ab absoluto pecuniam quam pactus erat. Non dantem detulit reum proditionis. Damnavit. Petitur in exilium.

1   DECLAMATIO

'Cum damnato proditionis et patronus exulet.' Damnatum esse proditorem certum est, et hunc fuisse patronum. Quomodo tamen defenditur? Quomodo proditorem defendit: hoc sibi[1] persuaserat etiam ante experimentum, nullam esse ingenio suo malam causam.

2   'Non fui' inquit 'patronus eo iudicio quo damnatus est.' Si verba legis intueri velimus, nihil hoc ad praesentem cognitionem pertinet. Satis est enim probare et illum proditorem et te patronum fuisse quandoque.

3   Sed videamus quid secuta sit lex. Non mehercule tantum putem providisse legum latorem quantum adversus te probamus. Patronum enim voluit exulare, non conscium. Illa prorsus locutus cum advocatis videtur: 'Sane suscipiatis alias temere causas ubi privatae leges erunt et ad unius commodum pertinebunt; cum vero de proditione agetur, diligentius intuemini. Etiamsi vobis nihil ipsi confitebuntur, at hoc, si non satis momenti publica pericula habent,
4 vestri respectu capitis inquirite.' Hoc igitur quod [de][2] lege cautum est: proditor advocatum habuit [licet illi nihil profuerit].[3] Nunc vero quam necessario[4] ex eventu ostenditur: proditor absolutus est. Has illi artes timuerunt, hanc calliditatem advocatorum. Constituit enim natura quae-

---

¹ *Aer.*: sic Aβ   ² *SB*³
³ *SB*³, *a Wi. monitus*   ⁴ *SB*³: -ium Aβ

---

² The legal provision.

The latter was acquitted. He claimed from the acquitted man the sum he had agreed upon. When the other did not give it, he charged him with treason and convicted him. Suit is brought to exile him.

DECLAMATION

"Along with one convicted of treason let the advocate too be exiled." It is certain that the traitor was convicted and that this man was his advocate. But how is he defended? The same way as he defended the traitor. He had persuaded himself even before the test that for a talent like his there is no such thing as a bad case.

He says: "I was not his advocate at the trial in which he was convicted." If we care to look at the words of the law, this has nothing to do with the present proceedings. It is enough to prove both that he was a traitor and that you were his advocate at some point.

But let us see what the law had in view. Upon my word, I would not think that the lawgiver foresaw as much as we are proving against you. He wanted the advocate to be exiled, not the accomplice. It is really as though he talked to advocates like this: "Granted that you take other cases at random in which the laws will be private and concern the good of an individual: but when it is a matter of treason, pay closer attention. Even if they themselves confess nothing to you, look into it, if public dangers are not reason enough, out of regard for your own survival." This then is what the law provided against: the traitor had an advocate. But now the event shows how necessary that[2] was: the traitor was acquitted. These were the skills they were afraid of, this cunning of advocates. For nature constituted certain

dam arma nequitiae per quae abducantur iudicum animi.

5 'Sed ipso' inquit 'iudicio quo damnatus est non fui patronus. Volo interim sic agere tamquam nullam rei publicae iniuriam fecerim.⁵' Etiamnum hoc satis est: advocatus proditoris fuisti. Fingamus igitur ampliatum fuisse iudicium et tantum primo iudicio patronum illum: nonne damnatio sequeretur quod omnino patronus fuisset? Non ergo tempus intueri debemus, sed causam, si homo idem

6 est, si crimen idem, si lex eadem. Putemus ab alio esse damnatum. Non enim proderit tibi istud quod imputas. Tunc enim diceres: 'ignoravi, et idem me quod iudices fefellit': nunc proditorem sciens defendisti.

7 Nihil dico de advocatione: testem perdidi. Tantane lucri cupiditas? Sic proditores corrumpuntur. Sic prorsus homo nocentissimus cum advocato suo locutus est: 'ego quidem prodidi, sed magnam pecuniam accepi: et tibi sufficit.' Quaeritis, iudices, quantum promiserit petenti?

8 Non potuit proditor solvere. Ergo quantum in isto est, proditor vivit, nec vivit tantum, sed etiam insidiatur et ad hoc necessitate solvendi urgetur: addidisti homini nocentissimo pecuniae necessitatem. Unde temporum mutata

---

⁵ *SB⁴*: -rit Aβ

---

³ Virtually repeated from s.2. He was in fact the prosecutor.

⁴ *Interim* should have been preceded by something like "we'll see about that later." An epiphany follows with the change of *fecerit* to *fecerim* and placing the sentence inside the quotation.

⁵ That you got him convicted at the second trial. On what follows see SB².

⁶ Could he not have claimed to have learned of the traitor's guilt after the first trial?

184

weapons for villainy, by which the minds of jurymen could be led astray.

He says: "But in the actual trial in which he was convicted I was not his advocate.[3] Meanwhile, I propose to take the line that I did no harm to the commonwealth."[4] Even so, this is enough: you were a traitor's advocate. Let us suppose that the trial was adjourned and that he was the advocate only in the first trial: would not conviction follow on the ground that he had been advocate at all? So we ought not to look at the time but at the case, if the man is the same, if the charge is the same, if the law is the same. Let us suppose he was convicted by somebody else. For this that you put to your credit[5] will do you no good. For then you would have said: "I didn't know and I was misled by the same thing that misled the jury." As it is, you knowingly defended a traitor.[6]

I say nothing about the advocacy;[7] I have lost my witness.[8] Such greed for gain? That is how traitors are corrupted. The guilty man talked to his advocate like this to be sure: "Yes, I was a traitor but I got a great deal of money—enough for you too." Do you ask, gentlemen, how much he promised his client? The traitor was unable to pay. So as far as this man is concerned, the traitor is alive,[9] and not only alive but plotting and driven thereto by the need to pay; you added need for money to the guilty man.[10] Whence

[7] The financial arrangement with his client before the first trial. He goes on to talk about it.

[8] The traitor, now in exile.

[9] Implying that he was dead. As Wi. points out, the speaker seems to forget that in this case the penalty was exile (theme), not the normal one for treason (death). [10] I.e. to his motive.

condicio est? Pecuniam non accipiebas; ita nunc ille quod punitus est, merces huius vindicata est? [Pecuniam non acceperat.][6]

335

Infamis in novercam vulneratus

Infamis in novercam cum patre peregre profectus est. Cum in latrones incidissent, fugerunt. Pater reversus adulteros inclusos in cubiculo deprehendit. Occidit uxorem, adulterum vulneravit; is fugit. Postea vulneratus filius venit. Interrogavit eum pater a quo vulneratus esset. Ille a latronibus dixit. Curavit eum pater et reddit[1] causas mortis voluntariae. Filius CD.

1

DECLAMATIO

Adversus mala et iniurias Fortunae et gravem plerisque vitam unum natura remedium invenerat, mortem. Nec quisquam potest tam crudelis legum lator fuisse qui hominem innocentem vita puniret, cum et hoc ipsum sit calamitatis

2 genus, mori velle. Necessaria tamen vestra cognitio est, [ut][2] non quia istud liberum esse innocentibus non oportet, sed quia multi sunt qui sic conscientiam emittunt; et ideo adiectum est damnum sepulturae ne se putent poenas effugisse. Ideo ego hanc vitam olim invisam tamdiu tuli

6 *SB*[3]
1 *Aer.*: reddidit A*β*
2 *Ro., Ri.*

---

1 Lit. "ill-reputed towards his stepmother."

have circumstances changed? You did not get your money: now that he has been so punished, has this man's fee been avenged?

335

Suspected of misconduct with his stepmother,[1] wounded

A man suspected of misconduct with his stepmother went abroad with his father. Falling in with robbers, they fled. The father returned and found an adulterous pair shut in his bedroom. He killed his wife and wounded the adulterer, who fled. Afterwards the son arrived wounded. The father asked him who had wounded him. He said it was the robbers. His father cured him and gives reasons for taking his own life. The son opposes.[2]

DECLAMATION[3]

For miseries and Fortune's injuries and life to many a burden nature found one remedy, death. No lawmaker can have been so cruel as to punish an innocent man with life when this too is itself a sort of calamity, the wish to die. But your enquiry is necessary, not because that should not be a free choice for the innocent but because there are many who in that way release their guilty consciences; and the loss of burial is added so that they don't think they have escaped punishment. I bore this life, which has long been hateful to me, until my son was healed lest it might seem

[2] The theme is incomplete; cf. 337 *thema*, init. The declaimer addresses the Senate.

[3] The speech is full of innuendos suggesting that the son was the wounded lover.

donec filius meus sanaretur ne viderer aliqua conscientia mori velle.

3   Mori volo. Nihil me commisisse manifestum est. Et iam satis rationem videor reddidisse. Mori volo senex; habet suos vita terminos, dum membra sufficiunt, dum in officio vires sunt. Quotamquamque partem habeo viventis? Cum adhuc haberem uxorem, matrimonio inutilis eram, nec mirum si quem concupivit iuniorem. Occidere adulterum non potui: non miraretur me mori velle si quis vidisset fugientem. Quam tarde feci! Felicissimus fuissem si me

4   latrones occidissent. Accedit illud: filium habeo. Mori volo dum salvus est, dum illum relinquere superstitem possum. Paene illum nuper amisi: quid futurum erat si non potuissem sanare? Bene dii quod leve fuit vulnus! Non accidet hoc mihi iterum. Ego scio in quibus cogitationibus fuerim: si in maius periculum filius meus venisset, non expectassem vos ut perirem. Nondum de adversis loquor; haec ipsa me ad mortem ducunt quae ex voto contigerunt.

5   Veniamus nunc ad querelas. Infelix sum: peregre proficisci volui, ⟨in⟩[3] latrones incidi, vivere me miror. Accessit dolor: a filio meo diductus sum. Non queror de ipso: omnis mihi ratio adversus Fortunam est. Intervenerunt latrones, non stetit mecum filius cum pro me pugnarem. Feci aliquid et ipse scelerate: solus reversus sum, tamquam sci-

6   rem filium salvum esse. Insecuta est alia fortuna: uxorem

[3] *ed. princ.*

---

[4] That his son's wound, which might have been fatal, had been inflicted by the father himself.

[5] "By saying the very words *mori volo*" (Wi.).

that I wanted to die because I had something on my conscience.[4]

I wish to die. It is clear that I have done nothing wrong. And I think I have already given reason enough.[5] An old man, I want to die. Life has its own limits; as long as the limbs hold up and the forces do their function. How small a part do I have of a living man! When I still had a wife, I was matrimonially useless and it's no wonder if she took a fancy to a younger man. I could not kill the lover; if somebody had seen me running away, he would not be surprised at my wanting to die. How slowly I did it! I would have been very fortunate if the robbers had killed me. There is another thing: I have a son. I want to die while he is safe, while I can leave him to survive me. Recently I almost lost him; what would have happened if I had failed to heal him? The gods[6] be thanked that his wound was slight! This will not happen to me again. I know what I was thinking about; if my son had come into greater danger, I should not have waited for your permission to perish. I don't yet speak of adversities: the very answers to my prayers lead me to death.

Let us come now to complaints. I am unlucky. I wanted to go abroad: I fell <upon> robbers. I am surprised to be alive. A grief ensued: I was separated from my son. I don't complain of *him*: all my case is directed against Fortune. The robbers intervened. My son did not stay with me when I was fighting for my life. I too did something criminal: I returned alone, as though I knew my son was safe. A different fortune followed: I found my wife in adultery.

---

[6] *Dii* is nominative, not vocative as assumed by Watt[2] on 315.23.

adulteram inveni. Quid accidere gravius huic aetati potuit?
Velut exprobrare mihi visa est Fortuna quare uxorem post
iuvenem filium duxissem. Ex eo quod deprehendi illud
quoque colligo, diu adulteram fuisse: paulo ante profectus
eram, statim in cubiculo adulter, tamquam sciret me non

7 reversurum. Quantum hinc ceperim dolorem ‹vel sic aestimate›[4]: deprehendi quod ipsos adulteros puderet: tene-
bris absconderunt tamquam nefas. Non est hoc ad mortem
satis? Adeo me laborasse iudicio ut nescirem quam ducere-
rem! Adeo me nescisse quid in domo mea ageretur ut non
fuerim deprehensurus nisi fugissem! Destituit me fides illa
quam speraveram fore solacium senectutis. Demens ego,
cum talem haberem uxorem, peregre profectus sum, ab-
ducebam mecum etiam filium!

8 Mori volo quia uxorem meam occidi qualemcumque.
Licuit, scio, sed non semper ad animum pertinent iura.
Occidere adulteros lex permittit: ego mihi sic irascor tam-

9 quam nefas fecerim. Aut si quid in hac parte consolari vultis, mori volo quod adulterum non occidi. Hoc tantum me
dicere putatis, quod me non vindicavi? [quod][5] Nescio
quis fuerit—et forte perstet hic mecum et quod has manus
evaserit gratuletur. Quod non occidi? Vulneravi; ita ille et
salvus est et beneficio meo vivet. Paenitet quod non ab
adultero coepi: circa uxorem moratus sum, tamquam illa
plus sceleris fecisset; interim fugit ille iuvenis et velox.

10 Mori volo quod adulterum non invenio. Unde venit?
Quis hominum fuit? Non inveniri in civitate hominem vul-

---

4 *Wi.* (aestimate *Aer.*)   5 *Ri.*

---

7 Hinting, as Wi. suggests, that he had had his suspicions—in
which case he was not so mad after all.

What worse could have befallen a man of my age? Fortune seemed to reproach me for having taken a wife after my son had grown up. From the fact that I caught her I also infer that she had had a lover for a long time. I had just left when, right away, a lover in the bedroom, as though she knew I would not be coming back. How that grieved me ⟨you can judge from this⟩: I caught what the pair themselves were ashamed of: they hid it in the dark like a crime. Is that not enough to make one die? To think that my judgment was so bad that I did not know the woman I married! To think that I was so ignorant of what was going on in my house that I would not have caught them if I had not escaped! The loyalty that I hoped would be the consolation of my old age forsook me. Mad that I was, I left for abroad when I had such a wife and took my son along with me.[7]

I wish to die because I killed my wife, whatever she was. It was my right, I know, but laws do not always concern the heart. The law permits me to kill adulterers· I am angry with myself as though I had committed a crime. Or if you wish to console me on this score, I wish to die because I did not kill the lover. Do you think I am only saying "because I did not avenge myself"? I don't know who he was—and perhaps he is still here with me and rejoices at having escaped these hands. Because I didn't kill him? I wounded him; so he is both safe and will live thanks to me. I am sorry that I did not begin with the lover. I took time over my wife, as though she was the more criminal; meanwhile, he fled, a young man and a fast mover.

I wish to die because I don't find the adulterer. Where did he come from? Who in the world was he? Strange that a wounded man is not found in the community. I called in

neratum? Quos ego non domi medicos adhibui? Omnes
illos interrogavi num quis alius. Nemo erat nisi quem latrones vulneraverunt. Et nunc ille me deridet ubicumque, et
fortasse iam sanus est.

Mori volo. Satis iusta moriendi causa erat si calamitas
11 mea hactenus stetisset. Accedit huc quod fortuna nostra
dedit malis suspicionem. Nihil est hoc loco, fili, quod me
suspicari putes: non habebam causam parcendi homo
periturus; ego te vere[6] innocentem puto. Ac si hoc non credis, curavi, sanavi; alioqui te et hodie occidissem. Constat
tibi innocentia; sed numquam potest constare tibi[7] fama.
Vis scire quae inimici nostri loquantur? Mirantur[8] me
⟨in⟩[9] latrones incidisse. 'Solet fieri, humanum[10] est, fre-
quens.[11]' Scio; et[12] nemo de hoc loqueretur si uxorem non
12 deprehendissem. Mirantur quod patrem in illo periculo
reliquisti. Ego te puto fecisse sapienter; et si crimen est istud, utrique commune est, nam et ego fugi. Non eramus
13 pares: quid attinebat periclitari? Utrumque nostrum fecisse summo consilio puto: in latrones incidimus et secessi-
mus,[13] fugimus; nemo persecutus est. Quid ergo est? Ego
gaudeo, cui non potuisti[14] aliud maius beneficium dare
quam ut salvus esses. Sunt qui te putent pro me pugnare
debuisse.

14   Querebar paulo ante de infirmitate corporis: mihi ne
mentem quidem satis constare credo. Cum domum venis-

    6 *Ro.*: vero Aβ
    7 c. t. *coni. Ri.*: c. sibi A: sibi c. β
    8 *Ranc.*: ira actus Aβ 9 *ed. princ.*
    10 *Obr.*: summum Aβ 11 *Gron.*: seq- Aβ
    12 *SB*[3]: sed Aβ 13 *SB*[2]: rec- Aβ
    14 c. n. p. *Ro.*: qui n. potui Aβ

all the doctors at my house and asked all of them whether there was somebody else. There was nobody except the man the robbers wounded. And now he is mocking me, wherever he is, and perhaps is already in good health.

I wish to die. There would have been cause if my misfortune had stopped here. There is the further fact that our fortune has given bad folk food for suspicion. My son, there is no cause for you to think that *I* suspect anything here. A man about to die, I had no reason to spare you;[8] I think you truly innocent. And if you don't believe me, I cured you, made you well. Otherwise I should have killed you even today. Your innocence is assured; but your reputation can never be assured. Do you want to know what our enemies are saying? They are surprised that I fell <in> with robbers. "Oh, it happens, it's part of life, happens often." I know; and nobody would be talking about it if I had not caught my wife. They are surprised that you left your father thus in danger. *I* think you did wisely; and if that is a reproach, it is one we share, for I too ran away. We were no match for them,[9] why take the risk? I think both of us acted with the greatest prudence. We fell in with robbers and we split up, fled; no one followed. So what? I am happy; you could have given me no greater boon than your safety. There are some who think you ought to have fought for me.

I was complaining just now of my physical infirmity, I believe my mind too is less than sound. When I had come

[8] Not in his speech (as Wi.: "taking us back to the time when he began (or wrote) the speech"), but when the son came to the house. He had already wanted to die because he had killed his wife (cf. s.8 init.).   [9] Not, as Wi., equal to each other ("the old man ran away more slowly").

sem,[15] uxorem adulteram occidissem, ‹adulterum vulne-
rassem,›[16] postea in domo viderem vulneratum, interrogavi quis te vulnerasset. [sed][17] Dignus sum morte: infamavi
te adulterio. In latrones incideramus: ego te interrogavi
quis vulnerasset! Non, fili, maligne, sed, quomodo exci-
dunt multa iis qui expaverunt, perculsus illo metu ignoravi
quid facerem. Mali istud aliter accipiunt. Irascor manibus
meis quod adulterum tantum vulneraverim: nulla ad te
pertineret infamia si occidissem. Nunc congruere haec inter se videntur: falso quidem, videntur tamen. Ego nescio
quem vulneravi, tu vulneratus es. Non prodest nobis quod
noverca est: hominum iniquitatem ne odio quidem defendimus. Ego te nunc si non curassem, viderer filium occidisse. Hanc ego infamiam ferre non possum. Tua alia ratio
est; tibi longa vita superest: poteris approbare innocentiam
cum duxeris uxorem, cum fidem illi maritalem praestiteris,
cum totius te vitae gravitas solvet.[18] Ego, etiamsi nolo mori, moriar antequam adulterum inveniam.

Vis adiciam adhuc causas moriendi? Irascor tibi. Nescio quem illum invenire non potes? Debet istud ignosci
meae senectuti: tu nec quaesisti.

15 c. d. v. *Wi.* (d. c. v. *Gron.*): cum conven- Aβ
16 *Ri.*
17 *Obr.*
18 *SB*³: res- Aβ: abs- *Gron.*

home and killed my adulterous wife, ‹and wounded her lover,› and later saw you wounded here in the house, I asked who had wounded you. I deserve death; I smeared you with adultery. We had fallen in with robbers: I asked you who had wounded you! Not, my son, with malice but as many things are let slip by people who have had a shock. I was so frightened that I didn't know what I was doing. Bad folk take it otherwise. I am angry with my hands because I only wounded the adulterer: no ill fame would have attached to you if I had killed him. As it is, there seems to be a fit between these two items—falsely, to be sure, but it seems so. I wounded somebody, you were wounded. It doesn't help us that she was your stepmother. We can't even use the hatred[10] to rebut people's unfairness. If I had not cured you, it would now be thought that I had killed my son. I cannot bear this ill fame. Your situation is different. You have a long life ahead of you. You will be able to establish your innocence, when you have taken a wife, when you have given her marital loyalty, when the strictness of your whole life will exonerate you. As for me, even if I decide not to die, I shall die before I find the adulterer.[11]

Would you like me to add further reasons for dying? I am angry with you. Can you not find that somebody? My old age should be forgiven for that: *you* have not so much as looked.

---

[10] The traditional ill will between stepmothers and stepsons. In this case, says the speaker, there was no ill will—far from it (another hint).

[11] Who will never be found. Wi. sees a second meaning : "I shall kill myself rather than find him." But in s.17 the father professes to want him found.

336

Ager communis et novae tabulae

Pactus cum fratre maiore ut agrum communem paternum ille susciperet et omni aeri alieno satisfaceret, tabularum novarum lege lata partem agri petit. Ille CD.

1   DECLAMATIO

Ager, quem communem nobis esse dico, patris nostri fuit. Is duos liberos reliquit, aequum utrique ius, ‹eadem utrique bona,›[1] eadem utrique onera aeris alieni, id est,[2] ut nunc est, nihil.

2   'Cessisti' inquit 'mihi.' Si hoc sine ulla conventione fecissem, si nulla opponi huic tuae voci posset exceptio, dicerem: circumscripsisti fratrem, nec difficile fuit, minorem. Quod si nulla vi coactus, nullis insidiis, id quod solum nobis pater reliquerat tibi uni concessi, debes referre animo

3   gratiam. Hoc fratri bene diceretur; sed quatenus exuis nomen istud et nos ad ius solum vocas, sub condicione cessi: sic enim tamquam alieni loquamur. Stari voce mea sit aequum[3] conventione pactorum. Quod quale fuit? Ut agrum possideres ita, ut opinor, ut aes alienum quod patris [tui][4] fuit solveres. Nullam igitur huius agri habuisti adhuc propriam possessionem, quia quaecumque sub condicione traduntur ita demum fieri possunt propria ac peculiaria si condicio consummata est. Fuit igitur usque ad tabulas no-

---

[1] SB[1] (cf. SB[2])
[2] i.e. SB[1] (cf. SB[2]): mihi Aβ
[3] in add. Hå.[2]: et coni. SB[3]
[4] Obr.

336

Common land and cancellation of debts[1]

A man agreed with his elder brother that the latter take over their common paternal land and settle all debts. When a law was passed canceling debts, he claims half the land. The other opposes.

DECLAMATION

The land which I say we held in common belonged to our father. He left two children. Their legal rights were equal, ⟨their properties were the same,⟩ their burden of debt the same, that is to say, as things now stand, zero.

He says: "You made over to me." If I had done so unconditionally, if no reservation could be set against this phrase of yours, I should say: "You cheated your brother and it was not difficult—your younger brother." But if I made over to your single self, not constrained by any violence or trick, all that our father had left us, you should be grateful for my good intention. That would be how to talk to a brother. But since you strip off that name and summon us only to law, I made over under a condition; for let us talk like non-relations. Let it be fair that we go by what I said when we agreed to the bargain. And what was that? You were to own the land provided, I think, that you paid your father's debts. So up to this point you have had no personal ownership of this land because whatever items are handed over conditionally can only become personal and peculiar if the condition has been fulfilled. So the land was common

---

[1] Lit. "new tablets," the standard expression for an across-the-board cancellation of debts.

4 vas communis nobis ager. Et ut facilius appareat, fingamus
te aes alienum noluisse solvere, egisse pacti huius paenitentiam: num dubium est quin ego venturus optimo iure in
hanc fuerim possessionem? Non quaeritur, ut opinor. Nam
etiamsi hoc inter nos convenerat, ut tu aes alienum patris
solveres, cogere ego tamen te non poteram: ⟨sed⟩[5] una so-
lutio erat pacti inter nos facti ut rursus omnia communia
essent, id est, ut et agrum possideremus et aes alienum
5 duo solveremus. Ergo convenit ut ager tuus ita esset si aes
alienum solveres: non solvisti. Quo iure vindicare potes
eam rem cuius pretium non dedisti? 'Ideo' inquit 'non solvi
aes alienum quia novae tabulae intervenerunt.' Equidem
querebar quod non solvisti; ceterum nihil mea interest qua
causa non solveris, cum agrum ita demum habere potueris
si solvisses. Sive istud tua voluntate factum est sive liberalitate creditorum sive, ut manifestum est, publica necessitate, non solvisti.

6 Quid si hae tabulae novae tam mihi factae sunt quam
tibi? Nam, ut paulo ante dicebam, communem agrum constat fuisse. Pater noster contraxerat cum multis. Non erubesco: non retinendum agrum habebamus. Habebamus[6]:
namque ego hoc ipso quod tibi cessi dominum egi. Igitur
7 cum essemus heredes patris nostri, debuimus ambo. Id
sic colligo. Finge esse aliquem ex creditoribus petitorem:
numquid petere a te totam summam potest? Minime, ut
opinor. Duos enim pater noster filios reliquit, et necesse

5 *SB*[2]   6 *Ro.*: habes A*β*

---

2 He should have said "until now" since he contends the cancellation did not fulfil the agreement, which required that the
debts *be paid*.

between us until the cancellation of debts.[2] And to make this more readily apparent, let us suppose that you had decided not to pay the debt, that you had come to regret this agreement: is there any doubt that I would have had a full legal right to enter into this possession? No question, I think. For even though it had been agreed between us that you should pay our father's debt, yet I had no means of compelling you; <but> the only way to cancel the agreement we made was that everything should again be common, that is to say that the two of us both own the land and pay the debt. So it was agreed that the land should be yours on condition you paid the debt: well, you did not pay it. By what right can you claim ownership of an asset for which you did not give the price? He says: "The reason I did not pay the debt was that the cancellation intervened." For my part, I complained that you did not pay; for the rest, it makes no difference to me *why* you did not pay, since you could only have the land if you had paid. Whether it was because you did not want to, or because the creditors were generous, or, as is clear, because of a public necessity, you did not pay.

What if this cancellation was made for me as much as for you? For, as I was saying just now, it is established that the land was common. Our father had borrowed from many people. I am not ashamed: we had land we could not keep—*we*, for by the very making over of it to you I acted as owner. Therefore, since we were both our father's heirs, we both owed. I infer this as follows: suppose one of the creditors claims, can he claim the entire sum from you? By no means, in my opinion. For our father left two sons, and

est, sicut bona, ita onera quoque esse communia. Partem
ergo tu debuisti, partem ego; quo efficiebatur ut partem
8 solveres. Faciamus hoc manifestius. Finge esse aliquem
ex creditoribus qui partem crediti sui a me petat: quid
respondere possum? 'Agrum fratri dedi, cum fratre meo
convenit mihi ut ille solveret'? Num dubium est quin dicturus fuerit[7] creditor: 'Partem tu debes mihi: patri tuo credidi, cuius ex parte dimidia heres es. Assem[8] non possum a
9 te petere, semissem petere [non][9] possum.' Ergo, etiamsi
conventione aes alienum transferebatur ad te, iure tamen
et veritate erat et meum. Igitur tabulae novae factae tam
me debito omni liberaverunt quam te. Id enim remiserunt
quod ex parte a me peti poterat, ex parte a te.
10   'Sed animus tamen is fuit pacti huius, ut totum aes alienum meum fieret.' Spectemus ergo [totum][10] animum.
Neque enim ego negaverim id intuitos esse nos et ita cogitasse, ut omne aes alienum tu solveres; num alioqui dubium est, aut deduci omnino in controversiam potest, an
ego tibi parte agri mea[11] cessurus non fuerim nisi quod
pretium soluturus viderieris, quin si ulla spes mihi novarum tabularum et huius necessarii in civitate nostra remedii fuisset, retenturus[12] fuerim id quod repeto[13]?
11   Ergo sive ius spectas, commune aes alienum fuit et
tabulae novae utrique profuerunt et tu non aliter totam
possessionem habere debes quam si aes alienum solveris;
sive animum spectas, is utriusque fuit, ut tu venditione agri
aes alienum solveres: ego aestimaram me onere a te libera-

---

[7] *Ranc.*: fuit Aβ   [8] *Aer.*: an Aβ   [9] *Aer.*
[10] *Castiglioni*   [11] *Ranc.*: mei Aβ
[12] *Gron.*: recept- Aβ   [13] *Gron.*: retineo Aβ

like the assets the liabilities too are necessarily common. So you owed half and I half: that meant that you paid half. Let me make this plainer. Suppose one of the creditors claims half his loan from me: what can I answer? "I gave the land to my brother, my brother agreed that he should pay"? Is there any doubt that the creditor will say: "You owe me half. I lent to your father, whose heir you are to half his estate. I cannot claim a twelfth from you, I can claim half." So although under the agreement the debt was being transferred to you, in law and reality it was mine as well. So the cancellation freed me of all debt just as much as you. For it remitted what could be claimed, half from me, half from you.

"But the intention of this agreement was that the entire debt become mine." Well, let us look at the intention. For I would not deny that what we looked for and had in mind was that you should pay all the debt. Is it doubtful anyway or can it even be disputed that I would not have made over my half of the land except that it appeared you would pay the price; that if I had had any expectation of a cancellation, of this forced remedy, in our community, I would have kept what I am reclaiming?

Well then, if you look at the law, the debt was common and the cancellation was for both our benefit and you should have sole ownership only if you pay the debt. Or if you look at the intention, it was the same with both of us, that you should pay the debt by selling the land. I had thought to be freed of encumbrance by you, to whom I was

ri, cui agrum dabam. Nunc id quod tu mihi praestaturus eras res publica praestat.

12   SERMO

Summae partes sunt aequitatis.

13   DECLAMATIO

Pater nobis idem fuit, eadem onera nobis, eadem bona reliquit: cur tu locuples es? Apud te ager totus, pro quo nihil impendisti, nihil numerasti; ego nudus, ego egenus. Erat hoc tolerabile cum viderer in aequo[14] tecum positus. ‹Nunc›[15] aufers mihi civitatis beneficium, et me sic relinquis tamquam pater praeter aes alienum mihi nihil reli-

14 querit. Tum quoque invitus feci: aetatis meae infirmitati consului. Si hereditate tibi ager iste venisset, inhumane cum fratre non partireris; non tantum sanguinis nos iura coniungunt: aliquid et ipsa necessitas, aliquid et ipsa societas.

337

Seditio populi et exercitus

Qui causas in senatu voluntariae mortis non approbaverit, insepultus abiciatur. Pauper et dives inimici. Utrique domus et uxor et liberi. Dux creatus bello dives cum bis acie victus esset, processit pauper, qui et disertus erat, et dixit prodi rem publicam a divite. Impetus in domum divitis

---

[14] *Ro., Ri.*: hoc Aβ [15] *Aer.*

---

[3] Now cancelled.   [4] "What is implied by *quoque*?" (Wi.). "I made our bargain reluctantly even at the time, let alone what I felt when the debts were cancelled" (SB[2]).   [5] I.e. poverty.

giving the land. As it is, what you were going to do for me is
being done by the commonwealth.

DISCUSSION

The final parts are about equity.

DECLAMATION

We had the same father; he left us the same liabilities, the
same assets. Why are you rich? You have all the land, for
which you have spent nothing, paid nothing down. I am
bare and needy. That could be borne when I appeared to
be on a level with you. <As it is,> you take the benefaction
of the community away from me and leave me as I would
have been if our father had left us nothing except debt.[3]
Even[4] at the time I did it unwillingly; I had regard to the
infirmity of my age. If that land had come to you by inheritance, you would not in human decency have failed to
share it with your brother. Not only are we united by the
ties of blood; necessity[5] itself is something, partnership
itself is something.

337

Sedition of the people and the army

Whoso shall not obtain approval in the senate for his reasons for suicide, let him be cast away unburied. A poor man
and a rich man were enemies. Each had a house and a wife
and children. Appointed commander in a war, the rich
man was twice defeated in battle. The poor man, who
was also a good speaker, came forward and said that the
commonwealth was being betrayed by the rich man. The
people made an onslaught on the rich man's house and

factus est a populo et domus incensa et interfecti liberi
cum uxore. Vicit tertia acie dives et in potestatem hostes
redegit. Exercitus divitis domum pauperis incendit et uxorem et liberos interfecit. Vult mori pauper ratione in senatu reddita. Dives CD.

1   SERMO

Quotiens hoc genus materiae dividam, necesse habeo id
dicere quod iam saepe dixi, me nullam voluntatem cuiusquam contra themata intellegere. Fortasse erunt aliqui qui
existiment a paupere id solum quaeri, ut invidiam diviti
faciat: quod illi contingere etiam citra mortis propositum
2   potest. Hic ergo pauper apud me mori vult; agere debet ut
moriatur. Quid ergo est? Non aliter invidiam diviti faciet
maximam.

Prima quaestio illa est, an causae mortis ideo tantum
sint approbandae ne turpes lateant.[1]

3   DECLAMATIO

Mori volo. Nullam tam inhumanam quisquam crediderit
esse legem ut hominem innocentem et invitum detineat in
luce; sed ita scripta lex est ut poenam mortis constituat.
'Insepultus abiciatur is qui non approbaverit causas.' Irascitur ergo lex ei qui non approbatis senatui causis perierit.
4   Quae profecto non hoc existimavit, quemquam mori velle
sine causa. Sed cum duplex genus causarum sit, alterum ex
iniuria Fortunae, alterum ex mala conscientia, hoc ipsum
voluit approbari senatui, causas non esse deformes. Graves

---

[1] *Ro., Ri.*: pat- Aβ

---

[1] Although this must not be the poor man's main motive, it will
in fact be best served by his dying.

the house was burned and his children killed along with
his wife. In a third battle the rich man won and brought
the enemy into his power. The rich man's army burned
the poor man's house and killed his wife and children. The
poor man wishes to die after giving his reasons in the
senate. The rich man speaks in opposition.

DISCUSSION

Whenever I divide this sort of material, I find it necessary
to say, as I have often said, that I recognize no intention
on anybody's part that conflicts with the themes. Perhaps
there may be some who think that the poor man's only object was to cast odium on the rich man: that he can achieve
even short of his proposed death. So in my book this poor
man wants to die; he should speak with the object of dying.
So what to say? He will not otherwise cast the maximum of
odium on the rich man.[1]

The first question is whether reasons for death are to
be approved only so that discreditable ones do not lurk
behind.

DECLAMATION

I wish to die. No one would believe that there is a law so in-
human as to keep an innocent man in life against his will.
But the law is so written that it lays down a punishment for
death: "Let him who does not gain approval for his reasons
be cast away unburied." So the law is angry with a person
who perishes without gaining the senate's approval for his
reasons. It surely did not think that anyone wishes to die
without good reason. But since there are two sorts of reasons, one from Fortune's injury, the other from a bad conscience, it wanted the senate to be satisfied on this very
point, that the reasons were not ugly. For that they are

205

enim esse manifestum est, cum homo mori velit. Ita senatui non de hoc cognoscendum est, hae graves causae mortis an non; graves enim putat[2] ille qui mori vult, hoc satis
est. Sed de eo cognoscitur, turpes sint causae an ex iniuria,
5 ut dixi, Fortunae proficiscantur. Aliquis metu iudicii mori
vult: dignus est qui insepultus abiciatur. Aliquis conscientia turpis alicuius flagitii admissi priusquam prodatur mori
vult: dignus est qui insepultus abiciatur. Adversus hunc
6 scripta lex est, †hoc cavetur de hoc†.[3] Ceterum quidem tu
ei qui tot lenocinia huic[4] constituta vitae contempserit, qui
non detineatur his voluptatibus, dices: 'non habes graves
causas moriendi'? Respondebit: 'Odi vitam, relinquere volo. Tu me nocentem probes oportet, ne sepeliri debeam.'
7 Si tamen de hoc quoque quaerendum est, an graves
causae sint videamus. Perdidi domum, fortuito incendio,
quomodocumque, tantum domum perdidi: ecquid possum videri iustas habere causas moriendi? Penates illos in
quibus natus sum, qui mihi cotidiana imagine adhuc versantur ante oculos, illos penates in quibus sacri aliquid esse
8 credimus, amisi. Hospes in civitate victurus sum. Perdidi
liberos quomodocumque, tantum liberos: ecquid iusta
causa mortis est orbitas, et orbitas non simplex nec tantum
geminata, verum etiam in unum tempus collata? Adferant
aliquid fortasse solacii mala divisa, et, sicut onera facilius
subeas si partiaris, ita hoc graves casus[5] allevare possis si
non ⟨una⟩[6] ingruant ac semel veniant. Uno tempore plu-
9 res liberos! Quid si et coniugem? ⟦Quod si per se grave est,

2 *Sch.*: inp- A(β)   3 *cruces posuit Wi.*
4 *Watt*[2]: haec Aβ
5 *Obr.*: causas Aβ
6 *Watt*[2]

weighty is clear, since a man wants to die. So the senate does not have to enquire whether these reasons for death are weighty or not; the man who wishes to die thinks they are, that is enough. But the enquiry is about whether the reasons are shameful or arise, as I said, from an injury of Fortune. Somebody wishes to die out of fear of a trial: he deserves to be cast away unburied. Somebody wishes to die because he has the commission of some shameful outrage on his conscience, before it is brought to light: he deserves to be cast away unburied. The law is written against him. It is about him that the provision is made (?). But to him who despises the many allurements allowed for this life, who is not held back by these pleasures, will you say: "You don't have weighty reasons to die"? He will answer: "I hate life, I wish to leave it. You ought to prove me guilty for me to forfeit the right to burial."

But if there has also to be an enquiry about this too, let us see whether my reasons are weighty. I lost my house in an accidental fire, no matter how, just lost my house: can I not appear to have just reasons to die? That house in which I was born, which still floats before my eyes pictured every day, that house in which we believe there is something sacred, it is gone. I shall live as a stranger in the community. I have lost my children, never mind how, just my children. Is bereavement not a just reason for death, and not simple bereavement, nor merely double, but brought together into a single time? Perhaps calamities divided bring a kind of consolation, and just as you can carry loads more easily if you separate them, so you might relieve the weight of misfortunes if they don't bear down <all together> but come one at a time. A number of children at one time! What if my wife too? [If that is weighty in itself, both loss

et quod liberos amisi et eodem tempore amisi, erant satis graves causae.]][7] Adice nunc: haec omnia simul amisi et omnia haec iniuria amisi: exercitus me expugnavit, sicut urbem hostis. Et haec ipsa causa satis iusta erat voluntatis meae: odit me exercitus, pars populi fortissima, pars popu-
10 li optime de re publica merita. Illi milites victores, illi hostium spolia referentes non me occiderunt sed liberos meos (puto illos his aetatibus hostium pepercisse) <sed>[8] coniugem meam (illa modo victa civitas nihil, quod ad feminas pertinet, passa est praeter captivitatem). Domum meam incendit: stant illae quas vicimus. Illud tamen inter omnia gravissimum est: cum haec fecerint, existimant se iure fecisse.

11 'Omnia' inquit 'haec et ego passus sum.' Scio quo pertineat: ut videar ego merito passus. Est et haec causa moriendi, si tantum peccavi, si eo me deduxit error ut filios meos occiderem. Confitendum est de hac gravissima calamitate: domum meam incendit exercitus, populus non de-
12 fendit. 'Omnia tamen eadem et ego passus sum.' Possum dicere hoc tantum: ferre fortius[9] potes, gratulor animo tuo. Sed ne mirum quidem est quod tu ferre fortius potes: locuples es. Quid horum quae perdidisti magnopere desi-
13 deras? Domum, opinor, hinc enim incipiam, perdidisti: infelix non habebis tectum quod subeas. In publico tibi manendum est, et sub caelo. Fortasse etiam contulerint ista detrimenta deliciis tuis: novimus animos vestros, novimus fastidia. Si non esset incensa domus, subinde diruere,

---

[7] *ita secl. SB*[4]: *del. Wi.*
[8] *Aer.*
[9] *Bu.*: pot- Aβ

of children and their loss at the same time, there were reasons weighty enough.]] Add now: I lost all these things at once and I lost them all by violence: the army stormed me like an enemy city. And this very reason was enough to justify my wish: the army hates me, the most gallant part of the people, the part of the people best deserving of the commonwealth. These victorious soldiers, carrying back the enemies' spoils, killed not me but my children (I think they spared enemies of that age), <but> my wife (that recently conquered community suffered nothing so far as women are concerned except captivity). It[2] burned my house—those we conquered are standing. But in all of this the worst thing is that in so doing they think they did right.

He says: "I too have suffered all these things." I know what that's about: I am to seem as though I deserved it. This too is reason for dying, if I went so far wrong that my mistake led me to kill my sons. I have to admit about this ghastly calamity: the army burned my house, the people did not defend it. "But I too suffered all these same things." I can say just this: "You can bear it more bravely, I congratulate your spirit. But it isn't even surprising that you can bear it more bravely: you are wealthy. Of all you lost, what do you greatly miss? Your house, I think, for I'll begin there: poor fellow, you won't have a roof over your head! You'll have to stay[3] in the open, under the sky. Perhaps these detriments actually contributed to your pleasures. We know how you folk are, we know how you get tired of things. If your house had not been burned, you

[2] The army. The singular seems to be a reflection of the theme (*exercitus divitis domum pauperis incendit*).

[3] I.e. "pass the night," cf. *TLL* VIII.282.59.

subinde mutare vos iuvat, et aliquid scilicet experimentis
adicere. Domum perdidisti: gravis iniuria Fortunae novam

14 habitare. Sed uxorem perdidisti. Ne in hac quidem tibi
multum desiderii est. Quomodo enim vos divites reficitis[10]
matrimonia! Reficitis[10]? Aliae vos rapiunt voluptates, illa
ministeria, illi imitati feminas pueri; inde fit ut ne liberos
quidem ametis. Ergo te possunt multa ‹ad vitam›[11] horta-
ri. Praeterea subeunt solacia: et uxorem tibi invenire facile
est et liberos tibi alios educare facile est. Non relinquunt

15 dolori locum tot circumfusae voluptates. Ego haec omnia
passus sum pauper. Si dicerem 'pauper domum perdidi',
exutus tamen omni censu viderer. Quomodo enim illa
apud me remanserat? Quia paterna erat. Pauper liberos
perdidi, pauper uxorem perdidi: solus relictus sum, solus

16 destitutus sum. Inimicum divitem habeo. Adhuc odia illa
quae contra me cotidie acuit fortius sustinebam spe liberorum. Iam mihi iuvenes erant, iam patrem tuebantur.
Etiamsi quando me aemulatio nostra in foro fatigaverat,
erat quae exciperet coniux. Si in hoc consisteret tota lis, an
mihi grave esset vivere, vel uno argumento probare poteram: inimicus me vult vivere. Hanc unam adhuc destinat
odiis suis ultionem.

17   Cur enim dicere aliquid ausus sum? Cur mihi suspec-
tum fuit quod fortissimi milites vincerentur? Cur indigna-
tus sum eorum bis terga caesa qui poterant etiam bis victi
tamen vincere? Intellego aversis auribus accipi hanc partem orationis. Vicit enim et bene etiam meritus de re
publica habetur. Et hoc inter causas mortis est.

---

[10] *SB*[2]: recipitis Aβ [11] *SB*[1]

---

[4] If he succeeds, he will pursue his vengeance further.

folk like to demolish from time to time, to change and add something no doubt by way of experiment. You lost your house: Fortune's grievous injury, to live in a new one! But you lost your wife. Even in her you don't miss much. For how you rich men remodel your marriages! Remodel? Other pleasures carry you off, those servants, those boys imitating women. So it comes about that you don't even love your children. Thus many things can encourage you ⟨to live⟩. Besides, consolations come: it's easy for you to find a wife and it's easy for you to bring up other children. So many pleasures all around you leave no room for sorrow. I have suffered all this as a poor man. If I were to say: "A poor man, I lost my house," I should still look as though I was stripped of my entire fortune. For how had it stayed in my possession? Because it was my father's. A poor man, I lost my children; a poor man, I lost my wife. I am left alone, forsaken. I have a rich man as an enemy. Until now I bore up more bravely against his hatred, sharpened every day, because of my hope in my children. They were already my young men, they were already protecting their father. Even if our rivalry in the Forum sometimes wore me out, I had a wife to go back to. If the point of the entire suit was whether it was hard for me to live, I could prove it with one argument: my enemy wants me to live. This is the one satisfaction for his hate on which he has so far[4] set his sights.

Why did I dare to say anything? Why did I find it suspicious that our gallant soldiers were defeated? Why was I aggrieved that men were twice stabbed from the back who even twice beaten could still win a victory? I realize that this part of my speech falls on deaf ears. For he won the battle and is regarded as having deserved well of the commonwealth. This too is a reason for death.

338

Lis de filio expositoris et repudiatae

Quidam, repudiata uxore ex qua iuvenem filium habebat
aut videbatur habere, duxit aliam. Frequenter iurgia erant
inter privignum et novercam. Quodam tempore adserere
coepit iuvenem pauper quidam et dicere suum filium. Is
qui pater videbatur torsit nutricem. Illa primis tormentis
domini esse filium dixit. Iterum torta dixit expositum esse
ab illo qui adserit, et inter haec mortua est. Cedit illi pater
iuvenem, repudiata vindicat sibi.

[De prohoemio et epilogi][1]

1   SERMO

Prohoemium propriam formam, propriam legem, proprium modum habet: neque narrationis forma cadit in prohoemium neque locorum. Uni parti declamationis solet
esse simile, epilogo: ideo autem simile, quod utraque
[res][2] frequenter extra quaestionem est. Nam et prohoemium rem praecedit et epilogus finita re dicitur. Praeterea
utraque [res][2] idem vult efficere, conciliare sibi iudicem.
2   Hoc differunt: prohoemia praestare debent ut intentum
iudicem faciant (haec pars oneris epilogo remittitur: dixit
enim), praecedere interim solet epilogum ‹enumeratio›,[3]

---

[1] Ri.   [2] del coni. SB[3]: pars Ro.   [3] Wi.

---

[1] As appears in what follows, the suit (lis) is brought by the
mother. Her legal adversary is the poor man (call him Father II),
who has claimed paternity of the son. The son has been ceded to
him by the natural father (Father I) at the urging of his present

338

Suit concerning the son of an exposer and a divorcée

A certain person divorced his wife, by whom he had or was thought to have a youthful son, and married another woman. There were frequent fights between stepson and stepmother. The time came when a certain poor man started to claim the youth and say he was his son. The putative father tortured the foster mother. In the first torments she said he was her master's son. Tortured again, she said he had been exposed by the claimant: and died in the process. The father gives the youth to the other man, the divorcée claims him for herself.[1]

[Concerning proem and epilogue]

DISCUSSION

The proem has its own form, its own rules, its own manner. The form of narrative is not appropriate to a proem nor is that of general topics. It is usually similar to one other part of a declamation, the epilogue: similar because both[2] are often outside the question at issue, for the proem comes before the matter and the epilogue is spoken after its termination. Furthermore, both aim at the same result, to conciliate the judge. They differ thus: the job of proems is to get the judge's attention (the epilogue is let off this part of the load, for the speaker has spoken). Sometimes an ⟨enumeration⟩ comes before the epilogue, to refresh the

wife, so the mother's advocate contends, their motive being to get rid of him. Indeed Father II's claim was engineered by Father I (s.13 and 28).

[2] *Pars* can be understood from *parti*; see crit. note.

qua[4] memoria iudicis renovetur; ita prima parte efficimus ut omnia audiat iudex, summa parte efficimus ut meminerit eorum quae audierit. Epilogus deinde inclinationem animi in se praestare debet: hoc illi cum prohoemio commune est, ⟨sed⟩[5] plus miserationis et plus libertatis habet pars summa. Nam prohoemium, cum precari debeat iudicem, fatigare non debet; nec epilogus quidem. Nam et illud verissimum est, lacrimas celerrime inarescere.

4   Prohoemia ex personis ducenda erunt, aut nostris aut adversariorum aut ipsorum interim iudicum: nostris ad conciliandum favorem, adversariorum ad odium iudici faciendum eorum contra quos dicimus; iudicum personae raro incidunt in scholasticas materias, in foro frequenter.

5   Nonnumquam etiam de rebus permittitur dicere nobis, illa ratione, quia scholastica controversia complectitur quidquid in foro fieri potest; in foro prohoemium aliquando ducitur[6] ex rebus, si iam singulae actiones praepositae[7] sint, iam causam iudex noverit. Quid ergo? Eo iure facimus istud quo illud etiam, ut narremus in isdem declamationi-

6   bus et contradictiones ponamus etiam a petitore. Quod tamen[8] in foro non secundum meum consilium fiet: is qui primo loco dicet et ponet causam contradictionem ipse non sumet, nisi si quae testationes praecesserint partis adversae et exceptae fuerint. In summa, numquam erit contradictionis loco sumendum quod adversarius dicturus fuerit sed quod dixerit.

7   Non est lis huic mulieri hodie cum marito suo; neque enim iudicium constitui potest inter eum qui cedit eam-

4 *SB*[3]: quo Aβ   5 *Aer.*
6 *Aer.*: dic- Aβ   7 D(?), *SB*[1]: prop- Aβ
8 *Sch.*: iam Aβ

judge's memory. So in the first part we make sure that the judge hears everything, in the last part that he remembers what he has heard. The epilogue further should produce a favorable inclination towards the speakers. It has this in common with the proem, ‹but› the last part has more pathos and more freedom. For the proem should plead with the judge, but not weary him—nor should the epilogue for that matter. For it is a very true saying that tears dry fast.

Proems will be derived from the personae, either ours or our adversaries'—or sometimes even the jury's—ours to win favor, our opponents' to make the judge dislike those against whom we speak. The jury's personae rarely come into academic materials, but often in the Forum. Sometimes we are allowed to speak of particulars too, on the reasoning that an academic controversy embraces whatever can be done in the Forum. In the Forum the proem is sometimes chosen from particulars if individual trials have already taken place and the judge already knows the case. What then? We do this by the same right as in the same declamations we also narrate and even produce counterarguments from the plaintiff. But that is something I do not recommend in the Forum; the opening speaker who presents the case will not himself assume a counterargument, unless testimonies of the opposite side have preceded and been received. In fine, what the adversary is going to say should never be assumed by way of a counterargument,[3] only what he has said.

The dispute today is not between this woman and her husband, nor can a trial be set up between the man who

---

[3] I.e. in order to demolish it. *Loco*, where *causa* might have been expected, seems odd.

que quae sibi adserit. Adulescens adseritur a paupere; pater[9] illi[10] cedit, mater non cedit.

8   DECLAMATIO

Etiamsi lis huic mulieri cui adsum, iudices, esset contra pauperem istum, infirmo loco pars nostra et dignior auxilio videretur, quia et per se imbecilla res est femina et adfert

9   infirmitati naturali non leve pondus quod vidua est. Huic etiam proprium illud accedit, quod in sollicitudinem[11] conversa sunt quae praesidia fuerunt. Haec enim, quamvis maritum habere desisset atque esset ea domo in quam[12] virgo nupserat pulsa, non sine auxilio tamen videri poterat,

10   cum haberet filium iuvenem. Cum vero hoc ipsum deducatur in litem et hoc tempore nihil matri praeter sollicitudinem adferat, iam[13] hoc confiteor, non eam cum ipso quem ex diversis videtis subselliis litigare: altior gratia premit. Esset quippe haec mater in lite utcumque felicior si maritus eius contentus esset filio cessisse; nunc adiecit testimonii[14] auctoritatem et infelicissimam nutricem, quam bis torsit quia verum dicebat, adversum nos mentiri[15] coegit. Cuius si vos auctoritas, iudices, movet, illud unum in prima parte causae dixisse contentus sum, vocem eius ab utraque parte recitari.

9 D: patre Aβ   10 *Ri.*: ille Aβ: *om.* D
11 *Sch.*: solit- Aβ   12 *Gron.*: qua Aβ
13 *SB*[3]: tamen Aβ   14 *Gron.*: -nio Aβ
15 *Ro.*: mori Aβ

---

4 This was before the trial.   5 As it *formally* is (s.7 and 10). "As it really is" Wi., apparently a *lapsus calami.*
6 Father II.   7 Father I, instigated by his present wife.

yields and the woman who claims. The young man is claimed by the poor man; the father yields to him, the mother does not.[4]

Even if the suit lay for the woman, my client, against that poor man,[5] gentlemen of the jury, our side would seem to be in a weak position and more deserving of help, both because a woman is a weak thing and because the fact that she has lost a husband adds no small weight to her natural infirmity. Something special accrues to this, the fact that what were her supports have been changed into anxiety. For although she no longer had a husband and had been driven from the house into which she had married as a virgin, even so she could seem to be not without help, since she had a youthful son. But since this is itself drawn into the suit and at the present time brings his mother nothing but anxiety, I confess it now, she is not in litigation with the person you see on the benches opposite,[6] a superior influence[7] loads her down. This mother would at all events be more fortunate in the suit if her husband had been content with giving up his son. As it is, he has added the weight of testimony and forced the hapless foster mother, whom he twice tortured because she was speaking the truth, to lie[8] against us. If her authority moves you, gentlemen, I am content to say just this in the first part of my case, that her words are read out by both sides.

[8] *Mori*, "to die against us," may be a startling phrase (Wi.: "to die to thwart us") but the foster mother's death was not aimed against the mother and *mentiri* is supported by its antithesis *verum dicebat*.

11   Quod si vindicare[16] filium mallet, satis eum vel sola
expositio causae tueretur. Fuit enim aliquando cupidus
liberorum, et propter hoc duxit uxorem et ad spem statim
futuri partus gratulatus est et natum educavit et in adulescentiam, quod satis est, sine ulla dubitatione perduxit.

12   Libentius in gravissima mariti iniuria, iudices, invehar in
novercam: sciit[17] enim quid vellet sibi cum in domum senis
iam et matrimonio occupatam et in qua iuvenis filius erat
irrupisset, sciit[18] hanc posse vacuari. Nolite quaerere quo
consilio, qua ratione fecerit [sola est].[19] Odia statim adversus adulescentem, nec haec occulta aut dissimulata saltem,
sed iurgia. Quod ipsum mehercule pro summa probatione
esse, iudices, potest: hunc iuvenem sic oderat tamquam

13   noverca. Nec huic libertas ex fiducia deerat, nec inveniri
poterat ullum crimen in vita quo abdicaretur. Inventum
est novum exheredandi genus: vilissimum istud caput et in
quamcumque litem pretio venale[20] testimonium adversus
se primum tulit: exposuisse se dixit, videlicet ne istum esse

14   malum patrem puderet. Testor deos, testor vestram, iudices, religionem: non satis putavit iste ipse qui expellere
filium volebat <id facere>[21] quasi aliquid sui credidisset:
infelicissimam nutricem (nam illam quoque oderat) omni

---

16 *Dingel*: -ri Aβ   17 *Wi.*: scio Aβ
18 C: se ut BD: scit A   19 *SB*4 (*cf. SB*2)
20 *Sch., Fr.*: vile Aβ   21 *SB*3

---

9 He goes on to say what it was: picking quarrels with the
youth.   10 *Sola est* makes sense in s.24, not here. Besides,
the stepmother was not alone, she had her husband, Father I.

11 With no doubt about his status and nothing to be ashamed
of, he used to speak his mind.

But if he preferred to claim his son, the mere exposition of the case would give him support enough. For he was at one time desirous of children and for that reason married a wife and congratulated her in the hope of imminent delivery and brought up the child and without any misgiving (which is enough) brought him to early manhood. The husband has done my client grievous injury, gentlemen, but I shall more willingly denounce the stepmother. She knew what she was about when she broke into an old man's house, already occupied by a marriage, in which there was a youthful son, she knew that his house could be emptied. Don't ask her plan, her method.[9] [She is alone.[10]] At once hostility to the young man, and not concealed or even dissimulated, but fights. This in itself upon my word, gentlemen, can be as good as convincing proof: she hated this young man as a stepmother. Nor did he lack the frankness that comes from confidence,[11] neither could any fault be found with his way of life for which he could be disowned. A new kind of disinheriting was discovered. This contemptible creature,[12] ready to sell his testimony in any suit, first gave evidence against himself: he said he had exposed the child, presumably to spare the other the shame of being a bad father. I call the gods to witness, I call your oath, gentlemen, to witness: this person, who himself wanted to drive out his son, thought it was not enough ⟨to do it⟩ as if he believed he had something of his own;[13] he tore the foster mother (for he hated her too) with every

[12] Father II.

[13] Information about the youth's parentage. This could have been put more plainly, and Wi. was misled ("as though he had believed him part of the family").

15   crudelitatis genere laceravit. Quaeritis qua causa? Scietis
cum iterum torquebit. Fatigaverat prima tormenta, et in
voce una manserat fides; exprobraverat isti sanguinem
suum. Revocatus est tortor, repetiti sunt cruciatus: manifestum est infelicissimae feminae factum futurum ut tam-
16   diu torqueretur quamdiu idem dixisset. Ego tamen illi non
irascor: dum aliquid virium, dum aliquid animi fuit, perseveravit; non est in mendacium coacta nisi moriens. Victor
his tormentis nihil aliud quaerendum putavit, nihil dubita-
vit. In tormentis (ut parcissime dixerim) paria nobis[22] vindico; sed rogo ut hoc velitis pertinere tantum ad istius[23]
causam.

17   Filium matri vindico contra eum qui adserere coepit
nuper. Ante omnia intellegitis, iudices, nullum onus probationis ad me pertinere. ⟨Quid? Filium esse probem⟩[24]
iuvenem de quo agitur cum hoc homine inventum per tot
annos qui ad robustam usque aetatem perducere eum [de
quo litigamus][25] potuerunt, numquam dubitatum[26]? Dicam nunc ego illa quae leviora sunt: 'nupsit et concipere
potuit'? Immo nisi concepisset non credidisset illi maritus.
18   Totum igitur onus redundat ad diversam partem. Adversarius multa probare necesse habet, habuisse se uxorem,
concepisse uxorem suam, peperisse, marem peperisse, eo
tempore quod ad aetatem eius de quo litigamus congruat
peperisse, exposuisse, vixisse expositum, ab hoc a quo

[22] tormentis . . . nobis *Sch.* (*cf. SB*[2]): -ta . . . non Aβ
[23] *SB*[2]: ipsius Aβ
[24] *SB*[3]
[25] *Sch.*
[26] *Sch.*: -atur Aβ: -atus C

kind of cruelty. You ask why? You will know when he tortures her again. He had exhausted the first torments and her honesty had held in a single saying. She had cast his own blood in his teeth. The torturer was recalled, the tortures repeated. It was made clear to the wretched woman that she would be tortured so long as she said the same thing. But I am not angry with her: so long as she had any strength, any spirit, she stuck to it, was not forced into a lie until she was dying. The victor in these torments thought there was no need for further enquiry, had no doubts. In the torments (to say the very least) I claim a draw for us. But I ask you to take this as relevant only to his[14] case.

I claim the son for his mother against the party who has recently started to assert paternity. To begin with, gentlemen, you realize that no burden of proof rests with me. ⟨Am I to prove⟩ the young man in question ⟨to be her son⟩? Found as he was with this man over so many years, years that brought him to his present vigorous age, and never doubted? Shall I now speak of lesser matters, as that she married and could conceive a child? Rather, if she had not conceived, her husband[15] would not have believed her. So the entire burden of proof recoils on the other party. My opponent must prove many things: that he had a wife, that his wife conceived, gave birth, gave birth to a male child, gave birth at a time which fits in with the age of the subject of our litigation, that he exposed him, that so exposed he lived, that he was picked up by the man[16] from whom he is

[14] Father II's; cf. SB[2].
[15] Father I.
[16] Father I.

repetit esse sublatum, aut[27] contra subiectum ab hac,
‹quae›[28] (quod praecedit) aut sterilis fuerit aut id quod

19 pepererat amisisset. Sterilem fuisse non dices: credidit
maritus. Amisisse non est satis dicere: probandum est.
Haec exigeremus in causa, iudices, si ‹esset›[29] de manci-
pio, si de pecunia: filium matri eripere conaris et partem
viscerum avellis, et contra maternos gemitus contentus es
alterius parentis neglegentia!

20 'Quid causae' inquit 'habeo? Cur adsero alienum?' Ut
nondum reddam rationem qua litiges, quod proposui[30] dicere illud est: nam si tibi causa adserendi alienum filium
non est, nec huic quidem retinendi. Quin immo facilius est
istud pauperi fingere: quid enim fortunae tuae interest an
heredem habeas? Sed reddemus postea rationem qua
fingas; interim instrumentum excutere causae tuae volo.

21 'Testimonio' inquit 'nitor eius quem tu patrem dicis.'
Putemus istius[31] esse testimonium: unus est, iratus est, alterius maritus est. 'Unus est' cum dico, succurrant vobis
Catones et Scipiones et tot clarissima civitatis nostrae nomina. Cum dico 'iratus est', succurrat vobis quidquid non

---

27 *Sch.*: et Aβ   28 *Ri., auct. Gron.*
29 *Ri.*   30 *Wi.*: -isti Aβ   31 *coni. Ri.*: istud Aβ

---

17 On this alternative theory either Father I had rescued the
exposed baby or his then wife, the present claimant, had found
and rescued the child having faked her pregnancy (impossible) or
lost her own baby (as by miscarriage). The declaimer, on the other
hand, holds that the youth was the son of Father I and his client,
and that the exposure was fiction. The theme allows this, though
the title does not.

18 In rebuttal of the mother's claim. the declaimer forgets that

reclaiming him, or, on the contrary,[17] put in by this woman, ⟨who⟩ previously was either barren or had lost her own child. You will not say that she was barren: her husband believed her. To say that she lost the child is not enough: it has to be proved. All this we should be demanding in the case, gentlemen, if ⟨it were⟩ about a slave or about money: but you are trying to snatch a son from his mother, you are plucking away part of her vitals, and against her maternal groans you are content with the negligence of the other parent.

"What motive do I have?" says he. "Why do I claim a stranger?" Even though I do not yet explain why you are going to court,[18] that is just what I proposed to say: for if you have no motive for claiming someone else's son, neither has she any for keeping him. Indeed the fabrication is easier for a poor man. For what does it matter to your estate in life whether you have an heir? But we shall explain later on why you are fabricating: meanwhile, I want to analyze the apparatus of your case.

"I rely," says he, "on the testimony of the man you say is his father." Let us suppose that it *is* his testimony: he is one man, he is angry,[19] he is the husband of another woman. When I say "he is one man," I want you to recall the Catos and Scipios[20] and so many illustrious names in our community. When I say, "he is angry," I want you to recall not only

he has already produced the motive, bribery by Father I (s.13 fin.).   [19] With his ex-wife and with his son because of the latter's behavior to his present wife (theme and s.13 init.).

[20] Cato the Censor and Scipio Africanus the elder. Even their testimony was not to be credited unless supported by other evidence: see Wi.

experimentorum in civitate sed in scaenis fabularum est,
quam multa fecerit hic adfectus, quam multos transversos
22 velut tempestate quadam egerit. Cum dico 'alterius maritus est', duo simul dico: et habet causam cur nocere huic
velit quam repudiavit et habet causam cur praestare ei ve-
23 lit quam duxit. Haec dicerem si istud testimonium esset
illius: testis tuus quid dicit? Scire se aliquid. Sequitur
ut interrogem: 'unde?' Ex nutrice illa. Nutricis ergo
testimonium est; non testis ‹est›[32] qui credit. Dimittamus
in praesentia maritum (reducemus[33] illum loco suo), de
nutrice dicamus.
24   Si ab initio mentita esset, id quod adversus hunc dicere
audeo magis auderem adversus nutricem dicere: sola est.
Nunc diversae quaestiones duae. Videamus utram verum
dixisse credibilius sit. Torta tuum esse filium dixit. Volo
adicere tormentis auctoritatem: anus torta. Una quaestio
adversus hunc sexum, adversus hanc aetatem non sufficit?
25 Deficientes[34] iam per se distendis artus lacerasque verberibus iam non cohaerentem cutem, et hoc dicis: 'mentiris'.
Tamdiu potest mentiri contra tuam voluntatem? Etiam
cum robustissimi torquentur, etiam cum animosos[35] asper-
rimus dolor temptat, plurimum tamen interest quid re-
26 sponderi sibi velit qui torquet. Durat[36] non dico contra
ignem, non dico contra flagella: contra ‹te›.[37] Hactenus

[32] *SB*[2]   [33] *Sch.*, *Gron.*: -camus Aβ
[34] *Aer.*: suffic- Aβ
[35] *Ro.*: -mus A[1]β: -mos A[2]
[36] *Wi.* (-avit *Sch.*): dura Aβ
[37] *Sch.*

---

[21] Anger. Theseus in the *Hippolytus* is an apposite example.

all we have experienced in the community but all the stories on the stage, how many are the works of this emotion,[21] how many the persons whom it has driven off course as by a hurricane. When I say "he is the husband of another woman," I say two things at once: he has a reason both for wanting to harm this one that he divorced and for wishing to help the one he married. All this I should say if that testimony were his. What does your witness say? That he knows something. It follows that I ask his source: "that foster mother." So it is the foster mother's testimony. Hearsay is not evidence. Let us dismiss the husband for the present (we shall bring him back in his place), let us speak of the foster mother.

If she had lied from the outset, what I dare to say against him I should dare all the more to say against her: she is on her own. As it is, we have two separate torturings. Let us see which is more likely to have told the truth. Under torture she said he was your son. Let me add authority to the torments: an old woman was tortured. Is not one torturing sufficient, considering the sex and age? You stretch limbs already failing by themselves and lacerate with lashes a skin already falling apart, and you say: "you're lying." Can she lie so long against your will? Even when the stoutest are tortured, even when the harshest pain assails the courageous, yet it makes a deal of difference what reply the torturer wants to get. She holds out, I won't say against fire, I won't say against stripes, but against ⟨you⟩.

But is the declaimer not off at a tangent? S.28 makes love for the present wife Father I's motive (cf. also s.22). What he says about the dramas could at least as well apply to that emotion, especially in Euripides.

veritatis inquisitio est, qua victum te sperat[38] si verum
dixerit. Cum vero repetas tormenta, cum reducas carnificem, quid aliud dicis quam illud: 'torque donec mentia-
tur'? Magna hercule tibi contigit, magna victoria: perdo-
muisti mulierem anum. Expressa vox est iam fugientis
animae: 'Miserere: non est tuus. Iam parce: verum dixi.[39]'

27 Hic iam, credo, tortor admonitus instaret perseveraretque
eamque adhiberet artem quaestioni ut moreretur mulier
dum hoc dicit, dum tu victor et hilaris adversario tuo quid
egeris nuntias. Rogo, cum mulier eadem in tormentis diversa dixerit, non est manifestum id te maluisse quod cre-
didisti?

28   Cui non mortalium patet totus hic mimus[40]? Quis non
videt artes novercales et pactum infelicis senis? Miserebor
enim; etiamsi nocet, ⟨nocet⟩[41] necessitate. Quaeritis quo
cedat animo? Quo matrem filii adulescentis domo expulit,
quo longam matrimonii concordiam nullo maledicto, nulla
suspicione dissolvit, quo in torum adhuc[42] uxoris prioris
vestigio calentem[43] adducta est nova nupta, quo ne hoc
quidem praestitit filio suo, ut vinceretur.

29   Alia est videlicet horum ratio quos brevis transitus vo-
luptatis fecit parentes, quos liberis suis extra posita[44] [vo-
luptates][45] conciliant; aliter amat[46] quae peperit,[47] quae

38 *Ro.*: -as Aβ   39 *Aer.*: dixisti Aβ
40 *Sch.*: ani- Aβ   41 *SB4*   42 *Ro.*: a. in t. A(β)
43 *Gron.*: -te Aβ   44 *Wi.*: -t(a)e Aβ
45 *Wi.*   46 *Aer.*: amant Aβ   47 *Ri.*: pepererint Aβ

---

22 Or "I told." *Dixi* is ambiguous.
23 Father II, whose claim Father I had not openly embraced
straight away. But "adversary" is bitter sarcasm.

So far, it's a search for the truth by which she hopes you are defeated if she is truthful. But when you repeat the torments, when you bring the torturer back, what else are you saying but "torture her until she lies"? You won a great, great victory, upon my word: you beat down an old woman. As her spirit fled, its voice was forced out: "Mercy! he is not yours. Spare me now: I have told the truth."[22] At this point, I believe, the torturer was admonished to press hard, not to let up, to bring such skill to his work that the woman die while she speaks, while you, joyous victor, report to your adversary[23] what you had done. I ask you, since the same woman said two different things under torture, is it not clear that you preferred[24] the one you believed?

To whom on earth is this whole charade not obvious? Who does not see stepmotherly tricks and the wretched old man's bargain? For I shall pity him, even though he hurts: <he hurts> because he must.[25] Do you ask how he felt when he yielded? Just as when he drove the young man's mother from the house, dissolved long-standing matrimonial harmony without any obloquy, any suspicion, brought a new bride into a bed still warm with the print of his former wife, did not even do so much for his son as let himself lose the case.[26]

Evidently those whom a brief passage of pleasure made parents, whom extraneous factors attach to their children, are in a different case; after another fashion loves she who has given birth, who brings to you, gentlemen, the memory

[24] An ironic euphemism for *coegisti* ("you forced") (SB[2]).
[25] His passion for his present wife drives him.
[26] He did not put up a legal fight.

227

30 memoriam decem mensum, quae tot periculorum, tot sol-
licitudinum recordationes ad vos, iudices, adfert. Numerate huius adulescentis annos, breve nimium videatur;
numerate omnes dies, singula temporum momenta: tamdiu mater testimonium dicit. Nulla potest esse tam longa
simulatio.

31 Si leges sinant permittatisque vos, se torqueri velit,[48] se
imponi ignibus, se verberibus lacerari postulet. Quid agis,
mulier? Temere facis: femina es et anus. Prima forsitan

32 tormenta sustineas: vincet dolor et ad suprema deficies. O
admirabilem, iudices, vocem! 'Torqueat' inquit 'modo:
mater sum. Aliud est nutrix et ancilla et torquente domino.' Age, cum in hac voce supremum posueris spiritum,
cui iuvenem reddituri sumus? Volesne illum ad hunc patrem reverti et ad illam novercam?

339

Rogatio Demosthenis

Rogationem fert Demosthenes ne illi qui apud Chaero-
neam capti erant a Philippo et gratis remissi consiliis publicis intersint. CD.

1 DECLAMATIO

Priusquam causas rogationis meae persequar, Athenienses, succurrit mihi laudare vos et accognoscere. Post ad-

---

[48] *Wi.*: volet Aβ

---

[27] Addressed to the mother, *ex hypothesi* dead, the question
has to be hypothetical (*velisne?*). But there is no obvious answer
and no obvious reason why the declaimer asks it. An idle flourish?

of ten months, the recollection of so many perils, so many anxieties. Count this young man's years, it might seem too short. Count all the days, the individual moments of time: for so long does his mother give her testimony. No pretence can last so long.

If the laws allowed and you permitted, she would ask to be tortured, demand that she be put on fires, lacerated with lashes. What are you doing, woman? You act rashly; you are a woman, an old woman. Perhaps you might bear the first torments, but pain will prevail and at the finish you will give up. Gentlemen, what wonderful words! "Just let him torture," she says, "I am a mother. A foster mother and a slave, and with her master torturing, that's another thing." Come, when you yield your last breath in this utterance, to whom shall we give the youth? Will you want him to go back to his father and that stepmother?[27]

339

Demosthenes' bill

Demosthenes brings in a bill barring those who were taken prisoner by Philip at Chaeronea[1] and returned free of ransom from taking part in public counsels. It is opposed.

DECLAMATION

Before I proceed with the reasons for my bill, Athenians, I am minded to praise you and give you your due. After the

One thinks of *voletisne*, addressed to the jury, but again to what purpose?

[1] Where Philip of Macedon defeated the Athenians and Thebans in 338.

versum proelium, quod quidem isti[1] qui rebus Philippi favent dolore ac[2] rumoribus in maius extollunt, non pacem petistis, non de condicionibus ullis cum hoste tractastis; ipsos etiam repetendo captivos hoc ostendistis, curam esse
2 vobis ut bellum geri posset. Id cum fecistis pro maiorum vestrorum opinione atque laude servataque usque ad hoc tempus gloria civitatis, tum etiam, ut arbitror, ratione quadam, quod nos victos non tam virtute hostis quam eorum qui pugnare noluissent timore existimabatis. Quamlibet igitur obliquis actionibus pars diversa, dum tueri mille istos captivos videtur, pacem suadeat, animum virtutemque civitatis debilitare conetur, ego loquor apud eos qui non defecerunt.
3   Sed multa me dicturum propter quae approbari possit rogatio mea oratoriis artibus impedire pars adversa conatur. Negat enim rogationem contra leges accipiendam, ne-
4 gat adversus singulos. Quorum ego utrumque confiteor. Verum neque adversus leges esse existimo quidquid pro opinione ac pro dignitate civitatis petimus[3] et cui nulla lex scripta ex contrario extat. Nam si quod est ius quo contineatur hoc, ut <tam>[4] mali et tam turpes cives utique consiliis publicis intersint, videar fortasse hanc rogationem contra leges scripsisse. Si vero nihil est quod ex contrario †coat†,[5] non potest videri hoc adversus id scriptum esse
5 quod non obstat. Illud vero aliquanto minus existimari possum, adversus singulos scripsisse legem, cum certe

[1] *SB*[1]: ipsi Aβ
[2] d. ac] damnorum *Watt*[2] (*cf. SB*[2])
[3] *Ro.*: patimur Aβ
[4] *Wi.*
[5] sit *vel* eat *coni. Wi., alii alia*

loss of the battle, which Philip's sympathizers exaggerate with distress[2] and rumor, you did not seek peace or negotiate with the enemy about any terms. Even by seeking the return of the prisoners themselves you showed your concern that there be means to wage the war. This you did both for the credit and good name of your ancestors and the glory of this community as maintained down to the present day and also, as I think, on a calculation, because you judged that our defeat was due not so much to the prowess of the enemy as to the cowardice of those who had been unwilling to fight. So however much my opponents advocate peace in disingenuous maneuvers and try to weaken the spirit and valor of the community, appearing to stand up for those thousand prisoners, I speak before those who did not fall away.

I have much to say as to why my bill could be approved, but my opponents try to hamper me with oratorical artifices. They say a bill must not be accepted in contravention of the laws nor against individuals. I admit both points. But I judge that whatever we seek on behalf of the credit and dignity of the community and to the contrary of which no written law exists is not against the laws. For if there is a statute providing that citizens <so> bad and so disgraceful take part in public counsels in all circumstances, I should perhaps be thought to have written this bill against the laws. But if there is nothing to the contrary, this cannot be seen as written against what does not stand in its way. As to the other part, much less can I be considered to have written my bill against individuals, since there are certainly a

----

[2] Show of distress to add to the general gloom (SB[2]). See crit. note.

mille sint de quibus agitur. Quamquam rationem etiam propter quam[6] non liceat rogationem contra singulos ferre illam video, quod peccata singulorum videantur habere leges suas. Homicidium fecit aliquis, sacrilegium, iniu-
6 riam, ceteraque his similia: suo iure punitur. Cum vero mille semel capiendos se alligandosque hosti praebuerint, haec, ut opinor, supersunt, ut aut nulla castigatione dignam rem qui contra dicunt putent, aut, si castiganda est,[7] ostendant legem qua castigari possit, aut, si non ostendunt, nihil aliud quam rogationem superesse fateantur.

7 Primum igitur hoc apud vos, Athenienses, dixisse contentus sum, aequissimum quidem ac iustissimum esse ut populo detur summa rerum potestas, consilium tamen non utique turba neque tumultu neque angustiis eorum qui consulantur constare. Utinam quidem fieri posset ut ex universo populo reicere ac seligere liceret eos qui parum
8 prudentes, parum digni consiliis publicis viderentur. Sed quoniam istud deprehendi nisi experimentis non potest, de his demum rogationem fero qui experti sunt. Atqui si hoc apud vos non male[8] constitutum est, esse aliquos qui consiliis publicis interesse non debeant, iam multo facilius ac pronius erit ut doceam hos esse, qui, etiamsi utiles consiliis futuri essent, indigni tamen propter dedecus proximae militiae erant.[9]

9 Ac mihi in haec dividenda videtur ratio istius orationis,

[6] *Gron.*: quod Aβ
[7] *Wi.*: sint Aβ
[8] *Obr.*: tale Aβ [9] erunt *Watt*[2]

---

[3] Unsound. One or a thousand, it makes no difference, and the objection to a *privilegium* is otherwise grounded.

thousand involved. All the same, I can see why it is not permitted to present a bill against individuals, namely that
wrongdoings by individuals are thought to have their own
laws. Someone has committed homicide, sacrilege, injury,
and the like: he is punished under his own statute.[3] But
when a thousand men have offered themselves to the enemy on a single occasion to be taken captive and tied up,
the following courses, I think, remain to my opponents:
either they think the thing does not merit punishment or, if
it is to be punished, they show a law under which it is pun-
ishable or, if they show none such, they admit that nothing
remains except the bill.

First then, Athenians, I am content to say to you that it
is eminently fair and just that ultimate power be given to
the people, but that counsel does not ultimately reside in
the multitude and noise and poverty[4] of those consulted.
Would it were possible to reject and set aside from the
whole people those who appear lacking in judgment, unworthy to take part in public counsels! But since that cannot be detected except by experiment, I present a bill concerning those and only those who have been tried out. But
if it is not unwisely established among you that there are
some who ought not to take part in public counsels, it will
be so much the easier and more straightforward for me to
show that these are such: even if they would have been of
use in our counsels, none the less they were unworthy because of the disgrace of their recent military service.

I think this speech of mine should be so divided that

---

[4] A rather awkward avoidance of the concrete "a noisy multitude of paupers."

ut pars ad ipsos de quibus loquor spectet, pars ad universam rem publicam.

10   Adversus istos hoc dixisse contentus sum: bellum
adversus Philippum suscepimus pro libertate totius
Graeciae, pro salute communi. Nam etiamsi in praesentia
amicam civitatem, nobiscum olim coniunctam, tueri vide-
bamur, eventus tamen belli ad omnes pertinebat. Et hoc
nobis, Athenienses, vetus atque a maioribus traditum est,
11   pro universa Graecia stare. Sic contra Persas semel ite-
rumque pugnavimus, ac privatis viribus defendimus publicam salutem. Iam igitur ex hoc apparet profecto vobis
numquam maiore animo, numquam concitatiore spiritu
fuisse pugnandum. Non enim nobis cum hoste ⟨ex⟩ Graecia[10] aliquo res erat, ubi, quamquam victi, leges tamen
similes linguamque certe eandem pateremur, sed cum homine barbaro, cum homine crudeli, cum homine infesto.
Quamquam quid necesse est ista diutius dicere? Pugnare
12   enim placuit et placet. In hoc igitur proelio, quod, ut dixi,
pro universa Graecia susceperamus, nondum dico quantum nocuerit istorum timor; interim cuius propositi fuerit
animum attendite. Longe felicissimum in bellis est vincere, fortissimum, si victoria non detur, pro causa mori.
Est tamen tertium aliquod inter ⟨decora positum et⟩[11]
dedecora: in patriam certe redire et, si vincere non detur,
13   effugere. Potest enim credi qui hoc fecit ad secundam[12] se
aciem reservasse et victum adversis animum reposuisse.

---

[10] ex (e *Obr.*) G. *Obr., Wi.*: -ciae Aβ: -co *Gron.*
[11] *coni. SB*3
[12] ad s. *Aer.*: s. ad Aβ

---

[5] Thebes.

part of it look to the persons themselves of whom I speak,
part to the commonwealth as a whole.

Against them I am content to say this: we went to war
against Philip for the freedom of all Greece, for the common welfare. For although at the present time we appeared to be championing a friendly community,[5] with
which we had ties of long standing, yet the result of the war
concerned everybody. And this, Athenians, is our ancient
tradition, handed down by our ancestors, to take a stand
for the whole of Greece. So once and again we fought the
Persians, defending the public welfare with our private resources. So from this it is surely already evident that you
ought to have fought with courage as great and spirit as
ardent as ever in the past. For we were not up against
some enemy <from> Greece, such that even vanquished
we should at least be under similar laws and the same
tongue; but a barbarian, cruel and hostile. But what need
to dwell on all that? It was our decision to fight and still is.
So in this battle, which as I have said, we had taken up on
behalf of the whole of Greece, I won't say yet[6] how gravely
the cowardice of these men has damaged us; meanwhile,
take note of the outlook underlying it.[7] In war to conquer is
far the happiest issue; the bravest, if victory is not granted,
is to die for our cause. There is, however, a third, interme-
diate between honor <and disgrace>, to return at least to
one's country and, if it be granted to win the day, to escape.
He that took that course can be believed to have reserved
himself for a second fight and laid up his courage, defeated
by adversity. But he that has given himself to the enemy

6 "Not that he ever does" (Wi.).

7 The decision aforesaid rather than the battle.

Ille vero qui se in servitutem[13] hosti dedit, qui abiectis[14] armis paratas[15] in vincula praebuit manus, quam tandem nobis spem[16] in posterum facit? Atque ego, Athenienses, eo tempore quo recipi istos placebat contradicturus fui nisi quod poterat honestum ex his receptis exemplum fieri. Sunt igitur digni poena aliqua, sunt ignominia, si hoc tantum ad ipsos referatur.

14

15 Sed redeo ad publicam utilitatem. Nihil esse quo magis disciplina militaris confirmari possit, Athenienses, quam exemplum adversus indignos[17] nemo dubitabit. Quae enim spes in bellis in milite nostro residua est si nihil[18] potius fuerit quam capi? Certum habeo nunc istos male sentire de iis qui in acie ceciderunt.

340

Novicius praetextatus

Qui voluntate domini in libertate fuerit, liber sit. Mango novicium puerum per publicanos traiecit praetextatum. Dicitur ille liber.

1 DECLAMATIO

'Qui voluntate domini in libertate fuerit, liber sit.' Quaerendum est nobis quid sit in libertate esse. *[1] 'voluntate domini est in libertate qui eo[2] volente liber est.' Nos finimus ita: 'voluntate domini in libertate est qui ius libertatis usur-

---

[13] in s. *Obr.*: inter virtutem Aβ
[14] *Pith.*: ab istis Aβ
[15] *Sch.*: -ta Aβ
[16] spem ⟨sui⟩ *coni. SB*[3]
[17] *Aer.*: d- Aβ [18] si n.] nisi nihil ⟨non⟩ *SB*[1]
[1] *lac. ind. Aer.*   [2] qui eo *Aer.*: quo Aβ

into slavery and thrown down his arms and offered his hands to be tied, what hope of him does he give us for the future? I myself, Athenians, at the time when you decided to take them back would have opposed it except that a good example might be made from their reception. So they deserve some punishment, deserve stigma, if this were related only to themselves.

But I return to the public interest. Nobody will doubt, Athenians, that there is nothing which can strengthen military discipline more than an example against the unworthy. For what hope in our soldiers is left in war if no choice is better than to be taken prisoner?[8] I am sure that they now resent the men who fell in battle.[9]

340

The new-come slave in a praetexta

Whoso shall be at liberty by will of his master, let him be free. A slave-dealer passed a newly-arrived slave through the customs[1] wearing a praetexta.[2] He is said to be free.

DECLAMATION

"Whoso shall be at liberty by will of his master, let him be free." We must ask what is meant by being at liberty. * "He is at liberty by will of his master who is free his master so willing." We define as follows: "he is free by will of his master who has used the status of liberty his master so willing."

---

[8] See crit. note.   [9] A tangential hit at the prisoners?

[1] Lit "tax farmers" (*publicani*), who bought from the state the right to collect excise.   [2] A toga with purple border worn by boys of free birth (also by magistrates and priests).

pavit domino volente.' Id primum scripto ipso colligemus.
Non enim difficile fuit ei qui hanc legem componebat id
scribere: 'qui voluntate domini liber fuerit[3]'; nunc hoc scri-
bendo: 'qui in libertate fuerit', satis ostendit aliud esse in

2 libertate esse, aliud liberum esse. Excutiamus etiam causas legis huius. Indignum putavit legum lator eum qui in
parte[4] aliqua rei publicae, qui in numero civitatis fuisset,
redigere in servitutem. Sed hoc quoniam sibi nequitia interim adserebat, adiecit ut ii liberi essent qui in libertate

3 voluntate domini fuissent. Vis scire quanto aliud sit in libertate esse, aliud liberum esse? Eum qui in libertate fuerit iubet lex liberum esse. Tanta rerum differentia est in

4 causa libertatis. In libertate est igitur quisquis caret forma
servitutis. Id, iudices, ex hac ipsa lege adhuc manifestum
est. Non enim legum lator putavit etiam eos qui a dominis
fuga abessent esse in libertate? Quod colligo scripto eius:
'qui voluntate domini in libertate fuerit': apparet aliquos et
non voluntate domini in libertate esse; quod si verum est,
potest in libertate esse etiam qui liber non est.

5 Nihil ergo prodest tibi cum dicis liberum eum non
fuisse. Non enim quaeritur an voluntate tua liber fuerit,
sed an voluntate tua in libertate fuerit. Si voluntate tua li-

6 ber [non][5] fuisset, quid nos postularemus? Depulsus hac
pugna transcendit eo, ut neget in libertate[6] saltem fuisse.
[Quomodo igitur colligemus?][7] Eum qui in libertate est

[3] *Ri.*: fuit Aβ
[4] *SB*[1]: fortuna Aβ
[5] *Gron.*
[6] in l. *Ri.* (in l. tunc *Gron.*): liberum tunc Aβ
[7] *SB*[3]

We shall first infer this from the text itself. For it would not have been difficult for the composer of this law to have written thus: "Whoso by will of his master shall be free." As it is, by writing "Whoso shall be at liberty" he has sufficiently shown that it is one thing to be at liberty and another to be free. Let us also shake out the reasons for this law. The lawmaker thought it improper to bring back into slavery one who had been in some degree part of the commonwealth, in the number of the community. But since villainy used sometimes to claim this for itself, he added that they were free who had been at liberty by will of their master. Would you like to know how great is the difference between being at liberty and being free? The law orders that he who has been at liberty shall be free.[3] So great is the factual difference in a freedom case. So whoever lacks the form of slavery is at liberty. That, gentlemen, is additionally clear from this very law. For did not the lawmaker think that even those who had run away from their masters were at liberty? I infer that from his text: "Whoso shall be at liberty by will of his master." It is apparent that some also are at liberty not by will of their master. If that is true, even one who is not free can be at liberty.

So it does you no good to say that he was not free. For the question is not whether he was free by your will but whether he was at liberty by your will. If he had been free by your will, why should we claim him? Dislodged from this contention, he shifts to denying that the boy was even at liberty. By what arguments shall we infer that he who is

---

[3] If to be at liberty *was* to be free, there would have been no need for the law. The order was in fact qualified ("by will of the master").

quibus argumentis colligemus esse in libertate? Signavit aliquis tamquam liber: si id voluntate domini fecerit, etiamsi maxime illum servum esse dominus voluit eo tempore, manifestum erit ⟨fuisse⟩[8] in libertate; sic[9] quisquis aliquid pro libero fecit.[10] Atqui hic puer non tantum pro libero sed etiam pro ingenuo est: praetextatus fuit. Si talem illum ad iudices produxissem,[11] hoc insigne non [tantum][12] libertatis modo sed etiam dignitatis esset. Ecquid[13] paves ne scelus feceris? Et alius fortasse tantum usurpaverit libertatem: hic et approbavit. Quibus? Publicanis, hominibus, ut parcissime dicam, diligentissimis. In summa velim ostendere totum tuum comitatum: quis habitus servorum fuit?

8   'Ego tamen' inquit 'non ea voluntate feci ut hic liber esset, sed ea ut publica non solveret.[14]' Saepius eadem dicenda sunt (etiam gratulamur si invito te liber est): liberum esse noluisti, sed in libertate esse voluisti. Nihil interest qua causa hoc feceris: id est, ut propius ad verba legis accedam, nihil interest qua causa in libertate esse eum volueris.

9   Verum ista causa quam praetendis digna poena est: circumscribere vectigalia populi Romani voluisti, specie praetextati imponere publicano voluisti. Postmodum dicam quantum intersit huius pueri; interim dicam, tua quid interest? Quod petieras non contigit tibi? Non fefellisti?

---

[8] *hic Ri., post* libertate *Aer.*
[9] *Aer.*: sit Aβ
[10] *Ri.*: facit Aβ
[11] *Wi.*: perdux- Aβ
[12] *Sch.*
[13] *Ro.*: equidem Aβ
[14] solverem *coni. SB*[1]

at liberty is at liberty? Someone has set his seal as though a free man: if he did this by will of his master, for all the master wanted him to be a slave at that time, it will be clear that ⟨he was⟩ at liberty; the same applies to whoever has done something as a free man. And yet this boy is not only quasi-free but quasi-freeborn: he wore a praetexta. If I had brought him before the jury so garbed, this would be a symbol not only of freedom but of status too. Are you not afraid you have committed a crime?[4] And another perhaps merely used liberty, *he* also had it approved. By whom? By the customs, most meticulous persons, to say the very least.[5] In fine, I should like to show your whole retinue: how were the slaves dressed?

"But I did not do it," he says, "wishing him to be free but to avoid paying the tax." I have to keep on repeating it (we even congratulate him if he is free against your will): you did not want him to be free but you wanted him to be at liberty. It makes no difference why you did it; that is to say, to come closer to the words of the law, it makes no difference why you wanted him to be at liberty. And yet that reason you put forward deserves punishment. You wanted to defraud the revenue of the Roman people, you wanted to cheat the customs officer by the appearance of a boy in a praetexta. I'll say later what difference it makes to this boy: meanwhile, I'll say: "What difference does it make to you? Did you not get what you were after? Did you not get away with it?"

[4] By claiming him as a slave.

[5] Not at all likely to forego their dues. *Diligens* sometimes connotes penny-pinching.

10   SERMO

Haec circa ius, illa iam circa aequitatem.

11   DECLAMATIO

Quae passurus est hic puer domino redditus? Sine dubio
‹novissima›.[15] Novimus istam negotiationem, et frequen-
tissima in foro videmus iudicia talium iniuriarum. Fortasse
etiam natus est ingenuus, fortasse rapto ex aliquo litore
praetextam Fortuna reddidit. Illud est tamen quod nos
magis confundat: videtur mangoni puer pretiosus, timuit
12 ne magno aestimaretur. Ista species in quacumque servi-
tute miserabilis foret. Rogamus vos, iudices, cogitetis[16]
quam multa facere possit adversus puerum mango iratus.
Aut illi fortasse pretium excisa virilitate producet, aut ob
†infelicis†[17] contumeliae annos venibit in aliquod lupanar.
Res est nobis cum homine qui non erubescit, nihil reser-
13 vat: etiam periculose avarus est. Quos cultus accipiet qui
praetextam habuit? Ego vobis allego etiam ipsum illud
sacrum praetextarum quo sacerdotes velantur, quo magistratus, quo infirmitatem pueritiae sacram facimus ac vene-
rabilem.

341

Res furtiva improfessa apud publicanos

Quod quis per publicanos improfessum transtulerit, commissum sit. Quidam rem furtivam transtulit per publica-

---

  [15] *Walter*
  [16] iudices (*Fr.*) c. *Ro.*: iudicetis Aβ
  [17] faciles *Opitz, alii alia*

This about law, the following now about equity.

What will happen to this boy if he is returned to his master? Doubtless ⟨the worst⟩. We know this business of yours, we see trials for this kind of injury in the Forum all the time. Perhaps he was actually born free, perhaps Fortune gave him back the praetexta after he had been snatched from some shore. But there's something that upsets me more: the slave-dealer thinks the boy valuable, was afraid that he would be assessed[6] at a high figure. Such looks would be pitiable in any sort of slavery. We ask you, gentlemen, to think how many things an angry slave-dealer can do to a boy. Either perhaps he will stretch[7] his price by cutting out his virility or because of his years, open as they are to abuse, he will be sold into some brothel. We are dealing with a man who doesn't blush, who stops at nothing; he is greedy even to the point of danger. What sort of dress will he get—he that had a praetexta? In my support I also bring you the very holiness of the gown: priests and magistrates are clothed in it, by it we make the weakness of boyhood sacred and revered.

341

A stolen article not declared with the customs

Let what somebody has passed through the customs undeclared be confiscated. A man passed a stolen article

---

[6] By the customs.   [7] "Make it last longer" (Wi.). Rather "heighten" ("boost"); see *TLL* X.1628.12.

nos, non professus est. Deprehensa res est. Publicani cum
domino contendunt. Illi tamquam commissam rem vindicant, ille tamquam suam.

1   DECLAMATIO

Rem non professam apud nos tenemus. Hoc ius quale sit
postea videbimus. Quod quis professus non est apud publicanos, pro commisso tenetur. Ea res de qua iudicatis in
professionem non venit. Omni iure condictionis nostra est.

2   'Mea est' inquit. Nihil istud contra ius nostrum est; alioqui
nemo non hoc de re non professa dicere possit: 'mea est.'
'At[1] is qui transtulit alienam rem transtulit.' Ante omnia,
nulla lege comprehensum est ut alienam rem non profiteri
liceret; alioqui publicum eversum est. ⟨Si⟩[2] leges permu-
tandae sunt ut transferantur aliena ⟨improfessa⟩,[2] tamen[3]

3   furtum profiteri debuit. 'At inicum est meam poenam esse
cum ille peccaverit.' Iterum dicam: si quid iniqui habet lex
nostra, postea viderimus; interim, lex est. Non adversus

4   homines sed adversus rem scripta est. Si ius accepissemus
aliquid[4] ab eo qui non ⟨professam rem⟩[5] transtulisset exi-
gendi, sic quoque sine dubio esset nostra causa melior, sed
tamen videretur ⟨non⟩[6] de re ipsa esse contentio. Nunc lex
hoc continet, ut rem teneamus quae translata est et professa non est. Quid interest quis professus non sit? Nobis res
dedita est.

   [1] *Wi.*: et A*β*: sed *Ri.*   [2] *SB*[1] (*cf. SB*[2])
   [3] *Sch.*: an A*β*
   [4] *Gron.*: -quod A*β*: ⟨aliud⟩ aliquid *coni. SB*[3]
   [5] *Ro., Ri.*   [6] *Ro.*

   [1] The usual "meanwhile" (*interim*) should have followed; cf.
e.g. s.3.   [2] Or "something ⟨else⟩"; see crit. note.

through the customs, did not declare it. The article was discovered. The customs officers are at law with the owner. They claim the object as confiscated, he as his property.

DECLAMATION

We hold possession of an article that has not been declared with us. We will see about the nature of this right later on.[1] What has not been declared with the customs officers is held as confiscated. The article as to which you are passing judgment was not put in declaration. By every legal right of claim it belongs to us. He says: "It's mine." That counts for nothing against our right; otherwise everybody could say about an undeclared object: "It's mine." "But the person who passed it through passed through somebody else's property." To begin with, no law provides that it is permitted not to declare somebody else's property; otherwise the public interest goes by the board. <If> the laws should be changed to allow passage of other people's property <undeclared>, still he ought to have declared a *stolen* article. "But it is unfair that I should be punished when he has done wrong." Again I say: if our law is in some way unfair, we shall see about that later; meanwhile, it is the law. It was written not with respect to persons but with respect to property. If we had been given a law empowering us to take something[2] from a person who had passed an <object> not <declared>, even so our case would undoubtedly be the stronger, but still the dispute would <not> appear to be about the object itself. As it is, the law lays down that we keep an object that has been passed through and has not been declared. What difference does it make who has not declared it? The article has been surrendered to us.

5   Haec de iure. 'Sed ius ipsum iniquum est.' Alio me vocas, de alio quereris. Dic istud rei publicae, dic senatui, dic magistratui: 'aerarium populi Romani vectigalibus iniquis repletur, et spoliantur provinciae et sublatum com-

6 mercium est.' Nos conduximus id quod locabatur. Sed res publica quoque, cum qua queri poteris, habet quod respondeat. Primum illud, necessaria esse vectigalia civitati. Exercitus stipendium accipiunt, bella cotidie geruntur adversus barbaras et bellicosissimas gentes, defendimus ripas et limites[7] et litora. Huc adice et illud: templa extruuntur, multum impendiorum sacra ducunt, aliquid et[8]

7 spectacula. Opus est vectigalibus. Inter vectigalia porro quid aequius inveniri potest et sine maiore hominum querela? Quanto illud iniustius videri potest quod[9] partem hereditatis sibi vindicat! 'At plurimum in hoc vectigal confert

8 negotiatio.' Quidquid est, de futuro lucro est, praeter id quod non potest videri iniquum ad quod acceditur. Et vectigal quidem ipsum necessarium, non iniquum: num haec iniusta poena est, in qua furta deprehenduntur, qua lex vindicatur, qua fraus transferentium detegitur? Aliter stare vectigal non potest.

9   Eodem revertimur iterum: hac ratione res publica locat, hac necessitate nos conduximus et pretio vicimus. Et adversus quales homines conduximus? Quamvis poena sit, quamvis in commissum veniant ea quae quis professus non

---

7 *SB*[3]: flumina Aβ   8 *Sch*.: ad Aβ
9 *Ranc*.: quo Aβ

---

3 Under which customs duties are levied.
4 And so are not concerned with wider issues.

So much as to the law. "But the law itself[3] is unfair." You are changing the ground, making a different complaint. Tell that to the commonwealth, tell it to the magistrate: "The treasury of the Roman people is being filled with unjust revenues and the provinces are being despoiled and commerce abolished." We bought the contract.[4] But the commonwealth too, to whom you will be able to address your complaint, has an answer: first, that a community must have revenues. The armies get their pay, wars are waged every day against barbarous and very warlike peoples, we defend riverbanks and boundaries and coasts. Add this too: temples are a-building, religious ceremonies draw large outlays, likewise shows cost money. Revenues are needed. And among them what fairer can be found, what causes less public complaint? How much more unjust it may appear that the commonwealth claims part of an inheritance! "But business contributes a lot to this tax." Whatever that is, it's about profit in the future,[5] besides that nothing that is voluntarily incurred[6] can be thought unfair. And the excise itself is necessary, not unfair. Is this penalty[7] unjust, by which thefts are caught, by which the law is vindicated, the fraud of those who pass items through detected? Otherwise the revenue can't hold.

I again return to the same point. The commonwealth farms out under this system, we made our contract with this requirement and our bid won. And in respect of what sort of people did we make the contract? Though there is a penalty, though articles that are not declared get confis-

---

[5] What businessmen pay in tax they expect to get back in profits.   [6] Lit. "is approached." People take things through the customs knowing what to expect.   [7] Confiscation.

est, tamen fallere nos volunt, tamen mille artibus circumscribimur. Quotaquaeque res est quae deprehendatur!

10 Poteramus tibi etiam imputare beneficium: istud quod tibi extorqueri quereris non apud nos perdidisti; interim, quod satis est, furem apud nos invenisti. Ignorares, nisi nos fuissemus, translata in aliam provinciam furta, inter ignotos homines, inter alienos.

11 In summa parte, quia[10] lex secundum nos est, aequitas secundum nos est, illud quoque dicendum puto, qua sententia possitis parti utrique consulere. Quid est aequius quam utrumque vindicari? Unus furtum fecit duobus; habet suam quisque legem. Nos nisi retinemus, nulla actione vindicari possumus; ille, etiamsi non ipsam rem acceperit, pro re tamen accipere poterit: habet actionem quidem de illa. Nam et in quadruplum litigatur.[11] Non irascitur furi

12 qui re contentus est. Adversus iniuriam[12] illius privata agi actione potest, a nobis ‹non nisi›[13] publica. Ille vobis commendat sarcinas suas; nos commendamus vectigalia vestra, commendamus reditus civitatis.

342

Ancilla in archipiratae nuptias missa

Qui voluntate domini in libertate fuerit, liber sit. Qui habebat patrem et sororem captus est a piratis. Scripserunt piratae patri ut mitteret vicariam filiam, futuram archi-

---

[10] *Gron.*: qua Aβ [11] *SB*[3]: -at Aβ
[12] *Ri.*: invidiam Aβ [13] *SB*[3] (tantum *SB*[1])

---

[8] The article.

[9] "The thief" (*furi*) might be better omitted. The owner's

cated, they still are out to defraud us, we are still cheated by a thousand tricks. How rare are the articles that are caught!

We could even say we have done you a favor. You did not lose what you complain you were robbed of with us; meanwhile, and it's enough, you found the thief with us. But for us you would be ignorant of a theft transferred to another province, among men unknown, strangers.

In conclusion, since the law is in our favor and equity is in our favor, I think I must also say what verdict you could give to be fair to both parties. What is fairer than that both be given satisfaction? One individual stole from two; each has his law. If we do not keep,[8] we cannot be satisfied by any legal action; whereas he can be paid in lieu of the article even though he does not get the article itself; he has an action about it, there is litigation for payment in quadruple. A man content with the substance is not angry with the thief.[9] There can be a private action against his injury, on our side <only> public. He commends his baggage to you, we commend your revenues, the returns of the community.

342

Slave girl sent to wed a pirate chief

Whoso shall be at liberty by will of his master, let him be free. A man who had a father and a sister was captured by pirates. The pirates wrote to his father to send his daughter as a substitute, to be the wife of the pirate chief. He sent a

anger would rather be with the customs officers who kept his property.

piratae uxorem. Misit ille matronali habitu ancillam. Remissus est adulescens. Illa, ab archipirata heres omnium bonorum relicta, rediit in civitatem. Ducitur[1] ancilla.

1

SERMO

Similes quaestiones sunt priori divisioni, eadem finitio. Dicit enim is qui petit in servitutem eum esse in libertate domini voluntate quem liberum esse dominus voluerit. Nostra pars dicit in libertate esse domini voluntate eos qui aliquid pro liberis ex voluntate domini fecerunt. Refellenda[2] est nobis finitio partis adversae, deinde nostra confirmanda. Finis partis adversae sic refelletur.[3]

2

DECLAMATIO

'Qui voluntate domini in libertate fuerit, liber sit.' Si de iis loqueretur lex quos dominus manumisisset et liberos esse voluisset, supervacuum erat. Nam etiam hac lege sublata non dubitabitur[4] quin manumissi liberi essent. Praeterea aliud esse in libertate esse, aliud liberum esse, etiam ex eo manifestum est quod eos qui in libertate fuerint liberos esse lex iubet. Ad quos ergo lex pertinet? Ut ad nostram finitionem redeamus: qui volentibus dominis fecerint aliqua tamquam liberi. Ut puta, signavit aliquid volente domino servus: liberum esse vult. Inicum enim erit tabulas auferri, et circumscriptum esse nescio quem cui signatae

---

[1] *SB*[3]: dic- Aβ   [2] *Ri., auct. Gron.*: repell- Aβ
[3] *Gron.*: repell- Aβ   [4] *SB*[4]: -batur Aβ

---

[1] Throughout this piece *matrona* has the wider meaning, mainly post-classical, of an upper-class woman, a lady. Obviously the daughter was not married.   [2] Referring to 340.

[3] See crit, note.   [4] I understand *auferri* in its normal

slave girl dressed as a lady.[1] The young man was returned.
She was left heir to all his possessions by the pirate chief
and returned to the community. The slave girl is taken to
court.

DISCUSSION

The questions are similar to the earlier division,[2] the
definitions the same. The party who claims into slavery
says that he is at liberty by will of his master whom his master wished to be free. Our side says that they who have
done something as though free men at the will of their
master are at liberty by will of their master. We have to re-
fute the other side's definition, then to confirm our own.
The other side's definition will be refuted thus:

DECLAMATION

"Whoso shall be at liberty by will of his master, let him be
free." If the law were speaking of persons whom their master had manumitted and wished to be free, it would have
been superfluous. For even with that law abolished there
will be[3] no doubt that persons manumitted would be free.
Furthermore, that to be at liberty is one thing, to be free
another, is clear also because the law requires that persons
who have been at liberty be free. To whom then does the
law relate? To return to our definition: to those who at their
master's will have done some things as free men. For example, a slave has sealed something, his master so willing: the
law requires him to be free. For it will be unfair for the tablets to be taken away[4] and he, whoever he is, for whom they

sense. "The persons for whom they were sealed" would take them
away without suspecting that they might be invalid. "Annulled"
(Wi.) would fit, but lacks parallel (300.5 is none).

sunt tabulae. Iudex inter duos convenerit et sententiam
tulerit volente domino: liberum esse hunc voluit, ut ea res
4 quae iudicata erat haberet suum finem. Denique neminem qui in aliqua forma libertatis fuisset, nisi fraude et culpa sua, redire in servitutem voluit. In libertate autem putavit esse legum lator etiam eos qui non voluntate domini in
libertate essent, sicut eos qui absentibus dominis aliqua
pro liberis egissent, et ideo adiectum est in lege: 'qui voluntate domini in libertate fuerit.' Ergo etiam invito domino potest aliquis esse in libertate, invito autem non potest
esse liber. Aliud est in libertate esse, aliud liberum esse.

5   Hanc igitur de qua quaeritur dico voluntate tua fuisse
in libertate. Hoc quo modo probo? Quo uno probari potest: fecit aliquid tamquam libera. Nondum dico 'ad piratas pervenit', dissimulo et illud, qua causa volueris eam in
libertate esse; interim et volente[5] te et spectante habitu
6 matronae fuit. Hoc satis erat, etiamsi postea nulla essent
consecuta. An vero maius in hoc putamus esse momentum, ut circumverteres mancipium aut si una voce liberum
esse iusseris quam si habitum dederis, stolam dederis?—
quod ne manumissis quidem omnibus contigit.

7   (Hoc loco poni solet illud.)

'Num igitur, si in scaenam misero et mimi partibus tamquam matrona processerit, poterit videri mea voluntate in
libertate esse?' Non est hoc[6] porro simile; nam ipsa statim
scaena rem fictam esse testatur. Stola illa mimi erit, non

---

[5] *Ro.*: vide- Aβ [6] hoc ‹idem, non› *Watt*[2]

---

[5] The law.
[6] As often, *invitus = praeter voluntatem*, consent not given.
[7] Done in a manumission.

were sealed to have been cheated. Suppose he was taken as arbiter between two persons and gave judgment, his master so willing: it[5] wished him to be free, so that the matter which had been judged should have a conclusion. In fine, it wished that nobody who had been in some shape of liberty should revert to slavery except by his own misdoing and fault. The lawmaker thought that even persons who had been at liberty *not* by will of their master, such as those who had done something as free men in the absence of their masters on behalf of the children, were at liberty and for that reason "whoso shall be at liberty by will of his master" was added to the law. Therefore a man can be at liberty without[6] his master's will, but without his master's will he cannot be free. It is one thing to be at liberty, another to be free.

So I say that the woman in question was at liberty by our will. How do I prove it? By the only way it can be proven: she did something as though she was free. I don't yet say "she went to the pirates," I say nothing either about why you wanted her to be at liberty; meanwhile, she was dressed as a lady with you so willing and looking on. That was enough even if nothing had followed later. Or do we think that your turning a slave around[7] or telling her in a simple utterance to be free counts for more than your giving her the get-up, giving her the robe—which does not happen even to all who are manumitted.

(At this point the following is usually placed:)

"Well then, if I put her on the stage and she comes forward as a woman of standing in a mime role, can she be thought to be at liberty by my will?" Now this is not similar; for the stage itself witnesses at once that this is a fictitious situation. That robe will belong to the mime, not the hu-

hominis. At eadem si hoc habitu extra scaenam fuerit et in civitate processerit, eadem illa quae solet mima esse nihilominus erit in iure libertatis. Ergo habitu satis testata est

8 libertatem. Quid si fecit aliqua tamquam libera? Profecta est, parum est dicere quasi ingenua: quasi honesta, quasi filia tua.

9 'Sed haec omnia' inquit 'feci non ideo quoniam eam in libertate esse volebam.' Lex non ad causam nos voluntatis tuae mittit sed ad ipsam. In libertate esse voluisti; quare volueris nihil ad iudicem, nihil ad voluntatem pertinet. ⟦Tu tamen illam in libertate esse noluisti? Ut parcissime

10 dicam, maligne.⟧[7] Quid si credibile est hanc etiam voluntatem tuam fuisse, ut illa libera[8] sit? Quid enim esse illam voluisti? Ancillam? Cuius? Num dubium est quin hoc votum tuum fuerit, ut matronam approbaret, ut filiam tuam approbaret? Noluisti eam in libertate esse de qua nihil magis timebas quam ne illa tibi tamquam ancilla remitteretur? Quamquam etiamsi remissa esset, iam tamen tua voluntate in libertate fuisset.

11 Sed processit ultra. Dicebam: 'habitum matronae te volente sumpsit, iter tamquam matrona ingressa est.' Te volente ad piratas tamquam filia venit tua, te volente approbavit se liberam et ingenuam, te etiam volente in matrimonio fuit tamquam libera, heres relicta est tamquam libera. Horum omnium ius a tua voluntate profectum sit necesse est, qui voluisti dimittere, qui voluisti tam-

---

[7] *ita secl. SB*[3]
[8] *Ri.*: in libertate Aβ

---

[8] The slave girl.

man being. But if the same woman is in this dress and comes out in the community, that same woman who is usually an actress will none the less be in the status of liberty. So by her dress she[8] has sufficiently borne witness to her liberty. What if she did something as a free woman? She set out—it is not enough to say as a free woman, but as a respectable lady, as your daughter.

"But," he says, "I did not do all this because I wanted her to be at liberty." The law does not send us to the reason for your willing but to the willing itself. You wished her to be at liberty; why you wished it does not concern the judge nor yet your willing. [[All the same, did you wish her not to be at liberty? That was nasty of you, to say the least.]][9] What if it is credible that it was actually your wish that she be free? For what did you want her to be? A slave woman? Whose? Is there any doubt that your prayer was that she pass as a lady, as your daughter? Did you not wish her to be at liberty when you feared nothing more than that she might be sent back to you as a slave? And yet, even if she had been sent back, she would already have been at liberty by your will.

But she went further. I was saying:[10] "She put on the dress of a lady, you so willing; she started her journey as a lady." With you willing she went to the pirates as your daughter, with you so willing she passed herself off as free and freeborn, with you likewise so willing she lived in marriage as freeborn, she was left as heiress as free. In all these situations the status must have arisen from your will, for you wanted to send her away, you wanted to send her away

[9] Surely an accretion, interrupting sequence.
[10] S.5 fin.

12   quam liberam dimittere. Haec dicerem etiamsi piratae
tantum vicariam petissent; nunc vero, cum adiecerint ut
eam vicariam mitteres quae in matrimonio archipiratae
esset, dubitari non potest quin tu eam miseris tamquam
liberam futuram.

13   Haec quod ad ius, illa quod ad merita. Digna est quae
sit libera: filium tibi restituit. Si tantum filii tui pretium
fuisset, videretur tamen bene meruisse; nunc quam multa
addidit ad fidem! Poterat et remanere apud piratas et obli-
gare illos hoc indicii sui beneficio. Sed non confessione
tantum effectum est ut filia tua videretur: quemadmodum
complexa est illa catenatum, quotiens fratrem vocavit,
quam veras lacrimas profudit! Optime meruerat de te et
hoc ipso, quod reversa est.

14   SERMO

Hic parce quidem stringendus erit pudor patris, stringendus erit tamen, tamquam cupidi et avari et hereditatem
istam adfectantis: hoc ideo non amare nec destricte[9] primum quod potest esse hic dominus illius, si ita iudicibus
videbitur, deinde quod nobis res cum eo est cui gratias agimus, cuius voluntate dicimus nos in libertate fuisse.

15   In summa parte declamationis[10] advocamus etiam adulescentem illum [quasi advocatum][11] qui nostro beneficio
redemptus est.

[9] *SB*[4] (*cf. TLL* V.1.772.13): dis- Aβ
[10] *Aer.*: advocat- Aβ
[11] *Wi.*

as a free woman. I should be saying all this even if the pirates had merely asked for her as a substitute; but as it is, they added that you should send a substitute to marry the pirate chief, so it cannot be doubted that you sent her as a woman who would in future be free.

So much as to the law, now as to deserts. She is worthy to be free: she gave you back your son. If she had only been the price of your son, she would still be thought to have deserved well. As it is, how much she added to make her story believed! She could have stayed with the pirates and obliged them by the favor of telling them the truth.[11] But it was not only by her acknowledgment that she was taken to be your daughter: how she embraced the chained captive, how often called him brother, how genuine were the tears she shed! She had deserved very well of you by the very fact that she returned.[12]

DISCUSSION

Here the honor of the father must be touched, sparingly to be sure, but touched all the same as a covetous, greedy man out for that inheritance; not bitterly though or with the knife out, first because he can be her master if the jury so decide, second because we are dealing with somebody we thank, by whose will we say we were at liberty.

In the final part of the declamation we call in the young man too, who was returned thanks to us.

[11] Before the captive was released. After that the pirates would not have been obliged. But *poterat . . . beneficio* would be better away or placed after *reversa . . . est* below (see Wi.).

[12] See s.16.

16   ‹DECLAMATIO›[12]

Promittit praeterea ista quae in hereditate relicta sunt illius esse. Quam causam revertendi habuit aliam? Licuit
illi, ignorante eo, in aliqua civitate subsistere.

343

Circumscriptor pauperis, divitis raptoris socer

Circumscriptionis sit actio. Pauper et dives eandem puell-
lam petebant in matrimonium. Capta est illa quae pete-
batur. Posuit condicionem petitoribus pater, eius esset qui
redemisset. Pauper profectus est et redemit virginem. Rapuit illam competitor dives. Educta ad magistratus nuptias
optavit. Circumscriptionis accusatur pater a paupere.

1   SERMO

Non tantum nobis in hoc laborandum est, ut circumscriptus sit adulescens, quantum in illo, ut circumscriptus sit a
patre. Esse enim iustam querelam eius qui redemit et reduxit, cum praesertim sub pacto redemerit, manifestum
2 est. Eximitur ex parte diversa rei persona: 'quod factum est
ne duceret ille, non pater fecit: rapuit dives, optavit puella,
pater tantum promisit.' Quomodo ergo fiet ut hic circum-
scripserit? Si probat omnia facta huius voluntate. Alioqui,
nisi hoc optinemus, frustra plorabimus apud iudices.

---

[12] *Ro., auct. Pith.*

---

[13] Why did she? Out of sheer probity, it seems.
[1] The prosecutor.

‹DECLAMATION›

She further guarantees that the property left in the inheritance is his.[13] What other reason did she have for coming back? It was open to her to live in some community or other without his knowledge.

343

Swindler of a poor man, father-in-law of a rich rapist

DECLAMATION

Let there be an action for swindling. A poor man and a rich man were courting the same girl. She they were courting was taken captive. The father made a stipulation to the suitors, that she would go to the one who redeemed her. The poor man set out and redeemed the virgin. His rich rival raped her. Brought before the magistrates, she opted for marriage. The father is accused of swindling by the poor man.

DISCUSSION

We do not have to be concerned so much to prove that the young man has been swindled as to prove that he has been swindled by the father. For it is clear that he who redeemed and brought her home, especially as he did so under a covenant, has a legitimate complaint. From the other side the persona of the defendant is eliminated: "That he did not marry her was not the father's doing: the rich man raped, the girl opted, the father only promised." How then shall it be established that he was the swindler? If he[1] proves that everything was done by his will. Otherwise, if this is not granted us, we shall whine to the jury in vain.

3

DECLAMATIO

Circumscriptum esse me probare prius volo quam ab isto circumscriptum. Pactus sum. Hoc pactum non servatur, nec potest repeti: pecuniam impendi sub pacto; neque pecuniam repetere possum neque id propter quod impendi habeo. Navigavi, laboravi (sic interim loquor) quoniam promittebatur aliquid; hoc quod promissum erat praestari non potest: curcumscriptio est.

4   Hactenus causa fundamenta cepit[1]; sequentia illa sunt, ut probem me et ab hoc circumscriptum esse et indignissime circumscriptum. Animadvertitis, iudices, fiduciam circumscriptoris: 'alius rapuit, alia optavit': ideo circumscriptio est. Neque enim umquam decurritur ad hanc legem nisi cum rectum ius nequitia exclusum est. Si non
5 alius rapuisset, ex pacto reprehenderem. Sed nihil haec cavillatio proderit tibi, qua crimen in generum et in filiam transfers. Nam si apparuerit iudicibus omnia te volente facta esse qui promisisti, manifestum erit a te esse circumscriptum eum qui tibi credidit.

6   Igitur ab initio propensiorem te fuisse diviti non suspicionibus probo, non eo quod credibile est. Capta filia tua, quam posuisti condicionem? Eius futuram qui redemisset. Id elegisti discrimen inter duos petitores quod facilius posset praestare dives. Deceptus es in hoc: ego redemi, ego
7 reduxi. Quo alio modo efficere potuisti ne mihi nuberet

---

[1] *Aer.*: c(o)episset Aβ

[2] "Looking to the elaboration of the dangers in 14" (Wi.).

[3] Taking up the father's words; cf. s.2.   [4] See SB[2].

[5] The father might *a priori* be expected to favor the rich man; the terms he laid down prove that he actually did so.

I wish to prove that I was swindled before proving that I was swindled by that man. I made a covenant. This covenant is not being observed, nor can it be reclaimed. I spent money under the covenant; and I can neither reclaim the money nor do I have what I spent it for. I took ship, I toiled (so I put it for the time being),[2] because something was promised me. What was promised cannot be delivered. It is a swindle.

So far my case has gained a foundation. What follows is to prove that I have been swindled by him and swindled most shamefully. You perceive, gentlemen of the jury, the swindler's confidence: "Someone else raped, someone else opted." That is why it is a swindle. For recourse is never had to this law except where straight justice is excluded by villainy. If someone else[3] had not raped her, I should have grabbed her according to the covenant.[4] But the quibble with which you transfer the charge to your son-in-law and your daughter will do you no good. For if it becomes plain to the jury that all was done at your will, who made the promise, it will be clear that he who trusted you has been swindled by you.

So I prove that from the start you favored the rich man, not by suspicions, but by what is credible.[5] When your daughter was captured, what stipulation did you make? That she would go to the one who redeemed her. You chose a criterion between two suitors which the rich one could more easily meet. In this you were disappointed. I redeemed her, I brought her back. In what other way than

nisi hoc? Dico ergo tua voluntate factum esse ut filia tua raperetur. Hoc quibus colligo? Rapuit eam qui non amabat. Petierit enim sane: non redemit, sub condicione hac non redemit. Cur diutius moror? Mihi cessit. Non est ergo quod illum cupiditate impulsum putes: carere illa poterat.

8   Adicio non fuisse illum rapturum nisi securum. Nihil loquor de patria severitate, nihil de lege quae pro pudicitia minatur, quae mortem denuntiat: ille rapuisset puellam alii destinatam, alii pactam, nisi fiducia tui? Non est credi

9   bile. Sed ne illud quidem credibile est, filiam nuptias optaturam fuisse nisi te volente: primum quod in nulla virgine tantum audaciae, tantum confidentiae est ut apud magistratum et de re summa audeat optare inconsulto patre. Et illa utique non fecisset: et noveram puellam et propius in

10 itinere cognovi. Adice quod numquam tam ingrata fuisset puella ut nuptias optaret eius a quo non erat redempta, relinqueret eius cui debebat libertatem, cui salutem. Hoc dico praeter illum iniuriae dolorem, cum id perpessa esset in civitate quod non inter latrones, non inter barbaros illos.

11 Non est, ut dixi, credibile ut aut rapuerit ille sine fiducia tua, qui non amabat, qui plurimum timere debuerat, aut haec optaverit sine auctoritate tua, et puella et contra eum qui de illa optime merebatur et pro eo a quo et contempta erat et rapta. Existimo animum tuum fuisse manifestum. Qui si apparet, a te circumscriptus sum.

12   Iam venimus ad illam tertiam partem causae nostrae, in

this could you prevent her marrying me? I say therefore that it was by your will that your daughter was raped. How do I infer this? The man who raped her did not love her. Granted that he courted her: he did not redeem her, in face of this stipulation he did not redeem her. Out with it! He yielded her to me. So you cannot reasonably think that he was urged by lust: he could do without her. I'll add that he would not have raped her unless he had felt safe. I say nothing of paternal severity, nothing of the law's menace in defense of chastity, its threat of death: would he have raped a girl intended for another man, engaged to another man, unless he relied on you? It is not credible. But neither it is credible that your daughter would have opted for marriage if you had not so willed: first, because no girl has the audacity, the self-confidence, to dare to opt before a magistrate, and about a matter of the first importance, without consulting her father. And most certainly *that* girl would not have done so. I knew her and got to know her at closer quarters on the journey. Add that a girl would never have been so ungrateful as to opt for marriage to a man who had not redeemed her and desert her engagement to the man to whom she owed liberty and life. I say this over and above the distress of the injury, when she had suffered in the community what she had not suffered among those brigands, those barbarians. It is not credible, as I have said, either that he did the rape without relying on you—a man who did not love her and had every reason to fear—or that she opted without your authority—a girl, against a man who had deserved so well of her and in favor of one who had despised her and raped her. I think your intention was clear. If it is apparent, I was swindled by you.

Now I come to that third part of my case in which I shall

qua ostendam vobis quam inique sim circumscriptus.
Nuptias filiae tuae pactus sum. Non dico qua mercede:
pactus sum. Fides supremum rerum humanarum vincu-
lum est, sacra inter hostes, sacra (quod nuper comperi)
inter piratas, tantae etiam apud malos auctoritatis ut, cum
tradere mihi filiam tuam nolles, negare aperte non susti-
13 nueris. Et qua mercede pactus eram? Ut redimerem. Non
dico a quibus, nondum dico quo periculo *[2] scilicet male
tecum agebatur nisi[3] cui coeperat plus debere quam tibi.
In summa qualis sit ista condicio sic aestimandum est: tu
14 posuisti. Hoc ad meritum pertinet, illud ad pericula. Navigavi ad piratas: in quos incidere miserrimum est, quaesivi.
Omnes scopulos scrutatus sum, omnia litora excussi. Accedit aliquid ponderis huic merito meo: pauper hoc feci, rem
15 diviti gravem, mihi <non>[4] necessariam. Et quare negata
est? Ut collocaretur ei qui non redemerat, qui contempse-
rat, qui piratis reliquerat. Tantumne pecunia valet, tantum
ille fulgor divitiarum contra veritatem potest? Nunc[5] ille
melior.
16 'Non tamen ego feci.' Quasi circumscriptio in hoc sit
solo quod non actum per te est[6]: est in illo quod promisisti,
est in illo quod me donec ille raperet distulisti. Non est hoc

---

2 *lac. ind. SB[3] ita fere supplendam*: condicio ipsa quam iniqua,
pauperi quidem!
3 *SB[3]*: si Aβ   4 *SB[3]*   5 hinc *Watt*[2]
6 actum . . . est *Ro., auct. Obr.*: acta per testem Aβ

---

6 The gift of life was given both by the father and the suitor,
but by the latter at cost to himself. As to the supplement, see crit.
note.

show you gentlemen how unfairly I was swindled. I was engaged to your daughter. I don't say at what price: I was engaged. Good faith is the highest bond in human affairs; it is sacred among enemies, sacred (as I recently discovered) among pirates, of such authority even among scoundrels that although you did not want to hand your daughter over to me, you did not have the gall to refuse openly. And at what price was I engaged? That I should redeem her. I don't say from whom, I don't yet say at what risk: <how unfair was the stipulation itself to a poor man!> I suppose you were hardly done by unless she began to owe somebody more than she owed you![6] In fine, what sort of a stipulation it was can be judged from the fact that *you* made it. That concerns my desert, this concerns my dangers: I took ship to the pirates. To fall in with them is the sorriest of luck, but I looked for them. I scrutinized every cliff, I rummaged every shore. This desert of mine weighs the heavier because I that did it was a poor man—a thing burdensome to a rich man and one that I was <not>[7] forced to do. And why was she denied me? So that she be married to a man who had not redeemed her, had despised her, had left her to the pirates. Is the prerogative of money so great? Is that gleam of riches so potent against truth? He is now the better man.[8]

"But I didn't do it." As though the swindle lay only in what you did *not* do. It lies in what you promised, in your putting me off until he raped her. This is not a case in

[7] Without the added negative we have to understand that the suitor was compelled by his love for the girl; but that would make his merit less, not more.

[8] Perhaps a question (Wi.).

genus causae in quo omnia crimina transferre possis. Initium a te est: promisisti. Si non erat in tua potestate, statim circumscripsisti. Scilicet ego stultus qui virginem reduxi, qui tantam curam egi verecundiae ut optari ‹non›[7] pos-

17 sem. Non in totum iactabo vobis, iudices, continentiam meam. Sine dubio perferre volui ad patrem integrum munus, nec corrumpere quod praestarem; aliquid tamen fecerunt et mores puellae: severam videbam et asperam. Ne me quidem tulisset.

344

Redempta meretrix a divite pauperis filio

Inscripti maleficii sit actio. Pauperis et divitis filii eandem meretricem amabant. Leno condicionem posuit ei traditurum se esse meretricem qui pretium prior attulisset. Pauperis filium in solitudine dives flentem stricto gladio invenit. Interrogavit causam. Ille dixit se mori velle ob amorem meretricis. Pretium ei donavit. Redemit adulescens meretricem. Agit pauper cum divite inscripti maleficii.

1 SERMO

De parte[1] legis inter utrumque litigatorem confessum est.

---

[7] o. n. *Ro.*: optare Aβ
[1] *anne* parte priore ?

---

[9] Implying that the "rape" which the girl forgave was a put-up job, i.e. she consented, not that "nothing happened." If the rescuer had attacked her, she would have resisted and she would not have forgiven.

[1] The first part (*inscripti*) of the law *inscripti maleficii*. Both sides agreed that the alleged offense was "unwritten." Not "the le-

which you can shift all the charges on to someone else. The initiative is yours: you promised. If it was not in your power, the swindle was immediate. No doubt I was a fool to bring back a virgin, to take such good care of her modesty that I could <not> be opted for. I shall not boast of my self-restraint to you, gentlemen, as though it was the only factor. Doubtless I wanted to bring her father a gift untouched and not to taint what I gave, but the girl's morals counted for something. I saw that she was strict and straightlaced. She would not have taken it even from me.[9]

344

Prostitute redeemed by rich man for poor man's son

Let there be an action for unwritten wrongdoing. The sons of a poor man and a rich man were in love with the same prostitute. Her pimp made a stipulation, that he would hand over the prostitute to the one who was first to bring the price. The rich man found the poor man's son in a lonely place weeping, with his sword drawn. He asked the reason. The other said he wanted to die for love of the prostitute. He gave him the price. The young man redeemed the prostitute. The poor man prosecutes the rich man on a charge of unwritten wrongdoing.

DISCUSSION

On part of the law,[1] there is admission between the two litigants.

gal question" (Wi.)—there were two legal questions. The speaker makes the case that the rich man's behavior was wrongdoing, so that the second part of the law did apply.

2

DECLAMATIO

Inscriptum esse id quod obicio non negatur: qua lege[2] comprehendi potuit hoc nocendi genus quod rem gravissimam fecit specie liberalitatis? Omnia igitur ista quaecumque ex adverso dicuntur, 'donavi enim[3] pecuniam et servavi' et 'quo iure prohibetur?', eo pertinent ut appareat inscriptum esse quod obicio.

3　　Hac parte finita et constituta, transeamus ad eam quae reliqua est, ut[4] ostendam[5] esse maleficium. Nihildum de animo divitis loquor, nondum prodo causas propter quas fecit. Solum fuisse filium meum credite amatorem meretricis, huic redemptam esse meretricem: dico hoc esse maleficium, et quidem omnium maleficiorum gravissimum. 4 Levia sunt illa quae patrimonium populantur, levia etiam quae adversus corpus excogitantur: hoc non est legis viribus vindicandum quod saevit adversus animum? 5 Utrum igitur dicis non esse deforme, non esse inutile, meretricem domi habere, an eum qui rem deformem atque inutilem effecerit non esse maleficii lege comprehensum? Cuicumque mortalium grave erat domi habere meretricem: hoc nomen suo loco tantum fortasse deforme est, 6 translatum in domum etiam periculosum. Dicam nunc ego hic interceptam spem nepotum, inquinatam filii mei famam, futurorum quoque annorum spem esse sublatam? Hoc igitur qui fecit non potest non admisisse maleficium.

7　　'Sed periturus' inquit 'erat nisi id fecissem.' Scio quae partes forent[6] severioris patris: diceret ille: 'Mallem: levior

---

[2] q. l. *Auratus*: quale Aβ
[3] meam *Gron.*: ei *Ri.*
[4] *Aer.*: et Aβ　　　[5] -amus *Gron.*
[6] *Ro.*: fuerint Aβ

DECLAMATION

That what I charge is unwritten is not denied. What law could have embraced this sort of injury, which did grievous harm under the guise of generosity? So all these pleas put up by the other side, as "I gave him money and saved him" and "what law forbids?", only go to show that what I charge is unwritten.

This part defined and established, let us pass to what remains and show wrongdoing. I say nothing as yet about the rich man's intentions, I don't yet bring forward his motives for doing what he did: only believe that my son was in love with a prostitute and that he redeemed the prostitute. I say this is wrongdoing and the most grievous of all wrongdoings. Those that devastate patrimony are slight, as also those that are devised against the person: is this that rages against the mind not to be avenged by the might of the law? Do you say then that it is not an ugly and injurious thing to have a prostitute in one's home or do you say that whoever brings about an ugly and deleterious thing is not included in the law of wrongdoing?[2] It would have been grievous for anybody alive to have a prostitute in his home. The thing so called in its own place is perhaps only ugly, but transferred to the home it is dangerous as well. Shall I now speak of the hope of grandchildren cut off, my son's reputation befouled, the hope even of future years cancelled? Therefore he that did this cannot but have committed a wrongdoing.

"But," says he, "he would have died if I had not done it." I know what the role of the sterner sort of father would be.

---

[2] He means *inscripti maleficii* and perhaps so wrote. But here he is thinking only of the second part—wrongdoing.

ad me dolor pervenisset ex morte. Felices[7] quidem qui liberos suos ad rogum deflent: summum orbitatis est malum desiderare. Hoc vero intolerabile est, lugere viventem, quotiens occurrit flere, diurnas[8] quasdam ducere exequias

8 dignitatis.' Ego sane hanc tibi remiserim partem qua colligis moriturum fuisse; utrum amore perisset non diu disputabo: vivunt qui amaverunt. Itane? Quid minus rationis habet quam ut is mori velit qui habet propter quod vivat?

9 'Stricto tamen gladio in secreto deprehendi.' Iam mihi narras moras: ipsum illud secretum quaerere et putare interesse ubi pereat non est ardentis in mortem impetus. Non fiunt ista nisi subito, nec quisquam, praesertim nulla

10 gravi praecedente causa, spiritum ratione deposuit. Et stricto tamen gladio et in secreto quid facientem vidisti? Aptantem iam iugulo mucronem, iam incumbentem, iam paene admotam usque ad sanguinem manum? Nihil horum. 'Flentem' inquit ['mirabar'].[9] Maius[10] fuisse periculum crederem si fleret antequam stringere gladium coepisset. Non est igitur quod dicas te fecisse causa mea quod ego non fecissem.

11 Et iam hoc, iudices, satis erat †nisi† et inscriptum et maleficium est. Quacumque a te mente factum est, ego

---

7 *Aer.*: inf- Aβ 8 *SB*[2]: plenas Aβ: perpetuas *Watt*[2]
9 *SB*[1]   10 *Ri.*: minus Aβ

---

3 "According to Wi., *ego . . . fuisse* "must be taken as a sarcasm, unless it is a question (*egone* for *ego sane*?)." But the point conceded for the sake of argument is that Poor Man's Son would have killed himself if Poor Man had not come on the scene. All right, says the speaker, let us suppose so; but I can show you that it would not have been for *love*: *vivunt qui amaverunt*. That point estab-

He would say: "I would rather he had: his death would have been a light sorrow to me. Fortunate are they who weep for their children at the grave. The worst evil of bereavement is the missing. But it is an intolerable thing to mourn a living son, to weep whenever he comes in one's way, to lead a kind of daily funeral procession for his good name." Suppose I concede you the part in which you infer that he would have died. [3] I shall not argue at length about whether he would have died for love; those that have loved live. Really? What can be less rational than for a man to want to die who has something to live for?[4] "But I found him all by himself with his sword drawn." Now you are telling me of deferments. To look for that lonely place in itself and think it matters where one dies is not suggestive of an ardent rush into death. Those things are not done except of a sudden, and nobody, especially where there is no grave prior cause, lays down his life with calculation. Already trying the point against his throat, already leaning forward, his hand already almost close enough to draw blood? Nothing of the kind. "Weeping," he says.[5] I should have thought the danger greater if he was weeping *before* he started drawing his sword.[6] So it is no use your saying that you did for my sake what I would not have done.

And now, gentlemen, this would have been enough. It is unwritten and it is wrongdoing. Whatever your motives,

lished, he goes back to his original position: there would have been no suicide" (SB[2]).

[4] *Itane? . . . vivat?* looks back to *colligis moriturum fuisse*.

[5] Rejecting *mirabar* ("I was surprised at") as an inept addition by someone who did not see that *flentem* still depends on *vidisti*.

[6] Answer: "who says he wasn't?"

laesus sum; etiamsi non vindicta dolori meo deberetur, debeatur tamen solacium. Videamus tamen et quare fiat ista
12 res. Eandem meretricem amaverunt duo iuvenes, filii nostri. Quaerebatur utrius esset. Volo te consulere an, cum scieris, pecuniam filio tuo dederis, volo scire an, cum vidisses filium meum (ut putas) mori volentem, tale aliquid de tuo timueris. Filius meus propter amorem dicit se mori velle: amat et tuus. Hic deprehendam patrem: tu si periculum mortis putasses, tum vero ad filium tuum cucurrisses.
13 Quae fuit ergo ratio? Non tu filium meum servasti, sed tuum emendasti. Una erat ratio, credo, illius ab eo quo flagrabat impetu ‹avertendi›,[11] si amor transferretur, si potestas illius deformitatis adimeretur.
14   Vivit itaque filius tuus et honeste vivit et iam sine fabula vivit. At tu mihi nurum meretricem dedisti, tu domum meam lupanar fecisti: et, ne parum sit has iniurias intulisse, etiamnum vis adfirmare iudicibus filium meum, nisi redempta meretrice, non fuisse victurum.

345

Pauper ad tyrannicidium mercede conductus

Tyrannicida optet quod volet. Dives adulescenti pauperi dedit pecuniam ut tyrannum occideret: [et][1] occidit. De praemio ambigunt.

11 *Ro.*
1 *Ri.*

I have been harmed. Even if no vengeance were due for my suffering, consolation[7] would be due. But let us see also why this thing is done. Two young men, our sons, were both in love with the same prostitute. The question was, which one would have her. I want to put it to you, whether knowing this you gave money to *your* son. I want to know whether, when you saw my son (as you think) wanting to die, you had any such apprehension about your own. My son says he wants to die because of his love: your son is in love too. Here I shall catch your fatherly feelings:[8] if you had thought there was a chance of death, then indeed you would have run to your son. So what was your calculation? You did not save my son, but reformed your son. There was one method, I believe, of turning him away from his burning impulse, if the love were directed elsewhere, if the power to commit that ugliness was taken from him.

So your son lives on, and lives respectably, and now lives without gossip. But you have given me a prostitute for a daughter-in-law, you have made my house a brothel, and as though it was not enough to have done me these injuries, you still want to assert to the jury that my son would not have lived if the prostitute had not been redeemed.

345

A poor man hired to kill a tyrant

Let a tyrannicide opt for whatever he will. A rich man gave a poor young man money to kill a tyrant. He killed him. They are at odds about the reward.

7 Compensation.
8 So Wi.

[QUINTILIAN]

1 SERMO

Duo efficienda sunt diviti, ut sit tyrannicida, ut dignior sit praemio. Ut tyrannicida sit non potest aliter efficere quam si κατὰ συναθροισμὸν dignum se praemio probaverit et pro eo sit ac si occiderit.

2 DECLAMATIO

Quod primum dici oportet pro eo qui praemium petit, occidit tyrannum. Num dubitari potest? Num de hoc controversiam ullam saltem adversarius movet? Viderimus ergo quae sit comparatio utriusque meritorum: interim, etiamsi maiora sunt divitis, alia sunt. Sit ille optimus civis, sit egregie de re publica meritus: hic tyrannicida est. Hodie porro de eo praemio contendimus quod lex tyrannicidae constituit. Isti fortasse quod fecit profuturum sit cum petet magistratum: interim vos ad hoc ius, ad hanc legem consedistis, interim rem publicam hic pro quo loquor verbis legis appellat.

Et mihi satis erat hoc apud vos approbasse, si tantum de eo quaereretur, an accipere hunc oporteat. Sed quatenus in hanc contentionem descendimus, videamus quomodo se tyrannicidam efficiat adversarius noster. De libertate patriae cogitavit: nondum tyrannicidium est. Hortatus est aliquem, pecuniam dedit, omnia fecit ut hic tyrannicidium faceret: simile esse hoc tyrannicidio ut confitear, hoc ipso tamen apparet aliud esse quod simile est. Quis autem vobis permittit inclinare leges et iura transferre? <Semel>[2] con-

---

2 *Wi.*

---

[1] The *sermo* introduces a declamation on behalf of the rich man, but the declamation following is on behalf of his opponent.

DISCUSSION

The rich man has two things to do:[1] make himself the
tyrannicide and the more deserving of the reward. He cannot be the tyrannicide unless by accumulation of detail
he approves himself as worthy of the reward and it is as
though he had done the killing.

DECLAMATION

The first thing to be said on behalf of the claimant to the
reward is: he killed the tyrant. Can that be doubted? Does
our opponent as much as raise any controversy about that?
Let us see later on then what comparison lies between
their respective deservings: meanwhile, even if the rich
man's deservings are greater, they are different. Grant that
he is an excellent citizen, has done outstanding service to
the community: my client is the tyrannicide. Perhaps what
the other did will be to his advantage when he stands for
office: meanwhile, you gentlemen are in session with re
spect to this law, this statute; meanwhile, my client appeals
to the commonwealth in the words of the law.

It would have been enough for me to have approved
this to you if the only question was whether he should be
the recipient. But since we have got into this dispute, let us
see how our opponent makes himself the tyrannicide. He
thought about the country's freedom but that is not yet
tyrannicide. He urged somebody on, gave money, did everything to make my client perform tyrannicide: although
I may admit that this is similar to tyrannicide, the very fact
that it is similar shows that it is something else. Who gives
you license to bend laws and transfer them? They were laid

stituta sunt, semel finita sunt, suis finibus, suis verbis continentur. Et fortasse utcumque[3] tolerabile esset[4] quaeri an
pro tyrannicidio habere deberetis voluntatem si tyrannicida non esset; nunc ut sit istud tyrannicidio simile, ipsi
tamen praeferri non potest cui simile est. Ergo lex nobis
dat praemium, tibi non dat. Quod ad religionem iudicum
pertinet, hactenus causam finiri satis esset.

6   Sed quare non iam etiam actioni[5] eius respondea-
mus?—cum illa quidem, iudices, prima confessione: esse
istum bonae voluntatis fatemur, cupidum libertatis conce-
dimus, dum et ille fateatur esse se parum fortem, fortasse
vitio infirmitatis vel naturali vel quod ipsae per se solent
7 adferre divitiae. Simus voluntate contenti, non exigamus
ab eo quantum non potest, ut sciatis hanc esse inter duos
differentiam, ut quidquid ille voluit hic fecerit. Volo enim
tecum loqui. Quid ad hanc legem sic[6] conscriptam audac-
ter venis? Tyrannicidium tuum non dico approba: ostende.
8 Quid fecisti? 'Pecuniam' inquit 'dedi.' Ita, iudices? Ista lex
emi potest? Ad summum in re publica nostra honorem non
animus, non virtus, non manus mittit, sed arca et dispensator? Bene hercule negotiaris, et[7] excogitasti non mediocre
non dico famae atque opinionis sed patrimonii etiam tui,
9 cum alioqui abundaret, compendium. Dic, dic quanti
emeris ⟨ut optes⟩[8] quod velis. Tu mihi dicis: 'pecuniam
dedi et ex otiosa iacente patrimonii parte aliquid numera-

---

3 *Aer.*: cumque Aβ   4 *Aer.*: est A: estis β
5 *SB*[3]: pa- A(β)
6 *coni. Wi.*: fu A: tu B: fuit C: pub. D: ita *Ro.*
7 n. et *Ri.*: -ri sed Aβ   8 *Gron.*

---

2 The rich man.

down ‹once for all›, defined once for all, they are cast in their own definitions, their own words. If there were no tyrannicide, perhaps it might be just tolerable that there be a question whether you ought to take the will for the deed; as it is, though we grant that what he did was similar to a tyrannicide, it cannot however be preferred to the thing to which it is similar. Therefore the law gives the reward to us, not to you. So far as the religious duty of the jury is concerned, it would be enough for the case to be concluded at this point.

But why should we not now answer his plea too?—with this admission at the outset, gentlemen of the jury: we confess that he is a man of good intentions, we concede that he is eager for freedom, as long as he on his side confesses that he lacks courage, perhaps because of weakness either natural or such as riches themselves are apt to bring in their train. Let us be content with the will, let us not demand of him what lies beyond his capability, so you gentlemen know that the difference between the two is that what the one wanted, the other performed. For I want to talk with you.[2] Why do you come boldly to this law, drafted as it is? I don't say approve your tyrannicide, show it! What did you do? "I gave money," he says. So, gentlemen? Can that law be bought? In the end, in our commonwealth is it not spirit, not courage, not the hand, that brings a man to the highest honor, but the strong-box and the steward? I like the way you do business; and you thought out a fine short cut—I won't say to fame and reputation but to property, of which you had more than enough anyhow. Tell me, tell me now, how much did you pay ‹to opt for› whatever you want? You say to me, "I gave money and put down something from a part of my fortune that was lying idle,"

vi', cum ego dicam: 'arcem conscendi, satellites stravi, ne-
farium corpus repetitis ictibus trucidavi.' 'Pecuniam dedi,
de tyrannicidio locutus sum.' Rem feceras periculosissi-
10 mam, nisi in tyrannicidam incidisses. Satis sit vobis, o divites, hoc vestras praestare fortunas, quod per dispensatores
faeneratis, quod familiam per procuratores continetis,
quod pleraque possidetis absentes, quod ignorantibus vobis et quiescentibus, si quis est tantae felicitatis labor, per
11 alienas manus transit. Contingat istud deliciis vestris,
contingat abundantissimae plerumque luxuriae: non dabi-
tis tyrannicidiis cognitorem, nec ad vos alienis periculis
12 veniet fama virtutis. Velim narres iudicibus, audiente populo, quem sermonem cum hoc adulescente habueris, qua
exhortatione sis usus. 'Premitur tyrannide civitas nostra;
cotidie gravia atque indigna patimur: opus est aliquo viro
forti, opus est aliquo bono cive, opus est liberatore tan-
torum malorum.' Si te haec cum maxime dicentem inter-
roget[9] cur non ipse facias, respondebis profecto: 'non possum, non is animus mihi, non id virium est', et adicies: 'tu
potes.'

13   Verum non contentus sibi acquisisse gloriam, etiam nobis detrahere conatur: negat enim hunc iuvenem ad tyrannicidium fuisse venturum nisi pecunia conductus esset. O
quantum erras, dives, ac falleris qui putas virtutem posse
conduci et animum pecunia fieri. In omnia enim sane lucro
trahamur, ducat nos spes ad laborem, ducat ad patientiam:
nemo futuri temporis cogitatione ⟨tantum⟩[10] periculum
14 subit. Iturus aliquis in id discrimen ex quo evasurum se

9 *SB*[3]: -gem Aβ
10 *SB*[1]

whereas I say: "I scaled the castle, I mowed down the guards, I butchered his wicked body with repeated blows." "I gave money, talked about killing the tyrant." That was a very dangerous thing to do, if you had not happened upon a tyrannicide. Let it be enough for you, you rich men, that your wealth enables you to lend money through stewards, that you manage your households through agents, hold most of your property in your absence, that if there is any work to such felicity, it goes through other hands while you remain unaware and inactive. Let that be contingent to your pleasures, your superabundant luxury, as a rule: you will not employ an attorney in tyrannicides, nor will the fame of courage come to you at other people's risk. I should like you to tell the jury, in the hearing of the people, what talk you had with this young man, what exhortation you employed: "Our community is oppressed by a tyrant; every day we suffer injuries and indignities. We need some brave man, some good citizen, someone to free us from these great evils." If he were to ask you as you speak why you don't do it yourself, no doubt you will answer: "I can't, I don't have the spirit or the strength" and you will add: "You can."

But not content with acquiring glory himself, he also tries to detract from ours; for he says that this young man would not have got to kill the tyrant if he had not been hired for money. Oh, how wrong you are, rich man, how much mistaken, to think that courage can be hired and spirit made with money! Maybe we are drawn into all manner of things by gain, maybe hope leads us to work, leads us to endurance, but no one takes ⟨so great⟩ a risk with thought of time to come. Has anyone ever had money in view when about to embark on a peril from which he does

non speret pecuniam spectavit? Scilicet ut locupletior
periret, ut, si destitutum in illis cogitationibus manerent
tormenta, si tyranni ira, haberet illud intra conscientiam
suam, accepisse se pecuniam et paulo ante gravem argento
15 manum fuisse. Ante igitur hae versabantur in animo huius
cogitationes, ante istud quod tu effecisse pecuniam putas
fecerat res publica, fecerat indignatio, fecerat ingenita virtus. Nec tu, nisi hoc intellexisses, ausus esses loqui aut
committere tam periculosum alieno secretum: videras vultum, audieras cum raperetur aliqua virgo ingemescentem.
16 Verumtamen cur non reponamus hanc contumeliam?
Non pro re publica dedisti. Scimus tyrannidem praecipue
ad divites pertinere. Illa quam dederas pecunia redimebas
fortunas, pecunias tuas, immo salutem, quandoquidem
plerumque perire vobis in lucrum crudelitatis alienae necesse est. Habes igitur satis magna istius liberalitatis tuae
pretia. Securus es nunc dominus, nunc dives; desisti for-
17 tunam tuam timere, desisti odisse quidquid iactas. 'Ego tamen' inquit 'dedi quod esset pro praemio.' Ideo ergo exigis
ut res publica non reddat, et, si quid tu privatus liberaliter
fecisti, universam civitatem vis facere sordide? Quamquam ne remittis quidem istud rei publicae, sed in te transfers; ut[11] ne voluntati quidem tuae obligati simus[12] si pecu-
18 niam ideo dedisti ut praemium acciperes. Hic porro si quid
avare, si quid cupide fecisset, tua potius pecunia quam ipsa
lege ad tyrannicidium conduceretur? Tu illi dicis: 'accipe
pecuniam'; res publica dicit: 'opta quod voles.' Ut avarus

11 at *Wi*.   12 *Aer.*: sumus Aβ

---

3 Of killing the tyrant, the attempt having failed.
4 The reward.

not hope to escape? To die wealthier no doubt; and if, left stranded in these thoughts,[3] torture and the tyrant's wealth awaited him, to have it in his heart that he had received money, that a little earlier on his hand had been heavy with silver. So these thoughts were in this man's mind earlier on, and what you think money accomplished had been done before by the commonwealth and by indignation and inborn valor. Neither would you have dared to talk or trust so perilous a secret to an outsider if you had not realized this: you had seen his face, heard him groan when some girl was being raped.

However, why should we not retort this insult? You did not give for the commonwealth's sake. We know that tyranny is of special concern to the rich. With the money you had given you were redeeming your fortune, your moneys, or rather your life, since you and your like must often perish by way of bonus to enrich another's cruelty. So you have large enough returns on your generosity. Now you, the owner, the rich man, are safe. No longer do you fear your good fortune, no longer hate all that you brag about. "Well, but I gave what was in lieu of a reward," he says. So on that account do you demand that the commonwealth not pay, and if you as a private individual acted with some generosity, do you want the entire community to act meanly? And yet you are not even taking that[4] off the commonwealth's shoulders but transferring it to yourself, so that we are not even obligated to your intention if you gave money in order to get the reward. As for him furthermore, if he acted in greed and avarice, would he have been hired for tyrannicide by your money rather than by the law itself? You say to him: "Take money;" the commonwealth says: "Opt for

sit et cupidus, utrum plus est?

19   Verum hic se adfirmat ne praemia quidem ista spec-
tasse cum faceret: 'Oblitus sum' inquit 'ante omnia salutis
meae. Commodum civitatis universorumque spectavi,
tum, si quid ad me proprie pertinebat, famam ituramque
in posterum gloriam huius quae subinde obicitur pauper-
tatis, si quidem facilius virtutem aluit.'

346

Tutor filii sui in adoptionem dati

Adversus patrem ne qua sit actio nisi dementiae. Quidam
dedit filium in adoptionem.[1] Moriens ille instituit patrem
eius naturalem tutorem. Ille tutelam gessit, rationes reddidit. Accusare ille vult patrem tutelae male gestae. Praescri-
bit ille quod actio non sit adversus patrem nisi dementiae.

1   SERMO

Natura rei fortasse hoc ferat,[2] ut hic pater, quem filius
reum vult facere, irascatur, atque eo magis irascatur quod
de filio bene meruit non tantum generando sed etiam dando in adoptionem. Sed non semper sequendi sunt adfec-
2   tus, et plerumque consilium his praeponendum est. Hic
enim pater, etsi revera irascitur, dissimulare hoc debet, et
agere mitem, indulgentem. Nam cum praescribat, hoc approbare debet iudicibus, idcirco praescribere se ne cum
filio gravius contendat; alioqui, si haec causa praescribendi
non est, supererit ut diffidentia videatur in causa.

[1] *add.* <amico> *Ro.*
[2] *Aer.*: fecerat Aβ

what you will." Greedy and avaricious though he be, which is more?

But he avers that he never even had those rewards in mind when he did it. "First of all," he says, "I forgot my safety, I looked at the good of the community, of everybody; then, if I had any personal concern, at fame and glory in time to come of this poverty that is sometimes thrown in my teeth—it reared courage more easily."

346

The guardian of his son given in adoption

Let no action lie against a father except for dementia. A man gave his son into adoption. Dying, he appointed his natural father guardian. He acted as guardian, rendered accounts. The son wishes to accuse his father of malversation. The other enters a demurrer on the ground that no action lies against a father except for dementia.

DISCUSSION

The nature of the case would perhaps allow that this father, whom his son wishes to prosecute, be angry, and all the more angry because he deserved well of his son, not only by begetting him but also giving him into adoption. But emotions are not always to be followed and often reasons must be preferred to them. For although this father is really angry, he ought to conceal it and play gentle, indulgent. For when he demurs, he should make the jury believe that he does so to avoid a more serious contest with his son. Otherwise, if this is not the reason for his demurrer, only lack of confidence can seem the reason.

3

DECLAMATIO

'Cum patre actio ne qua sit nisi dementiae.' Alio crimine
me reum fieri manifestum est. Nemo dubitabit quin id hac
lege non liceat, si ego pater sum. Atqui ne de eo quidem
dubitari poterit, quin pater sim. An hoc negas me esse qui
genuerim, qui educaverim, et, ut aliquod argumentum ex
eo ipso quod contra me ponitur ducam, me esse qui dede-

4 rim in adoptionem? Si haec parum firma sunt, lege[3] testamentum quo tutorem accepisti: patrem tibi tutorem dedit.
At enim dando in adoptionem ius omne translatum est *[4]

347

Absente marito rumor et nuptiae

Adulterum cum adultera liceat occidere. Uxor peregrinan-
tis mariti mortem rumore cognovit. Heres inventa nupsit
adulescenti cuidam et domum in dotem dedit. Supervenit
maritus nocte, utrumque occidit. Reus est caedis.

1

DECLAMATIO

Adulteros fuisse in matrimonio constat: nemo negat. Legitimum porro matrimonium nisi soluto priore esse non potest.[1] Matrimonium duobus generibus solvitur, aut repu-
dio aut morte alterius. Neque repudiavi et certe vivo.
Meae igitur nuptiae manserunt, illae non fuere legitimae.

---

³ *Sch.*: leges Aβ: legas *Aer.*   ⁴ *lac. ind. Aer.*
¹ legitimum . . . p. *post* legitimae (*infra*) *habent* Aβ: *transp.*
Wi.

---

[1] The son claims that the demurrer is void because the natural
father's parental status was permanently cancelled by the adoption.   [2] Declamation cut short.

"Let no action lie against a father except for dementia." It is clear that I am being prosecuted on another charge. Nobody will doubt that that is impermissible under this law, if I am his father. And yet it also cannot be doubted that I *am* his father. Or do you deny that it is I who begot you and raised you, and (to bring an argument from the very fact that is advanced against me)[1] that it is I who gave you into adoption? If all this is not solid enough, read the will under which you received your guardian. It gave your father as your guardian. "Ah, but by the giving into adoption all rights were transferred."[2]

347

In husband's absence, rumor and wedding

Let it be lawful to kill an adulterer along with the adulteress. A wife learned by rumor of the death of her husband, who was abroad. Found to be his heir, she married a young man and gave her house as dowry. The husband came along at night and killed them both. He is charged with homicide.

It is agreed that the adulterous couple were in matrimony; no one denies it. Now matrimony cannot be legitimate unless any prior marriage is dissolved. Matrimony is dissolved in two ways, either by divorce or by the death of one or the other. I did not divorce her and I am certainly alive. So my marriage was still in being; theirs was illegitimate.

2   'Sed rumor de morte venit.' Haec statim nupsit alio marito. Quid est hoc aliud quam improbius adulterium? An opinione contenti sumus? Isto genere, etiamsi caedis absolvar, omnibus tamen periclitor bonis: quippe testamentum meum lectum est et uxor omnium bonorum heres inventa est et ego scilicet testamento meo exheredatus. Quod si ius domini post hanc opinionem retinui, retinui etiam mariti.

3   Mihi ad defensionem hoc satis est: licuit. Possitis occisorum fortasse misereri quod decepti sunt, quod illos spes sua fefellit: adulteri tamen fuerunt etiamsi ignoraverunt. An ego si ‹non›² ignorassem quid diceretur³ non occidis-
4   sem? Utrum domum meam non fui intraturus, an me in aliud cubiculum iuxta adulteros meos collocaturus, an, cum venissem in cubiculum et iacentem cum adultero uxorem meam deprehendissem, excitaturus tantum? Quid deinde? Recepturusne an cessurus? Si talem habiturus
5   eram animum, diis gratias ago quod nocte veni. Vos profecto, dii coniugales, hanc illi mentem dedistis, ut domum in dotem daret, ut eadem familia excubaret, ut is ianitor esset qui me admitteret, ut reversus denique nihil novi invenirem praeter adulteros.

6   Ergo uxor sic a me amata, testamento relicta heres, audita morte mariti non inquisivit ubi perissem, non aliquos certiores nuntios, non reversuros a supremis officiis servulos expectavit, sed festinato quoque nupsit, et in novae

---

² *Ro.*
³ *SB¹, Watt¹*: quod diceret A(β)

---

¹ Belief in the rumor.
² And so killed them before I knew the facts.

"But a rumor came in about my death." She immediately married another husband. What is this but a more shocking adultery? Or are we content with a persuasion[1]? That way, even if I were acquitted of homicide, I am still in danger of losing all I possess: for my will has been read and my wife found to be heir to all my possessions and I, if you please, disinherited under my own will! But if I kept the status of owner after this persuasion, I also kept that of husband.

For me this is enough for defense: it was permitted. You might perhaps be sorry for those who were killed because they were misled, because their hope deceived them: still, they were adulterers even though they did not know it. Or would I not have killed them if I had <not> been ignorant of the talk? Would I not have entered my house, or would I have put myself in another bedroom next to my adulterers, or when I had gone into the bedroom and caught my wife in bed with a lover, would I merely have roused them? And then? Would I have taken them in or would I have just gone away? If that was to have been my attitude, I thank the gods I came at night.[2] Surely you, gods of wedlock, put it into her mind to give the house as dowry, so that the same servants should be awake, so that there should be a doorkeeper who would let me in, so that on my return I should find nothing new except the lovers.

So when the wife whom I loved so dearly, who was left heir in my will, heard of her husband's death, she did not make enquiry where I had died, did not wait for more reliable reports or for slaves to return from the final rites, but married, in haste too, and straightway transferred my dis-

libidinis amorem mea iudicia protinus transtulit? In eadem domo, in eodem cubiculo, in eodem lecto, adeo mariti
7 prioris etiam memoria abierat[4]? Desii ista mirari cum adulterum vidi iuvenem, propter quem tamdiu vidua esse non posset quamdiu peregrinari poteram ego qui uxorem sic amavi. Temere profecto, temere in longius ituri iter coniuges nostras domi relinquimus: subito absentium obliviscuntur, et paene cum ipsis toris uxorum pectora refri-
8 gescunt. Mirer nunc ego unde rumor, quae tam maligno mendacio causa, cui fingere istud expedierit? Ille profecto in causa fuit iuvenis qui ad[5] domum meam inductus est ‹cui›[6] quaesitus est locus. Iam vero bonorum meorum dira populatio, sicut notissimo Graeciae duci, qui felicior tamen solam in adulteris ultus est gulae voluptatem.
9   Scio, iudices, quam difficile sit alienorum malorum imaginem capere; sed[7] tamen, quantum cogitatione permittitur, unusquisque se illo loco ponat, ac primum illa quae intra animum meum volvi[8] mente concipiat, cum reverterer ex peregrinatione longa, quam mihi attulerit cogitationem primus aspectus.

4 A: -am abiecerat β
5 in *Ri.*: *del. Ro.*
6 *SB*4
7 *Obr.*: sit Aβ
8 *Gron.*: volvo Aβ

---

3 Testamentary.

4 An odd phrase. Something like *in novum amorem vel potius libidinem* might have been expected.

5 When he saw the young man's face he recognized him. It

positions[3] into the love of a new lust.[4] In the same house, in the same bedroom, in the same bed, had even the memory of her former husband so completely vanished? I stopped wondering about it all[5] when I saw the young lover on whose account she could not bear to be a widow as long as I, who loved my wife so much, could be abroad.[6] Surely we are rash, rash, when we leave our wives at home to go on a long journey. All at once they forget the absent, and wifely bosoms grow cold almost as fast as the beds themselves. Am I now to wonder what was the source of the rumor, who the reason for so malignant a lie, who had an interest in that fabrication? Surely the young man was behind it, who was brought into my house, ⟨for whom⟩[7] room had to be made. Now comes the terrible wastage of my possessions, as happened to a very celebrated Greek chieftain, who however, more fortunate than I, punished only the pleasure of gluttony in the adulterers.[8]

I know, gentlemen, how hard it is to form a picture of other men's calamities. All the same, so far as cogitation allows, let each one of you put himself in that place and first imagine what I turned over in my mind, when I came back from long absence abroad, what thoughts the first sight brought me.[9]

seems to be implied that he had suspected something before he went abroad. *Ista* refers to the situation he found in the house.

[6] But for her involvement with him, she would have remained a widow, as she mistakenly supposed, until her husband's return.

[7] Better add *cui* than delete *quaesitus est locus* (SB[3], Watt[1]).

[8] In Ulysses' case the suitors, loosely called adulterers, had not slept with Penelope.

[9] The declamation appears to be incomplete.

348

Cum proditoribus carcer incensus

Imperator in bello summam habeat potestatem. Imperator proditionis suspectos in carcerem coniecit. Ex transfuga comperit eadem nocte finitum iri proditionem. Incendit carcerem. Perierunt illi qui erant in carcere. Hostes
recesserunt. Accusatur quod de indemnatis sumpserit
supplicium.

1   DECLAMATIO

Si ratione defendi non possem, iure defenderer. 'Imperator in bello summam habeat potestatem.' Id quod obicitis
(ut nondum †obiciam†[1] propter bellum factum esse[2]) in
2   bello factum est. Usus sum igitur lege. Videamus[3] quam
utiliter[4] constituta et necessaria quoque. 'Imperator in bello summam habeat potestatem.' Ante omnia non id est
tempus quo iudicia exerceri, quo leges retinere vim suam
possint. Ista pax spectat, et diligentiorem rerum inquisi-
tionem securitas habet; non vacat in bello curam agere
3   singulorum. Ad hanc rationem accedit illud quoque, quod
administrare non potest bellum nisi tantam potestatem
habuerit imperator. Tot milia conscriptorum militum in
aciem educere, adsignare loca interim periculosa, tuendos
cives, expugnanda hostium castella ⟨curare⟩,[5] non potest

---

[1] dicam *coni. SB[3], alii alia*
[2] *Obr.*: est Aβ
[3] *SB[3]*: -erimus Aβ
[4] *Aer.*: -li Aβ
[5] *Watt[2]* (praestare *commentus eram*)

348

Prison burned along with traitors

Let the commanding general have supreme power in wartime. A general threw persons suspected of treason into prison. From a deserter he learned that the treason would be completed the same night. He set fire to the prison. Those who were in the prison perished. The enemy withdrew. He is accused of having punished persons uncondemned.

DECLAMATION

If I could not be defended by reason, I should be defended by law. "Let the commanding general have supreme power in wartime." The act which you charge me with (not to say yet that it was done because of the war) was done in wartime. Therefore I acted under the law. Let us see[1] how usefully constituted and even necessary the law is: "Let the commanding general have supreme power in wartime." To begin with, that is not a time in which trials can be held, in which the laws can retain their force. Peace has regard for that sort of thing, and security admits of a more thorough enquiry into happenings: in war there is no time to go into individual items. To this consideration accrues another, that the commanding general cannot conduct the war unless he has power thus great. To lead so many thousands of conscripted soldiers into battle, to assign stations sometimes dangerous, ⟨to provide for⟩ the protection of citizens, the storming of enemy forts, takes more than good

---

[1] Which he does immediately. *Viderimus* would postpone until he had dealt with some other topic (SB[2]).

sola ratio: opus est et metu. Quid si pleraque accidunt in quibus praesenti poena castigare necesse est eos qui peccaverunt? Ad haec igitur omnia provisum atque probatum est ut imperator summam potestatem haberet.

4 Quid tamen a nobis exigi oportet? Bonam voluntatem. Erraverim sane; sed[6] id satis probationi existimavi, si hoc ad utilitatem civitatis pertinere credidi: quis damnaverit eum qui duabus potentissimis rebus defenditur, iure et mente?

5 Quid si etiam ratio hoc faciendi fuit? Forsitan et lente et nimium periculose fecerim, quod suspectos proditionis tantum in carcerem duci iussi: nihil egeram, non satis civitati prospexeram, hostis idem speravit; tamen hoc ne ab accusatore quidem reprehenditur. Iam igitur de his, qui †in carcerem[7] duci† debuerunt, levius est supplicium, quacumque ratione sumptum est. Nunc quare sumptum?

6 Proditionis finis atque effectus omnis in proximam nobis noctem denuntiabatur. Puta falsum: quis non ignoscit rem tantam timenti? Non enim discrimen paucorum capitum agebatur:[8] an aliquid esset haec civitas, an templa, an vetustissimae vestigium saltem urbis relinqueretur, an liberi vestri coniugesque traditam a maioribus per manus in hoc usque tempus libertatem semel perderent. Pro his animadvertere in paucos indignum est? Et exercitus partem occidimus,[9] et, in aciem ductis militibus, certe innocenti-

---

6 *SB*[2]: si Aβ

7 in c. *fort. delendum*: ad supplicium *vel sim. add. coni. Wi.*

8 *add.* <, agebatur> *Aer.*: <sed> *Sch.*

9 *Wi.*: dicimus Aβ: caedimus *Watt*[2]: decimamus *Pith.*

---

2 By experience.

thinking: there's need of fear. What if cases often occur in which it is necessary to chastise offenders with an immediate punishment? Against all this, therefore, it has been provided and approved[2] that the commanding general have supreme power.

However, what ought to be demanded of me? Good disposition. Suppose I made a mistake: but I thought it enough for approval if I believed this concerned the good of the community. Who would condemn one defended by two very powerful factors: law and intention?

What if there was also reason for so doing? Perhaps I acted slowly and too dangerously in ordering persons suspected of treason only to be put in prison. I had done nothing effective, I had not taken enough thought for the community, it was what the enemy hoped for; and yet this is not blamed even by the prosecutor. Already then the punishment was too light, no matter why imposed, for men who should have been executed.[3] As it is, why was it imposed? I was told that the whole end and effect of the plot was timed for the coming night. Suppose it false: who does not forgive me fearing as I did so great a matter? It was not the fate of a few persons that was at stake, but the existence of the community, whether the temples, whether even a trace of the ancient city, should be left, whether your children and wives should lose once and for all the freedom passed from hand to hand by our ancestors down to the present day. In defense of all this is it shocking to execute a few individuals? We kill a part of our army too,[4] and when the soldiers, innocent as they assuredly are, are led into

[3] See crit. note.
[4] By decimation.

bus, multum contigisse imperatori videtur etiamsi non in-
cruentam victoriam referat. Pro hac securitate si perierunt
8   aliqui, ut parcissime dicam, non ignoscetis[10]? Equidem
intellego hanc esse condicionem omnium qui administra-
tionem rei publicae adgrediuntur, ut ea quae maxime pertinent ad salutem communem cum quadam sua invidia
efficere cogantur. Quanta vi adversus me inimici consur-
rexissent si istud sine causa fecissem!

9   Quid si proditores fuisse manifestum est? Putemus esse iudicium, et, quatenus mavultis illos indemnatos dicere
quam innocentes, excutite causam. Sane non consumma-
verint crimen[11] susceptum,[12] at certe transfugae hoc mentiendi causa quae fuit? Homo, relicto exercitu suo, relicto
imperatore suo, in civitatem nostram transgressus, cum
rem periculosissimam fecisset, mentiretur? Cum ad pro-
10   bationem rei caput suum obligaret? Eandem nobis noctem
denuntiavit. Manifestum est autem fuisse hostibus propositum civitatis nostrae per proditionem capiendae. Qui
proditores fuerint, recedendo confessi sunt. Quid enim est
causae cur qui ad illud usque tempus ‹ad portas›[13] civitatis
permanserant, post incendium carceris, post mortem sus-
pectorum nobis civium continuo discesserint?

11   Hic ratio illa quoque ‹reddenda›[14] est, quod sic exegi
supplicium ab illis (si modo hoc est exigere supplicium):
miratur aliquis si hos[15] timui educere, si, cum tanta conspiratio in civitate nostra nocentium esse diceretur ut pro-

10 *Aer.*: -cerem Aβ 11 *Obr.*: primum Aβ

12 *SB*[3], *duce Aer.*: -cipio CD: -cipi B: suspicio A

13 *Ro., auct. Aer.*

14 *SB*[2]

15 *Obr.*: non Aβ

battle, the general is considered very successful if he brings home a victory, even though it not be bloodless. If some persons have perished for the sake of this security, will you not, to say the very least, forgive it? For my part, I realize that all of us who come forward to conduct the affairs of the commonwealth have to expect that when they carry out measures of the highest importance to the public welfare, they will incur some personal unpopularity. How violently would my enemies have risen up against me if I had done what I did without good reason!

What if it is clear that they were traitors? Let us suppose there is a trial and, since you prefer to call them uncondemned rather than innocent, analyze the case. Granted that they did not consummate the crime they planned: but the deserter at least, what reason had he for lying about this? A man who had left his own army, his own commander, and passed over to our community, after so dangerous an action, would he lie? Though he was staking his own life on getting his story believed? He warned us of the same night. It is clear that the enemy planned to capture our city by treachery: who the traitors were, they confessed by their withdrawal. For having stayed ‹at the gates› of our city down to that time, why did they withdraw immediately after the prison fire and the death of the citizens whom we suspected?

Here I ‹must explain› also why I exacted punishment from them (if that is the right term)[5] in this way. Is anyone surprised if I was afraid to bring them out? If, when so extensive a conspiracy of criminals was said to exist in our community that they would commit treason even from jail,

[5] He might have said "eliminated them for the public good."

dere possent etiam ex carcere, vel cum tota sua custodia
12 eos obrui malui? His illud quoque adici potest, plurimum
differre utrum quis supplicium exigat ab indemnatis an si
aliquos securitatis publicae causa occiderit. Supplicium
vocetur quod civitati[16] praestiti[17]? Si vero hoc pro salute
communi fuit, non odio illorum factum est, imperatoris
fortasse consilium reprehendi potest, factum certe damnari non potest.

13   SERMO

In summa parte controversiarum talium quaeri solet haec
quo[18] animo fecerit imperator. In hanc partem satis
firmam causae fiduciam videtur habere: quod enim huic
obiecerunt[19] inimici odium praeter commune omnium
proditorum?

                            349

              Raptoris pater dementiae reus

Raptor, nisi et suum patrem exoraverit et raptae intra triginta dies, pereat. Rapuit quidam. Exoravit patrem raptae,
suum non exoravit. Dementiae accusat.

1   SERMO

Non dubie pater hic intellegi vult se filii sollicitudine esse
contentum et hanc triginta dierum moram pro ultione habere. Sed hoc si palam indicaverit, perdet artem; et si libe-

16 *Sch.*: -as Aβ
17 *Ro.*: -titit Aβ
18 h. q. (quo *iam Ri.*) *SB*[3]: ecquo A: ea quo β
19 *Watt*[1]: profec- A[1](β): -ferunt A[2]

I preferred that they be overwhelmed, even along with all their guard? It can be added that there is a great difference between punishing men uncondemned and killing some persons for the sake of public safety. Should what I did for the community[6] be called punishment? But if this was done for the general safety, not because I hated them, perhaps the general's judgment can be faulted, but the act certainly cannot be condemned.

DISCUSSION

In the final part of such controversies it is usual to ask what was in the general's mind when he acted. As to this part of the case he seems to have a sufficiently well-founded confidence. For what hatred have his enemies attributed to him other than the common hatred of all traitors?

349

Father of rapist accused of dementia

Let a rapist die unless he has won pardon both from his own father and the victim's within thirty days. A man raped. He has won the victim's father's pardon but not his own father's. He accuses his father of dementia.

DISCUSSION

Without doubt this father wishes it to be understood[1] that he is content with his son's anxiety and regards the thirty days' delay as a punishment. But if he intimates this openly, he will lose his device; and if he has once settled to

---

[6] According to Wi., *civitati* spoils the rhythm. The clausula $---\cup\underset{\smile}{}$ is not excessively rare (cf. 364.3 *dedisse qui deduceret*, 365.6 *singuli dissentiant*).   [1] By the jury.

rare filium sollicitudine semel destinavit, brevius habet
statim ignoscere. Varianda erit eius actio, ut filium dicat
2 morte dignum, an possit ipse perseverare dubitet. Non tamen praetereunda sunt illa, quamvis communia cum aliis
controversiis generis huius, quae circa ipsam quaestionem
dementiae versantur. Negabimus enim crimine uno posse
deprehendi dementiam, et hoc propositum nostrum adiu-
vabimus finitione, ut dicamus dementiam esse ablatum rerum omnium intellectum; alioqui neminem tam felicem
qui non aliqua paenitentia digna faciat, qui non subiectus
sit errori, et hoc proprium non dementis esse verum homi-
3 nis. Atque ad hoc, quod commune cum omnibus est, aliquid etiam proprie applicabimus, quod eius generis dicitur dementia esse, de qua iudicium est, ut emendari uno
verbo possit. Porro cum adeo confessum sit dementiam
non posse curari ut ne illud quidem adhuc inveniri potuerit, quae causa faceret dementiam, ubi animus consisteret,
profecto non poterit videri dementia quae est in hominis
potestate.

4   DECLAMATIO

Si exoratus fuero, statim non modo sanus verum etiam bonus pater et indulgens ero. Vis scire, fili, quid sit dementia?
Deducere se in periculum capitis cupiditate, non intellegere pacem, non intellegere leges, et, si quid supra hoc
momenti fortuna praesens [iudicium][1] habet, accusare

---

[1] *Watt*[2], *Wi.*

---

[2] Quicker no doubt, but keeping his son on tenterhooks is the
device he doesn't want to lose (or "waste"?). Double brackets?
[3] Of forgiveness.

free his son of anxiety, it is quicker for him to pardon him
straight away.[2] His pleading will have to be varied, so that
he says his son deserves death but doubts whether he himself can go through with it. But those points that have to do
with the question of dementia itself, though common to
other controversies of this kind, are not to be passed over.
For we shall say that dementia cannot be nailed by a single
charge and we shall support this proposition of ours by a
definition, saying that dementia is a loss of understanding
in all matters, that anyway nobody is so fortunate as not to
do some things worthy of regret, not to be subject to error,
and that this is not characteristic of a person demented but
of a human being. Add to this that in common with all such
cases we shall also add something specially, that the dementia concerned in this trial is said to be of a kind that can
be removed by a single word.[3] Further, since it is admitted
that dementia is incurable, so much so that it has not yet
been possible to discover what causes dementia or where
the mind settles,[4] what is in a man's own power surely cannot be considered to be dementia.[5]

DECLAMATION

If I am won over, I shall all at once be not only a sane but a
good and indulgent father. Do you want to know, my son,
what dementia is? It is to put one's life at risk because of
lust, not to understand the peace,[6] not to understand the
laws, and, if beyond this the present predicament counts
for anything, to accuse a man whom you need to win over.

[4] I.e. in what sanity consists; see Wi.
[5] As though madmen had control of their minds.
[6] As in "breach of the peace."

5   eum qui exorandus sit. Non est igitur dementia. Nec refert
ad praesens iudicium neque ad vestram pronuntiationem
an ego durus pater, an ego nimium severus. Non de hoc
quaeritur; satis est non esse furiosum.

6   'Non exoro te' inquit, 'cum rapuerim.' Miraris? Hoc
enim est quod te in hoc impulerit: adhuc quid feceris
nescis. Non dico illa quae fortasse tibi leviora videantur
†quae[2] ad materiam pertinent†: expugnasti domum, et vir-
ginis praetextam scidisti, et puellam usque in eam iniuriam
traxisti qua nihil gravius bella habent. Tu, qui in id te periculum demisisti ut tibi exorandus esset pater, miraris quod

7   non exorasti statim[3]? Si incidisses in illos felicioribus sae-
culis natos, [cum][4] quibus virtus magis commune bonum
erat, non expectasset[5] legem, non expectasset[5] tricesimum
diem. Nunc me merito contemnis: flentem aliquando vi-

8   disti: non auderes accusare patrem si timeres. Tu, si incidisses ‹in›[6] illum qui laureatas[7] filii sui cervices amputavit,
si incidisses in illum qui iudiciis propinquorum atque amicorum contentus fuit, opinor habuisses tempus querendi,
habuisses tempus non dico deferendi patrem sed diutius
rogandi. Illi vere fortes et viri fuerunt qui cum hoc memi-
nissent, liberos a se rei publicae gratia procreatos, bene

9   impendi crediderunt exemplo. Ego tacere contentus sum.
Cum exorari debeam, sic agis mecum tamquam etiam si

---

[2] quamquam *Ro*.
[3] *Hå.*[2]: patrem Aβ
[4] *SB*[2]: in *Watt*[2]   [5] *SB*[4]: -ssent Aβ
[6] D   [7] *Nic. Faber*: laudatas Aβ

---

[7] He would have killed the guilty son straight off.
[8] L. Manlius Torquatus Imperiosus and Spurius Cassius

So it is not dementia. Nor does it concern the present trial or your verdict whether I am a hard father, whether I am too strict. That is not the question. It is enough that I am not crazy.

"I don't win your pardon," he says, "when I have committed rape." Are you surprised? This is what made you do it. You still don't know what you have done. I don't speak of things which are relevant to our matter that may seem to you of slighter importance: you stormed a house, and you tore a virgin's gown and you brought a girl into an injury than which war holds nothing worse. Having brought yourself into a danger such that you have to get your father's pardon, are you surprised that you did not get it straight away? If you had fallen upon those born in happier times, in which virtue was more a common good, he would not have waited for the law, he would not have waited for the thirtieth day.[7] As it is, you are right to despise me; you once saw me weeping. You would not dare to accuse your father if you were afraid of him. Had you happened upon the father who cut off his son's laurelled beard or the one who was content with the judgments of relations and friends,[8] I imagine you would have had time[9] to complain, time, I won't say to prosecute your father, but to entreat him at length! They were truly brave, heroes; remembering that they had procreated children for the sake of the commonwealth, they believed them well sacrificed for the example. I am content to say nothing. When you ought to be winning my pardon, you behave to me as though even if I give you

Vecellinus (see Wi.). The case of D. Junius Silanus Manlianus (Val. Max. 5.8.3) might also be thought of, but he came later.

[9] Meaning of course the opposite.

praestitero tibi plus alii debiturus sis. Confutabit, opinor,
10 indulgentiam meam ille melior, ille mitior. Ego vero facilius frangerer si ille irasceretur. Aliquis, cum filia [illius][8]
rapta sit, tam cito exoratus est? Quis est ille tam demens?
Quid est istud quod vobis nimium convenit? Quid est istud
quod ille se accepisse iniuriam non putat, quod omnia[9] sic
agit tamquam exoratus ante tricesimum diem?

11   'Quid ergo?' inquit. 'Occides?' Debeo. Si quid in me
fuerit fortis animi, si quid virtutis incorruptae, faciam;
duret tantummodo animus, non deficiam, non deflectar.
Etiamnum fortis sum, etiamnum posse videor: sed supersunt dies. Non blandior tibi: cotidie me hortor et instigo
animum meum et totam sceleris tui deformitatem pono
ante oculos, et illud nescio quid quod persuasioni meae re-
12 pugnat volo perdomare. Bene facis quod accusas: turpiter
deficiebam, perdebamque[10] necessarium civitati exemplum, iamque in eam venturus eram hominum suspicionem tamquam me permittente fecisses.

13   Hoc age: dic insanum, dic furiosum, dic longe ab intellectu sanguinis sui positum. [vide][11] Ne rogaveris. Quid
enim acturus ‹es›[12] ad genua provolvendo, adhibendo
amicos, flendo in pectus meum? Insanus sum, nihil sentio.
I ad illum patrem tuum.

8 *SB*[3]
9 *β*: *om.* A
10 *ed. Bipontina*: prod- A*β*
11 *SB*[4]
12 *Ri.*

10 Implying a collusion between the girl's father and the rapist
to bring about their marriage; cf. 343.

what you ask you will owe more to someone else. That better, gentler father, I suppose, will put my indulgence to shame! But I should yield more readily if he were angry. Has anyone whose daughter has been raped ever been won over so soon? Who is that lunatic? What is that all too cozy agreement between you? What does it mean that he does not think he has received an injury? That he behaves throughout as though he had been won over before the thirtieth day?[10]

"So what?" he says. "Will you kill me?" I ought to. If anything of a brave spirit shall be in me, anything of uncorrupted virtue, I'll do it. Only let my spirit hold, I shall not fail, I shall not be turned aside. I am still brave, I still think I can; but there are days remaining. I do not flatter you; every day I exhort myself and goad my spirit and set the whole ugliness of your offence before my eyes and try to master that I don't know what which resists my intention. You do well to accuse me; I was faltering disgracefully, wasting an example necessary to the community, on the point of incurring a general suspicion that you might have done it with my permission.

Go on then. Call me insane, call me crazy, call me a man placed far from the understanding of his own blood.[11] Don't beg.[12] For what good will it do you to fall at my knees, call in friends, weep into my bosom? I am insane, I feel nothing. Go to that father of yours.

[11] I.e. "one far from being able to recognize his own kin" Wi. An ungainly phrase.

[12] *Vide ne rogaveris* should mean, if anything, "are you sure you haven't been begging?" or "see that you haven't begged," neither of which makes sense.

350

Aqua frigida privigno data

Qui habebat filium, amissa matre eius, aliam uxorem duxit. Incidit in gravem valetudinem filius. Convocati sunt medici; dixerunt moriturum si aquam frigidam bibisset. Dedit illi noverca aquam frigidam. Perît iuvenis. Noverca accusatur a marito veneficii.

1   DECLAMATIO

Veneficii ago. Filium meum perisse, et ea potione quam dederit noverca perisse, non difficile probabo. Nam et datam a se potionem non negat, et eam periculosam fuisse quae praedicta sunt ostendunt.[1] Ne ignorantia quidem de-
2 fendi potest: id quod accidit denuntiatum est. Itaque non tam in defensione fiduciam habet quam in lege, nec tam dicere potest scelus se non fecisse quam illud, impune fecisse. Negat enim se teneri posse veneficii, quoniam non dederit venenum.
3   Postea videbimus et quomodo intellegendum sit venenum et an hoc quod datum est illo tempore fuerit venenum; interim putemus nullam legem huic sceleri proprie
4 esse constitutam: nonne proxima[2] utendum est? Non ignoro esse frequentem huiusmodi in iudiciis minoribus dumtaxat contentionem, ut ‹petitor›[3] pecuniae[4] excidisse formula,[5] ut aliter quam oportuerit[6] agere dicatur. Sed haec tunc valent cum ostenditur ius aliud quo agendum sit.

[1] *Aer.*: -dit Aβ
[2] *Gron.*: -mo Aβ
[3] *Becher* (*cf.* 260.4 *fin.*)
[4] *Becher*: -am Aβ: petitor *Brisonius*
[5] *Ranc.*: -l(a)e Aβ   [6] *Ro.*: pot- Aβ

350

Cold water given to stepson

A man had a son. When he lost the boy's mother, he married another wife. The son fell gravely ill. Doctors were called in; they said he would die if he drank cold water. The stepmother gave him cold water. The youth died. The stepmother is accused of poisoning by her husband.

DECLAMATION

This is a poisoning charge. I shall have no trouble proving that my son died, and died of the drink that his stepmother gave him. For she does not deny that she gave him the drink, and that it was dangerous the warnings show. She cannot even offer ignorance as a defense: what happened was predicted. So she does not rely so much on a defense as on the law and she can't so well say she did not commit the crime as that she committed it with impunity. For she says that she can't be liable for poisoning since she did not give him poison.

Later we shall see both how "poison" is to be understood and whether what was given at that time was poison; meanwhile, let us suppose that there is no law specifically applying to this crime: don't we employ the one that comes closest? I am not unaware that in trials of this sort, those of lesser consequence at least,[1] it is often contended that <a claimant> has used the wrong form, is pleading incorrectly. But these arguments have force only when another law is pointed out under which the action should take place. So if

---

[1] Implying that legal quibbling would not be tolerated in matters of public importance.

Itaque si dicis qua lege alia accusare debuerim, merito
excludis hanc qua ago.[7] Sed neque hanc actionem meam
admittis neque aliud demonstras quo recedam ab hac lege
depulsus: hoc contendis, ut istud, etiamsi scelus sit, facere
5 licuerit. Atqui hoc etiamsi ‹sit›[8] non proprie conscriptum,
consuetudine iudiciorum consequens est, quotiens aliqua
propria actio in rem non detur, uti proxima et simili. Nulla
tanta esse potuit prudentia maiorum (quamquam fuit
6 summa) ut ad omne genus nequitiae occurrat.[9] Ideoque
per universum et per genera singula conscripta sunt iura.
Caedes videtur significare sanguinem et ferrum; si quis
alio genere homo fuerit occisus, ad illam legem reverte-
mur: si [inciderit in latrones aut][10] in aquas praecipitatus,
si in aliquam immensam altitudinem deiectus fuerit, eadem lege vindicabitur qua ille qui ferro percussus sit. Igitur et alia similia. Lex de aqua frigida scripta non erat: redeamus necesse est tamen ad eam quae venena coercet,[11]
cum aqua frigida id effecerit quod venenum.
7   Haec, ut remittam non fuisse hoc veneficium; nunc
vero venenum quomodo interpretari et intellegere possumus? Ut opinor, potionem mortis causa datam. Non quaeritur qualis sit, sed quid efficiat. Nam ipsorum venenorum
plura genera, plura nomina sunt, diversi etiam effectus.
Aliud ex radicibus herbarum contrahitur, aliud ex animali-
bus mortiferis reservatur; sunt quae frigore sanguinem ge-

---

[7] qua a. *Ro.*: quam lego Aβ   [8] *Ro.*
[9] occurreret *tempt. Wi.* (-rrerit *Gron.*)
[10] *Wi.*   [11] *Wi., auct. Aer.*: noceant Aβ

---

[2] In the several categories of offences, understanding *in
universum per singula genera*; for example, the law of *caedes* cov-

you tell me under what other law I should have brought my charge, you are right to exclude this one under which I am pleading. But you neither admit this action of mine nor show me another to which I can withdraw when I am dislodged from this law; your contention is that what she did was legal, even though it is a crime. And yet, though this <may> not <have been> drafted with specific reference, it follows in customary trial procedure that, whenever an action specific to the matter is not to hand, we employ the one that comes closest, one similar. The wisdom of our ancestors (though it was of the highest order) could not be so great as to meet every kind of wickedness, and for that reason laws were written comprehensively through the several categories.[2] "Murder" seems to signify blood and steel;[3] if someone is killed in some other way, we shall go back to that law. If he is flung into water or thrown down from an immense height, he will be avenged by the same law as the man who has been stabbed. And so on, therefore. No law had been written about cold water. However, we must go back to the law that punishes poisons, since cold water had the effect of poison.

This I say as conceding that this was not poisoning. But as matters stand, how can we interpret and understand poison? As I suppose, as a drink given to cause death. The question is not what it is but what it effects. For of actual poisons there are many varieties, many names, the effects too differ. One is drawn from the roots of herbs, another is put aside from deadly animals; some freeze the blood with

ers not only murder by a weapon but other forms of murder. Taking *singula* with *iura* (Håkanson) does not seem to help.

[3] *Caedes* has that connotation; cf. "butcher."

lent, sunt quae calore nimio vitalia exurant: omnia tamen
8 haec sub unam legem veneficii veniunt. Quin illud etiam in
rerum natura manifestum atque deprehensum est, alia
esse aliis venena: quaedam, mortifera nobis, etiam in remedium quorundam animalium cedunt; quaedam, quae in
voluptates etiam et luxuriam adhibentur, multis animali-
bus adferunt mortem. Similis ratio et remediorum est. Cur
igitur non sit differentia [cum veneno][12] etiam temporis?
9 Nihil interest quid faciat alias: nunc venenum est. Quomodo autem[13] comprobare[14] ista possumus? Ante omnia
animo dantis, deinde effectu. Animus dantis qualis fuerit,
mox[15] probabimus; interim de effectu constat. Vultis aestimare? Adeo certum fuit hoc venenum esse ut praedictum
sit. In summa, quid plus pati potuerat adulescens si venenum bibisset? Ponamus ex altera parte illam potionem
cuius tu nomen subinde iactas, pone ex altera potionem
quam tu dedisti: de utraque idem medici dicent. Si nihil
interest mortis, nihil interest criminis.
10   Haec ad ius; sed ad ream legi suae applicandam sane
scrutemur et animum. Non[16] dico quae sit quae dederit;
interim hoc respondeo, aquam frigidam dedit. Sane medici non vetuerint, non timuerint; satis est, non permiserunt.
Personam non onero, denuntiationem dissimulo: dedisti
11 aegro quod pater non dedisset. Si unus aliquis ex medicis

12 *Wi.*   13 *Sch.*: enim Aβ
14 *Ro.*: -parere Aβ
15 *Gron.*: non Aβ
16 *anne* nondum ?

---

4 *Venenum* according to Wi. Rather, I suggest, a particular poison (e.g. hemlock) which, he says, the defendant often brings up.

cold, others burn the vitals with excess of heat. But all these come under the same law of poisoning. Furthermore, it is clear and discovered in the Nature of Things that different organisms have different poisons. Certain of them, lethal to us, actually become remedial for certain animals, certain others, that are even used for pleasure and luxury, bring death to many animals. It is the same with remedies. So why should there not be a difference of time too? What it does at another time makes no difference: now it is poison. First, by the giver's intention, second, by the effect. What sort of intention the giver had, I shall prove presently; meanwhile, all agree about the effect. You wish to judge? That this was poison was so sure that it was predicted. In fine, what more could the young man have suffered if he had drunk poison? Let us put on one side that potion the name[4] of which you bandy about from time to time and on the other side the potion which you gave: the doctors will say the name of both. If the death is no different, the crime is no different.

So much as to law. But to attach the defendant to her proper statute,[5] let us by all means examine her intention too. I won't say *who*[6] the giver is; meanwhile, I reply that she gave cold water. Suppose the doctors didn't forbid, had no fears: it is enough that they didn't give permission. I don't stress the persona, I say nothing of the warning: you gave a sick person what his father would not have given. If just one of the doctors had said that the potion would only

[5] To show that this is indeed a case of poisoning.

[6] That it is a stepmother. *Interim* implies that the stepmother topos will come later, which it doesn't, the declamation being probably incomplete. *Nondum* would be normal.

nocituram tantum potionem esse dixisset, dicerem tamen: fortasse moriturum non putaveris, nocere voluisti. Nunc[17] inter omnes medicos constitit periturum esse si aquam fri-
12 gidam bibisset: dedisti postquam certum erat. Velim scire an aliquid tale in valetudine eius et ante feceris. Nam sive fecisti, apparet quomodo ad tantum periculum deductus sit; sive non fecisti, apparet fuisse causam propter quam faceres. 'Non putavi nocere, nec credidi medicis. Adeone ignota medicinae experimenta sunt?'

351

Exul index tyrannidis

Exulem intra fines deprehensum liceat occidere. Ex[1] suspicione tyrannidis sit actio. Exul, apud quem dives fuerat hospitatus, scripsit senatui se facturum indicium tyrannidis si reditus sibi decerneretur. In curia cum ageretur, solus dives contradixit. Decreto tamen reditu exul ille intra fines est occisus. Dives tyrannidis reus est.

1   SERMO

Exulem illum qui occisus sit dicemus, antequam damnaretur, fuisse civem seditiosum, omnibus sceleribus confossum; sed in illis quoque diu non fiducia innocentiae verum

---

17 *Ri.*: hoc Aβ   1 *ed. princ.*: et Aβ

---

7 To kill the boy.

8 The question is the stepmother's whether as discrediting the doctors' warning ("doctors are always experimenting") as SB[2], or as implying that the cold water was an experiment on her part; but I prefer the former. Wi.'s suggestion that the declamation is unfin-

harm, I would say in spite of all: perhaps you did not think he would die, you only wanted to harm. As it is, all the doctors agreed that he would die if he drank cold water. You gave it after there was a certainty. I should like to know whether you did anything like that before his sickness. For if you did, it is plain how he was brought into such danger; if you did not, it is plain that there was a reason why you did it.[7] "I did not think it was harmful, and I did not believe the doctors. Are medical experiments so little known?"[8]

351

Exile, informer on a tyranny

Let it be lawful to kill an exile caught inside the borders. Let there be an action from suspicion of tyranny. An exile, at whose home a rich man had been a guest, wrote to the senate that he could give information of a tyranny if his return was decreed. When the matter was debated in the senate house, only the rich man spoke against. The return, however, was decreed, but the exile was killed inside the borders. The rich man is accused of tyranny.

DISCUSSION[1]

We shall say that the exile who was killed had been before his conviction a seditious citizen, riddled with all manner of crimes; but that even in the midst of them he had kept

---

ished seems likely to be right ("it would be odd to give the opposition the last word"; and cf. on s.10 *interim*). His text, however, gives *adeone . . . sunt* to the prosecutor.

[1] In essence a declamation put into indirect speech. In the following pieces too *sermo* has replaced declamation. Calpurnius Flaccus 6 is on the same theme.

audacia nescio qua omnia fingendi atque dissimulandi la-
tuisse, et, quemadmodum multos inimicos habuerit, sic
2 non pauciores habuisse similes sui amicos.[2] Vix quidem
illum, quamvis in manifestis sceleribus, nescio qua audacia
repugnantem damnari potuisse. Expulsum autem (quod
fere sceleratis pectoribus eveniat[3]) graviter tulisse poenam
ac praecipue auctoribus eius fuisse infestum; quibus ut re-
3 ferre gratiam posset, quaesisse occasionem reditus. Quod
ut posset contingere, prius conterrere[4] voluisse patriam, ut
in communi servitutis metu non tanti unius exulis reditum
quanti securitatem omnium iudicaret. Dictitare igitur coepisse apparari tyrannidem, instare patriae gravem servitu-
4 tem: quaedam se comperisse. Has eius voces frequentes,
cum forte eadem iter faceret, ad divitem perlatas; et protinus motum tali rumore certius aliquid ex ipso voluisse
scire, quidnam [exul][5] loqueretur, an arma aliqua apud
eum, an vestigia saltem tyrannidis reperiri possent. Sibi
quoque exulem dixisse apparari tyrannidem, sed nihil
5 praeterquam inania verba se apud eum comperisse. Illum
autem hoc ipso accensum, quod fabulis suis iudicaret
etiam a divite haberi fidem, non distulisse quod diu cogi-
tasset: misisse ad senatum indicii epistulam. Ad nuntium
tam atrocis rei attonito universo senatu, divitem indicasse
quid ipse comperisset, quemadmodum sibi quoque eadem

---

[2] inimicos . . . similes sui a. *SB*[1]: similes sui amicos . . . inimicos
Aβ   [3] *Aer.*: v- Aβ   [4] *Pith.*: -terere Aβ   [5] *SB*[2]

---

[2] On this showing the rich man suspected the exile of plotting
tyranny; cf. Calp. 6 *pars altera*, where however text and interpretation are in doubt. Why the suspicion? Because of his bad character (cf. s.1)? In my Teubner edition I suggest eliminating *an . . .*

under cover for a long time, not in confidence of innocence but by a certain audacity in all kinds of falsehood and dissimulation, and that, just as he had many enemies, so he had friends like himself no fewer. It was with difficulty, although his misdeeds were clear, that he could be convicted as he fought back with a kind of audacity. When he was expelled, as generally happens with criminal mentalities, he bore the punishment hard and was especially hostile to its authors; and so that he could requite them, he sought an opportunity to return. And in order to get that, he first wanted to alarm the country so that in the general fear of enslavement she might judge the return of one exile as less important than the safety of all. So he began to talk about a tyranny plot, said heavy enslavement was threatening the country, that he had some information. This repeated talk of his was carried to the rich man, who chanced to be travelling in the same area. Moved by such a rumor, he wanted at once to know something more definite from the exile himself, what he was saying, whether weapons could be found in his home[2] or some trace at any rate of a tyranny. The exile had told him too that a tyranny was in preparation, but he had learned nothing in his home except empty words. The exile, however, fired by this very belief that the rich man too credited his fables, did not put off what he had long had in mind: he sent the senate a letter of information. The whole senate was in consternation at the report of something so atrocious, and the rich man informed them of what he himself had learned, how the exile had

possent or regarding those words as a stumble on the declaimer's part. In any case I see no virtue in deleting *apud eum* with Rohde and Wi. as an anticipation of the same words below.

6 denuntiasset. Intellexisse vanam illius, sine ullis argumentis, vocem; itaque dixisse nihil scire exulem, supervacuo
revocari. Ceteros autem, qui attoniti erant, decrevisse tanti non esse unius exulis reditum ut diutius tali metu sollici-
7 ta teneretur civitas. Hoc decretum senatus non omnibus
fuisse notum (etenim [festinatione quoque][6] in eiusmodi
metu praecipitari solere omnia), legem illam quae exulem
intra fines iuberet occidi nemini fuisse ignotam. Eum igitur qui multos inimicos haberet, non omnibus decreto senatus, omnibus iure exulis noto, intra fines occisum non
esse mirandum.

8 　　Multum adiuvat in defensione persona[7] divitem, quod
est integer; in qua parte etiam gloriari potest, ut dicat se
odisse etiam aliena scelera.

9 　　　　　DECLAMATIO

Tyrannidem paro. Vides enim: cum sceleratis mihi convenit, revocari exules volo, non etiam facta illorum, ‹non›[8]
consilia deprehendo. An ego, si hoc cogitassem, tam aperte omnia egissem et ipse potissimum ad exulem issem[9]?
Protinus me ac propositum meum innocenti[10] aperu-
issem? Non hoc ipsum timere debui? Adiecissem huic
suspicioni sententiam meam, ut viderer timere indicem?

[6] SB[3]　　　[7] SB[1]: -nae Aβ　　　[8] Sch.
[9] Becher: mis(s)i- Aβ　　[10] Hâ.[2]: no- Aβ

[3] It did not ordain, only permitted.

[4] So the prosecution's theory, that he had engineered the exile's death to block the information, is baseless.

[5] Meaning of course that his actions show just the opposite.

[6] Tyranny.

314

given the same warning to himself. He had realized that it was empty talk, without any proofs, and so said that the exile knew nothing, and there was no need for him to be recalled. But the others, who were in consternation, had decreed that the return of one exile was not of such importance that the community should be kept any longer in such fear. The decree of the senate was not known to everybody (and indeed in a scare of this sort everything is apt to be done in a hurry), but everybody knew of that law which ordained[3] that an exile within the borders be killed. So it was not to be wondered at that a man who had many enemies was killed inside the borders, when the senate's decree[4] was not known to everybody but the status of the exile was.

The rich man is much helped in his defense by his persona, in that there is nothing against him. In that section he can even boast, saying that he hates crime even in other people.

DECLAMATION

I am getting up a tyranny! For you see: I am in with criminals, I want exiles to be recalled, I don't catch their doings, their plots![5] If I had had this[6] in mind, would I have done everything so openly and gone myself of all people to the exile? Would I have revealed myself and my plan right away to an innocent man[7]? Ought I not to have been afraid of this very thing[8]? Would I have added my vote to this suspicion, so as to seem as if I was afraid of an informer?

---

[7] As the prosecution represents the exile, though the rich man too finds him guilty of nothing more than idle talk and a fraudulent proffer of information.

[8] Of his getting wind of what I was up to.

Nihil debui minus quam in metu ipse[11] metum prodere.

352

Reus tyrannidis qui deliberavit victor arma deponere

Ex suspicione tyrannidis sit actio. Quaedam civitas, quae bello laborabat, cum duobus proeliis victa esset, adulescens dives nobilis cum servorum et clientium manu armata processit in proelium. Fugavit hostes. Populus redeunti portas clusit. Cum aperturum promitteret si arma posuisset, respondit dives se deliberaturum. Triduo deliberavit. Rediit in civitatem positis armis. Reus est tyrannidis.

1   SERMO

Divitem hunc dicemus natum honesta domo, patre militari, forti viro; a primis statim annis adsuevisse studio armorum, magnum per se militiae usum collegisse. Cum autem subito bellum incidisset, factum alium ducem non iudicio sed quodam casu et incerta populi aura (nec sane vacasse tam ⟨in⟩[1] subito dilectum ducum agere)—factum ducem qui nullum militiae usum haberet; nec aliunde victam duo-

2   bus proeliis urbem. Tum demum intellexisse populum qualem haberet ducem; et ante omnes amicos paternos frementes venisse ad divitem, palam questos de duce,

[11] *SB*[4]: ipsum Aβ
[1] *SB*[2]

---

[1] "Martial arts."
[2] As distinct from his father's training.
[3] Lit. "breeze."
[4] *Tam in subito*: see SB[2].

The worst thing I could do in the scare was to show scared myself.

352

Accused of tyranny one who after victory considered whether to lay down his arms

Let an action lie from suspicion of tyranny. When a certain community which was in trouble in a war had been defeated in two battles, a rich young nobleman went into battle with an armed band of slaves and clients. He routed the enemy. As he returned, the people closed the gates against him. When they promised to open them if he laid down his arms, the rich man replied that he would consider. He considered for three days. He returned to the community after laying down his arms. He is prosecuted for tyranny.

DISCUSSION

We shall say that this rich man was well-born, his father being a military man, a hero. From his earliest years he was habituated to the pursuit of arms[1] and had himself gathered a great deal of military experience.[2] On the sudden outbreak of war, someone else was appointed to the command, not by judgment but by some chance and the people's fickle whim[3] (and to be sure in such an emergency[4] there was no time to pick and choose commanders)—a commander was appointed who had no military experience; and for no other reason the city was defeated in two battles. Then indeed the people realized what sort of a commander they had. Above all others, his father's friends came to the rich man in loud protest, openly grumbling

adiecisse: 'pater tuus, si viveret, pro patria arma cepisset: non esset passus vexari rem publicam et hostium armis et imperiti[2] ducis consiliis.' Accensum his vocibus pro salute ac libertate omnium pia arma cepisse, privatas quoque

3 adiecisse vires. Urbe egressum solutos laetitia victoriae hostes et nihil minus quam eruptionem timentes oppressisse. Hac victoria accensum, quasi in aemulum,[3] gravi dolore exarsisse ducem. Cum diceret malo exemplo militare privatos, et cum omnes amici divitis cum divite essent, non

4 difficile persuasisse ut portas cluderent. Milites autem confecto proelio ad gratulationem redeuntes portas clusas obstipuisse; posteaquam vero iussi sint arma ponere, aliquanto gravius exarsisse: veluti parricidas se excludi et armatis hostibus inermes obici. Hanc seditionem volentem sanare divitem tempus petisse, non magis deliberandi quam rogandi; et triduo illo nihil aliud egisse quam modo

5 singulos, modo universos rogasse. Illos quoque securiores fuisse posteaquam ex toto recessisse hostem crediderint. Redisse autem se a bello ad iudicium, et in conscientia maximi meriti gravissimum sibi crimen obici, ut qui solus rem publicam defenderit[4] opprimere voluisse dicatur.

353

Dispensatores torti

Quidam ab infitiante petebat depositum. Dispensatores

[2] *Fr., Obr.*: -tis Aβ
[3] *tempt. SB*[3]: -latione Aβ: -nem *Bu.*
[4] *Aer.*: -ret Aβ

about the commander, and adding, "If your father were alive, he would have taken up arms for our country. He would not have let the commonwealth be harried both by the enemy's arms and the counsels of an inexperienced commander." Fired by such words, he took up patriotic arms for the salvation and freedom of all, and also added his private resources. Issuing from the city, he surprised our enemy, who was relaxed in the joy of victory and apprehended nothing less than a sally. The commander, stirred by this victory, as though against a rival, flared up in fierce resentment. Saying that private armies were a bad precedent and with the rich man's friends all with the rich man, he had no difficulty in persuading them to close the gates. The soldiers, returning to be congratulated after wrapping up the battle, were astounded to find the gates closed; but after they were ordered to lay down their arms, their anger blazed up considerably more violently as they protested that they were being shut out like traitors and exposed to the armed enemy unarmed. Wanting to heal this sedition, the rich man asked for time, for entreaty as much as for deliberation, and in those three days he did nothing but beg his men, now individually, now collectively. They too felt safer after they believed that the enemy had totally retreated. He, however, had returned from war to a trial; in the consciousness of having performed a signal service he was facing a very grave charge, alleged to have wished to crush the commonwealth which he alone had defended.

353

Stewards tortured

A man was claiming a deposit from another who denied

utriusque torti contraria dominis dixerunt. De integro lis est.

1 Petitor necesse est infamet dispensatorem suum et dicat ab adversario corruptum, et ea fiducia esse illum infitiatum, cum promitteret dispensator negaturum se etiam in tormentis. Itaque ab adversario natum, cum lis esset: 'dis-
2 pensatores torqueamus.' Alterum hunc dispensatorem sani propositi dicet, qui semper accepisse se palam dixerit, et statim cum datus sit in tormenta, hoc sibi proposuerit[1]: 'quid? ego quo praemio mentiar?'; ⟨ideo⟩[2] confessum esse. Et hoc in locis valens est: 'Tuus dispensator accepisse se ait, meus dedisse negat. Huius potentior vox est: potest
3 enim etiam per alium numerata videri pecunia.' Initio autem dicet hunc[3] sibi placuisse servum, et ideo supra rationes esse positum; sed postea et licentia sua et securitate domini, qui illi plurimum crediderit, isse in vitia, a multis corruptum antequam ab hoc, et ideo se deposuisse. ⟦Hanc sibi deponendi fuisse causam, cum videret in malo statu rationes esse.⟧ Hoc necesse est adicere quia urgetur per interrogationem quam causam deponendi habuerit.
4   Infitiator dicat oportet dispensatorem suum finem tormentorum quaesisse: ideo confessum ut dimitteretur.

---

[1] *Aer.*: -rat Aβ   [2] *Aer.*   [3] *Sch.*: hic Aβ

---

[1] Perhaps to be deleted. But cf. *confessum* in s.4.

[2] If the money was deposited, the claimant's steward might still be telling the truth, supposing the deposit was made by somebody else, so that both can be believed. But that argument does not cover s.2, where the denier's steward says he received the deposit openly, in which case he would know, and say, who made it.

same. The stewards of both said under torture the opposite of their masters. The suit starts afresh.

The claimant has to discredit his steward and say that he has been bribed by his opponent, who has rejected the claim in reliance on the steward's promise to deny even under torture. Hence arose from the opponent, when the proceedings started: "let us torture the stewards." He will say that this other steward's intention was honest, for he always said openly that he had received the money and when handed over to torture he has this intention right away: "What? For what reward would I lie?" <Therefore> he confessed.[1] This too among common topics is effective: "Your steward received the money, mine denies that he gave it. The latter's word is more valid, for the money can also be thought to have been paid through someone else."[2] He[3] will say that initially he was pleased with the slave and therefore put him in charge of accounts, but later he went to the bad, what with his own license and the carelessness of his master, who trusted him a great deal; he had taken many bribes before this one and for that reason he himself made the deposit. [[This was his reason for depositing, since he saw that his accounts were in a bad way.]][4] This has to be added because he is pressed by questioning as to what reason he had for depositing.

The denier has to say that his steward wanted to end the torments: he confessed to be let go.

The claimant proceeds on the supposition that his steward was a scoundrel.   [3] The claimant.   [4] Either this or *et . . . deposuisse* calls for a double bracket (cf. SB[2]).

354

Morietur antequam nubat

Quidam nubilem filiam habens uxorem secreto loquentem
cum adulescente vicino formoso deprehendit. Quaesivit
quid locuta esset. Respondit mulier de nuptiis filiae se lo-
cutam. Ei maritus filiam despondit. Mater ait: 'morietur
antequam nubat.' Ante diem nuptiarum puella subito perît; livores et tumores in corpore fuerunt. Mulier rea est.

1   SERMO

Dicet haec mulier iuvenem illum numquam sibi placuisse,
et repugnasse se cum videretur illi puella destinari; illum
autem, utique volentem hanc uxorem habere, ad satisfac-
tionem venisse; tunc vero minus placuisse matri generum.

2 Itaque cum desponsam audisset filiam, cotidiana consuetudine vulgi iratam dixisse: 'morietur celerius quam nubat.' Ceterum de fato puellae una cum accusatore queretur. Causa fati[1] cruditate[2] fingitur.[3]

355

Tutor lenocinii reus

Pupillus cum tutore agebat tutelae, tutor cum pupillo
adulterii. Remiserunt invicem actiones. Lenocinii tutor
reus est.

---

[1] c. f. *Bu.*: -am f. Aβ: -a facti B   [2] *SB*[4]: -delitate Eβ:
-delitati A: cruditas *Bu.*   [3] fingetur *Bu.*

---

[1] By the husband, as in the elder Seneca's parallel case (*Contr.*
6.6).   355: [1] I.e. *tutelae male gestae* (346, *thema*).

354

She will die before she marries

A man who had a marriageable daughter caught his wife talking to a handsome young neighbor. He asked her what she had said. The women replied that she had talked about their daughter's marriage. The husband engaged the daughter to him. The mother says: "She will die before she marries." Before the wedding day the girl died suddenly; livid patches and tumors were on her body. The woman is accused.[1]

DISCUSSION

The woman will say that she never liked the young man and put up a resistance when it seemed the girl was intended for him. He, however, was determined to have her as his wife and came to make it all right. But then the mother liked him all the less as a son-in-law. So when she heard that her daughter had been affianced to him, she was angry and after the everyday fashion of common folk she said: "She will die sooner than she marries." As to the girl's death she will make moan along with the accuser. Indigestion is put up as the cause of death.

355

Guardian accused of pandering

A ward was going to law with his guardian over the guardianship,[1] the guardian with the ward for adultery. They mutually called off their actions. The guardian is accused of pandering.

1

SERMO

Fuisse quosdam utriusque inimicos hic tutor dicet, qui
ab initio moleste tulerint non ipsis potius relictam esse tutelam et, quoniam ab hac praeda exclusi sint, distulerint
spes suas in diem ultimum tutelae, ut rudem et imperitam
2 pupilli aetatem fraudibus suis circumscriberent. Se autem
tutelae rationes, ut debebat, reddidisse. Ceterum metuen-
tem ne dimissus a se pupillus fraudibus et insidiis inimicorum circumscriberetur, velut alteram eius tutelam gestu-
rum in domo retinuisse. Tunc vero consurrexisse illos qui
tutelam ipsis non commissam moleste tulerant, et graviter
excanduisse: ne peracto quidem tutelae tempore a domo
tutoris pupillum dimitti, nullam occasionem ad despoli-
3 andum imperitum iuvenem dari. Cogitasse igitur quemadmodum pupillum ac tutorem mutuo dolore distraherent.
Nam si rationes tantum infirmarent, videbant futurum ut
optima conscientia tutor non expectaret ultimam contentionem iudicii, sed per communes amicos propinquosque
4 pupilli satisfaceret. Invenisse illos rationem qua mutuo dolore distraherent: summisisse qui dicerent male tractatas
a tutore rationes; non omnia nosse pupillum qui taceat:
si litigare velit, futurum ut sua recipiat. Per alios deinde
internuntios sollicitatum maritalem animum, qui pupillum
5 falso crimine adulterii inquinarent. Se ut[1] maritum cre-
dulum nihil tanti putasse ut ‹non›[2] suspicioni suae satisfaceret. Diu hac fraude inimicorum pupillum tutoremque

---

[1] *SB*[4]: utique Aβ [2] *Gron.*

---

[2] In s.1–6. S.7 switches to the prosecution.   [3] If *utique*
is kept, the meaning will be "a husband who would believe anything." But the guardian would not be likely to say that of himself.

DISCUSSION

This guardian will say[2] that there were certain enemies of
both who were aggrieved from the start that the guardianship had not been left to themselves, and, having been shut
out from this plunder, put off their hopes until the final day
of the guardianship, in order to swindle the raw, inexperienced youth of the ward by their frauds. Himself, however,
had duly rendered accounts of his trust. But fearing that
the ward, once he let him go, would be swindled by the
frauds and snares of his enemies, he had kept him in his
house as though to exercise a second guardianship over
him. Then those who had been aggrieved because the
guardianship had not been entrusted to themselves rose
up in a great fury: even after the period of guardianship
had expired, the ward was not sent away from the guardian's home, no opportunity was given to fleece the inexperienced youth. So they thought of a way to drive a wedge
between ward and guardian with mutual rancor. For if
they only threw doubt on the accounts, they saw that the
guardian, whose conscience was clear, would not wait for
the ultimate contention of a trial but would make a set-
tlement through friends and relatives of the ward. They
found a way to drive a wedge between them with mutual
rancor. They suborned persons to say that the guardian
had cooked his accounts. The ward, they said, who was silent, did not know everything; if he would go to law, he
would recover his property. Then his mind as a husband
was disturbed through other go-betweens, who smeared
the ward with a false charge of adultery. A credulous husband,[3] he had to satisfy his suspicions at all costs. For a
long time ward and guardian were deceived by their ene-

deceptos. Sed posteaquam veriores amici intervenerint et se interrogaverint quam actionis haberet fiduciam, pupillum item seduxerint et querelae causas quaesierint, tum demum apparuisse mutuum errorem; et se[3] quaedam cer-

6 tius etiam ab uxore quaesisse. Detecta igitur fraude inimicorum facile depositas, quae nullis fundamentis niterentur, actiones et reditum in gratiam. Se tamen nondum inimicos effugisse, a quibus reus factus sit.

7 Accusator autem non committet si in pupillum dixerit: id enim crimen illi obiciet quod ille noluerit diluere. Dicet ergo propter amorem adulterae illum in domo tutoris remansisse (nam ante quattuordecim annos incredibile est crimen), remansisse ergo ‹propter›[4] amorem, nec illam indulgentiam in retinendo pupillo fuisse tutoris sed conscientiam, cum sciret male redditis rationibus non esse

8 offendendum pupillum. Mulieri autem multa donata, quaecumque desideraverit concessa. His sceleribus invicem cognitis, primo utrumque excanduisse, deinde tutorem ex conscientia rationum omisisse potius matrimonii vindictam quam mutuis caderent actionibus. Sic pares acceptasque factas rationes.

---

3 Eβ: sed A
4 *Gron.: anne* ob ?

---

4 Loving the woman, he will not want to deny their relationship. Hardly a convincing point, but perhaps better than Wi.'s: "because (it is hinted) he came to a compromise with his guardian rather than have the matter thrashed out."

5 He will therefore say nothing about the period when the boy was still in tutelage. The lawyers fixed the age of puberty as fourteen (see Wi. on s.1).

mies' trick. But after truer friends intervened and asked what evidence he had to go to law with, and likewise took the ward aside and enquired the grounds for his complaint, then indeed the mutual error came to light; and he himself got some more reliable information from his wife too. So the enemies' trick was discovered, the actions, unfounded as they were, readily dropped, and the two reconciled. But he himself has not yet escaped his enemies, by whom he has been charged.

The prosecutor will not go wrong if he speaks against the ward; for he will charge him with an offense of which he will not want to clear himself.[4] So he will say that the young man stayed on in his guardian's house because of his love for the adulteress (for before the age of fourteen the charge is unbelievable[5])—he stayed on, therefore <because of> his love, and that in keeping the ward the guardian was not acting out of affection but from his bad conscience, knowing that his accounts had been rendered improperly and so he must not offend the ward. As for the woman, she was given many gifts and granted anything she wished. When these crimes were mutually known, at first both flared up, but then the guardian with his guilty conscience over the accounts preferred to forego vengeance for his marriage rather than have both lose in their mutual actions.[6] So the accounts[7] were balanced and accepted.

[6] He was afraid that each would lose his case against the other. So the Latin seems to say. But given that both are at this point presented as guilty, the "Master" probably meant that each would be found guilty on the other's charge.

[7] Not the guardian's pecuniary accounts but metaphorically; see Wi.'s citations.

356

Filius pro meretrice patris suam redimens

Quidam luxurioso filio, amanti meretricem, dedit pecuniam ut sibi emeret eam meretricem quam ipse pater amabat. Ille eam redemit quam ipse adulescens amabat. Abdicatur.

1   SERMO

Hic senex dicet filium fuisse luxuriosum et non sine maximo patrimonii ac famae damno amasse meretricem. Cui malo voluisse mederi patrem: saepe obiurgatum filium, saepe secreto, saepe etiam palam castigatum. Cum iam nec sumptibus nec inverecundiae[1] finis imponi posset, habuisse cum cognatis consilium quidnam se facere oporteret. Abdicaret? Sed tanto liberior fuisset luxuria. Castiga-

2 ret? Sed nihil castigando profecerat. Succurrisse cognatis et amicis rationem qua putarent iuvenem posse emendari: si simularet pater amari a se meretricem et daret pecuniam potissimum ipsi filio ad redimendam; quod si fecisset, futurum ut meretrix redempta altera meretrice, deinde ab ipso adulescente redempta, indignaretur et illum amare

3 desineret. Nam initio statim dicendum est culpa meretricis iuvenem haesisse, et ideo quaesitam quae avocaret, et illa ratione datam iuveni pecuniam. At illum protinus cu-

---

[1] *Sch.*: ver- Aβ

---

[1] From the pimp.

[2] As indeed he was according to the theme.

[3] Not his mind off her. The prostitute had caught him and only she could set him free. The purpose of the buying out was to alienate the man's girl, not to provide a counterattraction.

356

A man buying out[1] his own prostitute
instead of his father's

A man gave money to his loose-living son, who was in love
with a prostitute, to buy out for him a prostitute whom
he himself, the father, loved. He bought out a prostitute
whom he himself, the young man, loved. He is disowned.

DISCUSSION

This old man will say that his son had been a loose-liver and
loved a prostitute not without great detriment to patrimony and reputation. The father had wanted to remedy
the evil. He often upbraided his son, often castigated him
in private, often even publicly. When finally no limit could
be set to the extravagance and shamelessness he took counsel with his relations on what he ought to do. Should he
disown? But the loose living would be so much the more
unbridled. Should he castigate? But castigating had got
him nowhere. A way occurred to the relations and friends
whereby they thought the young man might be reformed:
if the father pretended that *he* was in love with a prostitute[2] and gave money to the son himself of all people to
buy her out. If he did that, when the other prostitute had
been bought and bought out by the young man himself, the
prostitute would be outraged and stop loving him. For it
must be stated at the start that the young man had got involved by the prostitute's fault, and for that reason they
looked for something to take her mind off him[3] and that
was why money was given to the young man. But he ran

currisse ad meretricem suam; patrem autem, quoniam
nullo modo sanare filium potuerit, ad ultimam ultionem
confugere: abdicare filium quia emendare non potest.

357

Uxor non relinquens ob adulterium caecatum

Adulter excaecetur. Uxor virum in calamitate ne deserat.
Quaedam patri de marito ter questa et tacere iussa postea,
ab excaecato ob adulterium viro quia non recedit, abdicatur.

SERMO

1   Haec mulier dicet acceptum a patre maritum se ab initio
amare coepisse; adulescentem lenociniis adulterae illius
usque eo captum esse ut revocari a cupiditate non posset.
Ut necesse erat, moleste se tulisse, et eo magis quod mari-
2   tum diligeret. Voluisse ergo experiri quid de adulteriis[1]
pater sentiret; indicasse ei adulescentis errorem. Respondisse illum esse quaedam aetati[2] concessa, nec reprehendi
lusus in eiusmodi iuventa debere. Tum vero cariorem sibi
virum factum posteaquam lusibus eius patrocinari etiam
3   senex coeperit. Sed cum videret nequissimae mulieris illecebris maritum teneri, et iam vindictam adulterii atque occasionem captare adulterae maritum, iterum ad patrem
venisse, ut illius saltem auctoritate emendari adulescens

---

[1] *Ro.*: -ris A(Eβ)
[2] *Fr.*: -ibus A(E)β: -i huic *Ro.*

straight to his own girl. As for the father, since he had no
way to cure his son, he resorted to the ultimate punishment, that is, to disowning his son because he cannot re-
form him.

357

A wife who does not want to leave one blinded for adultery

DISCUSSION

Let the adulterer be blinded. Let a wife not desert her husband in adversity. A woman complained three times about
her husband to her father and was told to be quiet. Later
her husband was blinded for adultery and she is disowned
because she does not leave him.

DISCUSSION

This woman will say that from the beginning she fell in love
with the husband she had received from her father. The
young man had been so captured by the allurements of
that adulteress that he could not be recalled from his lust.
She bore it hard, as she was bound to do, all the more so
because she loved her husband. So she thought she would
see how her father felt about adulteries and told him of the
young man's error. He replied that certain concessions
were made to youth and that frolics in one so young were
not to be blamed. At that her husband became all the
dearer to her after the old man too began to excuse his frolics. But when she saw that her husband was trapped by the
seduction of that wicked woman and that the husband of
the adulteress was already watching for the opportunity to
punish the adultery, she came again to her father, hoping
the young man could be reformed by his authority if noth-

posset. In eadem voce illum perseverasse iterum ac tertio.
4 Accessisse novum amori suo sacramentum, et iudicio patris auctum[3] iuvenis adfectum.[4] Miserrimum ergo iuvenem fraude et insidiis deceptum eam fortunam sustinere
quam illi semper uxor timuerit.
5   Hoc colore optime defendetur mulier, alioqui lege imbecilla. Nam ex contraria parte infinitum potens est illud,
maritum esse damnatum.

358

Exposito pulsatori amputatae manus

Talionis sit actio. Qui patrem pulsaverit, manus perdat.
Quidam ‹ab›[1] exposito quem in locum filii sustulerat pulsatus tamquam pater manus incidit. Agnitus ille advocato
naturali patre talionem petit.

1   SERMO

Hic adulescens iure infirmus est: nam quod lege agitur non
solet vindicari lege. Cur enim potius ab educatore quam a
carnifice petatur talio? Sed praeterquam lege etiam facto
laborat, quod quamvis educatorem, tamen patris loco pul-
2 saverit. Dicat tamen educatorem fuisse hunc ab initio crudelem, et hinc suspicatum iuvenem non esse illum verum
patrem. Saepe amicis questum, quibusdam etiam man-

---

[3] *Sch.*: fac- AEβ   [4] accessisse . . . a. *huc transp. SB*[2]: *post*
timuerit (*infra*) *habent* AEβ
   [1] *Gron.*

---

   [1] The theme says otherwise: *uxor . . . ne deserat.*
   358: [1] *Talio*; cf. 297, theme. The case reappears in 372, where
the "Master" argues for the defense.

ing else. He stuck to the same answer a second and third time. A new sanction reinforced her love, and her affection for the young man was enhanced by her father's judgment. So the wretched young man, deceived by trick and treachery, endures the fate that his wife always dreaded for him.

The woman will best be defended by this color; her legal position is weak anyway.[1] For on the other side the fact that her husband was convicted carries infinite weight.

358

An exposed beater's hands cut off

Let an action of eye-for-eye[1] lie. Whoso beats his father, let him lose his hands. A man was beaten <by> one whom he had found exposed and adopted in place of a son. As a father, he cut off his hands. Recognized, the other calls in his natural father and claims eye-for-eye.

DISCUSSION

This young man is weak legally; for what is done according to law is not commonly punished by the law. For why should eye-for-eye be claimed from the foster father rather than from an executioner?[2] But he is in trouble not only in law but in fact, in that he beat one in a father's place, though a foster father. However, let him say that this foster father was cruel from the start and for that reason the young man suspected that he was not his real father. He had often complained to friends and actually commis-

---

[2] The question assumes that the law applies to foster fathers. What follows passes to the moral aspect, with the same result.

dasse ut inquirerent qui aliquando infantes exposuissent. Hac re validius offensum senem. Itaque dedisse operam ut se pulsandum praeberet; deceptum [certum habeo][2] etiam tempore ipso iuvenem incidisse in eum quem minime pro-
3 vocatum iniuria vellet. At illum confestim tamquam de alieno non deliberasse sanguine et, quasi[3] redditurus esset expositum, debilitasse. Certe eum lege patris usum qui sciret nec se patrem nec hunc filium. Adulescentem autem, quia nondum professum[4] illo tempore patrem habuerit, certe quia probare non potuerit, tacuisse; nunc petere talionem.

359

Lis publicani de unionibus

Praeter instrumenta itineris omnes res quadragesimam publicano debeant. Publicano scrutari liceat. Quod quis professus non fuerit, perdat. Matronam ne liceat attingere. Matrona iter faciens cum ad publicanos venisset, uniones habens quadringentos in sinum abdidit. Hos cum requi-

---

[2] *SB[3], auct. Wi.*   [3] *SB[4]*: quia Aβ
[4] *SB[1]*: prospectum Aβ

---

[3] That it was night is implied, though the theme does not say so. Wi. compares 364.4.

[4] "An astonishing glossing over of a beating" (Wi.). But the young man did not recognize the foster father and thought it was a chance encounter with a stranger—even though the foster father had deliberately put himself in the way.

[5] *Confestim* belongs with *debilitasse*, to which *tamquam . . . expositum* is prefatory.

sioned some of them to make enquiry as to persons who
had at one time exposed infants. That gave greater offense
to the old man. So he took care to put himself in the way of
a beating; deceived even by the time,[3] the young man fell
in with[4] the person whom he would have least wanted to
provoke by an injury. But the other, it not being his own
blood, did not pause to consider and immediately[5] mutilated him, as though he was about to repeat his exposure.[6]
Certainly he used a father's law when he knew that he was
not the father nor this man his son. As for the young man,
since at that time he did not yet have a professed father,
since he could not offer certain proof, he kept silent. Now
he claims eye-for-eye.

359[1]

Suit of an exciseman about pearls

Except for travelling gear, let all items owe 2½% to the exciseman. Let the exciseman have license to search. What
anyone does not declare, let him forfeit. Let it be illegal to
touch a lady.[2] When a lady travelling came to the customs
with four hundred pearls, she hid them in her bosom.

---

[6] See crit. note. With *quia*, "because he was about to return
the exposed one," there is a gap in the narrative, which had only
reached the point when the son had started to look for his real
father. And the prospect of transferring him hardly makes a reason
for the mutilation. *Quasi* gives a quip: "mutilated him (like Oedipus) as though he was about to subject him to a second exposure."
For *redditurus*, "repeat, reproduce," see *OLD reddo* 7.

[1] See 340 and 342.

[2] *Matronam*; see 342, *thema*.

reret publicanus, matrona scrutandi potestatem fecit. Publicanus noluit scrutari. Translatis manum iniecit et suos dicit.

1   SERMO

Quaestiones sunt: an instrumenta itineris videri uniones possint; an, etiamsi non possint videri, tamen, quoniam ad usum et ornamentum matronae parati sint, in commissum venire potuerint; an in usum parati sint; an, si in usum parati sint, non ostensi teneri possint, cum ostensi nihil de-
2 buerint; an, quamvis scrutari matronam non liceat, et ipsa permittente et publicano licuerit; ⟨an⟩[1] perinde sit scruta-tionem permisisse ac rem ostendisse; an dimissa res peti possit; an haec dimissa sit (dicit enim publicanus non rem sed controversiam dimissam).

360

Lis de dotibus socrus et nurus

Prius[1] ratio dotis habeatur. Quaedam apud filium amisso viro dotem reliquit. Adulescens ducta uxore dotata deces-sit. Res solvendo non est. Contendunt socrus et nurus utra prius dotem accipiat.

1   SERMO

Mulierem illam socrum nurus dicet hanc ruinam patrimo-

[1] *Ro.*   360: [1] *SB*[3]: primus A*β* (-um B): -ma *vulg.*

---

[3] How did he know about them?
[4] Presumably about whether they were subject to excise. That could be obviated by failure to declare them.
[1] A very tricky piece, calling for elucidation.

When the exciseman asked for them,[3] the woman gave him permission to search. The exciseman declined to search. After they had passed through, he laid hand on them, claiming them as his own.

DISCUSSION

The questions are: can pearls be considered travelling gear? Even if they could not be so considered, still, since they are there for the use and adornment of a lady, can they be confiscated? Are they there for use? Or if they are there for use, can they be seized not having been shown, although if shown they would not be subject to excise? Although it be illegal to search a lady, is it legal with her permission, and for an exciseman? Is permitting search tantamount to showing the item? Can an item let pass be seized? Was this item let pass? (For the exciseman says that what was let pass was not an item but an argument.[4])

360[1]

Mother-in-law and daughter-in-law in litigation about their dowries

Let the matter of dowry have priority. A woman having lost her husband left her dowry with her son. The young man married a dowered wife and died. The estate is insolvent. The mother-in-law and the daughter-in-law dispute which shall get her dowry first.

DISCUSSION

The daughter-in-law[2] will say that the woman, her mother-

[2] I now think the text sound and the note in my Teubner edition misconceived.

nii post mortem viri statim sensisse; non sumpsisse dotem
ne et filium decoloraret et dotem quoque perderet. Itaque
etiam dotatam filio quaesisse uxorem, quo facilius posset
ruentis patrimonii rationem fulcire. Addat donasse illam
filio petitionem, hodie, quia decessit, retractare. Sed et
praescribat.

2 DECLAMATIO

Sero petis, et illud[2] patrimonium est. Tu, dum heres mariti
tui erat, a filio petere debuisti; ego ex bonis mariti mei repeto. Nam duae mortes maritorum diversas successiones
habent. Bona mariti mei morte eius ⟨mea⟩[3] facta sunt;
dum viveret, patris fuerunt. Dos est si a viro aut ab herede
eius repetatur: tu amisso viro cum dotem non petisti, fecisti creditum ex dote.

3 SERMO

Circumscriptam se nurus queretur, et in ultimo quaeret in
quem usum anus dotem desideret.

Contra illa dicet hanc mulierem ambitiosam et profu-
sam fuisse: non minime propterea ad egestatem perduc-
tum virum.

---

[2] SB[2]: aliud Aβ   [3] SB[2] vel pro mei supposui

---

[3] The estate being insolvent, the dowry might not be repaid
even if claimed.   [4] The sentence is still part of what Nurus
might say.   [5] Rationem.   [6] Nurus. The following "she"
is Socrus, but Nurus is definitely the subject of praescribat.

[7] On the ground that the waiver precluded the claim.

[8] Nurus is speaking.   [9] Socrus' dowry, now part of her
son's estate inherited by Nurus.   [10] Nurus has inherited
these, but they are owing to the son's creditors, of whom she is in a

in-law, realized immediately after her husband's death that the estate was in ruin; she did not take her dowry for fear of casting discredit upon her son and losing her dowry into the bargain.[3] So[4] too she looked for a dowered wife for her son so that he might the more easily prop up the structure[5] of his collapsing patrimony. Let her[6] add that she waived her claim for her son's sake, but today, because he is dead, she takes it up again. But let her also enter a demurrer.[7]

DECLAMATION[8]

You claim too late, and that[9] is patrimony. While he was your husband's heir you should have reclaimed it from your son. I reclaim from my husband's possessions.[10] My husband's possessions became <mine> by his death; while he[11] lived, they were his father's. It is dowry if it be reclaimed from a husband or his heir. When you did not reclaim your dowry after you lost your husband, from a dowry you made it a loan.[12]

DISCUSSION

The daughter-in-law will complain that she has been cheated, and at the end will ask for what purpose the old woman wants the money back.

On the other side the other will say that this woman[13] was self-serving and extravagant. That was not the least of the reasons why her husband was reduced to penury.

sense one. Under the law in the theme a dowry would have priority over other claims, but see n.12.

[11] The father, who predeceased the son.

[12] She admits that Socrus' dowry belongs to Socrus, but it has the status of a loan, with no priority over other claims.

[13] Nurus.

4

[DECLAMATIO]⁴

Nurus oportet a viro dotem repetat, socrus a patri-
monio.

361

Depositi rapti quadruplum

Qui depositum perdiderit, iuret et sibi habeat. Quidam
cum depositum furto amisisset iuravit. Postea furem damnavit, exegit quadruplum. Dominus hoc quoque petit.

1

DECLAMATIO

Meae pecuniae accessio ad me pertinet. Quid si enim co-
gnitor meus, quid si procurator hoc idem respondeat? Denique, quid si damnatus fur non totum solvisset? Nempe
meum damnum erat. An iacturam debeo sentire, accessio-
nem non debeo? Ego enim a te recessi cum iurasti; iam
cum fure mihi negotium est: hic quidquid solverit ad me
pertinet.

2

SERMO

Contra ille suo nomine egisse se dicet, investigasse, laborasse. Illud praeterea potens est pro illo, non potuisse

4 SB⁴

---

14 Wi. gives up on this "epigram." It looks like part of the
sermo and I have secluded the heading. The second part repeats
the point made in s.2 init.: Socrus must claim her money as a loan,
not as a dowry, whereas Nurus claims hers as a dowry, with priority over other claims on the estate.

1 "The law is very strange" (Wi.). If he had really lost the de-

DECLAMATION 361

[DECLAMATION]

The daughter-in-law should reclaim dowry from her husband, the mother-in-law from the patrimony.[14]

361

Fourfold of a stolen deposit

Whoso loses a deposit, let him take an oath and keep it.[1] A man lost a deposit by theft and took an oath. Later he convicted the thief and exacted fourfold. The owner claims this too.

DECLAMATION[2]

The increment on my money belongs to me. What if my attorney or my agent were to make the same answer?[3] Finally, what if the convicted thief had not paid the full amount? I suppose that would have been my loss. Ought I to feel the loss but not the increment? For I left you when you took the oath. My business is now with the thief.[4] Whatever he pays belongs to me.

DISCUSSION

On the other side he will say that he acted on his own account, investigated, worked. An effective point in his favor

posit he would not be keeping it, but "keep it" must be understood as "not have to repay it." [2] On behalf of the depositor.

[3] I.e. claim any profits arising from matters they had handled.

[4] Apparently a sort of vivid present, representing not what is but what in equity should have been. The depositor could not take action against the thief (s.2); the holder had taken action and received the money with penalty. The present claim by the depositor is against him.

dominum illum furti agere: 'Itaque iudex quid pronuntiavit? Nimirum mihi furtum esse factum.'

362

Invicem pulsatores patrum

Qui patrem pulsaverit, manus ei incidantur. Duo adulescentes aequales iuraverunt ut alter alterius patrem caede-
rent. Ceciderunt. Petuntur manus; patres vindicant.

1   SERMO

Fuisse duos sodales, patribus ex austero indulgentibus.
Saepe coisse ad lusum, frequenter una fuisse. Quodam
tempore, cum alter ex his serius in convivium venisset,
dixisse alterum: 'Fortasse te, ut solet, ille senex retinuit.
Sed non feret impune: ego illum verberabo.' Hunc deinde
2   respondisse: 'et ego tuum caedam.' Cum alternis verbis
iactarentur minae, et uterque metueret ne inultum haberet patrem, iurasse in ultionem magis parentum quam
iniuriam.

363

Vestiplica pro domina

Malae tractationis sit actio. Quidam pauper, formosae ma-

---

⁵ And not the owner (Wi.).   ¹ Presumably the advocate
for the son. The action will have been against the fathers, but the
theme, as it stands, does not say so.

² Lit. "austerely loving." For the adverbial *ex austero* cf. *ex
lento* in Sen., *Dial*. 3.1.8 *et sim.* (*TLL* V.2.1123). Interpreters, unaware of the idiom, are at sea. *Indulgentibus* = "loving" rather
than "indulgent." See my Teubner apparatus.

is that the owner could not have taken action for theft. "So what did the judge pronounce? Surely that the theft was committed against me."[5]

362

Beaters of their fathers, mutually

Whoso beats his father, let his hands be cut off. Two young men of the same age took an oath that each would beat the other's father. They did. Their hands are claimed. The fathers punish.

DISCUSSION

He[1] says that there were two friends, whose fathers were loving but on the austere side.[2] One day, when one of them arrived at a dinner rather late, the other said: "Perhaps that old man kept you as usual. But he shan't get away with it. I'll whip him." Then this one replied: "And I'll thrash yours." So as they bandied threats alternately and each of them was afraid of having his father unpunished, they took an oath more to punish their fathers than to injure them.[3]

363

A wardrobe maid[1] instead of her mistress

Let there be an action of maltreatment. A poor man, hus-

---

[3] Presumably we are to understand that the beatings were only token. But according to the theme, *ceciderunt*, so it is hard to see any virtue in the "Master's" color.

[1] Lit. "clothes folder."

ritus, a peregrino vicino negotiatore ter de stupro uxoris adiecto pretio appellatus, vestiplicam dominae habitu misit. Malae tractationis reus est.

1   SERMO

Maritus illo colore defendendus est, ut dicatur fuisse diligens custos pudicitiae uxoris, natura quoque sollicitus et sedulus. Cum esset de stupro uxoris appellatus, admiratum tantam peregrini negotiatoris audaciam; cum deinde etiam repetitus, suspicari aliquid etiam de uxore coepisse; quantum nunc appareat, suae naturae potius vitio quam
2 culpa uxoris. Cum vero tertio quoque instaret adulter, non potuisse dissimulare suspicionem et sollicitudinem suam. Itaque quia putaret aliquid ante cum sua uxore locutum adulterum per vestiplicam, advocasse illam et quaesisse num aliquid de adulterio sciret. Illam respondisse innocentem esse dominam et ne notam quidem negotiatori: 'denique si dubitas, me uxoris tuae habitu mitte: videro an possit discernere.'

364

Conviciator pauper occisus

Pauper ad divitis domum nocte conviciari solebat. Quodam tempore dives processit, et insanire eum dicens decem servis imperavit ut eum domum ducerent. Cum isdem occisus postero die inventus est. Dives caedis reus est.

---

2 Presumably by the wife.   3 Would-be.
4 If the trick worked, it would prove the wife's innocence. If not, it would prove nothing either way.

band of a beautiful wife, was solicited three times by a foreign neighbor, a businessman, for his wife's favors, at a named price. The husband sent a wardrobe maid dressed as her mistress. He is accused of maltreatment.[2]

DISCUSSION

The husband is to be defended with the following color: Let him be said to have been a careful guardian of his wife's chastity, also naturally anxious and sedulous. When he was solicited about his wife's favors, he was surprised at the audacity of the foreign businessman. When he was approached again, he began to have some suspicion of his wife too; as far as now appears, more from a defect in his own nature than from any fault of his wife. But when the adulterer[3] urged him even for a third time, he was unable to hide his suspicion and anxiety. So because he thought that the adulterer had previously had some talk with his wife through the wardrobe maid, he summoned the latter and asked her whether she knew anything about an adultery. She answered that her mistress was innocent and not even known to the businessman. "In short, if you doubt my word, send me dressed as your wife. I'll see whether he can tell the difference."[4]

364

Jeering poor man killed

A poor man used to come to a rich man's house at night and jeer. One night the rich man came out and ordered the slaves to take him home, saying that he was out of his mind. The next day he was found along with them murdered. The rich man is charged with homicide.

1
SERMO

A parte divitis color ille introduci potest, ut dicatur pauper
fuisse factiosus aut turbulentus; habuisse eiusmodi furoris
sui comites, quibus ⟨in⟩[1] insidiis dispositis ipse tantum ad
concitandam rixam se ostenderet, ceterum illos in praesi-
2 dio haberet si quid forte dives moliretur. (Et hoc ipsa rei
condicio monstrat, cum sit incredibile pauperem solum et
praeterea nocte ad convicium diviti faciendum venisse.
Quare enim die tacuit? Quare in foro non maledixit?
Apparet illum noctem expectasse quo facilius comites abs-
3 conderet.) Paratum ergo ad rixam cum telo venisse. Divitem nihil tale suspicatum, magis insanire credentem, dedisse qui deducerent. Tunc vero pauperem quasi custodia
excanduisse; accessisse et ceteros eius conscios, qui, dum[2]
eripere pauperem vellent, rixam concitaverint, et fortasse
illum pauperem silentio occiderint, ne postea comprehen-
4 sus [pauper][3] auctores facinoris cogeretur fateri. (Et hoc
dubie ponendum est; quae constitutio in reliqua quoque
causae parte servanda est. Nihil enim pro certo adfirmare
debemus, sed tantum suspicionem iudicum a nobis alio
praevertere.) Ergo ab illis videri factam caedem qui adhuc
beneficio temporis latent; divitem super damna patrimonii
et tot servorum caedis[4] reum esse.

[1] *Aer.*
[2] A: cum β
[3] *SB*[1]
[4] *Sch.*: -dem Aβ

DECLAMATION 364

For the rich man the following color can be introduced:
the poor man is said to have been factious or turbulent and
to have had companions in such madness whom he placed
⟨in⟩ ambush, showing himself only to excite a brawl but
keeping them to back him up in case the rich man started
something (and this is shown by the very facts of the case
since it is incredible that the poor man would have come to
jeer at the rich man alone and at night too. For why did he
keep quiet in the daytime? Why not abuse him in the Forum? Evidently he waited for nightfall the more easily to
hide his companions). Therefore he came for a brawl with
a weapon. The rich man, suspecting nothing of the kind
and rather believing him to be mad, gave people to take
him away. But then the poor man flared up as though put in
custody and the others, his accomplices, came on the scene
and, wishing to rescue the poor man, raised a brawl, and
perhaps stealthily killed that poor man for fear lest he
might be arrested later on and forced to reveal the perpe-
trators (and this is to be presented tentatively, which ap-
proach is to be kept up in the rest of the case too. For we
should not assert anything positively, but only turn the
jury's suspicions in advance away from us to another quar-
ter). So the murder appears to have been committed by
those who are still in hiding, thanks to the timing.[1] The rich
man, over and above the loss of property and so many
slaves,[2] is on trial for homicide.

---

[1] Of the crime (at night).
[2] The slaves are the only loss mentioned.

347

365

De vi septem iudices

De vi septem iudicent. Quod maior pars iudicum statuerit, reus patiatur. Duo ignominiam statuerunt, duo exilium, tres mortem. Petitur ad mortem.

1 DECLAMATIO

'Quod maior pars' inquit 'iudicum statuerit.' Ego existimo maiorem partem esse in qua plures idem sentiunt, eandem poenam pronuntiant, in eadem verba iurant. Et hoc verum esse ab ipsis verbis legis disce: 'quam poenam'; non de pluribus suppliciis sed de uno loquitur. Etenim nemo potest 2 plura[1] supplicia unus nocens ferre. Scrutare et alia verba. 'Statuerit' inquit. Nonne tibi consentientis per omnia partis unius[2] videtur unam vocem includere? 'Quam poenam statuerit': id est, quod genus supplicii placere sibi pronuntiaverit, qua poena nocentem adfici voluerit.

3 'Sed quattuor' inquit 'iudices me noluerunt mori.' Tu nunc indicas quam poenam transierint, non quam statuerint; lex autem certam illorum sententiam exigit. Quid enim aliud diceres si nondum pronuntiassent, si negassent

1 D: -res Aβ
2 *SB*[3]: illius Aβ

---

[1] In Gell. 9.5.7 a closely similar problem is called insoluble; see Wi. The prosecutor argues from the words of the law, but these are inconclusive.

[2] Addressed by the prosecutor, not to the original jury but to another convened to pass sentence; cf. s.4 and 9. But most of the time he is arguing with the defendant or the defendant's advocate.

365[1]

Seven jurymen in a case of violence

In a case of violence let there be seven jurors. Let the defendant suffer what the greater part of the jury decides. Two were for stigma, two for exile, three for death. Death is demanded.

DECLAMATION[2]

"What[3] the greater part of the jury decides," it says. I conceive that the greater part is that in which more are of the same persuasion, pronounce the same punishment, take the same oath.[4] That this is true, learn from the very words of the law: "What penalty?"; it speaks not of several punishments but of one; for indeed a single guilty man cannot bear more than one punishment. Examine other words too: "Decides," it says. Don't you think it covers a single utterance of a single consentaneous part? "What penalty it decides"; that is, what kind of punishment it pronounces as its choice, what penalty it wants imposed on the guilty man.

"But four jurors," he says, "did not want me to die." You are now telling me what penalty they passed over, not what they decided. But the law demands their definite verdict. For what would you be saying if they had not pronounced yet, if they had said that they were not clear as to your pun-

---

[3] *Quod* as in the theme and s.8, changed (casually?) to *quam poenam* below and in s.2 and 5.

[4] "I know of no parallel to the swearing of a formula of sentence" (Wi.). Or does this refer (illogically) to the oath taken by any jury at the start of a trial?

liquere sibi de supplicio tuo? Numquid sententias illorum
numerares? Minime. Horum enim trium[3] iam verba signa-
vi: illorum quattuor quae signabo? Dubitare illos, nescire
quid pronuntient, etiamnum ergo suspensos? Cur dimitti
4 postulas si iudex deliberat? 'Plures' inquit 'me mori noluerunt.' Quid igitur velint pronunties oportet. Illorum sententiam signare volo, accusator recitare his iudicibus volo,
ut habeant quod sequantur. 'Duo' inquit 'exilium, ⟨duo
ignominiam⟩[4] mihi iniungunt.' *[5] 'Iam igitur ex parte[6] una
plures facis, iam turbam istam, quae universa noceret, di-
videndo extinguis.' Duo exilium, duo ignominiam pronun-
5 tiant: vis ego[7] illos iungam qui se ipsi dividunt? Revertere
nunc ad verba legis, ut paulo ante. 'Quam poenam' inquit
'maior pars iudicum statuerit.' Partem intellegimus eidem
numero applicatam, quemadmodum sententia coniunctam, sic turba. Alioqui si miscere tibi et iungere[8] dissen-
tientes licet, cur hos tres separas? Quomodo enim hi ab
illis quattuor discrepant, sic illi inter se pugnant. Ergo non
idem sentientes non potes iungere: idem sentientes com-
6 para. Ego qui mortem pronuntient tres habeo. Produc illos
qui exilium pronuntiant: vinco. Produc qui ignominiam:
aeque vinco. Dubitari potest valentiorem esse partem
quae composita neutri succumbit, utramque superat?

---

3 *Ranc.*: primum Aβ
4 *SB[1], Wi.*   5 *lac. ind. Wi.*
6 ex p. *Ro., auct. Aer.*: aperte Aβ: a parte D
7 ergo A[1]   8 *Obr.*: ingenere AC: ingerere BD

---

5 Sophistry; the four did vote. The anti-death argument, that
four jurors do not want him to die, would fail if the four included
nonvoters because nonvotes do not count.

ishment? Would you count their votes? By no means.[5] I have already stated the words of these three: what words shall I state for these four? That they are in doubt, don't know what to pronounce, still therefore in suspense? Why do you demand a dismissal if the judge is deliberating? "The majority," he says, "didn't want me to die." Then you should pronounce what they do want. I want to state their verdict, recite it as prosecutor to these jurors,[6] so that they have something to go by. "Two," he says, "sentence me to exile, <two to stigma>." * "So now you are making a majority from one part, now by dividing the group, which if united would hurt you, you extinguish it." Two pronounce exile, two stigma, do you want me to unite those who divide themselves? Go back now to the words of the law, as a little while ago. "The penalty," it says, "which the greater part of the jurors decide." "Part" we understand as brought under the same number,[7] joined by verdict as by group. Otherwise, if you are allowed to mingle and join those who disagree,[8] why do you separate these three? For just as these dissent from those four, so those four are at odds among themselves. So you cannot unite those who do not vote the same. Compare those who do vote the same. I have three who pronounce death. Bring forward those who pronounce exile: I win. Bring forward those who pronounce stigma: equally I win. Can it be doubted that the stronger part is that which when compared yields to nei-

---

[6] But what follows is from the defense. Proper sequence could be obtained by changing the active infinitives to passive *signari* . . . *recitari*).

[7] Three or two.

[8] Among themselves.

7 Quid si enim quattuor illi in totidem discreparent[9] sententias: numquid illos pro una parte opponeres? Nemo sine
dubio cum tribus meis staret, sed nemo alteri esset adiunc-
tus; numquid ex quattuor sententiis unum corpus effice-
res? Minime. At quid interest bini an singuli dissentiant?
Aeque numerari pars non potest si in partes scinditur.

8 Quid si duo ignominiam pronuntiarent, duo exilium, duo
mortem, unus (ut plerumque evenit) taceret? Sine dubio
pares essent sententiae. Si ergo detracto uno pares essent,
adiecto non sunt superiores? At enim, ut scias non utique
duas partes legem exigere, verba inspice. 'Quod statuerit'

9 inquit, non 'utrum statuerit.[10]' Denique, iudices, breviter
agendum est. Reus damnatus quam tandem poenam pati
debet si mortis poenam relinquitis[11]? Quam? Scilicet exilii.
Ergo cum tribus sententiis quattuor non cedant, duabus
quinque succumbent? <An ignominiae?>[12] At eadem est

10 iniquitas. Quid acturus es <in hac>[13] poenarum controversia? Utrumque ferre non potes: sive ignominiam sustines,
in patria morandum[14] est, sive expelleris, patriam relinquis.

11   'Quid ergo?' inquit. 'Moriar cum tres tantum me perire
voluerint?' Quid enim? an tam[15] inicum est te mori damnatum, confessum, etiam tuo iudicio supplicio[16] dignissi-
mum? Cui enim te reservabimus? Videlicet egregium
exemplum civibus[17] futurus es qui sic vivis ut damnari potueris.

[9] *Aer.*: dispartirentur (*"better* -pert-" *Wi.*) *vel* dispararent *Sch.*:
dissiparentur *Hâ.*[2]   [10] *Aer.*: potu- Aβ
    [11] *Obr.*: -uit Aβ   [12] *Ro., Ri.*   [13] *Aer.*
    [14] *Aer.*: narran- Aβ: manen- D[2]   [15] an t. *Aer.*: autem Aβ
    [16] A[2]: -ci A[1]: -cium β   [17] *Fr.*: civium Aβ

ther, beats both? For what if those four were split into as many verdicts? Would you then set them against me as a single part? Doubtless no one of them would stand with my three, but no one of them would be joined to another. Would you make a single block out of four votes? By no means. But what difference does it make whether the disagreement is by twos or by units? Equally it cannot be numbered as a part if it is divided into parts. What if two pronounced stigma, two exile, two death, and one (as often happens) abstained? Unquestionably the votes would be equal. So if they[9] are equal with one subtracted, are they not superior with one added? But, so you know the law does not necessarily require two parts, look at the words: "what the greater part decide," it says: not "which of two." Finally, gentlemen, I must be brief. What penalty ought the defendant to suffer if you leave out the death penalty? What penalty? Exile, I suppose. So when four votes will not yield to three, shall five succumb to two? ⟨Or stigma?⟩ But the unfairness is the same. What will you do ⟨in this⟩ controversy of punishments? You can't suffer both. If you bear the stigma, you must stay in the country; if you are expelled, you leave the country.

"What then?" he says? "Shall I die when only three wanted me to perish?" What about it? Is it so unfair that you die, when you have confessed[10] and even in your own judgment are eminently deserving of execution? For what shall we reserve you? Evidently you will be a splendid example to our citizens: your way of life is such that it was possible for you to be convicted.[11]

---

[9] The death votes.   [10] Not in our text.
[11] As he was by the previous jury.

366

Legatus filius proditoris occisus

‹Exulem intra fines deprehensum liceat occidere.›[1] Legatus sacrosanctus sit. Proditor cum liberis exulet. Cuius
filius legatus erat proditionis damnatus est. Revertentem
legatum quidam occidit. Caedis reus est.

1   SERMO

Fatetur caedem reus, sed iure defendit.

2   DECLAMATIO

'Exulem' inquit 'occidi.' Exul ille quando factus est? Quis
illum accusavit, quis damnavit, quis expulit? Atqui sic fieri
exulem pater illius exemplo est, et inde exul quoque dic-
3 tus est, quasi ex solo patrio expulsus. 'Pater' inquit 'illius
proditionis damnatus est; lex autem exulare et proditoris
liberos iubet.' Ut omnes lex puniat, huic tamen ignoranti
damnatio patris nocere non debuit. Puta in privatum
compendium peregrinatum: non ante exul erit †denique†
4 quam scierit se esse exulem. Aliquis poenam sustinet
quam ignorat, et eius est condicionis cuius se esse nescit?
Quem talem sacrilegum audistis, quem homicidam, quem
veneficum? Novi generis nocentem producis, tam secu-
5 rum ut se ne nocentem quidem sciat. Sed, quod paulo ante
remiseram, nego: non omnes lex punit, sed conscios, sed
participes sceleris; illis irascitur qui cum patre peccant.
Neque enim innocentes ulla lex punit. Et hic non solum in-

1 *SB*²

---

1 He became an *ex*ile by being *ex*pelled.
2 *Extra*, indeed *contra thema*.

366

An envoy, son of a traitor, killed

‹ Let it be lawful to kill an exile caught inside the borders. › Let an envoy be sacrosanct. Let a traitor be exiled with his children. A man whose son was an envoy was convicted of treason. Someone killed the envoy as he was on his way home. He is charged with murder.

DISCUSSION

The defendant confesses to the murder but defends himself with the law.

DECLAMATION

"I killed an exile," he says. When was he made an exile? Who accused him? Who condemned him? Who expelled him? But the father is an example that this is how a man becomes an exile, and that is why he was called an exile,[1] as having been expelled from his native soil. "His father," he says, "was convicted of treason and the law orders that a traitor's children too be exiled." If I grant that the law punishes them all, yet his father's conviction ought not to have hurt him when he was unaware of it. Suppose he had traveled for private profit: he will not be an exile before he knows that he is an exile. Does anyone suffer a penalty of which he is unaware, or is anyone in a status which he doesn't know he's in? Have you ever heard of such a temple-robber, such a homicide, such a poisoner? You are giving us a new kind of criminal, so confident that he doesn't even know himself to be guilty. But I deny what I conceded just now: the law does not punish them all, but the accomplices, the partners in the crime: it is angry with those who sin along with their father.[2] For no law punishes the inno-

355

6 nocens sed etiam honoratus fuit: legatus fuit. Ut proditoris
filium licuerit occidere, legatum non licuit. Quid enim lex
ait? 'Legatus sacrosanctus sit.' An hoc dubium est, fuisse
legatum? Creatus est, missus est. Atqui si fuit legatus, non
potuit antequam renuntiaret legationem desinere, tamquam magistratus intra suum annum, tamquam sacerdos.

7 'Patris' inquit 'damnatione desiit esse legatus.' Ad alium
forsitan filium pertineat paterna damnatio: ad legatum non
pertinet. Ante enim legatus hic factus est. Ita in eo iure fuit
in quo illum ‹esse›[2] res publica ante iusserat [id est, ante
legatus fuit quam damnati filius].[3]

Sed puta licuisse: non oportuit.

8   SERMO

Hic de iniuria publica querendum, quod ignoretur quid
renuntiaturus fuerit. Ultima descriptio, quam[4] nihil tale
merens occisus sit, etiam inter hostes tutus.

                                  367

                         Luxuriosi pater fortis

Luxuriosi pater fortiter fecit. Praemium non optavit ex
lege. Dementiae reus fit a filio.

1   DECLAMATIO

Dementiae reo quid obicis? Usitata fortasse crimina: trac-

    [2] *Ro*.
    [3] *SB*[3]
    [4] *Ro., Ri.*: qua Aβ

cent. And this man was not only innocent but honored: he was an envoy. If I grant that it was lawful to kill a traitor's son, it was not lawful to kill an envoy. For what says the law? "Let an envoy be sacrosanct." Or is there any doubt that he was an envoy? He was elected, he was sent. But if he was an envoy, he could not cease to be one before he had reported his mission, like a magistrate in his year, like a priest.[3] "By his father's conviction," says he, "he ceased to be an envoy." A father's conviction might perhaps pertain to another son, but not to an envoy. For he was made an envoy previously. So his legal status was that in which the commonwealth had previously ordered him ⟨to be⟩.

But suppose it was legal, it was not right.

DISCUSSION

Here we should complain of injury to the public because it is not known what he was going to report. Finally a description, how he was killed without having done anything to deserve it, safe even among enemies.

367

Hero father of a loose-liver

The father of a loose-liver became a hero. He did not opt for a reward according to the law. He is accused of dementia by his son.

DECLAMATION

He stands accused of dementia. What have you to say against him? The usual complaints perhaps: clothes trailed

---

[3] A bad example, since priests were usually appointed for life, not to undertake a particular mission.

tas per publicum vestes, non reddita salutantibus nomina,
non discretos ab inimicis amicos, aut dissipata luxuria bona
et aliena aetati vitia? Habet hoc crimen domus nostra, si
reum mutas. An vero desidiam obicis? Bellum non sentio,
2 hostem non intellego, patriam non vindico? 'Praemium'
inquit 'non optas.' Puta me rationem non posse reddere.
Non est unius criminis dementia. Ut hoc sit argumentum
dementiae, infirmum est quia solum est. ⟦Deinde num-
3 quam in uno dementia deprehenditur.⟧[1] Obice et alia. Sed
quid si ne hoc quidem obici potest? Quid? tu liberalitatem
dementiam vocas? Non expedit tibi, adulescens, hanc legem introducere. 'Non optas.' Age, quisquis non est avarus
4 demens est? Varii sunt mores. Puta me nolle optare, non
concupiscere praemium: non invenio quod optare possim;
deinde patriam onerare nolo bello adflictam; deinde gra-
tuitae debent esse virtutes; deinde hoc est praemium, intueri debitorem populum. Licet differre. Permittes et tua
5 causa: uxorem tibi opto, honores opto. 'Statim' inquit
'opta.' Ergo, si facio, sanus sum? En crimen quod statim
tolli potest! Quid vis optem? Opto statuas: vultum contra-
hit; dies festos: irascitur. Quid igitur? 'Pecuniam.' Et si
hanc desideras, cur non fortiter pugnabas? Descende in
aciem. An ego pro te pugnavi? Si perseveras in foro potius
militare quam in proelio, abolitionem[2] opto: tolle iudicium.

[1] *ita secl. SB*[3] (*del. SB*[1])
[2] *SB*[2]: absolut- Aβ

in public,[1] greetings by name not returned, friends not distinguished from enemies, or possessions squandered in loose living and vices inappropriate to his age? Our house lies open to this charge, if you change the defendant. Or is it laziness you bring against me? I don't feel the war, I don't understand the meaning of "enemy," I don't support the country. He says: "You don't opt for the reward." Suppose I can't explain: dementia is not a matter of a single charge. Even if this argued dementia, it is feeble because it is isolated. ⟦Further, dementia is never caught in a single item.⟧ Make other criticisms. But what if even this one cannot hold? Do you call generosity dementia? It's not in your interest, young man, to introduce such a law. "You don't opt." Come, is anybody who is not greedy demented? Characters differ. Suppose I don't want to opt, have no desire for the reward. I don't find anything to opt for; further, I don't want to burden my country, afflicted as she is by war; further, good deeds should be gratuitous; further, my reward is to see the people in my debt. I am allowed to defer. You will allow that, even for your own sake: I opt for a wife for you, honors.[2] "Opt right now," he says. Well, if I do, am I sane? Behold a charge that can be squashed right away! What do you want me to opt for? Statues? He frowns. Holidays? He gets angry. Money? Well, if that's what you want, why were you not a hero? Go into battle. Or did I fight for your sake? If you insist on soldiering in court rather than in combat, I opt for annulment. Away with the trial!

[1] Wi. cites Sen. *Contr.* 2.6.2, where a toga worn loosely down to the feet is a sign of loose living (*luxuria*).

[2] I.e. offices.

368

Alens patrem rapta abdicata

Rapta invito patre nuptias optavit. Ob hoc abdicata tacuit.
Egentem patrem quia invito marito alebat est repudiata.
Ingrati agit adversus maritum.

1 DECLAMATIO

Beneficium dedit: vitam donavit. Magnum beneficium est
lucem dare: ideo sunt parentes carissimi—et illi vitam dant
non sentientibus. Quid quod beneficium dedit cum accepisset iniuriam? Iam non tantum vitam tuam donavit tibi
sed etiam ultionem suam, nec tantum non exegit suppli-
2 cium sed etiam concessit matrimonium. Quid his vis adiciam? Exorata est. Solent dolere raptae et contineri non
possunt, nec a patribus. Dedit ergo beneficium. Quid si
etiam contra patris voluntatem te servavit? Illum offendit
ut tibi parceret. Et quam graviter! Etiam abdicata est.
Dum[1] tibi beneficium dat, ipsa accepit iniuriam. Donavit
3 tibi etiam testamentum patris. Accepisti ergo beneficium.
Non rettulisti gratiam. Quid si fecisti etiam iniuriam?
Expectatis ut dicam 'cultus negavit': viduam fecit. Quantum est vestis et ornamentum? ⟦Matrimonia sunt ab ipsa
rerum natura inventa. Sic mares feminis iunguntur ut im-
4 becillior sexus praesidium ex mutua societate sumat.⟧[2] Puta illam[3] habere patrem ad quem se recipiat: infamata est.

---

[1] *Ro.*: cum Aβ   [2] *ita secl. SB*[3]   [3] *Aer.*: illum Aβ

---

[1] Whoever wrote this title should have written *repudiata* (or
rapta abdicata alens patrem repudiata)

[2] Whereas the rapist did.

[3] Even so.

368

A rape victim supporting her father disowned[1]

A rape victim chose marriage against her father's will. Disowned on that account, she kept silence. Because she supported her father in need against her husband's will she was divorced. She brings suit against her husband for ingratitude.

DECLAMATION

She gave him a boon: she granted him his life. To give the light of day is a great boon. That is why our parents are most dear to us—and they give life to those who don't know it.[2] There is also the fact that she gave the boon after receiving an injury. So not only did she grant you your life but also her revenge, and not only did she not exact punishment but also conceded your marriage. What would you have me add? She forgave you. Rape victims are usually angry and cannot be restrained even by their fathers. So she gave you a boon. More, she saved you even against her father's wish. She offended him to spare you. And how gravely! She was actually disowned. In giving you a boon, she herself received an injury. For you she sacrificed even her father's testament. You did not repay it. More, you even did her an injury. Are you, gentlemen, waiting for me to say: "He refused her dress allowance"? He made her a widow. How petty are clothes and jewelry? ⟦Marriages were invented by the very Nature of Things. Males are joined to females so that the weaker sex gain support from the mutual partnership.⟧ Suppose she has a father to whom she can retreat: she has been disgraced.[3] As it is, she

Nunc bis vidua est, mendico patre. Ergo maritum eripis.
Quem tandem maritum? Quem tantopere dilexit ut patri
praeferret. Potuit tibi controversiam facere de nuptiis iuris
sui, si ad ingratum reverti vellet.

5   Quid huic[4] obicis? 'Patrem' inquit 'alit.' Accusas quod
miseretur. Patrem ali non solum oportet verum etiam necesse est. 'Sed me' inquit 'perire voluit.' [Ecquid ignoscitis,
iudices, si talem oderat qui ante cognoverat? Nam haec
ignoravit.][5] Perire voluit merito: rapueras. Lex te occide-
6 bat, non huius pater. Sed non defendo illum, qui non ad te
venit [peccavit idem],[6] te non rogat: filiam rogat, te uxor.
Nempe haec ei petit cibum seni cui alieni porrigunt. Nec
multum est quod detur, et haec misericors est. Sed expel-
lis, et cum patre mendicare cogis. Non es ingratus?

7   [Ergo matrimonium eripis. Quid quod matrimonium
iuris sui? Poterat iniusti repudii agere, <si reverti>[7] vellet.
'Inimicum' inquit 'meum alebat.' Miraris? Misericors est.
Et hoc accusas? Forsan non personam aestimavit sed fortunam. Est hoc vitium illius: nuper et raptoris miserita est.
8 Sed quid tam valde iste peccavit ut mori debeat? 'Me' inquit 'perire voluit.' Imitaris quod arguis. Ergo peccavit?
Idem facis. Crudelitatem et accusas et imitaris. Sed ille

---

[4] *SB*[3]: his Aβ
[5] *SB*[3]   [6] *Wi.*
[7] *SB*[3]: si *Bu., auct. Aer.*

---

[4] Not irrelevant. Her poverty was an added deprivation.
[5] The marriage is considered as protected by the law which
gave the rape victim the right to opt, so that the legality of the divorce could have been challenged; but if she had won, she would
have had to rejoin her husband. See s.7.

has been doubly widowed, with her father a beggar.[4] So you take away her husband. And what a husband? One she loved so much that she preferred him to the father. She could have disputed with you about the marriage, which was hers by legal right,[5] if she had wanted to go back to an ingrate.

What do you have against her? "She supports her father," he says. You're accusing her of taking pity. It's not only right but necessary that a father be supported. "But he wanted me to die," he says. Don't you forgive him, gentlemen, if he hated such a man, knowing him beforehand? For *she* did not know him.[6] He had good reason for wanting you to die: you had committed rape. The law was taking your life, not my client's father. But I am not defending him; he did not come to you, he is not begging you; he asks his daughter, your wife asks you. You could say that she begs food for an old man to whom strangers offer it. What is given isn't much and she is compassionate. But you drive her out and make her beg alms with her father. Are you not ungrateful?

⟦So you take her marriage away. Add that it is a marriage of her own right.[7] She could sue you for wrongful divorce, ⟨if⟩ she wanted to ⟨go back⟩. "She was supporting my enemy," you say. Are you surprised? She is compassionate. Well, do you accuse that? Perhaps she did not judge the person, but the plight. It is a foible of hers. Recently she took pity on a rapist too. But what did he do so very wrong that he deserves to die? "He wanted me to die," he says. You are copying what you accuse. So he did wrong? You are doing the same. You both accuse cruelty and copy

---

[6] Neither statement is in the theme.   [7] See above, n.5.

merito, quippe raptorem. Puta peccasse: satisfecit, rogat,
miser est; hostes quoque parcunt. Denique haec meruit:
9 hanc respice. 'Te quoque' inquit 'abdicavit.' Relinque aes-
timationem ipsi doloris sui, sine ipsa ⟨se⟩[8] vindicet. Sed
cur vindicet? Merito abdicata est. Te servaverat: meruit
exulare. Sed puta iniuste abdicasse: pater est. Non respi-
cimus in eiusmodi fortuna quid meruerit. Denique quid
faciet mulier cum ad ianuam venerit? Et quantulum est
quod praestat!
10   Quo nunc se misera conferet? Cum patre nimirum
mendicandum habet. Facile tamen maritum inveniet: tantum ne impune laesa sit solacium petit.]]

369

Armis sepulcri victor

Sepulcri violati sit actio. Quidam arma de sepulcro viri
fortis, suis consumptis, sustulit; victor reposuit. Reus est
violari sepulcri.

1   DECLAMATIO

Potui infitiari quod obicitur. Detracta arma dicis? Nego.
Mentior? Eamus in rem praesentem. Adnumerare volo; si
quicquam defuerit, damnari volo. Sed non corrumpam
gloriam meam, ut dissimulem propter quod vir fortis honoratus sum. Sed quid faciam? Non licet mihi ista narrare:
instat livor, et id quo salvus est odit.

---

[8] ipsa ⟨se⟩ *Wi., auct. Aer.*: ipse Aβ: ipsa (*sc. dolorem*) *Sch.,
Gron.*

---

[8] Well of you.   [9] Of the jury.
[1] Jealous folk would shout him down?

it. But he had a good reason—it was a rapist. Suppose he was wrong: he has made amends, he begs, he is wretched. Even enemies spare. Finally, she deserved:[8] consider her. "You too he disowned," he says. Leave judgment of her grief to her, let her be <her only> avenger. But why should she take any vengeance? She deserved to be disowned. She had saved you; she deserved banishment. But suppose he disowned her unjustly; he is her father. In a plight such as his we don't look at what he deserved. Finally, what will the woman do when he comes to her door? And how little it is that she gives!

Where shall the poor woman betake herself now? I suppose she has to go begging with her father. However, she will easily find a husband. She only asks[9] a consolation, so that she isn't harmed with impunity.]]

369

Victor with the arms of a tomb

Let an action lie for violation of a tomb. A man took arms from the tomb of a hero, having used up his own. Having won a victory, he replaced them. He is accused of tomb violation.

DECLAMATION

I could have denied the charge. Do you say that arms were pulled down? I deny it. Am I lying? Let us go to the very spot. I want to count; if anything is missing, I want to be convicted. But I shall not tarnish my glory by concealing how it was that I was honored as a hero. But what am I to do? I am not allowed to tell that story.[1] Envy is upon me and it hates the thing to which it owes its survival.

2   'Sepulcrum' inquit 'violasti.' Non utcumque attingitur sepulcrum violatur: alioqui nec inferre[1] mortuos licet nec collapsa reficere nec ornare. Aut, si utcumque attingitur violatur, bis ego peccavi, et cum sustuli et cum reposui. Sed non ita est. Et mens absolvitur. Sic Romani gloriose spoliarunt Iovem, sic Saguntini fecerunt parricidium. Si

3   ergo mens in factis spectatur, meam inspicite. Quare violo? Inimici sepulcrum est? Immo etiam commilitonis, amici; credibile enim est similes propositis amicos fuisse. Deinde, ut etiam vivo nocere voluerim, mortuo tamen parcendum est. Deinde, quo tempore? Bello, inter pericula odiis vacua. Sed quid sustuli? Aurum, credo, aut defossam pecuniam. Arma. Ista virtutis instrumenta, non sceleris sunt

4   pretia, quibus praemia merui. Nisi ista sustulissem, non accusasses: non haberes leges. Sustuli, confiteor, sed publicae salutis causa. Miraris? Ipsorum sepulcrorum ruina, si possem, hostem repellerem: tecta in subeuntes et sacra, quin etiam templorum fastigia desperantium tela sunt. Certum est omnia licere pro patria.

5   Denique vos interrogo: quid faciam? Magna pars exer-

---

[1] *Pith.*: inter Aβ

---

[2] Which is absurd.

[3] Wi. is troubled by *et*, but this is a fresh point: innocence of intention (state of mind), as well as innocence of act (when the "touching" leaves everything intact), is ground for acquittal (SB[2]).

[4] After Cannae (see Wi.).

[5] They "did not beat their fathers but killed them" (Sen. *Contr.*4.5). Besieged by Hannibal, the inhabitants destroyed the city and themselves. I do not think there is any allusion to the cannibalism alleged in Petron.141.9, surely a rhetorical fiction.

"You violated a tomb," he says. A tomb is not violated in whatever way it is touched. Otherwise it is impermissible to bring in the dead or to repair collapses or to decorate. Or, if it is violated in whatever way it is touched, I sinned twice, both when I removed and when I replaced.[2] But it is not so. Intention also is acquitted.[3] Thus the Romans gloriously despoiled Jupiter,[4] thus the Saguntines committed parricide.[5] So if intention is regarded in actions, look at mine. Why do I violate? Is it the tomb of an enemy? No, even of a comrade, a friend; for it is credible that persons with similar ways of life were friends.[6] Next, even though I wanted to harm him alive, one must spare the dead. Next, at what time? In wartime, among perils, void of hatreds.[7] But what did I take? Gold, I imagine, or buried coins. Arms. These are the tools of courage, not the yields of crime; with them I deserved a reward. If I had not taken them, you would not have accused me; you would have no laws.[8] I took them, I confess, but for the public survival. Are you surprised? I would thrust back the enemy with the falling masonry of the tombs themselves, were that possible: roofs descending upon the intruders and sacred things, ay, even the pediments of temples are the weapons of the desperate. Sure it is that all things are allowable for country's sake.

Finally I ask you, gentlemen, what am I to do? A great

---

[6] From this it would appear that he had not in fact known the tomb's occupant; but if he had, they would have been friends.

[7] *Inter arma silent inimicitiae.*

[8] The city would have been enslaved or placed under a tyrant.

citus in me cessat. Armati sunt interim etiam inertes, etiam
mortui: solus nudus steti. Quamquam quid[2] quaero? Habeo sententias vestras: honorastis, et sciebatis his me armis
vicisse. Nec sane aliud dedissetis consilium quam locus et
tempus. Visus est mihi emergere tumulo vir fortis.

370

Rapta competitrix divitis filiae

Inscripti maleficii sit actio. Qui ingenuam stupraverit, det
decem milia. Pauperis et divitis filiae petebant sacerdo-
tium. Rumor erat pauperis filiam futuram sacerdotem.
Eam parasitus sub diem comitiorum rapuit. Dives offert
pro eo decem milia. Inscripti maleficii reus est.

1   DECLAMATIO

'Non est' inquit 'inscriptum,[1] quia certa lege comprehensum est.' Hoc diceret raptor, si cum illo agerem. Sed aliter
mecum tibi consistendum est. Rapere enim usitatum
est, subicere raptorem novum: numquam hoc timuere
maiores.

371

Viri fortis pater reus proditionis

Abdicare liceat. Vir fortis optet quod volet. Qui proditionis
patrem reum habebat fortiter pugnavit. Rogante patre ut

---

[2] *Ro*.: quod Aβ [1] A[2]: sc- A[1]β

---

[9] His strength being as the strength of ten (or ten thousand):
an Achilles.   [1] Cf. 252.   371: [1] Cf. 287 and 375.

part of the army stands idle in my person.[9] Meanwhile, even cowards are armed, even the dead; I alone stood weaponless. And yet, who do I ask? I have your votes. You honored me, knowing that I was victorious with these arms. And surely you could have given me no other counsel than did the place and the time. Methought the hero came out of the tomb!

370[1]

Rape victim in competition with rich man's daughter

Let an action lie for unwritten wrongdoing. Whoso violates a freeborn woman, let him pay ten thousand. The daughters of a rich man and a poor man were candidates for a priesthood. There was a rumor that the poor man's daughter would be the priestess. A parasite raped her the day before the election. The rich man puts up ten thousand on his behalf. He is charged with unwritten wrongdoing.

DECLAMATION

He says, "It is not unwritten because it is covered by a definite law." That is what the rapist would say if I were suing him. But my case against you is different. For rape is familiar, suborning rape is novel. Our ancestors were never afraid of this.

371[1]

Hero's father charged with treason

Let there be license to disown. Let a hero opt for what he will. A man whose father was charged with treason became a hero. When his father asked him to opt for suppression of

369

optaret abolitionem suam, non optavit, sed in iudicio reo
adfuit. Absolutus pater abdicat filium.

1   DECLAMATIO

Quid peccavi cur abdicer? Num adversum patriam iners
sum? Luxuriae deditus bella fugio? An adversus patrem
impius? Reor. In qua parte filii cessat officium? 'Non op-
2 tasti' inquit 'quod volui.' Iam excedis legem tuam: pater
filio debes imperare, forti non potes. Potes peregrinatio-
nem, potes militiam, sed non sententiam iudici,[1] non decretum magistratui,[2] non praemium forti. Quid enim lex
ait? 'Fortis optet.' Me nominat, et aequum est hoc mihi
contingere: pugnavi.

Cum quo mihi res est? Cum patre: non est contumaci-
3 ter agendum. Ego vero etiam viri fortis optionem remitto,
si aequum petis. Quid petisti? Ut abolitionem optarem.
Memento non omnia, pater, nos posse petere: praemium
accipimus, non regnum. Nescis quantum sit abolitionem
petere: accusatori silentium indicere, reum eximere, leges
tollere. Nec pro te tenuissem et praemium perdidissem.
Sed cuius abolitionem? 'Meam' inquit. Animadvertitis
4 quodammodo parricidii reum. Agam potius causam. Hoc
praemium primum turpe est, deinde supervacuum. Turpe:

---

[1] *Sch., Gron.*: -cii Aβ   [2] *Sch., Gron.*: -us Aβ

---

[2] Lit. "his suppression."

[3] I.e., I think that's it, i.e. that is what you will say (SB[2])—unless a negative has dropped out (Burman). Surely not ironic.

[4] The law governing disownment, which at least by implication allowed a son to disobey in certain contexts. The next sentence seems out of place.   [5] We "heroes."

[6] Wi.'s note misses the point. The "hero" might from his fa-

the case,[2] he did not opt but appeared for the defendant at the trial. The father is acquitted and disowns his son.

What have I done wrong to be disowned? Am I a coward toward my country? Devoted to loose living, do I shirk fighting? Am I unfilial toward my father? I think so.[3] Where do I fail in filial duty? He says, "You did not opt for what I wanted." Now you are going beyond your law.[4] As a father you ought to dictate to your son, but you can't dictate to a hero. Travel, yes; military service, yes; but not his vote to a juror, his decrees to a magistrate, his reward to a hero. For what does the law say? "Let a hero opt." It names me and it is right that this be mine. I fought.

Who is my adversary? My father. I must not strike a note of defiance. On the contrary, I even leave to you the hero's option, provided you ask something fair. What did you ask? That I opt for suppression. Remember, father, that we[5] cannot ask for everything: we are given a reward, not a monarchy. You don't know how much it means to ask for a suppression. To muzzle a prosecutor, exempt a defendant, annul the laws. I would not have carried the point for you and I would have wasted the reward. But suppression for whom? "For me," he says. Gentlemen, you observe in some sort a man charged with parricide.[6] I would rather plead my case in court.[7] This reward is disgraceful in the first place and in the second superfluous. Disgraceful: you

ther's point of view be thought guilty of parricide in that he had refused to use his reward to relieve his father of a capital charge, treason—which itself came under the heading of parricide as committed against *patria*; cf. 322.4.   [7] If I were in his position. Or perhaps: even ask for a suppression.

damnaberis tuo iudicio in perpetuum. Quanto gravius est a
se damnari! Tamen alii possunt dicere: 'gratia victi sumus.'
5 Deinde supervacuum: innocens eras. At enim dubia est iudicii fortuna. Sed nobis non timenda: diluendum ‹crimen,
non›[3] iudicium est. ‹In›[4] invidia tantum criminis fiducia
erat et in timore tuo. Itaque apparuerunt iudicibus vana[5]
omnia, et profuit tibi quod abolitionem non optavi: appa-
ruit certa innocentiae fiducia.
6   Ergo advocatum tuum abdicas, participem laboris? De
me facile est: inveniam patrem. Sed tibi timeo: soles enim
periclitari.

372

Pulsator educatoris expositus

Qui patrem pulsaverit, manus ei incidantur. Talionis sit actio. Quidam expositum sustulit, pro filio educavit. Pulsatus
ab eo, tamquam pater manus incidit. Agnitus est adulescens. Advocato naturali patre cum educatore agit talionis.

1   DECLAMATIO

Sceleratissimus omnium, iudices, iuvenis, ingratus vel
quia lucem beneficio meo accepit vel quia [in][1] patrem, bis
parricida est, semel domi, iterum in foro. Quam merito
cruentas perdiderit manus si quis adhuc dubitabit, aspi-

[3] *SB*[3]   [4] *Gron.*   [5] *Wi.*: una Aβ
[1] *Ri.*

---

[8] It would be like an admission of guilt. He speaks as though
the father's request was still on the table.

[9] By adoption. A "hero" will be in demand.

will be convicted for all time by your own judgment.[8] How much more grievous it is to be convicted by oneself! And then, superfluous: you were innocent. "But the luck of a trial is doubtful." But we do not need to be afraid of it. ⟨The charge⟩ is to be dissipated, ⟨not⟩ the trial. They relied only ⟨on⟩ the odium of the charge and on your fear. So the jury found their whole case without foundation, and it counted in your favor that I did not ask for suppression. For sure confidence in your innocence became apparent.

So do you disown your advocate, the partner in your ordeal? I have nothing to worry about; I shall find a father.[9] But I am afraid for you; for you are apt to get into danger.

372[1]

A man exposed beats his foster father

Whoso beats his father, let his hands be cut off. Let an action of eye-for-eye lie. A man took up an exposed child, raised him as his son. Beaten by him, as his father he cut off his hands. The young man was recognized. He calls in his natural father and claims eye-for-eye from the foster father.

DECLAMATION

The young man, gentlemen, the worst of criminals, ungrateful because thanks to me he received the daylight and a father both, is a parricide twice over, once in my house, again in the Forum. If anyone is still going to doubt how richly he deserved to lose his bloody hands, let him behold:

[1] Cf. 358.

ciat: iterum me in conspectu vestro pulsat, et iam[2] truncus ac debilis, sola rabie integer, in miserum senem incurrit.

2 Quid si haberet manus? Ac ne quis illum coercitum poena putet, etiam audacior factus est: debilitatem meam concupiscit, et ei praecipue corporis parti irascitur per quam vivit. Fateor, iudices, fateor praecidendas fuisse has manus,

3 sed cum istum tollerent. Nec erubesco, quod ab isto minimum est, male audire et crudelitatis quoque reus fieri. Sane crudelem[3] me vocet, dum se ostendat: non timeo ne istud in me crimen credibile sit cum misericordiae meae

4 adversarius ipse monumentum sit. Nam quod pater parricidae adest, non miror. Debilem non timet. ⟦Aliquando crudelior cum exposuit.⟧[4] Neque enim dubito quibusdam illum somniis et prodigiis commotum, quia videlicet istum parricidio[5] defungi utique [in patrem][6] fatale erat, ut se metu liberaret proiecisse.

5 Ille ergo crudelis, iudices, quem solum[7] iste carnificem vocat, accessi miti vultu, miseritus sum, ad summam alienus sustuli quem proiecerat pater, nec contentus filii loco

6 habui. Quid hac indulgentia [quid][8] profecerim quaeritis?

---

2 et i. *SB*[3]: etiam Aβ 3 β: -litatem A
4 *ita secl. SB*[3]   5 *Sch., Gron.*: -dam Aβ
6 *SB*[3]   7 *Hå.*[2]: -us Aβ
8 *hoc loco del. Fr., priore mallet Wi.*

---

2 His hands; cf. s.13.

3 *Aliquando*; but *aliquanto* (Sch., Gron.), "considerably," a word much favored in these pieces, is very likely right.

4 *Neque enim = etenim non.*

5 With Oedipus in mind (cf. 358.3), along with the parricide that actually occurred, the declaimer assumes that the natural father exposed his son because paranormal indications had revealed

he beats me again in your sight and, mutilated now and crippled, whole only in his rage, he rushes at a poor old man. What if he had hands? In case anybody should think him subdued by the penalty, he has become even more audacious: he sets his heart on crippling me and directs his anger especially at that part of my body[2] through which he is alive. I confess, gentlemen, yes I confess that these hands should have been cut off—but when they took him up! I am not ashamed, gentlemen, to be reviled (the least to be expected from *him*) and even accused of cruelty. Let him call me cruel by all means, so long as he shows himself: I am not afraid that this charge against me may be found credible when my adversary is himself a living memorial of my compassion. That the parricide's father is here does not surprise me: he is not afraid of a cripple. ⟦He was once[3] more cruel when he exposed him.⟧ And indeed[4] I do not doubt that he was moved by certain dreams and portents and cast him forth to free himself from fear, because, evidently, it was destined that the fellow should discharge a parricide.[5]

So, cruel that I am, gentlemen, whom he calls "the one and only[6] executioner," I approached him with a gentle face, pitied him, in fine I, a stranger, took him up whom his father had cast forth, and, not content, had him in place of a son. Do you ask what I gained by my indulgence? The re-

---

that he would commit parricide. His beating of his adoptive father is viewed as "discharging" the sentence of fate—it fell short of murder and was visited on a surrogate. For *defungi* thus see *TLL* V.1.378 and my note on Cic. *Fam.* 8.1.4 (Cambridge ed.).

[6] *Solum* = *unicum, par excellence: OLD solus* 6. Not "the father being in fact no less of an 'executioner' because of the exposure" (Wi.).

Effeci ne deesset qui pulsaret senem: ille quem praesidio sustuleram, ille quem vindicem etiam adversus alienos speraveram, tam aperte pulsaverat ut ne infitiari quidem posset. Stultus eadem indulgentia etiamnum persevera-bam, et quaerentibus amicis ‹a›[9] quo essem pulsatus men-

7 tiebar. 'Quid tu?' inquiunt 'expectas donec occidat?'

Rapuerunt me in forum, ostenderunt verberati oris no-tas. Iste fassus est; iudex damnavit; carnifex manus abstu-lit: nihil in illo iudicio meum nisi fletus fuit. Dum iactatur tota civitate parricidium, invenit impietas originem suam. En, ut videtis, iterum pulsat: 'talionem' inquit 'peto.'

8 Quid agis? Crudelitatis arguis? Quem saltem[10] pulsavi? Misereri soleo etiam alienorum. Ego te, cum meus esses, debilitavi. Num per vinum? Num per furorem? Num ira-tus? Talio iniuriae ultio est; in hoc scripta est lex, ne quis

9 impune petulans sit. Hoc ergo dicis, ‹manus›[11] me iniuria abstulisse? Lege incidi: nec ego sed carnifex. Quidquid lege factum est vindicari lege non solet. Et qua lege? 'Qui patrem pulsaverit.' 'Sed tu' inquit 'pater non fuisti.' Puta: iudicia tamen iudiciis rescindi non possunt.

10   SERMO

Hic de sanctitate iudiciorum.

11   DECLAMATIO

Sera post damnationem innocentiae defensio est. Istud

[9] *ed. princ.*
[10] *anne* tandem ?
[11] *SB*[1] (*ante* abstulisse)

---

[7] The son found his real father.

sult was that I didn't lack someone to beat me in my old age. The one whom I had taken up to protect me, whom I hoped would be my champion even against strangers, had beaten me so openly that he could not even deny it. Foolishly, I still persevered in the same indulgence and when my friends asked me who had beaten me, I went on lying. "Come now," they say, "are you waiting for him to kill you?"

They haled me into the Forum, showed the marks on my battered face. He confessed, the judge found him guilty, the executioner took off his hands: I had no part in that trial except tears. While the parricide is talked about all over the community, impiety found its origin.[7] Look, as you see, he beats me again. "I ask eye-for-eye," says he.

What are you doing? Do you charge me with cruelty? Whom did I ever beat? My way is to pity even strangers. I crippled you, though you were mine. Was it in wine? Was it in madness? Was I angry? Eye-for-eye is retribution for injury. The law was written to the end that nobody should play the ruffian with impunity. So do you say that I took away <your hands> injuriously? I cut them off under the law; and not I, but the executioner. Anything done by law is usually not punished by law. And by what law? "Whoso beats his father." "But you," says he, "were not his father." Have it so:[8] still, trials cannot be rescinded by trials.

DISCUSSION

Here concerning the sanctity of trials.

DECLAMATION

After conviction the defense of innocence[9] comes too late.

---

[8] Cf. 382.2 init.   [9] The young man now claimed innocence under the law because his victim was not his real father.

quod nunc dixisti ante dixisses. Sed non potuisti dicere. Pater tuus eram, iure praesentis condicionis. Abdicare itaque potui, occidere potui, omnem potestatem tamquam in filio exercere. Miraris? Nec ille potuit contradicere qui

12 pater erat. 'Non eras' inquit 'naturalis.' Tanto igitur plus merueram: alienum sustuleram cum essent qui suos proicerent. Sed ut non fuerim, tu tamen putasti patrem: lex autem mentem punit. ⟦Ut scias verum esse hoc, impetravi.⟧[12] 'Sed tu' inquit 'sciebas non esse filium tuum.' Poteram quidem dicere[13]: 'sed meritis pater eram, sed tu tamquam patrem cecideras.' Sed, testor, nolui: expositum quoque collegeram. ⟦Indignati sunt amici; ipse fassus es.⟧[14]

13   Quid nunc facies? Praecides manus quae te sustulerunt?

373

Ornamentis redemptus

Abdicare liceat. Sepulcri violati sit actio. Amissa uxore et defossis in sepulcro eius ornamentis superduxit filio novercam. Captus a piratis pater de redemptione scripsit. Morante filio, uxor ex sepulcro prioris uxoris eruit ornamenta et misit. Ob hoc a privigno sepulcri violati accusata et dam-

---

[12] *ita secl. SB*[3]   [13] *Ro.*: scire Aβ
[14] *ita secl. SB*[3]

---

[10] "The reference is to the trial of the son" (Wi.), and such a trial is assumed in what follows, although the theme makes no mention of it either here or in 358.   [11] Because I loved you and did not wish to reveal that you are not my son.

What you have now said, you should have said earlier on. But you could not say it. I was your father, by right of the existing situation. Therefore I could disown you, I could put you to death, exercise all the power as upon a son. Are you surprised? Even he that was your father could not say anything to the contrary. "You were not my natural father," he says. So your obligation to me was all the greater; I had taken you in, a stranger, when there were some who cast out their own. But though I was not your father, still, you thought I was; and the law punishes intention. [[So that you know this to be true: I carried my point.[10]]] "But you," he says, "knew that I was not your son." I could have said: "But I was your father in virtue of my good deeds, but you had beaten me as your father." But I swear I did not wish to.[11] When you were exposed too, I had gathered you up. [[My friends were outraged; you yourself confessed.]][12]

What will you do now? Will you cut off the hands that took you up?

373

Ransomed by jewelry

Let there be license to disown. Let there be an action for tomb violation. A man who had lost his wife, whose jewelry was buried in her tomb, brought in a stepmother over his son. Captured by pirates, the father wrote about ransom. When the son delayed, the wife dug up the jewelry from the tomb of the former wife and sent it. For this she was accused by her stepson of tomb violation and convicted. The

---

[12] This sentence seems out of touch with what precedes.

nata est. Pater redit et abdicat filium.

1   DECLAMATIO

Antequam parricidium, inertiam obicio: non es peregrina-
tus, etiam me peregrinante. Coactus sum tuas vices sustinere. Sed dices non totam domum in periculum committi
2   debuisse. Remansisti ut redimeres? Redime. Patrem captum deseruisti: maximum crimen, immo parricidium.
Quantum in te fuit, occisus sum, et gravissimis quidem tormentis. Neque est quod paupertatem excuses: impietas
fuit. Moraris: et quid facis? Ut sciam otiosum, accusas.
Hoc vacat? Et quam accusas? Uxorem meam.
3   'Sepulcrum' inquit 'violaverat.' Quid ad te? Mea iniuria
est; ego vindicabo. Sed ne ego quidem debeo: recte viola-
vit. 'Ut scias' inquit 'peccasse, damnata est.' Miraris, absente viro? Ego te, uxor, damnavi, optima feminarum: sed
vindicabo.

374

Abdicatus heres ob tyrannicidium

Abdicatus de paternis bonis nihil habeat. Quidam hortatus
est in tyrannicidium filium. Nolentem abdicavit. Moriens
scripsit heredem qui tyrannum occidisset. Abdicatus occidit. Petit bona.

1   DECLAMATIO

'Abdicatus' inquit 'ne quid de bonis patris capiat.' Paterna

---

[1] The "Master" and the declaimer are against the son, who
must be supposed to have challenged his disownment (*CD* omitted in theme?).

father returns and disowns his son.[1]

Before parricide, I charge you with inertia. You did not go abroad even when I went abroad. I was forced to take on your role. But you will say that it would have been wrong to commit the whole family into danger. Did you stay behind to ransom me? Ransom me. You deserted your father in captivity: a heinous crime, or rather parricide. So far as lay in you, I was put to death and in terrible tortures at that. It no use for you to make lack of money your excuse: it was lack of filial feeling. You delay, and what do you do? To tell me that you had time to spare, you bring a prosecution. Time for this? And whom do you prosecute? My wife.

He says: "She had violated a tomb." What was that to you? I was the injured party; I shall take action. But no, I ought not either. She was right to violate. He says: "So that you know she did wrong, she was convicted." Are you surprised, when her husband was away? I convicted you, my wife, best of women. But I shall avenge.

374

A disowned son heir because of tyrannicide

Let a disowned son have nothing from his father's property. A man urged his son to kill a tyrant. On his refusal he disowned him. On his deathbed he wrote as his heir whoever killed the tyrant. The disowned son killed him. He claims the property.

"Let a disowned son have nothing from his father's prop-

haec esse bona constat, abdicatum te esse aeque patet:
quae ultra quaestio est?

2   'Heredem' inquit 'scripsit tyrannicidam, ego autem tyrannum occidi.' Nihil refert an aliquod ius postea acquisie-
ris: filii perdidisti. Lex enim quae abdicatis paterna bona
negat per omnia illos amovet: supervacuum namque erat
abdicatum summovere, qui alioqui perdiderat paternam
domum. Igitur lex ita[1] scripta est ne qua lege reverti in do-
3 mum posset. Licet ergo sis tyrannicida, non prodest tibi:
nec ulla lex reducit quem aliqua exclusit, et semper, iudices, potentior lex est quae vetat quam quae permittit ('ne
quid' inquit 'ex bonis capiat'). Hoc etiam in magistratuum
potestate servatur, et plus potest [inquit][2] unus qui vetat
quam omnes qui iubent. In permittente enim libera potes-
4 tas, in vetante poena est. Deinde haec lex publica est, ad
omnes pertinet: testamentum privatum est. Potentius est
quod in albo lego quam quod in testamento.

5   'Sed pater' inquit 'voluit me esse heredem, et ideo tyrannicidam scripsit quia sciebat me facturum tyrannicidium.' Falleris: te namque minime voluit. Nam si voluisset, scripsisset: 'filius meus, si fecerit tyrannicidium, heres

---

[1] *Sch.*: ista Aβ   [2] *Ro.*

---

[1] A disowned son was banished from his father's house and will
but could be reinstated (273.3 *al.*) in the absence of a law prohibiting that. If the law here in question (having no time limit) did not
prohibit in perpetuity, it changed nothing. Such appears to be the
argument; but s.5 implies that a father could bequeath to a disowned son even without reinstatement in the house. A tangled
skein.   [2] I have made this reminder a parenthesis, but perhaps it should be double-bracketed.

erty," says the law. It is accepted that this is his father's property. It is equally evident that you were disowned. What else is in question?

He says: "He wrote the tyrannicide as his heir, and I killed the tyrant." It makes no difference whether you acquired some right subsequently; you forfeited your right as a son. For the law that denies paternal property to disowned sons removes them in perpetuity. Otherwise it would be superfluous to remove a disowned son, who had in any case lost the paternal home.[1] So the law was written in order to stop such from returning to the house under any law. So tyrannicide though you be, it does you no good, nor does any law bring back one whom a law has excluded. And, gentlemen, a law that forbids always has more force than one which permits ("Let him take nothing from his father's property," it says).[2] This is observed even in the powers of magistrates, and one prohibiting always counts more than all ordering.[3] For in permission there is free choice, in prohibition there is penalty. Moreover, this law is public, applying to everyone; a will is private. What I read in an edict has more force than what I read in a will.

"But my father," he says, "wanted me to be his heir and he wrote 'tyrannicide' because he knew I was going to do tyrannicide." You are mistaken: he did not want you, far from it. For if he had wanted you, he would have written: "Let my son be my heir if he does tyrannicide." As it is, it is

[3] Laws that order (*iubent*) are carelessly equated with laws that permit, granting a privilege that can be declined, e.g. option for a reward. The argument here is that such permission has less force than a prohibition which allows no alternative and carries a penalty for noncompliance. *Omnes = ceteri omnes*.

mihi sit.' Nunc autem apparet dolentem iratumque scripsisse, et adoptare in locum filii tyrannicidam voluisse quia
6   in virtutem tyrannicidae filium excitare non poterat. Ira-
tum tibi dico fuisse: abdicavit. Numquam leviter excan-
descunt patres. Et qua causa? Quod tyrannum non occi-
deras. Vides quemadmodum inertiam execratus sit ne
iudiciis quidem malis excitatam. Tantum abdicavit? Immo
non reduxit. Passus est exulare, ne moriens quidem miseritus est, etiam testamento exheredavit, etiam alios adopta-
vit.

7   SERMO

Ultimae partes aequitatis.

8   DECLAMATIO

'Tamen' inquit 'tyrannum occidi.' Puta te meruisse: habes
praemium a re publica. Illud virtutis praemium debet esse,
hoc inertiae supplicium. Sed quando occidisti? Testamentum te excitavit.

9   SERMO

In ultimo tuenda mortuorum iudicia: commendabimus iudicibus testamenta: nullam autem maiorem illi fieri posse
iniuriam quam si hunc heredem habuerit.

---

   4 Such as disownment. As Wi. says, *iudiciis malis* cannot refer
to the will which came later—and a disowned son could not inherit anyway. He strangely prefers an allusion to the abolition (or
deformation) of law courts under a tyranny.

evident that he wrote in grief and anger, and wanted to adopt a tyrannicide in place of his son because he could not rouse his son to tyrannicidal courage. I say he was angry with you: he disowned you. Fathers never flare up lightly. And what was the reason? Because you had not killed the tyrant. You see how much he detested an inertia which was not even roused by declarations of disapproval.[4] Did he merely disown you? No; he did not bring you back. He let you be an exile;[5] even on his deathbed he took no pity on you, even disinherited you in his will,[6] even adopted others.

DISCUSSION

The concluding parts concern equity.

DECLAMATION

"After all," he says, "I killed the tyrant." Suppose you did a good service: you have your reward from the commonwealth. That should be the reward of courage, this is the punishment of inertia. But when did you kill him? The will roused you.

DISCUSSION

In the finale we must maintain the dispositions of the dead. We shall commend wills to the jury and say that there can be no greater injury done to him than if he shall have this man as his heir.

---

[5] From the family house.
[6] Forgetting that a disowned son was disinherited anyway.

375

Fortis filius proditionis rei, frater desertoris

Proditionis reo patre alter ex filiis deseruit, alter fortissime
pugnavit. Rogavit pater ut abolitionem suam optaret. Ille
fratris impunitatem optavit et in iudicio adfuit patri. Pater
absolutus abdicat. Ille CD.

1   DECLAMATIO

Fateor, non possum lusus arguere qui donari aetati possunt. Non est luxuriosus, sed contumax: haec minus feren-
da sunt vitia. Dicas licet 'fortis sum': quid mihi prodest si
2 magis patrem contemnis? 'Mea' inquit 'lex est.' Quicquam
tibi me vivo tuum est? Ego te in aciem misi: mea est virtus,
mea lex, mea optio. Non iniquam rem postularem si dicerem 'amicum reum vindica': quid si patrem? ⟦Etiam inno-
3 centem urget conspiratio.⟧[1] 'Sed turpis est' inquit 'abolitio.' Quid ad te? Ego meae condicionis arbiter sum. 'Sed'
inquit 'supervacua erat: innocens eras.' Quid autem? Ego
quia nocens eram petieram? Verebar fortunam iudiciorum
4 et exempla. Etiam innocentem[2] urget conspiratio.[3] 'Sed
fratris' inquit 'salutem optavi.' Iam ergo noli dicere 'supervacua abolitio fuit.' Alium enim mihi praetulisti, et innocenti nocentem, reo damnatum, qui certo perire debebat;
si misereris tuorum, eos saltem adiuva de quibus iudex

---

[1] *vide* 3 *fin*.   [2] -tes *Gron*.
[3] etiam . . . c. *huc transtulit ex* 2 *SB*[4]

---

[1] Cf. 287.   [2] I.e. for me, on my side.
[3] As he had. Perhaps delete the question or double-bracket.
[4] Of innocent persons found guilty.

375[1]

Hero, son of a man accused of treason, brother of a deserter

A father was accused of treason. One of his sons deserted, the other fought heroically. The father asks him to opt for suppression of his trial. He opted for impunity for his brother and appeared for his father at the trial. The father is acquitted and disowns his son. He speaks in opposition.

DECLAMATION

I admit it, I cannot bring against him the frolics that can be forgiven his age. He is not loose-living, but contumacious: these are faults less to be borne. You may say: "I am brave." What good is that to me if you defy your father all the more? He says: "The law is mine.[2]" Is anything yours for you while I am alive? I sent you into battle: it is my courage, my law, my option. I should not be asking too much if I said: "Champion my friend on trial." What if I said: "Your father"?[3] ⟦Conspiracy bears hard even on the innocent.⟧ "But suppression is dishonorable," he says. What is that to you? I am the judge of my own situation. "But it was superfluous," he says. "You were innocent." What then? Had I asked you because I was guilty? I was afraid of the luck of trials and the examples.[4] ⟨Conspiracy bears hard even on the innocent.⟩ "But I opted for my brother's life," he says. So don't go on saying: "Suppression was superfluous." You preferred someone else to me, a guilty man to an innocent, a convicted man, who certainly deserved death, to an accused man. If you pity your kin, at least help those on whom the judge has not yet decided. "What

5   etiamnum dubitat. 'Quid ergo?' inquit 'perisset?' Si me in-
terrogas, occupatus sum, non audio; si patriam, desertor
est. Quaedam, iudices, comparatio minuit: per se crudele
fuit perire fratrem, sed comparatum mihi tolerabile. Quid
6   ergo? Ego perissem? 'Fratrem' inquit 'servavi.' Itaque
nunc pater te abdicat[4]: ille beneficii gratiam debet, ego
peccati poenam. Sed quid si non pietati servisti,[5] sed ut me
occideres? Quantum in te fuit, damnatus sum. 'Adfui' inquit. Alioqui abdicareris tantum?

376

Expositus iuratus ob nuptias educatoris filiae

Quidam moriens adulescenti, quem pro filio educaverat,
indicaturum se veros parentes pollicitus est si iurasset se
filiam quam relinquebat ducturum uxorem. Iuravit adulescens. Ille dixit. Post mortem educatoris a naturali patre
receptus, quia non vult orbam divitem ducere uxorem, abdicatur.

1   DECLAMATIO

Abdicat tam cito? Si non eram idoneus, non eram recipien-
dus. Tam exiguo tempore quid peccare potui? Etiamsi
quid peccavi, ignosce: nondum novi mores tuos. Noviciis
etiam servulis ignoscitur. Sed quid obicis? 'Uxorem' inquit

---

[4] pater te a. *Pith.*: frater te a. A(β): f. te alat *Bu*.
[5] pietate servasti *Gron*.

---

[5] But Burman's *frater te alat*, "let your brother feed you," is
very tempting.
[6] He would have been charged with parricide.

then?" he says. "Would he have died?" If it's I you ask, I am busy, I don't hear; if it's our country, he is a deserter. Certain things, gentlemen, are reduced by comparison. In itself it was a cruel thing for your brother to die, but compared to me, it was tolerable. What then? Would *I* have died? "I saved my brother," he says. So now your father disowns you.[5] He owes you gratitude for a boon, I penalty for a wrong. But what if you were not doing it for family feeling but to kill me? As far as you were concerned, I was found guilty. "I appeared for you," he says. If you had not, would you merely have been disowned[6]?

376

Exposed, on oath[1] to marry his foster father's daughter

A man on his death-bed promised a young man whom he had brought up as a son that he would tell him who his true parents were if he swore to marry the daughter whom he was leaving. The young man swore, the other told him. After the death of the foster father he was taken in by his natural father and is disowned because he refused to take a rich orphan as his wife.

DECLAMATION

Does he disown me so quickly? If I was not to his liking, he should not have taken me in. In so short a time, what could I have done wrong? Even if I did something wrong, forgive me: I don't yet know your ways; even new slaves are forgiven. But what do you have against me? "You don't marry

---

[1] The construction *iuratus ob nuptias* = *iuratus ducere* (cf. Plaut. *Rud.* 1372ff.) seems unexampled.

2 'non ducis quam volo.' Quid tum? nescis nostri arbitrii esse
matrimonia? Adfectus nostri vobis[1] non serviunt: non potes efficere imperio ut vel amem quem velis vel oderim.
Matrimonium vero tum perpetuum est si mutua voluntate
iungitur. Cum ergo quaeratur mihi uxor, socia tori, vitae
consors in omne saeculum, mihi eligenda est. Alioqui quid
3 proficis invitum cogendo? Repudiabo. 'At enim' inquit
'lege cogeris orbam ducere.' Quid? tu illius patronus es?
Sine me illi respondere. Si potest, lege illa cogat. Interim
noli mihi patriam maiestatem opponere. Sed nimirum non
potest cogere, et ideo non cogit. Alioqui forsitan illi re-
sponderem [non][2] habere orbas privilegium, sed vacuis
indicere nuptias, non occupatis.

4 'Quid ergo?' inquit 'orbam non ducis?' Gaudeo, pater,
quod misereri fortunae potes: et haec orba est, et haec patrem perdidit. Fortuna similis, indulgentia propior[3] est. In
eadem domo educati sumus: novi mores, probo verecun-
5 diam, probo genus. Quid si mihi a patre commendata est?
Quid si rogatus sum? Quid si etiam iuravi? Vis me fidem
non praestare? Et cui? Qui me sustulit, qui patrem egit,
qui te mihi patrem dedit. Quemadmodum rogavit? Non
est quod dicas: 'ego cogo'; aeque tamen peiero. Et quales
futurae nuptiae quae periurio iunguntur?

---

[1] D: no- Aβ   [2] *Gron*.   [3] *ed. Leid*.: proprior Aβ

---

[2] Sons.

[3] An Athenian law obliging an orphan (*orba*) to marry her next
of kin (Ter. *Phorm*. 125). It should have been in the theme.

[4] He could refuse, paying a fine.

[5] In that both were orphans, though one was wealthy, the
other penniless.

the wife I want," he says. What then? Don't you know that marriages are for us[2] to decide? You fathers are not masters of our affections; you cannot make me love or hate whom you want by an order. Matrimony is in perpetuity only if it is joined by mutual will. So when we are looking for a wife for me, to share my bed, to be my life-companion for every generation, *I* must choose her. Otherwise, what do you gain by forcing me against my will? I shall divorce her. "But the law[3] compels you to marry an orphan," he says. What? Are you her advocate? Let me answer her. Let her force me by that law if she can. Meanwhile, don't block me with paternal majesty. But I'll wager she can't force me[4] and that is why she doesn't. Otherwise I should answer her that orphans do have a law to themselves but that perhaps it imposes marriage upon the available, not the already bespoke.

"So what?" he says. "Don't you marry an orphan?" I am delighted, father, that you can pity the unfortunate. This one too is an orphan, she too has lost her father. In fortune[5] she is alike, in love closer. We were brought up in the same house, I know her ways, I like her modesty, I like her family. Add that she was commended to me by our father. Add that he asked me. Add that I even took an oath. Do you want me to go back on it? And to whom? Why, the man who took me up, who was a father to me, who gave me you as a father. How did he ask me?[6] It's no use your saying: "I am forcing you." It's perjury all the same. And what sort of marriage will it be, based on perjury?

[6] Following Wi.'s suggestion, I formerly obelized. But the son may mean: "I would never have known you if he had not asked me the way he did (promising to reveal my real parents)."

6 SERMO

Ultima comparatio puellarum: illam esse divitem, facile
inventuram maritum, hanc in totum destitutam, et nunc
vere orbam si eam hic quoque deseruerit. Referendam
esse gratiam expositos colligentibus.

377

Vocatus a patre in militiam venenum terens

Parricidii sit actio. Pater filium in militiam vocavit. Ille or-
natus donis ad patrem rediit. Adhibitis amicis petît a patre
ne se amplius mitteret; non impetravit. Iterum fortissime
pugnavit; rediit. Terens venenum a patre deprehensus est.
Interrogatus dixit se mori velle. Parricidii reus est patri.

1 DECLAMATIO

Parricidii reus sum. Quaedam crimina ipsa magnitudine
fidem non impetrant. Parricidium aliquando legem non
habuit, nec immerito: quis enim se facile vinclis naturae
exsolvat? Vos estis qui nascentes excipitis. Itaque ad tantum nefas magna oportet serie parricida veniat, et per
hominum deorumque contemptum ad ultimum nefas
2 conscendat. Quid hoc est, iudices? Maximum omnium
reo crimen obicitur, et solum: non circumscriptus amicus,
‹non ∗›,[1] cessant etiam familiaria adulescentiae crimina et
ne in scortis quidem ‹parricidii›[2] reus male audio. Plus
fortasse quam putatis, iudices, pollicebor; non quemlibet
ex illis subselliis sed accusatorem ipsum laudatorem dabo:

[1] Wi.
[2] SB²

DECLAMATION 377

Finally, comparison of the girls: one, we'll say, is rich, will easily find a husband, the other is altogether destitute, and now truly orphan if he too deserts her. Gratitude should be shown to those who gather up the exposed.

377

Summoned by father to join the army, mixing poison

Let action for parricide lie. A father summoned his son to join the army. He returned to his father with decorations. Calling in friends, he asked his father not to send him out again; he was refused. A second time he fought heroically. He returned. He was caught by his father mixing poison. Questioned, he said he wanted to die. His father accuses him of parricide.

DECLAMATION

I stand accused of parricide. Certain charges gain no credence because of their very enormity. Once parricide had no law, and for good reason: for who would easily release himself from the bonds of nature? It is you fathers who take us up when we are born. So a parricide must come to such an atrocity by many stages and ascend to the final wickedness through contempt for men and gods. What is this, gentlemen of the jury? I am charged with the greatest of all crimes, and with that only. I have not cheated a friend, <not * >, even the familiar charges against youth don't appear and, accused <of parricide> as I am, I don't have a bad reputation even for whoring. I shall promise you more than you perhaps suppose, gentlemen: I shall offer as testimony to character not just anybody from these

3   numquam abdicavit. Quidni non abdicaret cuius non solum innocentiam sed etiam virtutem cognoverat? Facinus indignum! Inter speciosa militiae opera impietatis privatae reus sum, sponsor salutis publicae. Non sunt eiusdem pectoris vitia et virtutes. Etiam pro alienis patribus dimicare soleo.

4   Sed forsitan non solum puram sed etiam speciosam innocentiam gravet [in parricidium]³ causa. Numquid abdicaveras, et exuere naturalem indulgentiam prior docueras? An etiam [in]⁴ hereditatis cupiditate volebam te occidere, scilicet immensis luxuriae oneratus damnis? An infeliciter te iubente pugnaveram et inertiae poenam verebar? 'Immo' inquit 'invitus militabas.' Sic fit ergo ut quisquis hostem timet patrem occidat? Ergo iners sum: atqui parricida non solum audax debet esse sed etiam temerarius. Invitus ‹militabam›.⁵ Quid ergo? Rogare non possum, ad preces decurrere, non ad venena? Iterum allegare amicos non possum? Denique, ‹si›⁶ perseveras, mori non possum? Finge enim qualem te velis esse. Crudelem? Et hunc iudex vindicabit, et propter hunc occidet filium. Sed melius ego de te iudico: puto te omnia indulgenter imperare filio. Avida est gloriae paterna pietas: nostra tirocinia timidiora sunt. Numquid offenderis si te laudo? Sed ne tali quidem patri parco?

7   Quemadmodum occidere volo? Conducam percussorem, insidiabor peregrinanti? Nihil horum est: meas ma-

---

³ SB³   ⁴ *Aer.*   ⁵ *Aer.*   ⁶ *Aer.*

---

¹ The prosecution.
² A proposition advanced in order to be contradicted. Wi.'s note is astray. For *gravet* see *TLL* VI.2314.70.

benches[1] but the prosecutor himself: he never disowned me. And why would he, knowing as he did not only my innocence but my valor even? For shame! Amid brilliant military exploits I am charged with private impiety, I the guarantor of public safety! Vices and virtues do not belong in the same heart. I am used to fighting even for other people's fathers.

But perhaps the case would weigh down innocence not only pure but shining.[2] Had you disowned me, and taught me first to strip off natural affection? Was it even out of greed to inherit that I wanted to kill you, loaded no doubt with immense sums lost in loose living? Or had I fought on your orders unsuccessfully and was I afraid of punishment for cowardice? "No, but," you say, "you fought unwillingly." So is that the way of it? Whoever fears the enemy kills his father? So I am a coward. And yet a parricide ought to be not just bold but temerarious. <I served> unwillingly. What then? Can I not beg, resort to entreaties, not poison? Can I not call in friends once again? Finally, <if> you insist, can I not die? For imagine what kind of father you want to be. Cruel? Even such a one will the judge avenge and kill a son on his account.[3] But I judge better of you: I think you give all your orders to your son lovingly. Your fatherly feeling is greedy for glory: I am a raw recruit and rather timid. Are you offended if I praise you? But don't I spare even such a father?

How do I propose to kill you? Shall I hire an assassin, ambush you travelling abroad? Nothing of that sort. I stain

[3] Not a question, I now think. He could be a cruel father and still win his case, but no, he had not been cruel. *Et* surely = "even."

[QUINTILIAN]

nus inquino, et sic paro venenum ut deprehendar. Secreta sunt parricidarum scelera.

8 'Cur ergo' inquit 'venenum habuisti?' O miseram liberandae adulescentiae meae sortem et malis quoque ipsis tristiora remedia! Excusandum est quod ne diluerem mori volueram, et ultimae cogitationes revocantur ad iudices: paulo minus quam post fata arcessor reus. Sed ne fallam te, pater, respondebo verbis fortunae meae, respondebo quod

9 soleo, id est: non alius reus quam filius, mori volo. O quanto facilius tibi mortis causas quam parricidii reddam! Immo passim obiectas et publicatas tantum non transibo. Mori volui. Quaeris quare? Quia natus sum ad miserias hominum, incendia, naufragia, bella. Felices qui suo arbitrio moriuntur. Scipio '<imperator>[7]' inquit 'bene habet': puto quia ultra pugnaturus non erat. <Quid>[8] Cato? Num et ille peccavit? Idem feci quod Cato. Ad quietem hoc iter est et

10 dulcis quaedam ad securitatem via. Quare mori voluerim quaeris? En quia vivam reus sum! Quare mori volui? Vides enim: ex voto adulescentiam egeram, nihil umquam me offendit, quamquam interim et secunda adversum me[9] faciunt: quidquid rogavi te,[10] pater, etiam solus exoravi.

7 *Aer.* 8 *SB*[1] 9 a. me *Sch.*: ad usum meum Aβ
10 r. (*Sch.*) te *Obr.*: -vit et Aβ

---

4 By suicide. Not "from the charge against him" (Wi.).
5 Cowardice. 6 Wi. renders "I shall virtually omit mention of the reasons brought up against me publicly, i.e. cowardice." But that reason (singular) is staple to his defense and he has as good as already given it (s.8). There are, however, other reasons which he goes on to advance, the miseries of the human lot. *Obiectas* = "charged (against human life"; add *vitae*?).

my own hands and prepare poison so as to be caught. The crimes of parricide are secret.

"So why did you have poison?" he says. Miserable indeed is the lot of my youth, a youth I have to free![4] Remedies sadder than woes! I have to excuse myself for something I had wanted to die rather than explain away,[5] and my last thoughts are brought before a jury. I am put on trial almost beyond the grave. But not to deceive you, father, I will reply in the words of my plight, I will reply as is my habit, that is, no differently as a defendant than as a son: I want to die. Oh how much easier it is for me to give you reasons for death than for parricide! Or rather, I shall virtually pass over those everywhere advanced and publicized.[6] I wanted to die. You ask why? Because I was born to the miseries of mankind, fires, shipwrecks, wars. Happy are they who die of their own choice! Scipio says: "It is well <with the general>."[7] I think because he was not going to fight any more. What of Cato? Did he too do wrong? I did[8] the same as Cato. This is the road to peace,[9] a sweet path to freedom from fear. You ask why I wanted to die? Look, because I live, I am on trial. Why did I want to die? For you see: I had spent my youth just as I would have prayed. Nothing ever upset me, although sometimes even successes[10] make against me. Whatever I asked of you, fa-

---

[7] The famous last words of Metellus Scipio (not "a general of Cato's"). On the omission of *se* with *habet* see (with Wi.) my notes on Cic. *Att*. 2.8.1 (Cambridge ed.).

[8] Or rather "meant to do."

[9] Correct the misprint *quietam* in my Teubner text.

[10] Referring to his "heroism."

11 Pace maiestatis tuae dictum sit: non omnes tam fortes sumus, non omnes bella sustinere possumus. Sed non quisquis occidere hostem non potest continuo patrem potest.
Varia sunt ingenia: alii ⟨negotio, alii⟩[11] otio delectantur:
ego tecum volebam militare. En parricidam! Sub iudicio[12]

12 tuo vivere volo. In hoc etiam ambitiosus apud te, pater,
amicos adhibui. Sed postquam iussus sum, 'obsequendum
est' inquam 'patri, eamus in bellum; quid habeo quod pro
me timeam si de filio pater securus est?' Vidi alios sterni,
alios fugari, universos exercitus caedi. Dedi me periculo,

13 subieci, tamquam vilis mihi, fortunae. Et ideo, puto, miser
vici. Tum vero in aestimatione periculorum ac vulnerum
'quid? hic' inquam 'nemo vincere potest nisi mori voluerit?' Redii in domum patris: nulla erat missio, ne post victoriam quidem. 'Si necesse est, moriamur,' inquam 'sed

14 domi: ibi certe pater sepeliet.' Inter haec tamen paternam
dementiam sperans 'videat' inquam 'pater, deprehendat:
qui roganti non credidit, morienti credat.' Ipse me cum veneno optuli, ut essem miserabilis. Sed, ut video, crudelio-
rem feci patrem. Et nunc intellego: filium perire voluisti
cum in aciem misisti.

15 Si perseveras, venenum redde: liceat meis instrumentis
mori. Sed miserere heredis, miserere viri fortis: iudicio
impetrem quod per amicos exorare non potui.

---

11 *Ri.*   12 β: dicio A: *anne* dicione tua ⸮

---

[11] On the contrary, even with friends he was refused. The
passage is ironical, as Gronovius saw (*contra* Wi.).   [12] A sly
reproach? The father is not said to have done any soldiering.

[13] Hasty writing, one supposes; he means *rogantem non au-
divit*, "paid no attention when I begged."

ther, even alone, I obtained.[11] Let it be said, saving your majesty: we are not all so brave, not all of us can bear fighting. But not everybody who cannot kill an enemy is automatically able to kill his father. Dispositions vary: some enjoy <business, others> leisure. I wanted to be a soldier along with you.[12] There! A parricide: I wanted to live under your judgment. Eager to show it, I even called friends into your presence. But after I was ordered: "I must obey my father," I said. "Let us go to war. What should I have to fear for myself if my father has no fears for his son?" I saw some struck down, others put to flight, whole armies slaughtered. I gave myself to the peril, submitted me, as though cheap in my own eyes, to Fortune. And therefore, I think, I was victorious, poor wretch! Then it was that, considering my perils and wounds, "What?" I said. "Can no one be victorious here, unless he wants to die?" I returned to my father's house: there was no discharge, not even after the victory. "If it is necessary, let us die," I say, "but at home. There at least my father will bury me." Yet still hoping the while for a father's clemency: "Let my father see," I said. "Let him catch me. He did not believe[13] me when I begged, let him believe me when I die." I put myself in his way with the poison to make him take pity on me. But, as I see, I made my father more cruel. And now I understand: you wanted your son to perish when you sent him into the battle.

If you insist, give me back the poison. Let me die by my own means. But pity your heir, pity the hero: let me get by your judgment what I could not win from you through friends.[14]

[14] I.e. drop the case and let me stay out of the army.

16

Hoc est difficillimum in hac controversia, quod in eadem condicione et parricidii et mortis est militiae metus: quem si infitiamur, non habuimus cur ipsi vellemus mori, si fatemur, habuimus cur patrem vellemus occidere. Medio igitur temperamento opus est.

378

Auctor pacis abdicandus

Victa duobus proeliis civitate, tertia instructa acie, pollicitus pacem adulescens si permitteretur sibi cum duce hostium loqui, post discessum eorum quia non indicat patri, abdicatur.

1

Non esse privilegium parentibus datum (mentior?), datam[1] esse video liberis respondendi potestatem, et de abdicatione iudicem cognoscere. Dico igitur certa esse quae imperent patres, navigationem, militiam, quaedam excipi, senatoris, magistratus, iudicis sententiam, et libe-
2 ros ‹nos›[2] esse qua[3] cives: hanc vero novam legem, silentium crimen esse. Cum abdicetur procacitatis petulantia, sub hoc patre tacere non licet. Finge te quaerere quid amico deliberanti suaserim: extorquebis? Quare iudex reum damnaverim? Quam rationem senator in sententia secutus

---

[1] A: datum β [2] SB^2 [3] SB^2: quia Aβ

---

[15] "Clumsily expressed" (Wi.). "If he denies cowardice, he had no reason for suicide; if he confesses it, he had a reason to kill his father."   [1] Meaning apparently a law giving them in special

DECLAMATION 378

The most difficult point in this controversy is that fear of military service operates in the same way both for parricide and for death.[15] If we deny it, we had no reason to want to die ourselves; if we admit it, we had a reason to want to kill the father. So we have to strike a balance.

378

Peacemaker to be disowned

When the community was defeated in two battles and a third battle line drawn, a young man promised peace if he were permitted to speak with the enemy commander. After their meeting ended he gives his father no information and for that reason is disowned.

DECLAMATION

I do not see a special law given to fathers[1] (do I lie?). I do see that children are given the right to respond and that a judge holds a hearing on the disowning. I say then that there are certain things that fathers may order, travel by sea, military service; and certain things excepted, vote of senator, magistrate, juror; and that ⟨we⟩[2] are free *qua* citizens; but that this is a new law, making silence an offense. Whereas truculent effrontery is disowned, under this father one is not allowed to hold one's tongue. Suppose you ask what advice I gave to a friend with a problem: will you force it out of me? Or why as a juror I found a defendant guilty? Or for what reasons I gave a vote in the senate?

---

cases a right to disown without legal challenge, their right to disown subject to challenge being part of the system.   [2] Sons.

3 sim? Isto modo levissimis quoque causis expellemur, et utcumque delicatis visum fuerit testamenta perdemus. Abdicas. Amavi? Potavi? Et fortasse ista donare potuisti.[4] Tanti supplicii quod crimen est?

4 'Non indicas' inquit 'quid locutus sis.' Finge nolle: licet. Magistratus non exigit, patria non exigit. Si proditorem putas, accusa. Sunt quaedam secreta, iudices, et animi parentum imperiis vacant.

379

Dives a parasito sacrilego reus caedis

Pauper et dives inimici. Dives pauperem quodam tempore cum uxore occisum adulterii crimine in publicum abiecit. Postea dimissus ab eo parasitus, in sacrilegio deprehensus, e lege tortus inter alia dixit a divite pauperem illum inimicum iniuria occisum. Dives caedis reus est.

1 DECLAMATIO

Reo caedis quid obicitur? Petulantia, improbitas, circumscriptio? Ista ne pauper quidem obiecit: nec potuit latere ante acta vita sub eiusmodi inimico, quem usque eo vehementem dicitis ut mea manu esset iugulandus.

---

[4] d. p. *SB*[3] (*cf. Wi.*): donasti Aβ

---

[1] Another loose title. The parasite was informer, not prosecutor. Much is left murky.

[2] The prosecutor, whoever he was, based his charge on the parasite's evidence, alleging that the adultery killing was a smokescreen and the poor man victim of a plot on the part of his enemy the rich man, who had presumably forced or lured him into the adultery scenario. But details are withheld.

That way we shall be expelled even on the most trivial of pretexts and lose our wills just at our touchy fathers' whim. You disown me. Was I in love? Did I drink? And perhaps you could have waived that sort of thing. What is the crime deserving so drastic a punishment?

"You don't tell me what you spoke about," he says. Suppose I don't want to: it's allowed. The magistrate doesn't require it of me, neither does the country. If you think I am a traitor, charge me. Some things are secret, gentlemen, and minds are free of parental commands.

379

Rich man brought to trial for murder by temple-robbing parasite[1]

A poor man and a rich man were enemies. The rich man one day killed the poor man along with his wife on a charge of adultery and threw him into the street. Later on a parasite whom he had dismissed, caught in temple-theft and tortured under the law, said that the poor man had been wrongfully killed by the rich man, whose enemy he was. The rich man is accused of murder.

DECLAMATION[2]

Standing trial for murder, what is said against me? Offensive behavior, rascality, fraud? Even the poor man did not accuse me of such things; and my past life could not be hidden with such an enemy, so bitter, as you people say, that I had to slaughter him with my own hand.

[QUINTILIAN]

2 Sed inimicum occidi. Quem? Pauperem, qui nihil in curia, nihil in contione[1] poterat. Inimici sunt ex pari. Sed puta inimicum fuisse: statim ad caedem confugiendum est? Verborum contentiones armis finiuntur? Etiam hosti-
3 bus parcitur: Caesar Catoni voluit ignoscere. Deinde mea manu occido? Tam efferati animi sum? Non venenum est, non percussor? Et dives sum. Deinde cum uxore? Ne illi quidem parco? Deinde quemadmodum? Rapio de publi-co? Non clamat, non Quiritium fidem invocat? Et tanti facinoris parasitum conscium advoco, et eundem postea eicio? Non timeo indicem?
4 'Quemadmodum ergo' inquit 'uxorem corrupit?' Alieni facti rationem a me exigis. Qui scio an hoc genere vindi-care se voluerit qui aliter non poterat? 'Pauper' inquit 'fuit.' Quasi tantum pretiis[2] mulieres corrumpantur, prae-sertim divites: immo illecebris et blanditiis magis capiun-tur. Utique, si quis domesticorum adiuvit, per parasitum factum; et ideo eiectus, ideo a nullo receptus, quod eum laesisset a quo liberalissime exceptus est.
5 'At enim dixit parasitus.' Primum unus testis est, deinde parasitus. 'Tortus dixit.' Eo minus credo: mentiuntur ple-rumque torti. Deinde hic habuit mentiendi causam, quod expulsus est, quod sacrilegium propter inopiam admisit, nec fefellit. Hinc reus factus sum.[3]

---

1 *Pith.*: contenti- Aβ
2 A: -ii β: -io *Aer.*
3 nec . . . sum *transp. SB*3: *post* validius (*infra*) *habent* Aβ

---

3 In promoting the adultery.
4 Because he had been concerned in the adultery; cf. s.4.

But I killed my enemy. Whom? A poor man, with no power in the senate-house or the assembly. Enemies stand on equal terms. But suppose he was my enemy: do I have to resort to murder straight away? Are verbal arguments ended with weapons? Even public enemies are spared: Caesar wanted to pardon Cato. And then, do I kill him with my own hand? Am I such a savage? Isn't there poison, an assassin? And I am rich. And then, along with my wife. Don't I spare her even? And then, how? Do I haul him out of the street? Doesn't he cry out, appeal to the citizenry? And do I call in a parasite as my accomplice in such a crime, and throw him out afterwards? Am I not afraid of his informing on me?

"How then," he says, "did he seduce your wife?" You ask me to account for another person's action. How do I know whether this was his way of getting even since he had no other? "He was poor," says the prosecution. As though women are seduced by money only, particularly rich ones. They are more taken by allurements and endearments. At all events, if any of the household helped,[3] it was done through the parasite; and that was why he was thrown out[4] and why nobody took him in—because he had injured the man who had taken him up most generously.

"But the parasite said so." First, he is only one witness; second, he is a parasite. "He said so under torture." I believe him all the less. People often lie under torture. Further, he had a reason for lying, because he had been sent packing, because he committed temple-theft by reason of poverty and did not get away with it.[5] Hence I am on trial.

[5] He had been caught.

⟦Adstiti praesens: inde ille exarsit validius.⟧[4]

380

Crux scripta servo non danti venenum

De iniusto supplicio tribunos appellare liceat. Aeger a servo, cui libertatem scripserat, venenum petît. Nolenti dare crucem scripsit. Heredes volunt supplicium sumere. Servus appellat tribunos.

1
DECLAMATIO

'Testamento' inquit 'cautum est.' Ideo tribuni cognoscunt non utrum scriptum sed quare scriptum sit. Crux scripta est. Quare? Quid commisit? Ante actam vitam scrutemur. Video illi prius libertatem fuisse scriptam. Quid igitur tam subito peccavit? Numquid venenum dare domino voluit quo citius libertate frueretur? In contrarium incidi. Non periclitaretur si dedisset. 'Petenti' inquit 'domino non dedi.[1]'

2
SERMO

Quaestio an omnibus imperiis parendum, an aegri,[2] an huic[3] imperio. Hic, primum non debuisse, deinde non potuisse parere. Ultima supplicii figuratio, sub eiusmodi titulo.

[4] *ita secl.* SB[3] [1] *SB*[4]: -it AE*β*
[2] *Sch., Gron.*: -ro AE*β*
[3] an h. A[2]CD: adhuc B: huic A[1]

---

[6] At the torture.
[1] Directed in his will that the slave be crucified.
[2] Presumably the dead man's heir.

⟦I stood by,[6] present: that made him all the more furious.⟧

380

Cross written for slave who would not give poison

Let it be lawful to appeal to the tribunes concerning unjust punishment. A sick man asked his slave, to whom he had left freedom in his will, for poison. On the slave refusing to give it, he wrote down the cross.[1] The heirs want to punish him accordingly. The slave appeals to the tribunes.

DECLAMATION

He[2] says: "It is prescribed in the will." Therefore the tribunes investigate not whether it was written but why it was written. The cross was written. Why? What had he done? Let us examine his past life. I see that earlier on freedom had been written for him. What did he do wrong so suddenly? Did he want to give poison to his master so as to enjoy his freedom the sooner? I have got it upside down.[3] He would be in no danger if he had given it. He says: "When my master asked for poison I did not give it."

DISCUSSION

Question: are all commands to be obeyed, are those of a sick man, is this a command? Here first we say that he should not have obeyed, then that he could not. Finally comes a description of the punishment under the appropriate placard.[4]

[3] Lit. "fallen into a contrary proposition," i.e. one that stood the facts on their heads.   [4] Placed at the top of the cross, like the scriptural "king of the Jews."

407

381

Noverca torta filiam consciam dicens

Venefica torqueatur donec conscios indicet. Quidam filio superduxit novercam et ex illa [aliam][1] filiam suscepit. Amisso filio ambiguis signis uxorem ream fecit. Confessa illa in tormentis communem filiam consciam dixit. Adest filiae pater.

1   DECLAMATIO

Ut sciatis, iudices, nocentes tantum a me veneficii reas fieri et hanc non immerito praeteritam, proferte a sinu nutricis ream. Non peccant hi anni, ne in novercis quidem. Parvulae serpentes non nocent, ferae etiam mansuescunt. Persona virgo est, causa soror. Quam valde a fratre dilecta est, quemadmodum mortuum flevit!

2   'Sed mater' inquit 'consciam habuit.' Primum sceleratis naturale est alienam conscientiam fugere, deinde, si quaerant, adiutores quaerere. Quod autem adiutorium in puella esse potuit? Emit venenum? An confecit, ut fratri daret? Quid? Ipsa privigno non potuit dare?

[1] *Ri.*

---

1 Same case in Sen. *Contr.* 9.6 and Calp. Fl. 12.

2 Suggestive of poison, as in 319, *thema*.

3 She is too young to poison anybody, even a stepmother.

4 When they are small. *Mansuescunt* improperly= *mansuetae sunt*.

381[1]

Stepmother under torture saying daughter accomplice

Let a female poisoner be tortured till she gives up her accomplices. A man brought in a stepmother over his son and acknowledged a daughter by her. When he lost his son with ambiguous signs,[2] he accused his wife. She confessed under torture and named their joint daughter as her accomplice. The father is the daughter's advocate.

DECLAMATION

Gentlemen of the jury, to let you know that I accuse only guilty women of poisoning and had good reason for not charging the girl, bring the accused forward from her nurse's lap. Such years do not sin, not even where stepmothers are concerned.[3] Little snakes are harmless, even wild beasts are gentle.[4] By persona she is a virgin, by the case a sister.[5] How dearly her brother loved her, how she wept for his death!

"But her mother," he[6] says, "had her as an accomplice." First, it is natural for criminals to avoid other people's complicity;[7] second, if they look for such, to look for those who will assist them. But what assistance could there be in a girl? Did she buy the poison? Or make it up to give to her brother? Could she not have given it to her stepson herself?

---

[5] Both her youth and the relationship should exempt her from suspicion.

[6] The prosecutor.

[7] I.e. *conscios*.

3

SERMO

Hic verba matris appellantis filiam, illius expavescentis timorem.

4

DECLAMATIO

Ego certe interrogavi. 'Quid est' inquit 'venenum?'

Cur ergo dixit consciam? Ut me orbaret. Nihil dulcius est ultione laesae. Et prorsus non frustra hoc cogitavit: certe, si non aliud, iudicio patrem torquet.

382

Tyrannicida conductus

Cuius opera tyrannus occisus fuerit, praemium petat. Dives senex adulescentem robustum in tyrannicidium pecunia data conduxit. Occidit adulescens tyrannum. Certant de praemio.

1

DECLAMATIO

'Cuius opera' inquit. Operam puto laboris esse, proelii, armorum. Tu quam dicis operam? Consilii? Atqui nemo, ut proposuit sibi tyrannicidium, continuo tyrannicida est. Tuum ipsum consilium quid profuisset citra manum meam? Ergo operam lex desiderat, ideo tantum concedit praemium; atqui si haec opera est, ⟨cur⟩[1] ego pugnavi?

---

[1] SB[3]

---

[8] Whoever put these scraps together misattributed the question in the declamation below to the girl's mother.

[9] I see no problem (cf. Wi.). It is easy enough to imagine why the girl might be frightened. But the declamation does not mention her fear.

DECLAMATION 382

Here we give the words[8] of the mother as she approaches her daughter and the latter's fear as she panics.[9]

DECLAMATION

I certainly questioned her. "What is poison?" she said.

Why then did she say she was her accomplice? To make me childless. Nothing is sweeter than vengeance to a woman harmed. And to be sure she did not think this up for nothing: if naught else, she is torturing her father[10] with a trial.

382

Tyrannicide hired[1]

Let him by whose doing a tyrant has been killed claim a reward. A rich old man hired a strong young man with money to kill a tyrant. The young man killed the tyrant. They dispute about the reward.

DECLAMATION

"By whose doing," says the law. "Doing," I take it, implies work, fighting, weapons. What "doing" are you talking about? Counsel? But nobody is a tyrannicide just by forming the notion of it. What good would your counsel itself have been short of my hand? So the law requires "doing," allows a reward for that only. But if *this* is "doing," ⟨why⟩ did I fight?

---

[10] The speaker himself. Thus she avenges her own torture.
[1] Cf. 345.

2 'Sed ego' inquit 'conduxi.' Puta: nempe conduxisti ut
tyrannicida essem tamquam si conduxisses ut gladiator aut
histrio essem. Si conduxisses ut hominem occiderem,
nempe et ego tenerer. 'Non tua sponte tyrannicidium fecisti.' Istud omnibus dici potest: illum sororis raptus ac-
cendit,[2] hunc uxoris[3] stuprum. Age, si hortatus esses in
3 tyrannicidium, praemium peteres? Sed tu me propter
mercedem tuam putas tyrannicidium fecisse, tantum meritum mercennariae operae imputas? Non est humilis pectoris libertatem publicam capere. Etenim si tua merces
movere me potuit, multo magis praemium movit; et ideo
ad me venisti quia intellexisti a vultu cogitationem tyran-
4 nicidii.[4] 'Cur ergo' inquit 'mercedem accepisti?' Non cupi-
ditatis causa, sed pignoris, quia temptari me putavi et te a
tyranno summissum.
5 'Quid ergo? duo praemia feres?' Ideo tyrannicida sum.
Et[5] tu iam habes praemium[6]: patrimonium, liberos, tyranni mortem desideratam.

383

Rapta male tractata

Quae virum malae tractationis damnaverit, duplam dotem
recipiat; si indotata nupserit, litem aestimet. Rapta nuptias

---

[2] CD: -endet A: -edit B [3] *Ro.*: soro- Aβ
[4] *coni. Wi.*: -dae Aβ
[5] *Ro.*: ut Aβ: tria ("*viz* III") *Watt*[2] [6] -ia *Sch., Watt*[2]

---

[2] Killing a tyrant was a very different matter.
[3] So I have at any rate a share in the tyrannicide. "A man"=
somebody or other (not the tyrant).

"But I hired you," says he. Suppose you did. I imagine you hired me to be a tyrannicide as though you had hired me to be a gladiator or an actor.[2] If you had hired me to kill a man, I suppose I too would be held responsible."[3] "You did not slay the tyrant of your own accord." That can be said to everyone: one man was fired by his sister's rape, another by his wife's dishonor. Come, if you had encouraged such to slay the tyrant, would you be claiming the reward? But do you think I slew the tyrant for your price? Do you credit so great a service to a paid job of work? A low mind has no space for public freedom. And indeed, if your hire could motivate me, the reward motivated me far more. And you came to me because you sensed from my face that I was thinking of tyrannicide. "Why then," he says, "did you take the pay?" Not out of greed, but as a pledge[4] because I thought it was a trap and that you were put up by the tyrant.

"What then? Will you take two rewards?" That's why I am a tyrannicide.[5] You too already have your reward: your property, your children, the tyrant's death that you desired.

383

Rape victim maltreated

Whoso convicts her husband of maltreatment, let her get back double her dowry; if she married without a dowry, let

---

[4] With the notion that if his suspicions turned out to be true he could abscond with the money.

[5] Ironic. If I am in it for money, as you say, then the more the better (SB[2]).

optavit, postea virum malae tractationis damnavit. Litem
morte aestimat.

1   DECLAMATIO

Nimio amore et sollicita inquisitione hic offendit uxorem.
Venit illa in forum gratiosa; ne nos quidem obstitimus quo
minus vinceret, ut sciremus quanto dotem[1] aestimaret.
Iudices dixerunt: 'Quid nos intercedimus? Optime ipsis
conveniet. Haec tamen, ne sine causa in forum videatur
venisse, ferat aliquid solacii: bene credimus illi eius patrimonium cuius capiti pepercit.' Veneramus hilares ad aesti-
2   mationem. At ista 'quid mihi' inquit 'cum pecunia est?
Mortem desidero.' Putat se ut occideret vicisse quae vicit
quia non occiderat. Obsequendum est tibi, adulescens: nihil in mulierem dicam. Sed patiaris causam tuam defendi.
3   Dicimus pecuniarias lites esse, litigatorem esse non
reum, non qui de capite sortiatur: illud iudicium vocari,
quaestionem, quidlibet potius quam litem. 'Aestimet' inquit. Quam familiare, quam cotidianum verbum est! Si
quid commodatum non redditur, nota sunt verba postulan-
tium: 'quanti aestimet.' Ergo pecuniarium verbum est.

---

[1] litem *SB*[3]

---

[1] His jealousy.   [2] Because of her option.

[3] I now keep *dotem*, with some misgiving, as implying that the
damages would be double a (putative) dowry. But as a reason this
can hardly be taken seriously. He (the husband's advocate) implies, I think, that his side was not worried about the money because the marriage was not going to break up.

[4] They assumed that the couple would stay married. Otherwise it would not be a matter of trusting—the ex-husband would
be out of the picture.

her assess damages. A rape victim opted for marriage then later convicted the husband of maltreatment. She assesses damages at death.

He annoyed his wife by too much love and anxious enqui-ries.[1] She came to court a popular[2] lady. We too did not put up a fight to prevent her winning—we wanted to know at what figure she would assess the dowry.[3] The jury said: "Why do we interfere? They'll settle between themselves, fine! Still, just so she doesn't seem to have come to court for nothing, let her have some consolation. We may well trust the wife with the property of the man whose life she spared."[4] We had come cheerfully to the assessing. But she says: "What do I care about money? I want death." She thinks she won in order to kill; actually she won because she hadn't killed.[5] I must do as you wish, young man. I won't say anything against the woman. But please allow your case to be defended.

We say that litigations are about money, that he is a liti-gator, not a defendant on trial for his life[6]: that is called a trial, an enquiry, anything rather than a litigation. "Let her assess," says the law. What a familiar, everyday word! If a loan is not repaid, we know the words of the claimants: "the amount assessed."[7] So the word is about money. Do

[5] When she had the option.

[6] *Sortiatur*= "takes his chance"? But there seems to be no par-allel.

[7] Lit. "at how much (the claimant) assesses." Or is the judge the subject? Anyway the word implies that only money is involved.

4 Huic tu mortem putas subici? Veneficus exulat, alii scelerati mitius puniuntur: malae tractationis damnatus occidetur? 'Mea' inquit 'aestimatio est.' Immo iudicum: tua in una lege est, quam habuisti. Et lex ubi perire vult hominem, aperte significat: 'desertor occidatur.'

5   SERMO
Ultimae sunt preces, ut exoretur mulier.

6   DECLAMATIO
Serves munus. Nam removeas licet secures, si irasceris morietur alioqui. Putas illum †delaturum†[2] nuptias tuas? Denuntio, iterum rapiet.

384

Virgo immolata pestilentiae

In pestilentia responsum est virginem immolandam. Sorte ductam pater virginem negavit, magistratus immolavit. Non finiebatur pestilentia. Iterum sortiti sunt. Altera immolata est. Sedata est pestilentia. Prioris patri magistratus caedis reus est.

---

[2] relicturum *Ro.*: desert- *vel* dimissurum *coni. Wi.*

you think it covers death? A poisoner is exiled, other criminals are punished more mildly. Shall a man convicted of
maltreatment be killed? "The assessment is mine," she
says. Say rather the jury's; yours is in the one law that you
had.[8] And when the law wants someone to die, it makes
that clear: "Let the deserter be put to death."

DISCUSSION

Last come entreaties to make the woman relent.

DECLAMATION

Preserve your gift.[9] For though you remove the axes, he
will die anyway if you are angry. Do you think he will aban-
don (?)[10] your marriage? I warn you, he will rape you again.

384

Virgin sacrificed for plague

In a plague it was responded[1] that a virgin must be sacrificed. A virgin was chosen by lot, but her father denied
that she was a virgin.[2] The magistrate sacrificed her. The
plague did not end. They drew lots again. A second was
sacrificed. The plague subsided. The magistrate is prosecuted for murder by the father of her predecessor.

---

[8] Tentatively: if the jury disallows the death assessment, it will
substitute another (cf. 385.7n.). The one law is the rape law (so
Wi.), which gave her, as the law in the theme did not, power of life
and death.

[9] Life.

[10] See crit. note.

[1] By an oracle.

[2] Not "refused to agree to her being killed" (Wi.).

417

[QUINTILIAN]

⟨SERMO⟩[1]

Colorate: 'Sortem filiae meae[2] deus inter virgines esse noluit, sed tamquam alienae turbae exemit.'

385

Lenoni reus qui meretrici amatorium dedit

Damni iniuria dati sit actio. Adulescens cum amaret ancillam meretricem et multa ei donasset, amatorium ei dedit. Videbatur amare ancilla adulescentem. Agit leno cum eo damni iniuria dati.

1

DECLAMATIO

Si quis utramque partem inspexerit, intelleget profecto ex utra parte sit damnum. Nam lenonis impudentiam satis admirari non possumus qui, non contentus in lupanari venditare ancillam, in foro venditat quo plures amatores inveniat. Quod si aliquid valet amatorium, fateor, hic bibit.

2

SERMO

Rei gestae ordinem quia necesse est exponere, in eiusmodi persona ⟨advocato opus est, cui non⟩[1] necesse est erubescere.

[1] *coni.* Wi.
[2] *SB*[4]: tuae Aβ
[1] *SB*[4], *duce* Ri.

---

[3] Addressed to the prosecutor by the magistrate if *tuae* is right. But how would this "color" work for the defense? The change to *meae* appears to me unavoidable. The magistrate had ignored the allegation of the prosecutor (father of the first victim sacrificed)

DECLAMATION 385

Use the color: "The god did not want my[3] daughter's lot to be among the virgins, but took it out as though from an alien group."

385

A man who gave a prostitute a love philtre prosecuted by her pimp

Let an action lie for loss caused by injury. A young man in love with a slave-girl prostitute to whom he had given many presents gave her a love philtre. The girl seemed to be in love with the young man. Her pimp goes to court with him for loss caused by injury.

DECLAMATION

If anyone looks at both sides, he will surely realize on which side is the loss. For we cannot wonder enough at the impudence of the pimp, who, not content to hawk the slave girl in his brothel, hawks her in the Forum to find more lovers. But if a love philtre has any power, I admit it,[1] *he* drank it.

DISCUSSION

Since it is necessary to set out the order of events, with a persona of this sort 〈an advocate is needed,〉 who does not have to blush.

---

that his daughter was no virgin and should not be in the lottery. The gods by rejecting the sacrifice had confirmed it.

[1] Not "I declare." To drink a love potion knowingly (cf. s.6 fin.) was something one would not admit to willingly. This item is not in the theme.

Quaestiones illae sunt: an leno damni iniuria dati agere possit, an impune illi iniuria[2] fieri; an, cum suam iniuriam non possit vindicare, mancipii possit; an, si mancipii [non][3]

3 potest, prostituti[4] possit; quid sit damnum datum esse? ⟨An⟩[5] cum quis non habeat quod ante possederit? Etiamnum, ut in primo loco ⟨sit⟩[6] comparatio personarum, utrum credibilius sit adulescentem intulisse damnum an accepisse: felicem esse ⟨hanc⟩[7] aetatem si servare possit sua; et lenonem circumscriptum quis crediderit?

4 DECLAMATIO

Quamquam, ut feceris[8] damnum, merito relata tibi talio est, propter quem damna omnes faciunt: leno est publicum damnum. Atqui tuam ancillam habes. 'Malo' inquit 'exemplo datum est.' Quidni ait civitatem stare non posse quia meretrix amet? 'Amatorium' inquit 'dedisti.' Damni agis et veneficium obicis?

5 SERMO

Hic, an amatorium effectum habeat. Quid enim si deformis det, si debilis, si caecus, si pro absente? Numquid enim mandata medicamentum accipere? Et illud prius: quomodo animum mutet[9] quod corpori non noceat per quod transit, et mutet animum[10] ut indulgentiam praecipiat? Isto modo lenonem divitias in manu habere.

6 'Cur ergo' inquit 'dedisti?' Multa miseros etiam sine

---

2 -am *coni.* SB[3]   3 *SB*[3]   4 -tutae *Gron.*
5 *SB*[1]   6 *Aer.*   7 *Sch.*   8 *Ri.:* -im Aβ
9 *Aer.:* mutat Aβ   10 et ⟨ita⟩ mutet [animum] *coni. Wi.*

---

2 "The *leno* might lack legal rights as an *infamis*" (Wi.).
3 He could make his customers fall in love with his girls.

The questions are as follows: can a pimp sue for loss caused by injury or is injury done to him with impunity? Since he cannot avenge injury to himself,[2] can he avenge one done to his chattel? If he can to his chattel, can he to a prostitute? What is "loss caused"? <Is it> when someone does not have what he previously possessed? Furthermore, if <we put> a comparison between the personae at the outset, which is more credible, that the young man caused a loss or took one? At <his> age, we shall say, he is lucky if he can keep what is his; and who would believe that a pimp was defrauded?

DECLAMATION

All the same, even if you suffered a loss, you were deservedly repaid eye-for-eye, since everyone suffers loss because of you; a pimp is a public loss. And yet you have your slave girl. He says: "Giving it set a bad example." Why doesn't he say that the community cannot survive because a prostitute is in love? He says: "You gave her a love philtre." You sue for loss and charge poisoning?

DISCUSSION

Here we ask whether a love philtre has any effect. What if an ugly fellow gives it, or a cripple, or a blind man, or for somebody absent? For can a drug take instructions? And this first: how could something change the mind which does not harm the body through which it passes, and so change the mind as to prescribe affection? That way a pimp holds riches in his hand.[3]

"Then why did you give it?" he says. We say that unhappy folk try many things even without a reason. When he

ratione temptare. Huic, cum tristis esset, supervenisse anum, monstrasse. Hunc, antequam daret monstratam potionem, ne quid noceret priorem bibisse. Reum autem sub hac culpa esse, quod nocuerit.[11]

7 Ultima figuratio quemadmodum leno damnum aestimaturus sit: nimirum voluisse illum aestimare[12] ancillam, et fortasse huic vendere.

8 Supra etiam illud quaeremus, unde intellegat amare ancillam. Quod saepius veniat? Hoc illum saepe fecisse dicet: nempe amat, sine illa non potest vivere; hoc est miseri iuvenis amatorium. Et illo loco dicemus non posse illum[13] aliquando damnum sentire, qui nullo labore tantos quaestus faciat: invidendum illi, nisi leno esset.

386

Iphicrates[1] cum gladio

Reus est Iphicrates[1] quod vim iudicio fecerit, cum Cotyn Thracum regem in id adduxisset et gladio cinctus ipse venisset.

1 DECLAMATIO

Non tulimus tabellas, sed fugientes proiecimus; non iudices reum absolverunt, sed reus iudices. Quid est vis? Haec

---

[11] *Ro.:* non tac- Aβ   [12] -ari *coni. Wi.*
[13] *Aer.:* illam Aβ   [1] *Gron.:* epic- Aβ

---

[4] Not in the theme, but see s.l fin.   [5] *Non tacuerit* in the manuscripts seems irrelevant. What did he tell?

[6] I now keep *aestimare* (see crit. note), understanding that while the plaintiff would make the assessment if the jury found in

was sad, an old woman came to him and showed him. Before he gave the potion that had been shown him, he drank it first in case it might be harmful.[4] But he is under prosecution on this charge on the ground that he did harm.[5]

Finally, a description. How is the pimp going to assess the damage? Presumably he wanted to assess[6] the girl and perhaps sell her to my client.

Beyond this we shall ask what makes him think the girl is in love. Because she visits rather often? She will say that *he*[7] often did that; for he loves her, can't live without her— this is the poor young man's love philtre! And at this point we shall say that the pimp can't ever feel a loss, making all that money with no work. One would have to envy him if he were not a pimp.

386

Iphicrates[1] with a sword

Iphicrates is on trial for bringing violence to bear on a court when he led in Cotys, king of the Thracians, and came himself wearing a sword.

DECLAMATION

We didn't cast our voting tablets but threw them away in our flight. The jury didn't acquit the defendant, the defendant acquitted the jury. What is violence? It happens

his favor, it could be challenged and submitted to the jury. Cf. 383.3 *"aestimet" inquit.*   [7] The young man.

[1] Fourth-century Athenian commander who married the daughter of the Thracian king Cotys. His name is corrupted here to Epicrates, notably supporting a conjecture of Tyrrell's in Cic. *Att.* 2.3.1.

fit alias patientia, alias metu: quorum alterum ad corpus, alterum ad animum pertinet. Si male iudicatum est, fuit aliquid quod iudex timeret. Hoc sic[2] probo: qualis in iudicium venis? Ego illum habitum reorum ⟨non⟩[3] noveram. Ad summam, id solent rei a iudicibus petere quod nuper iudices petiere a reo, ut sibi parceret.

2   SERMO

Reus dicit: 'non' inquit 'hoc animo feci, ut vim facerem; ideo' inquit 'gladium attuli[4] ut illo me, si innocens oppressus essem, interficerem.'

387

Fortis abdicans servatum desertorem

Filium, cuius desertoris salutem ipse fortis optaverat, abdicat.

1   DECLAMATIO

Duas leges habui, viri fortis et patris. Viri fortis legem transtuli in patrem, patris in virum fortem.

388

Avia testis

Qui habebat matrem duxit uxorem, ex qua natum filium

---

    [2] *Aer.*: si Aβ   [3] *Aer.*
    [4] *Gron.*: ret(t)uli Aβ

---

    [2] Defendants normally wore mourning.
    [1] I.e. I felt as a father when I opted for his life ("hero's" law), as a "hero" when I disowned him (disownment law).

sometimes by suffering, sometimes by fear; the one pertains to the body, the other to the mind. If the judgment was bad, the judge was afraid of something. This is how I prove it: in what shape do you come to court? I did \<not\> know of defendants dressed like that.[2] In fine, defendants usually ask from juries what a jury recently asked from a defendant: mercy.

DISCUSSION

The defendant says: "I didn't do it," he says, "with any intention of using violence. I brought the sword," he says, "to kill myself with it if I had been overcome, an innocent man."

387

Hero disowning deserter he had saved

A man disowns his son, a deserter whose life he himself, as a hero, opted for.

DECLAMATION

I had two laws, for a hero and for a father. I transferred the hero's law to the father, the father's to the hero.[1]

388[1]

Grandmother witness

A man who had a mother married a wife and had a son by

388: [1] By its length, novelettish quality, and descriptive touches the piece might seem to have strayed from the *Major Declamations* if we disregard the two scraps of *sermo*, which look more like a reader's marginal notes than *sermones*.

aviae nutriendum dedit. Moriens heredem filium fecit,
substituit uxorem; dispensatorem suum manumitti iussit.
Puer reductus ad matrem et ab ea in fundo maritimo, visis
piratis, relictus non comparuit. Post paucos dies cadaver
confusis lineamentis, quod filii putaretur, in idem litus
eiectum mater ductis sepelivit exequiis. Dispensator manumissus ab ea, post aliquot annos negotiatum profectus,
adulescentem, quem dominum diceret, apud venaliciarium repertum iudicio adserens evicit. Cum eo revertit in
patriam. Puerum agnoscit avia, negat suum mater.

1   DECLAMATIO

Causam, iudices, probatam peregre, probatam domi, propinquis, domesticis, libertis, aviae, (facinus indignum!)
matri tantum probare non possumus: usque eo se libenter
2   credit orbatam ut suos non nisi mortuos agnoscat. Quod
si antea ignotum fuit quantum pecuniae cupiditas possit,
victrix etiam de natura triumphat: mulier, modo cadaver
tamquam filium complexa, nunc filium tamquam cadaver
fugit. Quae funus suum tantum sibi credidit, gratulationem nemini credit[1]! Infelicem puerum sola non agnoscit

---

[1] *Lat.*: -didit Aβ

---

[2] The theme at this point is inadequate and misleading. From
the declamation it appears that the boy and his mother and a large
party were bathing off shore when the pirates were sighted. In the
ensuing *sauve qui peut* the boy was abandoned and his fate became a subject of dispute.

[3] Her son being a minor, she would administer the estate on
his behalf? But the manumission may have been after the boy's
presumed death and his mother's assumption of the inheritance.
How long after her husband's death that took place is not stated.

her whom he gave to his grandmother to be reared. On his deathbed he made his son his heir, his wife alternate heir. He ordered that his steward be manumitted. The boy was brought back to his mother, and, pirates being sighted, left[2] by her in a house by the shore. He disappeared. After a few days a corpse with battered features, thought to be the son's, was cast up on the same shore and buried by the mother with funeral rites. The steward, manumitted by her,[3] after a few years set out on business and found a young man, whom he said was his master,[4] in a slave mart. He claimed freedom for him and won.[5] He returned with him to their country. The grandmother[6] recognizes him, the mother says he is not hers.

DECLAMATION

Gentlemen of the jury, we[7] proved our case abroad, proved it at home to relatives, domestics, freedmen, grandmother; only to this mother (for shame!) we cannot prove it. She is so happy to believe herself bereaved that she doesn't recognize her own unless they are dead. If the power of greed for money was not known before,[8] it triumphs even over nature. A woman who recently embraced a corpse as her son now flees her son as though he were a corpse. For her loss she believed only herself: for congratulation she believes nobody. Alone of his relations she does not recognize

---

[4] Had been, before the manumission.

[5] *Evincere* has the legal sense of successfully asserting someone's free status in court.

[6] No mention of the slave girl (s.21).

[7] A relative is speaking as the young man's advocate.

[8] "We know it now" must be supplied, at least mentally.

ex propinquis. Causam quaeritis? Quia vivit.

3 Narratio

Habuimus adulescentem optimum propinquum, mitissimum patronum, fidelissimum amicum, maritum vero nimium quoque uxorium: quod ignovimus—filium sustulerat. Puer continuo ad aviam translatus est: scilicet et ab[2] illa matris indulgentia occupata est et haec ablatum non indignata est. Toto illi corpore innotuit; non tamen ulteriorem aviae notitiam profiteor: nepotem suum optime
4 ‹quaeque›[3] facie novit. Moriens igitur propinquus noster testamentum scripsit breve et simplex: nam neque diu de primo herede cogitandum fuit habenti filium, neque de secundo habenti priorem. Nec sane invidimus isti honorata viri iudicia, quibus utinam gratiam referret. Neque avia captare testamentum eius fas putavit cui destinaverat
5 suum. Haec est nostra narratio: ista narret suos piratas.

Non insequar eam malignis suspicionibus, nisi quod suos libentius mortuos agnoscit. Habetis narrationem pueri, habetis et matris[4]: audite liberti.
6 Interposito tempore libertus notae probitatis, deorum credo numine, quod rebus humanis etiam qua non apparet intervenit, peregre negotiandi causa profectus est. Cum forte videt puerum venalibus interpositum, simul et agno-

---

[2] et ab *SB*[3]: ad A: et *β*: ab *ed. Leid.*
[3] *coni. SB*[3]   [4] *Aer.*: -rem A*β*

---

[9] "The father was duly grateful to his wife for providing him with a first heir" (Wi.). Rather, since (hopefully) the son would inherit, the second heir was not important.

[10] *Iudicia* referring to testamentary bequests.

[11] Scornfully, as though she had made them up; a false touch,

the unfortunate boy. You ask the reason? Because he is alive.

Narrative

We had a young man: the best of relatives, the gentlest of patrons, the most loyal of friends, as a husband even *too* uxorious, something we forgave him: he had acknowledged a son. The boy was at once transferred to his grandmother. No doubt she forestalled his mother's love, and the other woman did not resent his removal. His whole body came to be known to her, but I don't claim the grandmother's knowledge further than this: every grandmother knows her grandson best by his face. So on his deathbed our relative wrote a will, short and straightforward; for he did not have to think long about his first heir, having a son, nor about the second heir, having a first.[9] Nor did we grudge her the honorable judgment[10] of her husband; would that she had been grateful! Neither did the grandmother think it right to hanker after the will of one for whom she had destined her own. This is *our* story: let her tell us about her pirates.[11]

I won't pursue her with malign suspicions, except that she is better pleased to recognize her own when they are dead. You have the boy's story, you have the mother's: listen to a freedman's.

After a while, a freedman of known probity, by the power of the gods, I believe, which intervenes in mortal affairs even where it is not apparent, set out on business abroad. When he happens to see the boy among those on sale, he both recognized him and was recognized by him.

whether original or not, since the pirates' reality is essential to the boy's case.

vit et agnitus est. 'Quis' inquit 'vobis narravit in quas terras
7 delatus essem? Num avia vivit?' Itaque habuit puer adser-
torem, adsertor sponsorem, peregrinus advocatos, cum
ipse vultus causam ingenuitatis suae ageret. Filium istius
quid aliud dicam quam agnoverunt? Nec mirum: nihil erat
confusum. Fateor multum absentium quoque profuisse
nomina, cum diceremus: 'habet matrem, habet aviam.' In
una re, iudices, mentiti sumus: adfirmavimus enim futurum ut hunc mater agnosceret.

8   Bona paterna filio peto. 'Sed ego' inquit 'heres sum.'
Sed hic prior heres. 'Periit' inquit. Quando? Apud aviam
valuerat: ad mortem arcessitus est? Diutius captivi apud
9 piratas vivunt. 'Visis' inquit 'piratis relictus fluctibus obru-
tus est.' Quid ais? Relictus? Ulli metus filii memoriam tibi
excutiunt? Matrem non agnosco. Quaedam animalia ipso
ore in periculis catulos suos transferunt, novasque illis
indulgentia manus commenta est: noxios alioqui morsus
huic uni officio mitigant. Nidulorum, si infestantur, crebra
mutatio est: nec quicquam usque eo ferum est ut non cum
progenie sua migret; adeo illis quibus omnium rerum in-
10 tellectus negatus est hic tamen adfectus relinquitur. Romani generis auctor, divisis inter patrem et filium pietatis
officiis, cum utrumque ad fugiendum anni deficerent, alterum tulit, alterum traxit. Mater, disce fugere. Puto, non
miramini cur mater non recipiat quem tam vilem habet ut
tamquam cadaver relinquat.

---

[12] The steward, to "assert him into freedom" (*adserere in
libertatem*). The sponsor and the backers are not identified. Cf. s.
11 fin.   [13] Cf. Juv.11.154 *ingenui vultus puer*, Petron.107.6.
[14] As were the features of the cast-up corpse.
[15] Aeneas.

"Who told you people," says the boy, "what land I had been brought to? Is my grandmother alive?" So the boy had a claimant,[12] the claimant a sponsor, the foreigner backers, while his face itself pleaded the cause of his free birth.[13] What else shall I say but that they recognized him as that gentleman's son? Not surprising: nothing was confused.[14] I admit that the names of absent persons helped a lot, when we said: "He has a mother, he has a grandmother." On one point, gentlemen, we lied: we affirmed that his mother would recognize him.

I claim his father's possessions for the son. "But I am the heir," she says. But he is the first heir. "He died," she says. When? With his grandmother he had been healthy: was he sent for to his death? Captives live longer with pirates. "Pirates were sighted," she says. "Left behind, he was overwhelmed by the waves." What are you saying? Left behind? Do any fears drive out from your mind the memory of your son? I don't recognize a mother. Some animals when in danger carry their cubs away in their own mouths and love creates new hands for them. They soften their bites, otherwise harmful, for this one office. Nests are often changed if they become unsafe; and no creature is so savage that it does not migrate with its progeny. So true it is that to those to whom understanding of all things is denied this one emotion is left. The founder of the Roman race[15] divided his pious offices between father and son and since the years of both lacked strength for flight, he carried one and led the other by the hand. Mother, learn how to escape. I think you are not surprised that a mother does not receive a son whom she holds so cheap that she leaves him like a corpse.

431

11 'Primus' inquit 'heres periit.' Nisi fallor, iudices, in hoc controversia est, utrum fluctibus submersus sit puer an a piratis raptus sit. Si doceo non perisse, nimirum raptus est; si raptum ostendo, doceo etiam vivere. Si vivit, nimirum hic est quem invenit libertus, evicit adsertor, iudex remisit,
12 avia recepit. Verum, ut propositum ordinem sequar, nego in mari perisse. Litus, amoenitate notum, numquam elato alluitur mari, sed molliter devexum aequali planitie, paulatim superveniente pelago, subsidit.[5] Longo spatio ingre-
13 dientem fatigat antequam destituat. Porro tu tranquillo mari an aestuante progressa es? ‹Illud›[6] credibilius; scilicet ad haec oblectamenta laetiores eligimus[7] dies, horridus vero decidentium undarum fragor ‹vitatur›[8] et exaestuantis fluctus minax facies. Et tibi, oportune[9] secundum ipsa habitanti[10] litora, non rapienda sed expectanda occasio[11] est: ita habitas ut tibi etiam tranquillitates eligere fasti-
14 diose liceat. Sane tamen adversis tempestatibus et saevientibus se undis offerre libuerit, ne hoc quidem periculosum: venientis enim fluctus et consurgentis [antequam] freti[12] facies ante terret quam decipit.[13] Utinam quidem eiusmodi tempestatibus productus esses, puer! Tu potius
15 matrem[14] reliquisses. Denique quo tempore summersus?

[5] *Sch.*: -sedit Aβ   [6] *SB*[3]   [7] *Aer.*: eleg- Aβ
[8] *SB*[2]   [9] *Ro.*: -na Aβ   [10] *Aer.*: -ndi Aβ
[11] *Pith.*: obsessio Aβ   [12] *Aer.*: a. fracti Aβ: *del. Hå.*[2]
[13] AD: -cepit β   [14] *Sch., Gron.*: pa- Aβ

[16] The advocate seems to forget that the freedman and the claimant were one and the same.   [17] Actually he deals only with the first point: the boy was not drowned.

[18] Contrast s.14 *consurgentis freti facies* and 16 *undarum*

"The first heir," she says, "is dead." If I am not mistaken, gentlemen, the controversy lies in this, whether the boy was submerged in the waves or carried off by pirates. If I show that he did not die, then presumably he was carried off; if I show that he was carried off, I tell you that he is still alive. If he is alive, surely he is the one the freedman found, the claimant[16] vindicated, the judge sent back, the grandmother took back. However, to follow my proposed sequence:[17] I deny that he died in the sea. The beach is noted for its amenity. The sea that washes it never rises high.[18] The shore slopes down gently in an even spread, gradually sinking as the water covers it. It tires the walker in its long stretch before it fails him. Further, was the water calm when you went out or rough? ⟨The former⟩ is more plausible. We naturally choose pleasant days for these diversions, ⟨we avoid⟩ the horrid crash of breakers and the threatening aspect of a sea in turmoil. And you, living conveniently close to the beach, would wait for the right time, not snatch at it; your location allows you a fastidious choice even of calm days. But granted that it might have pleased a person to offer herself to unfavorable weather and raging billows: even this isn't dangerous. The aspect of advancing surf and rising water alarms before it seizes.[19] A pity you were not brought out in such weather, boy! It would rather have been you who left your mother behind.[20] Finally,

saevientium. The sea can get rough on this beach but is never very deep.   [19] The bather has time to retreat. For *decipit* = *occupat* see my (Teubner) apparatus to Mart. 14.217.

[20] But actually the sea was calm. Had it been rough, the boy would have been first to get back to land. Such at least is the best I can make of this cryptic remark.

433

Dum applicant piratae an ante? Necdum scis? Tam secura es? Hoc matri non credo. *[15] Cur enim nemo ex paedagogis vidit? Si vidit, cur laboranti auxilium non tulit? Dum applicant? Necesse est utique tunc fluctus vitaverit et ipse quoque piratas fugerit. An vero eodem tempore et pirata applicat et fluctus praedatur? Rogo vos: qui ante adventum 16 tutus fuit, adventu piratae perît? 'Cur ergo' inquit 'nemo clamantem audit?' Primum vicinus undarum saevientium fragor audientium auribus minorem excludebat sonum; deinde in tanto tumultu fugientium praeterisse vocem non mirum est. Quid ita non auditus est? Ne, quaeso, infelici puero vilitatem sui imputaveris,[16] quod relictus, quod de-17 sertus est. Cur non audisti? Longius fugeras. 'Sed post paucos dies corpus expulsum est.' Quid mirum, ubi piratae vagantur? Quid? Tu porro impune semper[17] maria traici putas? Non minus possum dicere alienum fuisse quam ⟨tu⟩[18] tuum filium: signa confusa sunt. Immo credibilius est naufragi fuisse (litus enim amoenum, non infestos scopulos habet), utique post paucos dies cum dicas expulsum; illud vero longo tempore non expulsum sed advolutum.

---

[15] *lac. ind. Wi.* (non ante *fort. supplendum*)
[16] sui (*Aer.*) i. *Sch.*: suum (*ex corr.* A) putaverit Aβ: suam p. D
[17] *Sch.*: s(a)epe Aβ   [18] *SB*[3]

---

[21] No mother could be so callous.
[22] Excised by Wi. (and in my Teubner ed.). But the advocate is repeating this possibility and rejecting it. The boy would have fled, not drowned—an assertion rather than an argument.
[23] Now the sea is rough again. But the declaimer's assertion makes no apparent sense.
[24] The mother's question, implying that the boy was already

when was he drowned? While the pirates were pulling in or before? Don't you know yet? Are you so unconcerned? I don't believe this from a mother.[21] ‹ It was not before. › For why did none of the tutors see it? If one saw, why did he not go to help the boy in trouble? Then while they were pulling in?[22] It must needs be that he then got out of the waves[23] and himself too escaped the pirates. Or does the pirate pull in and the sea devour the boy at the same time? I ask you: if he was safe before the pirate's arrival, did he die *at* his arrival? She says: "So why did nobody hear him shout?"[24] First, the noise of the raging waves close by shut out the lesser sound from the hearers' ears; then in such a tumult of fugitives it is not surprising that a voice went unheard. Why was he thus unheard? Don't, I beg, blame the unfortunate boy for holding himself so cheap, for the fact that he was left behind, abandoned. Why did you not hear him? You had fled too far. "But after a few days a body was expelled." No wonder, when pirates are abroad. Do you really think the seas can always be crossed in safety? I can say that it was someone else's body as easily as ‹you› can say it was your son's. The features were battered. Or rather, it is *more* likely to have been a shipwrecked sailor's (for the coast is pleasant, without dangerous rocks); definitely so, since you say it was expelled after a few days; but that body was not expelled, but washed up after a long time.[25] And

drowned. The advocate makes the obvious reply, but then repeats the question and answers it by blaming the mother.

[25] As shown by its battered condition. *Litus . . . habet* would go better after *advolutum*. Even the mother admits that the body had been in the water for a few days, but actually it had been for a long time.

18 Quomodo autem potuit confusa facie agnosci? 'Aetas' inquit 'conveniebat.' Hoc inter argumenta mea minimum est. 'Statura.' Hoc ratione pari.[19] 'Quare ergo mater sepelivit?' Nescio; hoc unum dico, non poterat agnosci. Festinavit in bona.[20]

19 <center>SERMO</center>

Summovimus peregrinum cadaver; restat ut inducamus filium.

20 <center>DECLAMATIO</center>

'Primus' inquit 'heres sepultus est.' Hic ergo quis est? Unde? Qua fiducia? 'Aetas eadem est.' Quid si solet quidem hoc argumentum apud te valere? Sed cur ex aequalibus nemo alius hanc spem vindicat? Hoc argumentum transeo. 'Statura suffragatur.' Nec[21] hoc me movet: et tu haec dicis. Sed haec valeant ubi confusus est vultus; ubi lineamenta oris, oculorum et coloris proprietas capillo-

21 rumque habitus, [omnia staturae][22] levia. 'At similitudo fecit illi animum.' Age, quid si ancilla cognoscit? Est quidem humilis persona et ei fortuna gravitatem detrahit. Sed saepe magnorum fides ex ⟨non⟩ magnis[23] venit. Quid si frugi, probata domino? Sunt etiam in his morum discrimi-

---

19 r. p. *SB*³: in actione loci Aβ
20 *Pith.*: bono Aβ
21 CD: ne Aβ
22 *Wi.*
23 non m. *SB*²: parvis *Pith.*

---

26 A reader's addition?
27 As when you identified the body on the shore (s.18).
28 A point in the boy's favor, but not worth pressing.

how could it be recognized with the face battered? "The age matched," she says. This is one of the least of *my* arguments. "The figure." The same goes for this one. "Why then did the mother bury him?" I don't know, I say only this: he could not have been recognized. She was in a hurry for the property.[26]

DISCUSSION

We have got rid of the foreign corpse; remains to bring in the son.

DECLAMATION

"The first heir," she says, "was buried." Who is this then? Where from? What makes him confident? "His age is the same." Well, doesn't this argument usually carry weight with you?[27] But why does no one else among his coevals assert the same hope?[28] I pass over this argument. "His figure is in his favor."[29] This too does not impress me: you too say as much. But let points like these carry weight when the face is battered: where we have the features, the particular eye color, the character of the hair, they are trivial. "But it was the resemblance that emboldened him." Come, the slave girl recognizes him, doesn't she?[30] A humble persona to be sure, and her fortune detracts from her credibility. But proof of great matters often comes from persons ⟨not⟩ great. Is she not honest, well thought of by her master?[31] Even in these folk there are differences

---

[29] Like the compatible age, both sides could use this argument in favor of their identifications (it could also be used against either as a reason for making a false claim).

[30] Not in the theme.

[31] When he was alive.

22 na. Quid—ad fontem causae per gradus venio—‹si›[24] libertus paternus agnoscit? Frugi servos libertos facimus:
sortimur genus, non eligimus, nec ante nos nostri arbitrii
sumus. Et nescio an maius sit facere genus. Libertus viri
tui, mulier, cuius iudiciis gloriaris. Qui te filio substituit,
hunc etiam a filio manumisit. Quod tibi dedit, nulli abstu-
lit; quod huic, etiam filio subduxit: et facilius est viro pla-
23 cere quam domino. 'Sed pro se mentitur[25]': agnoscit patronum; servitutem sibi manumissus imponit. 'Huic' inquit
'debeo manus,[26] operas, testamentum.' Vindictam magno
24 redimere solent. 'Colludit' inquit 'cum avia.' Bene agis:
dum evertere vis testem, alterum dedisti. 'Convenit' inquit
'illis.' Proba convenisse. ‹Quem›[27] speraverunt effectum
mendacii? Qui potuit esse sermo? 'Nepos meus periit fluctibus et sepultus est. Tu tamen vade, aliquem venalem ad-
duc, ego agnoscam.' Perfectum est: non timent deprehen-
25 di? Non omnia signa confusa sunt. Si odit, testamentum
potius dementiae accuset, dicat subiectum, dicat falsum;

[24] *SB*[1] [25] *β*: -itus A
[26] *ed. Leid.*: minus A: munus *β* [27] *SB*[1]

---

[32] Manumitted by his widow as directed in his will. So *libertus viri* below.

[33] Cf., with Wi., Sen. *Contr.* 1.6.3 *quidam ignobiles fecere posteris genus*. But the relevance is not obvious and *sortimur . . . genus* should perhaps be double-bracketed.

[34] Whose slave he would otherwise have been. For *a filio* see my commentary on Cic. *Fam.* 13.52.1, *a Caesare liberavi* (different however in that the son's consent was not required).

[35] He would expect the successful claimant to be grateful.

[36] Seemingly, a brash exaggeration referring to the freedman–patron relationship (see Wi.). Or would the manumission become

of character. Doesn't his father's freedman[32] recognize him?—I am getting to the bottom of the case step by step. We make freedmen of honest slaves. We get our family by hap, we don't choose them and we're not at our own disposal before we exist. Perhaps it's a greater thing to *make* one's family.[33] He is the freedman of your husband, madam, of whose will you are so proud. The man who put you down as alternate heir also made him free of your son.[34] What he gave you, he took from nobody: what he gave him he took away even from his son. And it is easier to please a husband than a master. "But he is lying for his own sake."[35] He recognizes his patron. Freed, he imposes slavery[36] on himself. "To him," says he, "I owe my hands, my services, my will.[37]" They generally buy their freedom at a high price.[38] "He was in collusion with the grand-mother," she says. Good for you! In trying to overturn our witness, you have given us another. "It was arranged between them," she says. Prove it. <What> did they hope to achieve by the lie?[39] What could they have said to one an-other? "My grandson was drowned and has been buried. But you, go along and bring some boy from the market, I'll recognize him." It's done: are they not afraid of being found out? Not all the features were battered. If she hates you, let her rather accuse[40] the will of dementia, say it

void if the status of the wife as heir was invalidated? If so, the point is a technicality, since the son would repeat the procedure.

[37] Freedmen were expected to remember their patrons in their wills.   [38] Presumably an observation by the advocate: manumission does not come cheap.

[39] A naïve question surely.   [40] There were easier and safer ways for the grandmother to get at the mother.

accuset te quod filium ad mare duxeris, dicat tua culpa perisse. Quare deinde tam sero, post annos, consilium initum est eiusmodi? Res inter initia urunt, et livor mora solvitur. Sed ad hoc proficiscitur: qua ratione alienum servum evincit?

26 Modo dicebam, testem[28] habeo; at iam praeiudicium habeo. Si testis honestior iuraverit, conficitur controversia: at ego multos iudices iuratos dabo. Causa cognita, excussa et absoluta est. Nego solvenda esse iudicia: hunc esse puerum inventi sunt qui iurarent. ⟦'Peregre' inquit. Illic, dicis, ubi non gratia, *[29] ubi citra[30] haec omnia nuda veritas stabat. Hoc meum argumentum est.⟧ Quid quod non tantum iudicatum sed etiam peregre iudicatum est, ubi non propinqui, ubi vix quisquam erat qui patrem huius nosset? At hercules quale domi iudicium est? Ibi solus libertus evicit[31]: hic et avia defendit. 'Dedit' inquit 'libertus pecuniam venaliciario ut praevaricaretur.' Sane nec avia libertum timuerit nec libertus venaliciarium. Proba libertum habuisse pecuniam, tulisse, dedisse. Necesse est multum venaliciarius poposcerit: aestimavit enim non rem suam sed spem nostram. Age deinde, non timet libertus ne ille qui

27

28

---

28 *SB*[4]: libertum Aβ   29 *lac. ind. Ro.*
30 *Ro.*: contra Aβ
31 *SB*[3]: v- Aβ

---

41 "But . . . slave": perhaps to be double-bracketed. The point of the question is not clear. "Rather than just buying him" Wi. Or perhaps: "why pick on the slave of a stranger, who would have to be squared?" The need to fit the alleged son into the pirate story seems left out of sight.

42 The sworn jury.   43 But cf. s. 7.

was substituted, forged. Let her accuse you because you brought your son to the sea, let her say his death was your fault. Then, why embark on such a plan so late, after years? Things burn us at the beginning, even jealousy dissolves with time. But that's the object of the journey: what reason had he to win freedom for somebody else's slave?[41]

I was saying just now: "I have a witness." But I already have a prejudgment. If a respectable witness swears, a controversy is resolved: but I shall produce many sworn jurors. The case was heard, investigated, and wrapped up. I say that judicial findings are not to be undone: persons[42] were found to swear that this is the boy. [["Abroad," she says. Yes, where influence * , where without all these things the truth stood naked. This argument makes for me.]] Add that the case was not only judged but judged abroad, where there were no relatives, where there was hardly anyone who knew this boy's father.[43] And yet, upon my word, what sort of trial do we have at home? *There* the freedman by himself won him free: here his grandmother too defends him. She says: "The freedman gave money to the slave dealer for his collusion." I'll grant you that neither the grandmother feared the freedman, nor the freedman the slave dealer.[44] Prove that the freedman had money, brought it, gave it. The slave dealer must have asked a lot: he assessed not his property but our hope. And then, come, isn't the

[44] He waives two possible arguments: the grandmother would not have put herself into the freedman's hands and the freedman would not have put himself into the dealer's hands, risking exposure or blackmail. None the less he goes on to elaborate the latter point. But the apparent concession ("all right, they weren't afraid . . .") really makes the argument· they were not afraid because there was no collusion.

puerum vendidit tibi[32] vendat indicium, ne veniat, ne scri-
29 bat? Si corruptum iudicium non probas, vici.

Agnoscit avia, quae maiorem temporum partem huius
oblectatione consumpsit. 'Filius meus' inquit 'in hac aetate
talis fuit.' <Fide> digna[33] est testis notitia: de nepote dicit
causam; nullum testamentum captat, etiam suum pigno-
rat.[34] 'Sero hoc placuit.' Hoc et meum[35] argumentum est.
Filium sustulit (pudicae argumentum est), hunc curiose
30 educavit, in nullum litus duxit. 'Sed filius illam notavit.' Si
merito, huius crimen; si immerito, illius. Dic quare: immo
noli mortuum illius criminari filium. Non queritur. 'Sed
sperat pecuniam.' Primum eius aetatis est ut debeat con-
31 temnere. 'Odit me' inquit. Quam habet iniuriam tuam?
Nihil queritur, nisi quod filium tuum in litus duxisti. Deos
peierat.[36] Nimirum oscula sua †venaliciario†[37] inquinat.
'Non debeo' inquit 'videri invita filium agnoscere: mater
sum.' In multis nihil matris ultra titulum est: nec novercae
omnes <novercae>.[38]

32   SERMO

In matrem et illa Cicero dixit: 'mater enim a me, tametsi in

[32] *Pith.*: ubi Aβ: *anne* tibi vendidit ?
[33] f. digna *Hå.*[2], *Watt*[1]: magna *Ro.*: idonea *coni. Wi.*
[34] *Obr.*: -atur Aβ   [35] *tempt. Ri.*: tuum Aβ
[36] d. p. *Opitz*: deo peri- Aβ   [37] venalicii (*melius* venalis
(*Wi.*); *anne* venalis pueri?) ore *Opitz*
[38] *SB*[4]: <oderunt> *Wi.*

[45] See crit. note. *Notitia* could be nom. and *testis* (possessive)
gen. or *testis* nom. with *notitia* causal abl.
[46] Cf. s.4 fin.

freedman afraid that the man who sold you the boy might sell his information, might come, might write? If you don't prove that the trial was corrupt, I have won.

The grandmother recognizes him; she spent the greater part of her time in the pleasure he gave her. "My son," she says, "was just like him at his age." The witness's knowledge deserves credence.[45] She pleads the case about her grandson. She is not after any will, she even pledges her own.[46] "It was late in the day to take this course." This argument works my way too. She took up her son (sign of chastity[47]), raised him with care, did not bring him to any shore. "But her son censured her."[48] If she deserved it, that is against her: if not, against him. Tell me why: no, don't find fault with her dead son; she doesn't complain. "But she hopes for money." First, at her age she should despise it. "She hates me," she says. What wrong have you done her? She makes no complaint except that you brought your son to the shore. "She swears falsely by the gods." I suppose she taints her kisses with the mouth of a bought boy! She[49] says: "I ought not to be thought unwilling to recognize my son. I am a mother." In many cases there is nothing of a mother except the title. All stepmothers too are not really such.[50]

DISCUSSION

Cicero too said against a mother: "I shall call her his

---

[47] Her husband presumably died shortly before he was born.

[48] By sending the boy to his wife. Why he did so is nowhere stated.

[49] The mother.

[50] Such as the name commonly suggests. See crit. note.

hunc hostili odio et crudelitate est, mater, inquam, appel-
labitur.' Sub hoc tamen titulo insidiatam filio dicit quaesisse pericula, ut filii sui bona sector possideret.

33   DECLAMATIO

Nihil quidem ultra haec timendum fuit, et supra fidem laesus est. Gratulari tamen tibi inter calamitates tuas, cruen-
34   ta, possum, quod avia secunda heres non fuit. Multa sunt
quae animum tuum sollicitent: ingentis patrimonii hereditas, et gravior possessionis quam spei iactura [est],[39] et
<quod>[39] diu cum ea fuisti.[40] Illa tecum (habeo certum)
cogitas: 'si recipio, ducet uxorem, quam fortasse cariorem
habeat quam matrem.' [Ergo <non>[41] sola obstat patrimonii cogitatio.][42]

35   A piratis dimissum, a Fortuna—o te, liberte, inofficio-
sum!—reduxisti non ad imagines, sed ut propius amissam
dignitatem aspiceret. 'Etiam' inquit 'fortunam meam noveram.' Non est, puer, quod cum liberto queraris: omnia
tibi reddidit praeter matrem.

[39] *SB*[3] (iactura quod diu *Sch.*)
[40] *Sch.*: fuit Aβ
[41] *SB*[4]
[42] *SB*[3]

---

[51] *Cluent*. 12.
[52] Cicero. Is what follows a grossly garbled version of *Cluent*.
176 ff?
[53] Of mother.
[54] Could he be thinking of the present case? But the property
went to the mother, from whom the claimant was claiming it and
no reason is given why she should have intended to sell it.

mother, yes, his mother, though in hatred and cruelty she is his enemy."[51] But he[52] says that under this title[53] she laid a trap for her son, seeking to endanger him so that her son's property should go to the auctioneer.[54]

DECLAMATION

Nothing worse than this could have been feared, and he has been harmed beyond belief. But amid your misfortunes, bloody madam, I can congratulate you in that the grandmother was not second heir. You have many things to disturb you: the inheritance of an enormous property, the loss of possession worse than the loss of expectation, and ⟨the fact that⟩ you had it for a long time. You think to yourself (I am sure of it): "If I take him back, he will marry a wife whom he will perhaps love more than his mother." [So the thought of the property is ⟨not⟩ the only impediment.][55]

Dismissed by the pirates and by Fortune[56] (freedman, you failed in your duty[57]) you brought him back, not to the masks, but to get a closer view of lost status.[58] "I still knew my fortune,"[59] he says. My boy, you have no cause to complain of the freedman. He has given everything back to you except your mother.

---

[55] Probably a reader's comment.

[56] Like Wi. I do not see the point, unless it be that having brought the boy back home Fortune had cast him off.

[57] The reproach is merely rhetorical and presently recanted.

[58] Not to rejoin his family but only to see what a fine position he has lost.

[59] Obscure to Wi., but perhaps he means "I recognized Fortune, always my enemy." See *OLD nosco* 5.